THE TALK OF THE CLINIC:
Explorations in the Analysis of Medical and Therapeutic Discourse

LEA'S COMMUNICATION SERIES
Jennings Bryant/Dolf Zillmann, General Editors

Selected titles in Applied Communication (Teresa L. Thompson, Advisory Editor) include:

Cissna • Applied Communication in the 21st Century

Nussbaum/Coupland • Handbook of Communication and Aging Research

Ray • Case Studies in Health Communication

Ray/Donohew • Communication and Health

For a complete list of other titles in LEA's Communication Series, please contact Lawrence Erlbaum Associates, Publishers

THE TALK OF THE CLINIC:
Explorations in the Analysis of Medical and Therapeutic Discourse

Edited by
G. H. MORRIS
Texas Tech University
RONALD J. CHENAIL
Nova Southeastern University

LEA   LAWRENCE ERLBAUM ASSOCIATES, PUBLISHERS
1995   Hillsdale, New Jersey   Hove, UK

Copyright © 1995, by Lawrence Erlbaum Associates, Inc.
All rights reserved. No part of the book may be reproduced in
any form, by photostat, microform, retrieval system, or any other
means, without the prior written permission of the publisher.

Lawrence Erlbaum Associates, Inc., Publishers
365 Broadway
Hillsdale, New Jersey 07642

Library of Congress Cataloging-in-Publication Data

The talk of the clinic : explorations in the analysis of medical and
  therapeutic discourse / edited by G. H. Morris, Ronald J. Chenail.
    p. cm.
  Includes bibliographical references and index.
  ISBN 0-8058-1372-1 (cloth : alk. paper). — ISBN 0-8058-1373-X
(paper : alk. paper)
    1. Communication in medicine. 2. Discourse analysis. 3. Content
analysis (Communication) 4. Communication in psychiatry.
5. Physicians—Language. 6. Patients—Language.
7. Psychotherapists—Language. 8. Psychotherapy patients—Language.
I. Morris, G. H. (George Howard) II. Chenail, Ronald J.
  [DNLM: 1. Communication. 2. Physician-Patient Relations.
3. Physician's Practice Patterns. W 62 T146 1995]
R118.T35   1995
610'.14—dc20
DNLM/DLC
for Library of Congress   95-3833
                                                               CIP

Books published by Lawrence Erlbaum Associates are printed on acid-free paper,
and their bindings are chosen for strength and durability.

Printed in the United States of America
10 9 8 7 6 5 4 3 2 1

For our wives and our parents

Contents

Contributors   xi

Introduction: The Talk of the Clinic   1
   Ronald J. Chenail and G. H. Morris

PART I: THERAPY AND CONVERSATIONS ABOUT THERAPY

1. **Telling Problems in an Initial Family Therapy Session: The Hierarchical Organization of Problem-Talk**   19
   Richard Buttny and Arthur D. Jensen

2. **Therapists' Techniques for Responding to Unsolicited Contributions by Family Members**   49
   Charlotte M. Jones and Wayne A. Beach

3. **Resourceful Figures in Therapeutic Conversations**   71
   Ronald J. Chenail and Liana Fortugno

4. **Behind the Looking Glass: Tinkering With the Facts on the Other Side of a One-Way Mirror**   89
   David A. Todtman

5. **Marital Therapy and Self-Reflexive Research: Research and/as Intervention**   105
   Jerry Gale, Mark Odell, and Chandra S. Nagireddy

CONTENTS

6. Telling How to Say It: A Way of Giving Suggestions in Family Therapy Supervision ... 131
   Dan A. Ratliff and G. H. Morris

PART II: THE DISCOURSE OF MEDICAL CARE

7. Precepting Conversations in a General Medicine Clinic ... 151
   Anita M. Pomerantz, Jack Ende, and Frederick Erickson

8. Two Types of Institutional Disclaimers at the Cancer Information Service ... 171
   Robert Hopper, Jo Ann Ward, W. Ray Thomason, and Patricia M. Sias

9. Educating the Patient: Interactive Learning in an OB-GYN Context ... 185
   Sandra L. Ragan, Christina S. Beck, and Martha D. White

10. Discussing Health-Related Quality of Life in Prenatal Consultations ... 209
    Richard L. Street, Jr., William R. Gold, and Tony McDowell

11. Some Answers About Questions in Clinical Interviews ... 233
    Richard M. Frankel

12. Preserving and Constraining Options: "Okays" and 'Official' Priorities in Medical Interviews ... 259
    Wayne A. Beach

13. Implications of Relational Communication for Therapeutic Discourse ... 291
    Kelly S. McNeilis, Teresa L. Thompson, and Dan O'Hair

Author Index ... 315

Subject Index ... 325

Acknowledgments

Many people helped us bring together this collection. We thank the contributors for agreeing to orient their chapters to the novel character and demands of this volume, tailoring it to our specifications, honoring our suggestions during the process of revision and working so diligently to finish on schedule. Many clinical practitioners also lent a hand on the various projects and we appreciate their help. Our thanks to Teresa L. Thompson, whose idea it was to consider Lawrence Erlbaum as our publisher and their Series in Applied Communication as the platform for our book. The series editor, Jennings Byrant, and our Lawrence Erlbaum editor, Hollis Heimbouch, and editorial assistant, Amy Olener, were superb in their attention to detail, flexibility, and enthusiastic support of the project. Thanks go to Sondra Guideman for seeing the book through production. We wish to express our gratitude to Bill Kirkpatrick, Harold Lucas, Brad Keeney, Liana Fortugno, Richard Buttny, Ann Noble and Karen Wampler for their inspirational, constructive and encouraging comments on the project. Robert Hopper encouraged us to showcase some of this work at conferences of the International Communication Association and Speech Communication Association and urged us to seek the participation of Len Hawes and Harlene Anderson as critics of these presentations. We sincerely appreciate Robert's advice and their illuminating commentary. The faculties, staffs and students of the Department of Communication Studies at Texas Tech University and Nova Southeastern University's School of Social and Systemic Studies deserve gold medals for their interest, support and toleration. A research assistant, Sharmila Surendran, was especially helpful, and her fine work is really appreciated. Finally, we want to acknowledge the loving, resourceful and plentiful help we were given by our spouses, Pat and Jan, and our children Christopher, Ellen, and George.

Contributors

Wayne A. Beach — School of Communication, San Diego State University, San Diego, CA 92182-0300

Christina S. Beck — School of Interpersonal Communication, Ohio University, Athens, OH 45701

Richard Buttny — Department of Speech Communication, Syracuse University, Syracuse, NY 13244

Ronald J. Chenail — School of Social and Systemic Studies, Nova Southeastern University, Ft. Lauderdale, FL 33314

Jack Ende — Department of Medicine, Hospital of the University of Pennsylvania, Philadelphia, PA 19194-4283

Frederick Erickson — Graduate School of Education, University of Pennsylvania, Philadelphia, PA 19122

Liana Fortugno — Tressler Centers of Delaware, 1304 N. Rodney Street, Wilmington, DE 19806

Richard M. Frankel — Primary Care Internal Medicine, University of Rochester School of Medicine and Dentistry, Highland Hospital, Rochester, NY 14620

xii CONTRIBUTORS

Jerry Gale	Department of Child and Family Development, University of Georgia, Athens, GA 30602
William R. Gold	Institute for Health Care Evaluation, Scott & White Clinic, 2401 South 31st Street, Temple, TX 76508
Robert Hopper	Department of Speech Communication, The University of Texas, Austin, TX 78712
Arthur D. Jensen	Department of Speech Communication, Syracuse University, Syracuse, NY 13244
Charlotte M. Jones	Department of Communication Studies, Carroll College, Helena, MT 59625
Kelly S. McNeilis	Department of Communication, The Ohio State University, Columbus, OH 43210-1217
Tony McDowell	Department of Obstetrics and Gynecology, Scott & White Clinic, 2401 South 31st Street, Temple, TX 76508
G. H. Morris	Department of Communication Studies, Texas Tech University, Lubbock, TX 79413-3083
Chandra Nagireddy	Department of Child and Family Development, University of Georgia, Athens, GA 30602
Mark Odell	Department of Child and Family Development, University of Georgia, Athens, GA 30602
Dan O'Hair	Department of Communication Studies, University of Oklahoma, Norman, OK 73019
Anita Pomerantz	Department of Rhetoric and Communication, Temple University, Philadelphia, PA 19122
Sandra L. Ragan	Department of Communication, University of Oklahoma, Norman, OK 73019
Dan A. Ratliff	Department of Counseling and Human Services, St. Mary's University, San Antonio, TX 78228-8527
Patricia M. Sias	Department of Speech Communication, Washington State University, Pullman, WA 99164

Richard L. Street, Jr.	Department of Speech Communication and Department of Internal Medicine, Texas A & M University, College Station, TX 77843
W. Ray Thomason	Department of Speech Communication, East Tennessee State University, Johnson City, TN 37614
Teresa L. Thompson	Department of Communication, University of Dayton, Dayton, OH 45469-1410
David A. Todtman	Family Therapy Institute of Vancouver Island, 1434 Thomson Terrace, RR#5, Duncan, British Columbia V9L 4T6, Canada
Jo Ann Ward	Cancer Information Service, University of Texas M. D. Anderson Cancer Center, Houston, TX 77030
Martha D. White	Division of Arts and Humanities, Oklahoma City Community College, Oklahoma City, OK 73159

Introduction:
The Talk of the Clinic

Ronald J. Chenail
Nova Southeastern University

G. H. Morris
Texas Tech University

This book is a collection of original chapters about how speech is used in therapy and medicine. The contributors closely examine how practitioners in such positions as physician, therapist, telephone hot line operator, clinical supervisor, and medical preceptor "fix the world with their voices" (Weick & Browning, 1991). Their focus is on how practitioners' talk with clients, patients, co-workers, and trainees addresses and works through recurrent clinical problems.

The contributors share an orientation to clinical encounters as communication events, a commitment to careful analysis of recorded and transcribed data, and a concern to illuminate and, in some cases, to reform clinical practices. In other ways, the contributors diverge. Some are communication scholars studying clinical encounters. They use research methods that range from the analysis of institutional talk as a derivative of conversation (Drew & Heritage, 1992) to a form of interaction analysis long used to explore dominance in relationships. Others are clinician-researchers trained to use comprehensive discourse analysis, conversation analysis, or interpersonal process recall to better understand clinical practices. Four chapters were co-authored by teams consisting of conversation or discourse analysts and clinicians. In all, there are six analyses of talk in or related to marriage and family therapy, followed by seven analyses of talk in medical encounters.

Our purpose for bringing together this collection is to document, celebrate, and invigorate collaborations between communication-oriented researchers and medical and therapy practitioners and researchers. Today, researchers and practitioners working collaboratively are constructing what may comprise "a basic science of listening-and-talking" (Percy, 1954/1987, p. 159) and are applying it in such settings as therapy sessions, diagnostic interviews, referrals, calls to medical information services and emergency hot lines, mediation sessions, doctor–patient interactions, and home visits. There has been a tremendous increase in the interchange of ideas about medical encounters and therapeutic interaction among clinicians and researchers since the early 1980s that culminates a revolution in the understanding and practice of clinical interaction.

The revolution began when audiotape recorders, movie cameras, and videocameras were first used to capture clinical encounters for repeated review and analysis, and skilled observers used these records to understand how clinical interaction works. Philosophical investigations into the linkage of speech and action, linguistic excursions beyond the level of the sentence, anthropological explorations of speech events, activities and identities, and the emergence of conversation analysis in sociology are the cornerstones of the robust new approach (Labov & Fanshel, 1977).

Although there is considerable variety among discourse-based approaches to clinical interaction, there is also a commonality among them that is of vital importance. Discourse and conversation researchers focus on naturally occurring talk and use recordings and transcripts of the talk to reach a level of detail that would otherwise be impossible. (See the appendix for a key to the transcription symbols used by analysts in this volume.) The validity and richness of descriptions produced by these means are unmatched by other ways of working. What may be more important in the long run, however, is that doing research by recording, transcribing, and analyzing clinical encounters puts researchers and practitioners on an equal footing that fosters productive collaboration. Neither group has a privileged understanding of what happens in the clinic. Rather, the clinicians' insight into the tasks and activities that are being performed meshes well with the analysts' penchant for systematic observation and intricate detail.

The study of clinical talk on the part of clinical researchers and researching clinicians can be conducted both as private and as public research. By private research, we mean the type of inquiry that is done every day by reflecting practitioners in the course of their practices as they re-search their interactions both during conversations with clients and afterward. The purpose of such research is to share the results of the inquiry with practitioners and clients. These studies are usually conducted informally and their results are used to make decisions in and about treatment. This research can be conducted in silence, but most likely clinicians as private researchers report the findings orally to clients during a session or possibly in the form of a letter. Results also may be shared with other professionals, team members, supervisors, referral sources, and so on. Poring over a recording and a detailed transcript of an important moment in clinical interaction can be a useful supplement to more usual forms of private research.

By public research, we mean those studies that are more formal in intent, structure, and execution. These are the types of research that are presented at professional conferences and that are published in professional journals. The methods employed are clearly articulated, contexts of talk are analyzed in intricate detail, and descriptions of clinical moments are rich and exhaustive. The turn-around time between starting a public research study and its having an impact on anyone's practice may be months or even years. However, the science of talk-and-listening has yet another revolutionary impact: Rather than relying on data that can be used only once, collections of discourse and transcripts are being made. This makes it possible for researchers and practitioners to share data and to use it repetitively to study different phenomena. Archiving recordings and transcripts amplifies the productivity of discourse researchers tremendously and brings discourse and conversation analysis into the realm of possibility for private researcher-clinicians.

An explanation for the present recognition and appreciation of communication research in the clinical world is that it uniquely combines the best of both research worlds, the public and the private. From the public style, health-care providers can "private-ize" a whole range of methodologies and techniques that may help them to articulate that which may have been beyond their private lenses. In addition, clinicians can learn how to make their private research results public by adopting and modifying some of the written reporting forms found in communication research (e.g., the display and analysis of exemplars) and by engaging in collaboration with nonclinicians who are specialists in discourse.

In the privatization of a heretofore public communication research method in clinical practice, the research becomes part of the clinical practice, not a postsession or posttreatment inquiry, but an in-session, real-time integral part of the therapy; and sometimes the research itself can become therapeutic. A "practice-wisdom-as-research" trend has recently emerged in the clinical fields (e.g., family therapy: Chenail, 1992; psychology: Hoshmand, 1991; Hoshmand & Polkinghorne, 1992; social work: Scott, 1990; medicine: Shapiro & Talbot, 1991) and practitioners are exploring new and more informative ways (i.e., communication theory, literary theory, narrative, ethnography, discourse analysis, etc.) to express that which they do in clinics and hospitals. With the studies presented in this volume, we hope to build upon this dialectical process between practitioner and researcher and to help the conversation to continue.

In making public the clinician-as-researcher point of view, practitioners can ask their clients to join them in this in-session inquiry; if clients accept, they have taken an important step in de-constructing the clinician–client relationship and re-constructing it as a co-researching one. These co-researchers, practitioner and client alike, have their own methods, their own ways of knowing in the world: They share the results of their observations with each other in dialogue, sharing double descriptions and differences that make a difference for themselves and the other in conversation.

COMMUNICATION AND THE CLINIC

Arguably, the start of modern day inquiry into clinical interaction can be traced to two major projects that stretched from the 1950s to the late 1970s: The Natural History of the Interview (NHI) and the Double Bind project. These two studies, along with their successors, helped to establish the strong ties between the fields of communication and clinical practice.

The NHI (McQuown, 1971b) was an inter-multidisciplinary investigation that included some of the most brilliant investigators from psychiatry (Frieda Fromm-Reichmann and Henry W. Brosin), linguistics (Charles F. Hockett and Norman A. McQuown), anthropology (Gregory Bateson), and kinesics (Ray L. Birdwhistell) (Leeds-Hurwitz, 1987). These researchers were brought together in 1956 by Fromm-Reichmann to produce "a fine-grained analysis, transcription and interpretation of the speech and body motion of participants in a sound-filmed (and tape-recorded) family interview" (McQuown, 1971a, p. 1).

McQuown (1971a) set forth the purpose of the group's investigation of the film by stating that NHI was to serve as

> a general introduction to the theory of microanalysis of interviews with a focus on overt behavior, to the individual systems of analysis of the speech and body-motion of participants in such interviews, to the techniques of manipulating taped and filmed materials in order to facilitate such analysis, and to the theoretical frame suitable for the interpretation of the materials and for the use in psychotherapeutic and other practical applications. (p. 2)

According to Leeds-Hurwitz (1987), NHI directly influenced many other seminal studies of interaction in psychotherapy including *The First Five Minutes: A Sample of Microscopic Interview Analysis* (Pittenger, Hockett, & Danehy, 1960), *Communicational Structure: Analysis of a Psychotherapy Transaction* (Scheflen, 1973), and *Therapeutic Discourse: Psychotherapy as Conversation* (Labov & Fanshel, 1977).

The other major communication study of clinical process from this time period was Bateson's (1972) Double Bind project during which a team investigated a number of clinical approaches: Don Jackson's post-psychoanalytic work, Milton Erickson's clinical hypnosis and John Rosen's direct analysis. Many of these research notions were spelled out in Bateson's (1972, 1979) own work, as well as in the widely used communication book, *Pragmatics of Human Communication: A Study of Interactional Patterns, Pathologies, and Paradoxes* (Watzlawick, Beavin, & Jackson, 1967). Also, a maturation of these ideas as applied to therapy can be found in books like *Change: Principles of Problem Formation and Problem Resolution* (Watzlawick, Weakland, & Fisch, 1974) and *The Tactics of Change: Doing Therapy Briefly* (Fisch, Weakland, & Segal, 1983).

Following these earlier projects, a number of other noteworthy ventures in which clinical practice was informed by communication theory occurred. These language-informed therapy projects include Richard Bandler and John Grinder and their Neuro-Linguistic Programming (NLP) work, the Milan Systemic Therapy-Coordinated Management of Meaning (CMM) collaboration, and Bradford Keeney's cybernetic project.

In Richard Bandler and John Grinder's NLP studies, a close scrutiny of the work of Virginia Satir, Milton Erickson, and others (Davis & Davis, 1982) from a linguistics and grammar metaphor led to an innovative therapy model that embraced some of the Satir–Erickson style of clinical practice, but added some interesting metacommunicative distinctions. The new clinical approach, NLP, was explicated in numerous works such as *The Structure of Magic[1]: A Book about Language And Therapy* (Bandler & Grinder, 1975) and *Trance-formations: Neuro-Linguistic Programming and the Structure of Hypnosis* (Grinder & Bandler, 1981) and has reached a notable level of popularity in the clinical fields.

In the Milan-CMM project, Karl Tomm put together a conference in 1982 at the University of Calgary that allowed for an interesting exchange between a group of Milan-style therapists (e.g., Gianfranco Cecchin, Luigi Boscolo, and Tomm himself) and a number of communication theorists and researchers from the CMM project (e.g., Vernon Cronen, W. Barnett Pearce, John Lannamann, and Sheila McNamee) (McNamee, Lannamann, & Tomm, 1983). This meeting lead to a number of projects and papers created from a juxtaposition of the circular notions of Milan therapy (e.g., Selvini-Palazzoli, Boscolo, Cecchin, & Prata, 1980) with the circularity of communication approach of CMM (Cronen, Johnson, & Lannamann, 1982; Pearce & Cronen, 1980). As a result, Milan-style circularity in therapy took a reflexive turn evident in Tomm's (1987) subsequent work and a turn toward curiosity exemplified in Cecchin's (1987) therapy. As for a change in research, the notion of questions as interventions in therapy (Tomm & Lannamann, 1988) helped lead to the suggestion that research questions may also be seen as interventions and, possibly, as therapy (McNamee, 1988).

In a Batesonian-style metalogue with James Morris, Bradford Keeney gave a short and concise description of his extensive clinical research into therapeutic practice: "My own work concerns the development of cybernetic ethnographies of communication in the context of systemic therapy" (Keeney & Morris, 1985, p. 102). This approach to understanding clinical discourse has led to a number of works, *Aesthetics of Change* (Keeney, 1983), *Mind in Therapy: Constructing Systemic Family Therapies* (Keeney & Ross, 1985), *The Therapeutic Voice of Olga Silverstein* (Keeney & Silverstein, 1986) in which Keeney juxtaposed a science of patterns (i.e., cybernetics) to study a practice of patterns (i.e., systemic family therapies).

The latest development in this cybernetic project has been the creation of Recursive Frame Analysis (RFA), an analytic tool for describing and organizing patterns of frames in conversation. RFA has been used as a researching method to study discourse in a variety of contexts: therapy and supervision (Keeney, 1990; Rambo, Heath, & Chenail, 1993), domestic violence (Keeney & Bobele, 1989), and parents' concern over their children's heart murmurs (Chenail, 1991; Chenail et al., 1990). It also has been employed as a prescription for practicing therapy (Keeney, 1990; Rambo et al., 1993).

THE RISE OF HEALTH COMMUNICATION

Since the publication of Labov and Fanshel's (1977) *Therapeutic Discourse,* arguably the last of the NHI-style opuses, the general field of discourse analysis and several of its currents have matured, and this maturation can best be seen in the growth of health communication as a distinct and influential subfield of communication. With journals like *Health Communication* and *Qualitative Health Research,* and basic texts such as Kreps and Thornton's (1992) *Health Communication* and Silverman's (1987) *Communication and Medical Practice,* the work of health communication researchers and theoreticians has emerged as a rich and diverse voice in both the health-care and communication fields.

Some of the new generation of discourse researchers (e.g., Fisher & Todd, 1983, 1986; Todd, 1984; Waitzkin, 1991; West, 1984) take a critical/interpretive stance toward medical discourse, concentrating on issues of ideology and power. By contrast, other researchers strive to achieve work that is more descriptive and microscopic in character (e.g., Frankel, 1984a, 1984b; Waitzkin & Britt, 1993). Discourse analysts and conversation analysts (e.g., Levinson, 1983; Nofsinger, 1991) are becoming very sophisticated in how they grapple with the particulars of discourse practices. The same can be said of discourse/conversation analysts who have begun to research talk in the clinic (e.g., Freeman, 1987).

With increasing frequency, detailed analyses of clinical discourse are appearing in scholarly journals and in the form of conference presentations. Studies of the use of accounts in marital therapy (Buttny, 1990), presentation of disappointing test results to clients in a speech and hearing clinic (Pomerantz, Mastriano, & Halford, 1987), information giving in medical encounters (Waitzkin, 1985), the potentially hazardous organization of practices used by a poison control hot line (Frankel, 1989), the importance of communication in the medical intake process (Heller & Freeman, 1987), and conversation techniques used by particular therapists (Gale, 1991; Gale & Newfield, 1992) are just a few examples of this expanding movement.

At the same time, a communication focus is becoming more important in the clinical practice arena. The biopsychosocial model (Engel, 1977) has helped health-care providers recognize and appreciate the role communication plays in their practices (Helman, 1985) and their training (Branch et al. 1991). Whether it is the basic medical interview (Billings & Stoeckle, 1989; Hein & Wodak, 1987), or physician-to-physician discourse (Prince, Frader, & Bosk, 1982), or doctor–nurse interaction (Dixon, Wilcox, & Wilcox, 1991), or doctor–patient relations (Tannen & Wallat, 1983, 1986; Waitzkin, 1984; Youssef & Silverman, 1992), physicians, nurses, and other health-care professionals are now more aware of communication in their everyday interactions. Also, they are beginning to be more sensitive to the multichannel aspects of this interaction (e.g., Freidman, 1979; Shreve, Harrigan, Kues, & Kagas, 1988).

THE TALK OF THE CLINIC

As part of this growing trend toward communication research-informed health care and health-care-informed communication research, the studies in this volume have been conceived and collected as state-of-the-art descriptive analyses and as exemplars that bear practical import for clinicians. Each contributor delves deeply into clinical practice and its wisdom; so each is positioned to identify alternative clinical practices and techniques and to appreciate practitioners' means of performing effectively. When reflective practitioners (Schön, 1983, 1987) encounter these pieces or work, productive alterations in how their work is done can be stimulated.

OVERVIEW

The chapters in Part I focus on talk occurring in marriage and family therapy clinics. For readers unfamiliar with how these clinics are usually organized, the key idea is that the therapist tries to work with couples or families, rather than with individuals. When someone calls the clinic for assistance, he or she is interviewed to determine the general nature of the problem, and arrangements are made for an initial session with a therapist and the "family system," that is, those people who plausibly have a stake in the problem and its resolution.

At least in university training settings such as those studied in this book, therapy is conducted in a room designed to allow monitoring by a team of co-therapists and supervisors who may call into the room to give instructions or to ask questions of the therapist. Therapy is routinely videotaped for purposes of reflection, supervision, and research.

Different styles of marriage and family therapy divide the time devoted to a session differently. The session itself is often divided into an initial portion, a mid session break and a final portion. The session may be bracketed by pre- and post-session discussions of what should occur and what has been accomplished. During the midsession break, the principal therapist and the observing team meet to discuss how to proceed. Finally, therapists and supervisors hold periodic supervision sessions. These sessions involve review of what is happening with the therapists' cases. Attention is directed to particular cases and moments within them by replaying portions of sessions on video. This process is termed *videotape supervision*.

The therapy-oriented contributions to this volume span the various activities we have just described. The first two chapters relate to kinds of talk that occur within marriage and family therapy sessions. In the first chapter, Richard Buttny and Arthur Jensen describe how clients tell therapists the nature of their problems in initial sessions. Buttny and Jensen examine six episodes of talk occurring in the first 9 minutes of a session, and address how the talk is organized hierarchically into a coherent narrative. In chapter 2, Charlotte Jones and Wayne Beach address how therapists order therapeutic conversations by constraining who has the floor to speak. Their chapter is based on videorecordings and transcripts of 8 hours of sessions conducted by three therapists with five families. It principally concerns one aspect of how turns are managed: How therapists respond to the contributions of family members who have not been asked to speak.

Ron Chenail and Liana Fortugno, in chapter 3, examine a "practicum group" of student therapists and more experienced clinicians discussing a case during a midsession break. The chapter is reminiscent of Weick and Browning's (1991) observation that "conceptual" therapists "fix the world with their voices." These contributors show how the practicum group discovers how the language in use by the family, which binds them into their problem and blinds them to alternative ways to escape it, can be "loosened" and "reconfigured" to foster therapeutic change. This chapter exemplifies the practice-wisdom-as-research orientation to which we alluded earlier.

The three remaining therapy papers relate to activities after sessions are complete. David Todtman uses the method Labov and Fanshel (1977) established (comprehensive discourse analysis) to explore how an observing team and therapist deliberate about the progress being made on a case. By examining an episode from a postsession discussion, Todtman, in chapter 4, reveals how conflict among team members can influence the group's perspective on therapy cases and even their determination of whether or not therapy has been successful.

In chapter 5, Jerry Gale, Mark Odell, and Chandra Nagireddy offer a glimpse at what can happen when the border between research activities and therapeutic activities is blurred. These contributors delve into the talk of the initial session of a marital therapy session and interviews with clients and therapist about significant moments occurring within the initial session. Results from these interviews (e.g., what each party felt had been significant and why) were revealed to the clients in a final "Reflexive Process Analysis." The chapter addresses four interpretive themes that emerged from consideration of the entire process of therapy/research, including one that may be quite provocative: The research seems to have been more therapeutic than the therapy.

The final chapter in Part I is an investigation of how supervisors give suggestions to trainees about what to do in upcoming sessions. Dan Ratliff and G. H. Morris (chapter 6) base their observations on 12 supervision sessions conducted by three supervisors in a top-ranked marriage and family therapy program. The analysis shows how, in 39% of 117 suggestion cases, supervisors go beyond telling trainees to do things—actually telling how to say things to clients or to other mental health personnel. Ratliff and Morris coin the term, *how to say its* to refer to this phenomenon and describe the circumstances that call them forth in family therapy supervision.

Chapters in Part II all concern the discourse of medical clinics. Five of the seven chapters pertain to the interaction of physicians or other practitioners with patients. The initial two chapters, however, pertain to other kinds of medical encounters. Anita Pomerantz, Jack Ende, and Frederick Erickson, in chapter 7, look into precepting conversations. In these conversations, the structure of which is similar to the supervision sessions just mentioned, experienced physicians ("preceptors") assess and guide interns' activities with patients. In particular, the medical history and physical exam, the diagnosis, and the plan for treatment are examined and modified as necessary. The focus of this analysis is on how preceptors correct interns who are perceived to be wrong. Particular techniques of correction are described. In contrast to the blatant and harsh corrections one might expect on the basis of prior research or anecdote, these are performed much more supportively.

The second chapter in this part (chapter 8) is about a kind of "aligning action" that can be found in calls to a cancer information service. Robert Hopper, Jo Ann Ward, Ray Thomason, and Patricia Sias explore what we can call *natural* and *institutional* varieties of disclaimers in these calls. When information specialists give what the authors refer to as *early* disclaimers, they tell callers that, although they are not doctors, cannot give medical advice, and so on, they do have useful information to provide. The thrust of this contribution is its contrast of such institutional disclaimers with how disclaimers occur in natural conversation, in which they are embedded more fittingly into the ongoing stream of talk. Accordingly, this chapter, like the preceding one by Jones and Beach, exemplifies how conversation analysts have begun to approach institutional talk (Drew & Heritage, 1992) by seeing institutional discourse as constrained or structured in ways that ordinary talk is not.

Chapter 9 by Sandra Ragan, Christina Beck and Martha White presents an analysis of health-care interviews conducted by a nurse practitioner with 22 Native American women who were being seen for routine pregnancy exams. The authors explore how the nurse practitioner diplomatically sets about educating the women, while the exam is ongoing, about how best to take care of themselves. Specific measures are utilized to give patients information without calling patients' competence into question. These techniques fit a model of "interactive learning" that is offered as a possible strategy for educating patients and thereby improving health-care outcomes. Readers who have grown tired of "doctor bashing" in writing about health communication and who want to see examples of the work of practitioners who are performing talk very skillfully will appreciate this chapter especially.

Richard Street, William Gold, and Tony McDowell's chapter (10), like the preceding one, examines prenatal visits. In this case, seven medical residents interviewed 56 women during the very early stages of pregnancy. The study combines qualitative analysis with quantitative measures of the women's preferences for doctors to inquire about their health-related quality of life, women's perceptions of whether or not these matters were addressed, and their satisfaction with the health care they received. The qualitative portion of the report is based on recordings of 43 interviews in which health-related quality of life was in fact discussed.

The analysis focuses on the variety of ways that health-related quality of life is brought up for discussion or avoided by patient or doctor. Finally, the authors address several clinical implications of the analysis, including recommendations about the kinds of quality of life issues that it might be most appropriate to explore.

Richard Frankel (chapter 11) laments the lack of theoretical discussion upon which to base understandings of the clinical interview and offers two avenues for theoretical exploration. Via case analysis of clinical encounters, Frankel argues that neither linguistic analysis focusing on questions and answers as preconstituted speech acts, nor sequential analysis focusing on question–answer chains adequately come to grips with the realities of how questions and answers emerge and are interpreted in clinical interviews. Two cases illustrate how it might be possible to construct more adequate approaches to the interview that retain sensitivity to local, sequential contexts while also attending to the structure provided by clinical tasks and activities.

Sometimes well-intended rules for clinical practice handicap interaction rather than improving the quality of clinical work. One instance of this is the idea that physicians should not say "okay" in clinical encounters because patients might be misled seriously. Wayne Beach (chapter 12) describes the rationale others have given for this proscription, then exposes the lack of understanding of discourse such a proscription evidences. Beach begins by showing that fictive illustrations of the use of "okay" do not display that patients are actually confused. He then shows, based on conversation analysis of actual interviews, many of the ways that "okays" are used appropriately in institutional talk. For instance, "okays" are part of the way other's turns are treated as complete and topics are averted or changed. Thus, rather than being speech act nuisances, "okays" are shown to be indispensable to clinical interaction.

The concluding chapter (13) by Kelly McNeilis, Teresa Thompson, and Dan O'Hair addresses how physicians and patients negotiate control over their relationship during clinical encounters. Based in the tradition of relationship communication originated by Bateson and his associates, this chapter examines the control functions served by individual utterances and interacts in clinical interviews, especially how they combine into patterns of interactional symmetry or complementarity. The analysis illustrates different kinds of interaction patterns that occur within the negotiation of a therapeutic plan. Part of the innovativeness of this chapter is that it moves beyond the analysis of these patterns to also explore role negotiation between physician and patient and global patterns of control. Especially illuminating is the identification in these interviews of control "switchpoints" at which global patterns shift from one type to another. The discussion of these switchpoints is a point of intersection with several of the other chapters in this volume, most notably Ragan and colleagues' approach to educating the patient, (chapter 9), Street and associates' exploration of circumstances in which quality of life is talked about (chapter 10), and Frankel's analysis of windows of opportunity in clinical interviews (chapter 11).

Overall, the distinctive features of this work are that its authors present a variety of state-of-the-art descriptions of clinical talk in which they focus on several key moments, achievements, and practices, and display analyses of clinical talk in ways that can have an impact upon future solutions to the recurrent problems of the clinic. We hope this work will garner reflective practitioners' attention to new ways of considering their talk and that new possibilities for communicating effectively and conducting clinical research will result.

APPENDIX: TRANSCRIPTION KEY

The following symbols are used in the transcriptions in this volume:

[ ]	Brackets are used to indicate overlapping utterances. Left brackets note the beginning of an overlap, and right brackets close or end the overlap.
=	This sign denotes a "latching" of two contiguous utterances that do not overlap.
____	Underlining represents stress/emphasis.
:	A colon stands for the extension or stretching of the sound that it follows.
-	A hyphen following a sound marks a cut-off, a definite stopping of sound.
?	A question mark indicates rising pitch at the end of a word or phrase ending, *not* necessarily a grammatical question.
↑	An arrow pointing upward shows a marked rise in pitch.
.	A period indicates a sliding or falling pitch at the end of a word or phrase, *not* necessarily a grammatical sentence.
,	A comma denotes a continuing intonation, a subtle or slight stretching of sound with a small upward or downward pitch that shows possible completion.
^ ^ ° °	A carat sign or degree sign preceding and following a word or phrase indicates that it was said more quietly than the surrounding talk.
» «	The sideways chevrons bracket talk that is spoken *faster* than the surrounding talk.
« »	The sideways chevrons bracket talk that is spoken *slower* than the surrounding talk.
(0.4)	Single parentheses enclosing numbers represent pauses in a conversation. The numbers express seconds and tenths of seconds. Brief pauses are expressed as (.).
( )	Single parentheses enclosing words or blank space surround doubtful hearings.
hhh	Hs indicate audible outbreaths, sighing, or nonverbal laughter.

˙hh   A superscripted period followed by hs denotes audible inbreaths.
y(h)es   An "(h)" displays speech with laughter embedded.
pt   This symbol indicates an audible lip smack.
*   The asterisk indicates a gravelly voice, break, or catch in pronunciation.
(( ))   Double parentheses are used for descriptions of nonverbal behavior or nonspeech sounds.

These transcription symbols are adapted from the notation system developed by Jefferson (Sacks, Schegloff, & Jefferson, 1974).

REFERENCES

Bandler, R., & Grinder, J. (1975). *The structure of magic[1]: A book about language and therapy.* Palo Alto, CA: Science and Behavior Books.

Bateson, G. (1972). *Steps to an ecology of mind.* New York: Ballantine.

Bateson, G. (1979). *Mind and nature: A necessary unity.* New York: Bantam.

Billings, J. A., & Stoeckle, J. D. (1989). *The clinical encounter: A guide to the medical interview and case presentation.* Chicago: Year Book Medical Publishers.

Branch, W. T., Arky, R. A., Woo, B., Stoeckle, J. D., Levy, D. B., & Taylor, W. C. (1991). Teaching medicine as a human experience: A patient-doctor relationship course for faculty and first-year medical students. *Annals of Internal Medicine, 114,* 482–489.

Buttny, R. (1990). Blame-accounts sequences in therapy: The negotiation of relational meanings. *Semiotica, 78,* 57–77.

Cecchin, G. (1987). Hypothesizing, circularity, and neutrality revisited: An invitation to curiosity. *Family Process, 26,* 405–413.

Chenail, R. J. (1991). *Medical discourse and systemic frames of comprehension.* Norwood, NJ: Ablex.

Chenail, R. J. (1992). A case for clinical qualitative research. *The Qualitative Report, 1*(4), 1, 3–7.

Chenail, R. J., Douthit, P. E., Gale, J. E., Stormberg, J. L., Morris, G. H., Park, J. M., Sridaromont, S., & Schmer, V. (1990). "It's probably nothing serious, but . . . ": Parents' interpretation of referral to pediatric cardiologists. *Health Communication, 2*(3), 165–187.

Cronen, V. E., Johnson, K. M., & Lannamann, J. W. (1982). Paradoxes, double binds, and reflexive loops: An alternative theoretical perspective. *Family Process, 21,* 91–112.

Davis, S. L. R., & Davis, D. (1982). NLP and marital and family therapy. *The Family Therapy Networker, 6*(3), 19–21, 46.

Dixon, L., Wilcox, J. R., & Wilcox, E. M. (1991). *Playing the doctor-nurse game.* Paper presented at the International Communication Association Annual Conference, Miami, FL.

Drew, P., & Heritage, J. (Eds.). (1992). *Talk at work.* Cambridge: Cambridge University Press.

Engel, G. L. (1977). The need for a new medical model: A challenge for biomedicine. *Science, 196,* 129–136.

Fisch, R., Weakland, J. H. & Segal, L. (1983). *The tactics of change: Doing therapy briefly.* San Francisco: Jossey-Bass.

Fisher, S., & Todd, A. D. (Eds.). (1983). *The social organization of doctor-patient communication.* Washington, DC: Center for Applied Linguistics.

Fisher, S., & Todd, A. D. (Eds.). (1986). *Discourse and institutional authority: Medicine, education, and law.* Norwood, NJ: Ablex.

Frankel, R. M. (1984a). From sentence to sequence: Understanding the medical encounter through microinteractional analysis. *Discourse Processes, 7,* 135–170.

Frankel, R. M. (Ed.). (1984b). Physicians and patients in social interaction: Medical encounters as a discourse process [Special issue]. *Discourse Processes, 7.*

Frankel, R. M. (1989). "I wuz wondering—uhm could Raid uhm effect the brain permanently d'y know?": Some observations on the intersection of speaking and writing in calls to a poison control center. *Western Journal of Speech Communication, 53,* 195–226.

Freeman, S. H. (1987). Introduction. Verbal communication in medical encounters: An overview of recent work. *Text, 7,* 3–17.

Freidman, H. S. (1979). Nonverbal communication between patients and medical practitioners. *Journal of Social Issues, 35,* 82–99.

Gale, G. E. (1991). *Conversation analysis of a marital therapy session: Pursuit of a therapeutic agenda.* Norwood, NJ: Ablex.

Gale, J. E., & Newfield, N. (1992). A conversation analysis of a solution-focused marital therapy session. *Journal of Marital and Family Therapy, 18,* 153–165.

Grinder, J., & Bandler, R. (1981). *Trance-formations: Neuro-linguistic programming and the structure of hypnosis.* Moab, UT: Real People.

Hein, N., & Wodak, R. (1987). Medical interviews in internal medicine: Some results of an empirical investigation. *Text, 7,* 37–65.

Heller, M., & Freeman, S. (1987). First encounters: The role of communication in the medical intake process. *Discourse Processes, 10,* 369–384.

Helman, C. G. (1985). Communication in primary care: The role of the patient and practitioner explanatory models. *Social Science and Medicine, 20,* 923–931.

Hoshmand, L. T. (1991). Clinical inquiry as scientific training. *The Counseling Psychologist, 19,* 431–453.

Hoshmand, L. T., & Polkinghorne, D. E. (1992). Redefining the science-practice relationship and professional training. *American Psychologist, 47,* 55–66.

Keeney, B. P. (1983). *Aesthetics of change.* New York: Guilford.

Keeney, B. P. (1990). *Improvisational therapy.* St. Paul, MN: Systemic Therapy Press.

Keeney, B. P., & Bobele, M. (1989). A brief note on family violence. *Australian and New Zealand Journal of Family Therapy, 10*(2), 93–95.

Keeney, B. P., & Morris, J. P. (1985). Family therapy practice and research: A dialogue. In L. L. Andreozzi (Ed.), *Integrating research and clinical practice* (pp. 98–107). Rockville, MD: Aspen.

Keeney, B. P., & Ross, J. M. (1985). *Mind in therapy: Constructing systemic family therapies.* New York: Basic Books.

Keeney, B. P., & Silverstein, O. (1986). *The therapeutic voice of Olga Silverstein.* New York: Guilford.

Kreps, G. L., & Thornton, B. C. (1992). *Health communication: Theory & practice* (2nd ed.). Prospect Heights, IL: Waveland.

Labov, W., & Fanshel, D. (1977). *Therapeutic discourse: Psychotherapy as conversation.* New York: Academic Press.

Leeds-Hurwitz, W. (1987). The social history of the natural history of an interview: A multidisciplinary investigation of social communication. *Research on Language and Social Interaction, 20,* 1–51.

Levinson, S. C. (1983). *Pragmatics.* Cambridge: Cambridge University Press.

McNamee, S. (1988). Accepting research as social intervention: Implications of a systemic epistemology. *Communications Quarterly, 36,* 50–68.

McNamee, S., Lannamann, J., & Tomm, K. (1983). Milan clinicians and CMM theoreticians meet: Was it a fertile connection? *Journal of Strategic and Systemic Therapies, 2*(1), 57–62.

McQuown, N. A. (1971a). Forward. In N. A. McQuown (Ed.), *The natural history of an interview* (pp. 1–5. Available from Microfilm Collection of Manuscripts on Cultural Anthropology).) Chicago: University of Chicago, Joseph Regenstein Library, Department of Photoduplication.

McQuown, N. A. (Ed.). (1971b). *The natural history of an interview* (Available from Microfilm Collection of Manuscripts on Cultural Anthropology). Chicago: University of Chicago, Joseph Regenstein Library, Department of Photoduplication.

Nofsinger, R. (1991). *Everyday conversation.* Newbury Park, CA: Sage.

Pearce, W. B., & Cronen, V. E. (1980). *Communication, action, and meaning: The creation of social realities.* New York: Praeger.

Percy, W. (1987). *The message in the bottle: How queer man is, how queer language is, and what one has to do with the other.* New York: Farrar, Strauss and Giroux. (Original work published 1954)

Pittenger, R. E., Hockett, C. F., & Danehy, J. J. (1960). *The first five minutes: A sample of microscopic interview analysis.* Ithaca, NY: Paul Martineau.

Pomerantz, A. M., Mastriano, B. P., & Halford, M. M. (1987). Student clinicians' difficulties while conducting the summary diagnostic interview. *Text, 7,* 19–36.

Prince, E., Frader, J., & Bosk, C. (1982). On hedging in physician-physician discourse. In R. J. Di Pietro (Ed.), *Linguistics and the professions: Proceedings of the second annual Delaware symposium on language studies* (pp. 83–97). Norwood, NJ: Ablex.

Rambo, A. H., Heath, A. W., & Chenail, R. J. (1993). *Practicing therapy: Exercises for growing therapists.* New York: W. W. Norton.

Sacks, H., Schegloff, E. A., & Jefferson, G. (1974). A simplest systematics for the organization of turn-taking in conversation. *Language, 50,* 696–735.

Scheflen, A. E. (1973). *Communicational structure: Analysis of a psychotherapy transaction.* Bloomington, IN: Indiana University Press.

Schön, D. A. (1983). *The reflective practitioner: How professionals think in action.* New York: Basic Books.

Schön, D. A. (1987). *Educating the reflective practitioner: Toward a new design for teaching and learning in the professions.* San Francisco, Jossey-Bass.

Scott, D. (1990). Practice wisdom: The neglected source of practice wisdom. *Social Work, 35,* 564–568.

Selvini-Palazzoli, M., Boscolo, L., Cecchin, G., & Prata, G. (1980). Hypothesizing—circularity—neutrality: Three guidelines for the conductor of the session. *Family Process, 19,* 3–12.

Shapiro, J., & Talbot, Y. (1991). Applying the concept of the reflective practitioner to understanding and teaching family medicine. *Family Medicine, 23,* 450–456.

Shreve, E. G., Harrigan, J. A., Kues, J. R., & Kagas, D. K. (1988). Nonverbal expressions of anxiety in physician-patient interactions. *Psychiatry, 51,* 378–384.

Silverman, D. (1987). *Communication and medical practice.* London: Sage.

Tannen, D., & Wallat, C. (1983). Doctor/mother/child communication: Linguistic analysis of a pediatric interaction. In S. Fisher & A. D. Todd (Eds.), *The social organization of doctor-patient communication* (pp. 203–219). Washington, DC: Center for Applied Linguistics.

Tannen, D., & Wallat, C. (1986). Medical professionals and parents: A linguistic analysis of communication across contexts. *Language in Society, 15,* 295–312.

Todd, A. D. (1984). The prescription of contraception: Negotiations between doctors and patients. *Discourse Processes, 7,* 171–200.

Tomm, K. (1987). Interventive interviewing: Part I. strategizing as a fourth guideline for the therapist. *Family Process, 26,* 3–13.

Tomm, K., & Lannamann, J. (1988). Questions as interventions. *The Family Therapy Networker, 12*(5), 38–41.

Waitzkin, H. (1984). Doctor-patient communication: Clinical implications of social scientific research. *Journal of the American Medical Association, 252,* 2441–2446.

Waitzkin, H. (1985). Information giving in medical care. *Journal of Health and Social Behavior, 26,* 81–101.

Waitzkin, H. (1991). *The politics of medical encounters: How patients and doctors deal with social problems.* New Haven, CT: Yale University Press.

Waitzkin, H., & Britt, T. (1993). Processing narratives of self-destructive behavior in routine medical encounters: Health promotion, disease prevention, and the discourse of health care. *Social Science & Medicine, 36,* 1121–1136.

Watzlawick, P., Beavin, J. B., & Jackson, D. D. (1967). *Pragmatics of human communication: A study of interactional patterns, pathologies, and paradoxes.* New York: Norton.

Watzlawick, P., Weakland, J., Fisch, R. (1974). *Change: Principles of problem formation and problem resolution.* New York: Norton.

West, C. (1984). Medical misfires: Mishearings, misgivings, and misunderstandings in physician-patient dialogues. *Discourse Processes, 7,* 107–134.

Weick, K. E., & Browning, L. D. (1991). Fixing with the voice: A research agenda for applied communication. *Journal of Applied Communication Research, 19,* 1–19.

Youssef, V., & Silverman, D. (1992). Normative expectations for medical talk. *Language & Communication, 12,* 123–131.

THERAPY AND CONVERSATIONS ABOUT THERAPY

1 Telling Problems in an Initial Family Therapy Session: The Hierarchical Organization of Problem-Talk

Richard Buttny
Arthur D. Jensen
Syracuse University

Communicators continually attend to the evaluative significance of their own and others' actions. When actions fail in various ways this may lead to the emergence of troubles or problems. To conceive of something as a problem opens up the need for a response of some sort to solve, reframe, or at least cope with the problem (Buttny, 1985; Morris, 1985). In short, to frame an action, event, or relationship as problematic makes a response practically necessary (Scott & Lyman, 1968). In close relationships, such as marriage, the perception of and talk about relational problems are characteristic of the disintegration and alienation phases of relational change (Conville, 1991).

Problems that are seen as serious and without a ready solution may lead one to seek out the help of a specialist, such as a therapist. Therapy sessions are a specialized communication context that involves intensive talk about problems and candidate solutions guided by a therapist (Labov & Fanshel, 1977). Therapy sessions offer a particularly interesting form of communication because participants are oriented to the description and explanation of problems and the search for, and evaluation of, solutions (Bergmann, 1992; Buttny, 1990; Buttny & Cohen, 1991; Gale, 1991; Gale & Newfield, 1992; Lannamann, 1989; Peyrot, 1987; Wodak, 1981). How do participants construct problems through talk? How is language used to allocate responsibility and blame? How are problems responded to? We need to look more closely at how persons talk about problems and how responses to problems are accomplished.

This chapter begins with an analysis of discourse about problems and responses. Because therapy sessions offer a context in which participants talk intensively about their own and other's problems, part of a family therapy session is used as a text. Family therapy sessions, in particular, are interesting in view of the fact that each participant can present his or her telling of problems as well as respond to other participant's tellings. We conceive of *problem-talk* as an issue of global coherence, that is, how problems are accomplished and organized as a whole. The case is made that the construction of problems has an underlying hierarchical structure. Furthermore, we attempt to integrate our analysis of the therapeutic discourse with the larger body of interpersonal communication theory. In this study, an analysis of discourse about relational problems is located within a model of relational transition (Conville, 1991). A hierarchical model of meaning is posited as the dynamic, recursive link between these two levels of analysis and action.

GLOBAL COHERENCE

Coherence in discourse is generally thought of as a function of both local coherence and global coherence (see G. Brown & Yule, 1983, chapter 7, and McLaughlin, 1984, chapter 2, for reviews). Local coherence concerns how discourse parts are chained together, for example, turn-taking in conversation (Sacks, Schegloff, & Jefferson, 1974), the sequencing of lexico-syntactic parts (Halliday & Hasan, 1976), or the telling of "what happened next" in a narrative (Labov & Waletsky, 1968). Global coherence concerns the overall point or goal of the discourse, for example, the plot structure in a narrative (Meyer, 1975), the goals in a plan (Hobbs & Evans, 1979), or the point from an informant in an ethnographic interview (Agar & Hobbs, 1982).

Discourse must cohere at both the local and the global level. Discourse coheres globally by seeing its "macrostructure" (Van Dijk, 1980). Macrostructure is used to frame the intuitive sense of the gist or point of a discourse. The notion of macrostructure provides an abstract semantic description of the global content and, hence, of the global coherence of discourse. Macrostructures are derived from the text by semantic mapping rules or "macrorules": deletion, generalization, and construction (Van Dijk, 1980). Macrostructures may be hierarchically arrayed as a function of their level of abstraction from the text. For instance, at the highest level, the whole text may be abstracted into a single macroproposition. For Van Dijk, global coherence may also be conceived of by the notion of "superstructure": "the schematic form that organizes the global meaning of a text" (pp. 108–109). Texts such as narratives, arguments, scholarly papers, and newspaper articles will consist of both macrostructure and superstructure. Macrostructure involves the higher order structures of the semantic content of the text, whereas superstructure involves the conventionalized, schematic form of the text. Narratives typically are organized around the superstructure categories of setting, episode, complication, resolution, plot, and the like; whereas, at the same time, these schematic forms need to be filled in by the content categories or macrostructure of the particular narrative. Global coherence may be seen as the overall goals the participants are attempting to achieve in the discourse (Hobbs & Evans, 1979; Levy, 1979; Schank

& Abelson, (1977). A person's actions can be seen in a means–ends framework to achieve his or her main goals. The global notion of goals or plans can be broken down into strategies or subgoals, which likewise may be further broken down. But each level of subgoal needs to be seen in terms of the communicator's main goal(s).

Hinds (1979) claimed that there are two basic types of discourse organization: linear organization (e.g., turn-taking rules) and hierarchical organization. As the text unfolds in a linear progression, a hierarchical structure can be imposed on this linear progression. All discourse can be organized by *paragraphs:* "a unit of speech or writing which maintains a uniform orientation" (Hinds, 1979, p. 136). Paragraphs subsume other levels of organization such as *segments, events,* and *performatives*. For instance, Hinds shows how the discourse type—interview—can be hierarchically arranged by paragraphs (e.g., eliciting background information) that subsumes the segments (e.g., place born, place raised, arrival in Hawaii, etc.), and so on. The communication theory, the coordinated management of meaning, conceives of a person's meanings as hierarchically organized (Cronen, Johnson, & Lannamann, 1982; Pearce, Cronen, & Conklin, 1979). A model of hierarchical organization of meanings is based on the premise that any specific level of organization is simultaneously whole and part (Cronen et al., 1982). That is, any discourse unit (e.g., the speech act) is itself a whole, but it is simultaneously part of a larger whole (e.g., maintaining a relationship with an acquaintance). A hierarchical model is used to explain how various parts of the discourse contribute to the whole and, in turn, are only understandable in terms of the whole. A hierarchical conception is used to capture the multiple levels of meaning in discourse, but each level may simultaneously influence the other. The model is hierarchical in that increasing degrees of generality and contextual influence are represented at each level. The model is reflexive in that lower levels of context may alter higher levels of context. The extent to which interactants coordinate the definition of context is the extent to which a sequence of utterances is judged to be coherent.

The Global Coherence of Problem-Talk

Labov and Fanshel's (1977) detailed examination of problem-talk during a therapy session stands out as an exemplar of discourse analysis. Here we just review their sense of global coherence in discourse. Labov and Fanshel claimed that "most utterances can be seen as performing several speech acts simultaneously" (p. 29); conversation is not so much a "chain of utterances" but "a matrix of utterances and actions bound together by a web of understandings and reactions" (p. 30).

To understand the matrix or multiple levels of actions leads to a "cross-sectional analysis" (p. 37). This is achieved by a "close reading" of the text to ascertain "what is really going on" in the discourse (p. 59). A close reading allows an expansion of the text to make explicit what is implicit. This is accomplished, in part, by seeing a portion of the text in terms of what has already been said and what will be subsequently said. The expansion of the text (what is said) is transformed into the mode of interaction (what is done) by rules of speech actions (see Labov & Fanshel, 1977, p. 68 for a schema of this approach). It is at the level of actions that Labov and Fanshel examined global coherence. Multiple actions may be performed by a single utterance. To present one example of this approach, Labov and Fanshel looked at the client's recounting of what she said to her mother as performing six actions simultaneously at various levels of abstraction. From the client's utterance, "Look, you've been there long enough," Labov and Fanshel inferred six actions: the *assertions* to her mother, (a) you have fulfilled secondary obligations and (b) you have neglected primary obligations; an *assertion* to the therapist, (c) I have carried out the suggestion of therapy; a *request* to her mother, (d) come home and help with primary obligations; a *challenge* to her mother, (e) you have not performed your role as mother properly; and an *admission* to mother and therapist, (f) Rhoda (i.e., the client) may not be an adult member of the household. Each of these actions at various levels of abstraction contribute to the global coherence of the therapeutic situation.

The Accomplishment of Global Coherence in Problem-Talk Through the Hierarchical Organization of Meanings

Intermediate between "what is said" and "what is done" is the level of "what is meant." Labov and Fanshel (1977) approached this level of meanings through their expansion of the text to make what is implicit, explicit. However, instead of using Labov and Fanshel's method of reading forward into the text to use future information to interpret the present, we present a model that examines the interactants' underlying logic as they tell their problems. That is, we approach the level of meaning by looking at how global coherence is accomplished through problem-talk. A problem may be seen as a configuration of events, conditions, wants, goals, and intentions that can be told to another. Our concern here is with the telling of the problem—discourse about problems or how persons construct a problem through talk. In a therapy session, the telling of a problem becomes an object of examination and discussion. What is the underlying logic or structure of this object (i.,e., the problem)? How do persons organize the telling of a problem? Building on the work of Cronen et al. (1982), Buttny (1985), Hinds (1979), and Van Dijk (1980), the case is made here that the underlying logic of discourse about problems is hierarchically organized.

Rationale for a Hierarchical Organization. An organizational feature found in problem-talk, or in any discourse type, is that of *importance* or *salience*. Participants, as well as researchers, recognize that certain parts of a discourse are more salient or important than other parts. This notion of importance is reflected by discourse categories such as topic (Keenan & Schieffelin, 1976), formulations of the gist (Heritage & Watson, 1979), issue, theme, and the like. The criterion for importance may vary from speaker to listener, or from reader to reader, but the point is that we do distinguish among levels of importance. This notion of levels of importance in discourse needs to be seen as hierarchically organized. Higher order and lower order levels of importance suggest a hierarchical or cross-sectional configuration of the whole.

On our conception of hierarchy, the various levels of the configuration are not a fixed schema or prototypical forms as we find with Hinds (1979) where a paragraph topic subsumes segments that subsume events, or with Longacre (1979) where a story subsumes paragraphs that, in turn, subsume sentences, or with Cantor and Mischel's (1979) work on person perception where the prototypical form, "cultured person" subsumes "patron of the arts" that then subsumes "donator to repertory theater" and "supporter of community orchestra," and so on. Instead of conventional, fixed levels in a hierarchical relation, we conceive of a hierarchical organization as context-dependent and emerging from the person's meanings in the discourse. That is, higher order meanings will reflect the speaker's ascription of importance or salience in the discourse. These higher order meanings cannot be known a priori or as a schema, but are a function of interpretation of discourse. Higher order levels of meaning reflect importance or salience in the speaker's discourse. Importance may be recognized by three kinds of criteria. First, speakers can indicate importance by *repetition* or *recurrence* of a proposition in the discourse. Speakers may use different words to make the same underlying point. Second, speakers may mark importance by various *verbal devices,* such as "so my point is . . . "; "what I'm trying to say is . . . "; "it all boils down to . . . "; and the like. Importance may also be marked *paralinguistically* by devices such as vocal emphasis through increased pitch or volume, drawl on words, or pausing before or after important points. Although these devices are conventionalized ways to signal importance, they are highly context-sensitive. Third, conversational partners may indicate importance by what they respond to in the prior speaker's turn. Although listeners may respond, rather than reply (Goffman, 1976) to practically anything suggested by the speaker, responding to the speaker's main point or "issue" is generally perceived as more competent (Tracy, 1985).

Importance or higher order levels of meaning imply a hierarchical organization to discourse. For instance, telling a problem in a therapy session may be seen as hierarchically configured. To account for the person's meanings, we need to examine the global coherence or whole of the discourse. Lower order levels of meaning can only be understood in the context of the higher order levels. That is, the higher order levels subsume the lower order levels, such that the latter needs to be seen in conjunction with the former. In Cronen et al.'s (1982) terms, the meaning of a part can only be understood in the context of the whole. Or, in Van Dijk's (1980) terms, the macrostructure allows us to interpret the meanings of lower order macrostructures and microstructures. In short, this internal relation of higher order levels subsuming lower order levels is the key to the notion of the hierarchical organization of discourse.

This conception of hierarchical organization is applied to discourse about problems during a therapy session. There are culturally recognized ways in which persons can talk about problems: causes, consequences, solutions, examples, descriptions, narratives, and the like. These relations do not allow for a schematic hierarchical ordering. However, once we examine actual problem talk, we see that certain higher order meanings arise as a function of importance and configure lower order meanings. The hierarchical relations among the parts constitute the speaker's meanings. This provides the rationale for our first research question: How are problems constructed through discourse?

Given that problems become constructed, how do participants orient themselves toward these problems? The construction of a problem makes a response of some sort conditionally relevant or practically necessary. A response to a problem may involve numerous types of moves, such as denying, conceding, justifying, excusing, blaming, and the like, while the therapist may respond by questioning, doubting, supporting, and so on. By seeing these various moves in response to the hierarchical organization of the problem, we may be better able to understand the functions of these moves. Our second research question is: How do speakers orient responses to the hierarchical organization of the problem? (For further discussion of the methodology used to investigate these research questions, see the appendix.)

THE ORGANIZATION OF PROBLEMS IN FAMILY THERAPY DISCOURSE

Our research questions of how problems are constructed and how problems are responded to in discourse suggests that we need to examine the progression or development of the problem through the therapy session. This approach of looking at how the problem is constructed over time is contrasted to looking at the therapy session as a whole.

Our analysis is taken from episodes in the first 9½ minutes of the therapy session. We divided this opening section into six episodes. The notion of an episode reflects a sequential organization of discourse that is bounded by a principle of unity (Harré & Secord, 1972). This principle of unity is frequently topic focused (Labov & Fanshel, 1977), but also episodes may be marked by shifts in structure (e.g., narrative or interactional discourse) or by changes in conversational style (e.g., formal to informal). We distinguished six episodes in the opening 9½ minutes: Episode 1: initial presentation of the problem; Episode 2: elaboration upon the initial presentation of the problem; Episode 3: wife's narrative about relationship with brother-in-law; Episode 4: wife's narrative about past happiness and present problem; Episode 5: wife's blaming and husband's defending; Episode 6: husband's decision to stay or go.

A complete account of problem-talk involves the examination of each participant's hierarchical organization of meaning. In the present study, we focus on the clients' sense of the hierarchical structure of their problem. Therapists attempt to avoid placing blame on a single family member, attempting instead to help clients discover the interactive nature of family problems. Clearly, the therapist's orientation to the problem will influence the problem's negotiation during the session. Our concern here, however, is with the clients' construction of problems as told to the therapist. The intricacies of client–therapist problem negotiation are discussed elsewhere (Lannamann & Buttny, 1985).

Episode 1A: Husband's Initial Presentation of the Problem

It is a well-known feature of therapeutic sessions that participants are oriented to the presentation, discussion, and solution of problems. How is discourse about problems organized in therapy sessions? The therapist makes requests for information and feelings, probes and asks for clarification, doubts or confirms participants' descriptions. The therapist's utterances function to provide direction for the discourse; the therapist's request for the problems to be worked on leads the husband and then the wife to present their problems. But this request–comply pair merely scratches the surface of organizational features of the discourse. We need to look at how the problem is constructed through the telling, that is, the internal relations of the problem as presented.

The husband initiates the telling of the problem in reply to the therapist's request.

```
1    H:    Um. I don't know, it's just that well I've been
2          you know I've been dealing with her illness for
3          such a long time . . . and it's just that sometimes
4          I gotta get ( ) myself in my own way
5          too you know, I gotta I gotta have my feelings
6          too in a way in a way (T: Uh huh) uh just going
7          out and she's going to instead of just being
8          together constantly all the time like that ya
9          know how she acts and stuff ya know sometimes it
10         puts a little pressure on me too ya know, I just
11         gotta get away from her for a while ( ) it's
12         something that ah ya gotta under- ya gotta
13         handle whatever her illness is and stuff like that
14         I realize that ya know, it's just that we've been
15         together for a long time, we've been married for
16         a long time too, but it's just that sometimes a
17         person myself I gotta get away ya know I just
```

18	can't tolerate having her at times things that
19	she does and we argue and stuff and it all
20	builds up ya know I just gotta get it going.
21	So that's how it's been doing so far we
22	haven't been communicating too well.

The husband begins his telling of the problem by citing a constraint, "dealing with her illness for such a long time" (lines 2–3), which leads to his need for independence, "I gotta get ( ) myself in my own way too you know, I gotta I gotta have my own feelings too" (lines 4–6). The husband uses this presentational form of citing a *constraint* that justifies his *need for independence*. This claim is made at four points in this episode. His needs are indicated by the locution, "I gotta"; these locutions have the logical form, "I gotta do X" (see lines 4, 5, 10–11, 17, 20). For instance, the husband expresses the needs: "I just gotta get away from her for a while" (lines 10–11); "I gotta get away" (line 17); and "I just gotta get it going" (line 20); "I gotta have my own feelings too" (lines 5–6). This expressed need or complaint reflects a common tension or problematic in interpersonal relationships: the need for independence in a dialectical relation to the need for mutuality (Bochner, 1984; Rawlins, 1983a, 1983b, 1992). We frame the husband's expressed need to get away from his wife and have his own feelings as his need for independence.

In his presentation, the husband prefaces his need for independence by a constraint or problem in their relationship. This problem is presented as making necessary his need for independence. These constraints include: "dealing with her illness for such a long time" (lines 2–3), "just being together constantly all the time like that" (lines 7–8), and "we've been together for a long time, we've been married for a long time too" (lines 14–16). A common feature of these prefaces is the time factor—time in the relationship that is problematic—what we call *problematic relational time*. This is used to justify his call for independence. For instance, citing the duration of wife's illness (lines 2–3) intensifies it as problematic. This justification draws upon our taken-for-granted assumptions about time (Hewitt & Hall, 1973; Hopper, 1981). A short period of time caring for one's wife through her depression would not seem to warrant a call for independence, but caring for her for a lengthy period of time provides more of a justification. The second instance of problematic relational time concerns their being together for too much time. The locution, "just being together constantly" (lines 7–8), reflects his perception of its problematic character. Why it is problematic is specified somewhat in the subsequent utterance, "how she acts and stuff ya know sometimes it puts a little pressure on me too" (lines 9–10). The third instance of time being used as a preface to his need for independence is his mention of how long they have been together as couple (lines 14–16).

The point here is that the husband constructs his problem by prefacing his need for independence by the constraining nature of problematic relational time. Not only does problematic relational time precede his call for independence, but more importantly is used to justify it. A second constraint that the husband uses to justify the need for independence is that his wife's negative actions adversely affect him. This complaint is used to elaborate upon the problematic relational time of "being together constantly" (lines 7–8)—"how she acts and stuff ya know sometimes it puts a little pressure on me too ya know" (lines 9–10). Also, "things that she does and we argue and stuff and it all builds up" (lines 18–20). These utterances may be seen as part of the same theme because they have a similar underlying logic: *wife's actions adversely affect husband*. This reflects a common pattern in discourse about relational problems: One's partner is said to be the agent of various actions that emotionally hurt the teller. The teller portrays him or herself as unjustifiably wronged. The teller is the passive recipient of the partner's actions. This organizational feature in the presentation of problems reflects an implicit ascription of responsibility to one's partner (Scheff, 1968; Semin & Manstead, 1983, chapter 4).

These two claims are abstracted out as the main points of the husband's presentation of his problem. These two claims are not discrete, but related. We frame the underlying logic of the husband's presentation as justifying his need for independence. As shown, the assertion of problematic relational time precedes each call for independence and recurs three times. The second claim, wife's actions adversely affect husband, is used in support of his need for independence. Thus, we may frame these two claims into a hierarchical configuration to represent the husband's underlying logic (see Fig. 1.1).

This hierarchical model represents the underlying logic and structure of the husband's problem as presented in his discourse. The higher levels of meaning are abstracted from the text by the criterion of recurrence (see earlier). More importantly, the superordinate level, need for independence, subsumes problematic relational time and wife's actions adversely affect husband, because the latter two are used as reasons to justify the former.

Episode 1B: Wife's Initial Presentation of the Problem

The wife initiates her telling of the problem by picking up on the husband's point in his coda, "lack of communication," as a local coherence device.

```
1    W:    The lack of communication has gotten worse
2          especially on my part because um knowing that
3          he's leaving me and all I don't want to share
4          anything with him (T: Uh huh) and it's hard
5          for me to share.
```

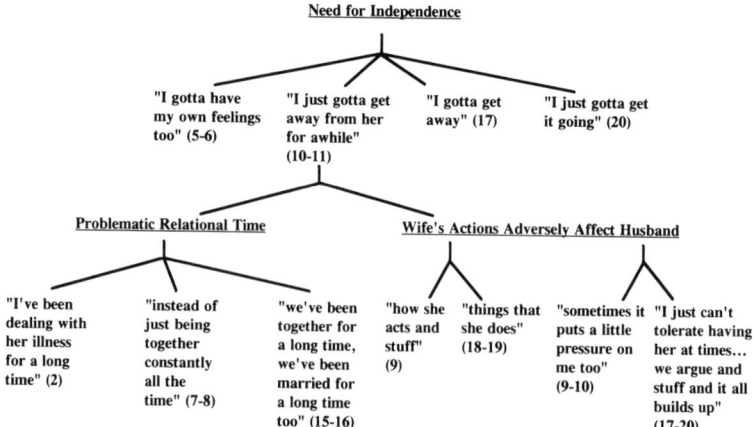

FIG. 1.1. Episode 1A: Husband's initial presentation of problems.

The typified marital difficulty, "lack of communication" (line 1), is sufficiently broad to allow her to agree with it as the problem. She will use this typification as a lead into her telling of the problem. Notice the taken-for-granted assumption in relational problems that each party will not only have a different side of the problem but even a different telling of the problem, and, hence, a different problem. In the present case, each participant is oriented toward an initial presentation of the problem.

Just examining line 1, the wife appears to be blaming herself for the lack of communication. But then as she begins to explain the reasons for this lack of communication, the more fundamental level of blame is allocated onto the husband: "because um knowing he's leaving me and all" (lines 2–3). In other words, the communication is "worse" (line 1) and she doesn't "want to share anything with him" (lines 3–4) because "he's leaving me" (line 3).

This allocation of blame to the husband is restated again a few moments later. After a short narrative on needing the right moment to share with others, she concludes with the accusation:

```
6   W:   and him and I bein' going to be separated I don't
7        share anything with him
8   T:   You're going to be separated or
9   W:   I don't know
```

The repetition of this point marks it as salient. The therapist orients toward this repeated charge by a question of clarification. Both the *repetition* and the *therapist's response to it* are indicators of its importance in understanding the wife's presentation of the problem. That is, according to the wife, the problem is the husband is leaving her, which leads to the consequences that she does not want to share with him.

Problems call for solutions. The second main dimension of her presentation concerns her lack of a solution to the problem.

10	W:	It's like whenever I get frustrated I just say
11		to him well then bring me up to my sister's
12		if that's the way ya feel about it bring
13		me up to my sister's house and ya don't
14		have to deal with me any more you know
15	T:	Uh huh uh huh
16	W:	And then I go out my sister's house and she
17		acts like she don't want me out there and
18		stuff so

The wife's narrative here has the structure of: "problem—possible solution—obstacle to solution." Given the practical necessity that problems require solutions, not having a solution or an apparent direction seems to intensify the problem for the wife. This is accentuated even more because the husband's main problem, the need for independence, can also be read as his proposed solution.

The underlying logic of the wife's initial presentation of the problem is represented (see Fig. 1.2) by a hierarchical ordering of levels of meaning. The superordinate level is the main problem, husband is leaving. The subordinate levels are:

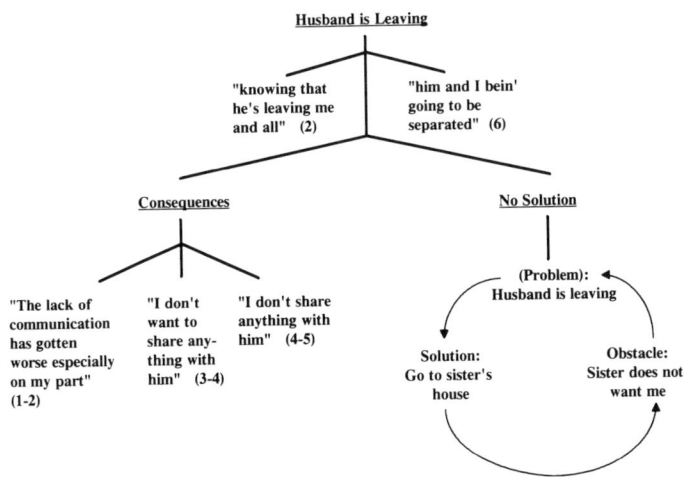

FIG. 1.2. Episode 1B: Wife's initial presentation of problems.

consequences (she does not want to share with him) and no solution (glossed as problem solution–obstacle). The superordinate level subsumes lower order levels by providing a frame for them. That is, the level, consequences—the wife does not want to share with the husband—needs to be understood in the context of the higher order level, husband is leaving. There is no schematic hierarchical relation between husband leaving and consequences, but in terms of the wife's telling of the problem, the consequences are meaningful only as they relate to the larger problem of the husband leaving. Problem-consequences suggests a sequential organization, and surely this discourse may be conceived of in this way. But for our goal of mapping the underlying logic of problem-talk, the hierarchical framework seems more useful because it models the global coherence of the problem as an object constructed through discourse.

Episode 3: Wife's Narrative

In Episode 1, the husband and wife have presented their version of the problem. Throughout the therapy session, the construction of the problem progresses: The questions and comments of the therapist lead to further elaboration and examples from the couple. Also, the participants respond to each other's presentation of the problem to defend, justify, or excuse their actions. In Episode 2 (which we do not examine here due to space limitations), the husband elaborates upon the nature of his wife's negative actions and how they adversely affect him.

Episode 3 beings as the therapist asks when the wife's illness began; the wife answers with a narrative.

```
 1    W:   Four years well he ah a long long time
 2         ago when I was in Connecticut I was ah we were
 3         with his brother and his brother was really high
 4         on God and stuff like that–he was a paranoid
 5         schizophrenic and my manic depression must have
 6         tooken over because I wasn't in love with him
 7         but I was in love with the fact that he was in
 8         love with God, so that was but I didn't get
 9         hospitalized for it but that happened way back
10    T:   Um huh that was before four years ago (W: um
11         huh) so that was the first sign of something
12         not being right (W: Um uh huh)
13    W:   But we never-he just thought I was makin' that
14         I was in love with his brother and that I was so
15         headstrong about it but that wasn't the case it
16         was that I was in love with God and what he was
17         saying about God so I wanted to be with him to
18         be closer to God ((cough)) but it was a manic
```

19		phase I know it was because it wasn't me
20	T:	How are you when you're you?
21	W:	I've forgotten it's been so long. I'm happy
22		go lucky usually

We are not interested in the structures of a narrative as such, but rather in how the narrative is used in the construction of her problem and in response to her husband. Narratives can be used to argue a position and to defend oneself (Bruner, 1985). In this narrative, the wife directly refers to her illness or manic depression for the first time: "my manic depression must have tooken over" (lines 5–6). Also, at the conclusion or coda, "it was a manic phase I know it was because it wasn't me" (lines 18–19). Her illness is used in this discourse as a happening or "phase" that takes over and controls her such that she acts out of character. By claiming that her illness controlled her so that she was not herself during this course of events, she is able to mitigate the potentially discrediting implications of this episode. She presents her illness as a physiological or psychological cause to deny or qualify her responsibility. In short, she excuses her actions by portraying her illness as a cause that takes her over (lines 5–6) and prevents her from being herself (lines 18–19).

The wife's most important claim in this narrative is that her husband misunderstands her actions. She accomplishes this claim by first stating that her husband misinterprets her relationship with her brother-in-law and second, provides the correct interpretation. For instance, at lines 13–14 she makes explicit her husband's misinterpretation. This passage allows us to respectively understand her previous denial—line 6: "I wasn't in love with him" (i.e., the brother-in-law). A misinterpretation requires a "correct" interpretation, which she offers at lines 16–17 and also at lines 7–8.

Her presentation of the problem uses repetition to emphasize and make her main points explicit. The therapist initially asks when did her illness begin. The wife responds with 4 years (line 1) and then begins her narrative. After the first telling (lines 1–9), the therapist seems to take her point as dating the first signs of the illness as earlier than 4 years (lines 10–12). The wife agrees and then repeats her main points, this time making them more explicit and clear (lines 18–19). Here again we see the use of repetition as a lingual device to indicate importance.

The underlying logic of this narrative may be seen as hierarchically organized under the superordinate meaning, *husband misunderstands wife* (see Fig. 1.3). Her *husband's interpretation* of that relationship needs to be seen as justifications for her claim that her husband misunderstands her actions. The terms we use, *misunderstand* and *misinterpret,* seem to be nearly synonymous, but we are using them to reflect the wife's meanings: a general pattern of the husband misunderstanding her in this episode in contrast to a specific misinterpretation of her relationship with his brother. A third branch of this hierarchical tree involves the claim (discussed earlier) that her illness is a cause that overcomes her and prevents her from

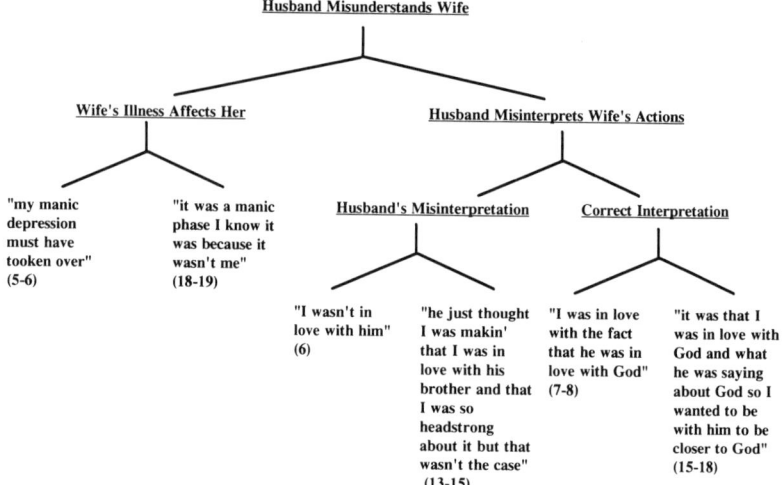

FIG. 1.3. Episode 3: Wife's narrative.

being herself. This also needs to be seen as subsumed under the higher order claim that the husband misunderstands her because the illness is used as a reason to support this claim. The point here is that this hierarchical organization maps the wife's construction of the problem: The three subordinate levels are used to support her implicit superordinate claim.

The underlying logic of the wife's narrative in Episode 3 can be seen as an addition to the problem presented in Episode 1B. That is, the hierarchical organization of Episode 3 can be subsumed under the superordinate problem of Episode 1B, husband is leaving. There are various levels of hierarchical organization that can be mapped to see the global coherence of the discourse (the progression of the problem throughout the whole therapy session could be represented as hierarchically organized). In this case, the higher order level, husband misunderstands wife, along with its subordinate levels, can be seen as a branch under the superordinate level, husband is leaving. The claim husband misunderstands wife is used as an implicit explanation for husband is leaving.

In addition to the further telling of her problem, the wife's narrative can be seen as responding to the husband's blaming her for *negative actions* (Episode 1A). The wife defends herself in two ways, by a *justification* and by an *excuse*. As we have seen, she justifies her actions by claiming that the *husband misinterprets* her relationship with his brother along with providing the *correct interpretation* that she "wanted to be with him to be closer to God" (lines 17–18). She denies that anything reprehensible occurred with her brother-in-law and justifies that sequence of events under a frame of religious involvement. This justification functions as a response to the husband's initial presentation of her negative actions by claiming that he misinterprets her actions, at least in this case. A second response she makes to the husband is to excuse her actions because her illness overcame her (lines 5–6) and she acted in a way that was not herself (lines 18–19). In other words, this excuse functions as a response in that the husband has to understand that she cannot be held fully responsible for her negative actions due to her illness—because when she is depressed, she is not herself.

Episode 5: Wife Blaming and Husband Defending

Episode 5 is organized around the therapist's question to the husband about how he can decide whether to stay with his wife or leave her. The episode begins with the therapist asking how can a decision be made whether to remain in the relationship or leave it.

1	T:	They're wondering because this is something that's
2		going on what would have to happen to affect a
3		decision about staying or leaving?
		(1.0)
4	W:	That's on his part.
		(3.0)
5	H:	I don't know it's just that see I don't I:::
6		don't know
7	W:	He's got this don't give a care attitude lately
8		you have haven't you? I could care less like
9		((cough))
10	H:	( ) it's not just you you know it's me myself
11		too I gotta
		[
12	W:	it's you
13		he's had three weeks off in the hospital I was in
14		the hospital for three weeks and he was hanging
15		around with his friends and having a old time
16		even thought he still had to come up and visit me
17		and worry about me he was still having a good old
18		time ((cough)) right?
19	H:	Yeah but I didn't have to come and see you at all
20		if I didn't want to
21	W:	Yeah I know
22	H:	All right then (1.0) Does that mean I don't care
23		about ya?
24	W:	Yeah but ya can't live like that honey ya can't
25		live me at my sister's house and you can come up

```
26            and see me when ya want you can't live a marriage
27            like that: we have to live together
                       [
28   H:                I never said
29            I know that
```

The therapist's question (lines 1–3) addresses the wife's superordinate level of meaning in the construction of her problem (see Fig. 1.2). The therapist's question provides a retrospective confirmation of the superordinate level of our hierarchical organization. That is, another person's responses provide a criterion for indicating importance in the original speaker's utterances. Other's responses are not an invariant or context-free criterion for importance, because other may respond to some minor point. But when other's responses are combined with other contextual criteria, such as the internal relation of subsuming as well as the reoccurrence of the point, these three together provide criteria for distinguishing among levels of importance.

This episode is particularly interesting because the wife and husband respond directly to each other over an eight-turn sequence. After the therapist's question and the wife's turning the question over to the husband (line 4), the husband appears unable to give an answer (line 5). The wife then identifies the husband's response as characteristic of his recent negative "attitude" (lines 7–9). This labeling is also an implicit blaming of the husband for failure to have an "appropriate attitude" toward their relationship. The husband's response (lines 10–11) is not directed toward the wife's preceding blame, but to the therapist's original question. He puts his previous blame of the wife into perspective (e.g., her negative actions) and begins to cite his own needs that he has to decide for himself. The wife interrupts him before he completes his point (lines 10–12) but given the context and the reoccurrence of the theme, it is likely that he was going to cite his need for deciding what he wants to do. That is, the husband appears to be going to cite his superordinate point—the need for independence (see Fig. 1.1).

The wife seems to anticipate the husband's superordinate point and interrupts him with a narrative that illustrates that he already does have independence (lines 12–18). She argues that he does have independence by indicating that they were apart for 3 weeks while she was in the hospital (lines 13–14) and that he was having a good time with his friends (lines 14–18). The husband's relationship with his friends is presented here as in conflict with his obligations toward their relationship (lines 16–18). On a more abstract level, this narrative throws into bold relief the previously mentioned tension between the need for mutuality and the need for independence in interpersonal relationship. In short, this narrative constructs a hierarchical ordering of tensions in their relationship: At the most abstract level, the tension between the need for independence and the need for mutuality; and at the level referenced in the narrative, the tension between his relationship with his friends and his concern for his wife (see Fig. 1.4).

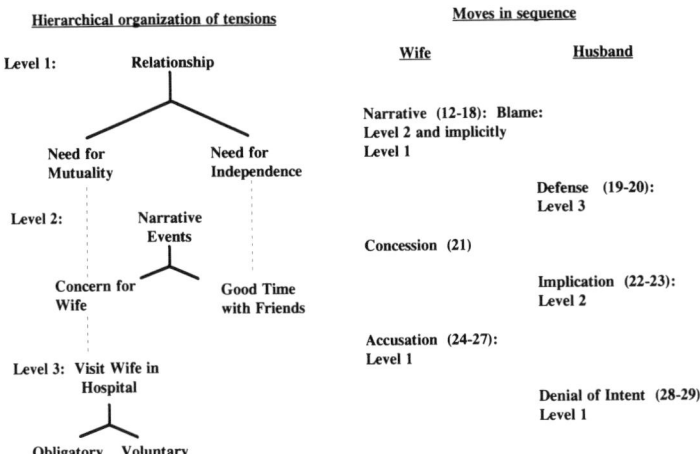

FIG. 1.4. Episode 5: Blame-defense sequence.

This implicit hierarchical organization of the problem presented by the wife in the narrative is responded to in the subsequent five-turn sequence. These responses (i.e., defenses, explanations, and accusations) are oriented toward the hierarchical levels of the problem. The husband responds to the wife's narrative by the justification that visiting her in the hospital is voluntary, not obligatory (lines 19–20). She concedes his point (line 21). The husband then makes a second response to her narrative by moving to the higher level tension that being with his friends does not mean that he does not care about her (lines 22–23). His utterance uses the indexical term *that:* "Does that mean I don't care about ya?" (lines 22–23). The *that* may be seen as referencing the conflict in her narrative between having a good time with his friends and caring about her. In short, his response (lines 22–23) is a denial of her accusation; that is, having a good time with friends does not count as not caring about her. The wife then responds by moving to yet a higher level by framing his need for independence as incompatible with what it means to be married (lines 24–26). This is the highest level of tension between the need for independence and the need for mutuality. In this blame-defense sequence (lines 12–29), we can see how the hierarchical organization of the problem provides a frame for each partner to orient his or her claims. The construction of "the problem" becomes an object for the partner to respond to—by denials, justifications, defenses, counter accusations, and the like. The hierarchical levels of the problem provide the structure toward which the partner will direct responses. As we have seen, the husband denies the wife's claim that having a good time with his friends means he does not care about her (lines 22–23). Also, the wife criticizes the husband's need for independence as being incompatible with their relational needs in her narrative (lines 12–18) and her attribution about living arrangements (lines 24–27).

A MODEL OF RELATIONAL TRANSITION

Thus far we have seen how two partners construct their relational problems through talk to a therapist. An analysis of the hierarchical macrostructure of semantic content reveals how global coherence is accomplished during the first 9 minutes of a therapy session. Now we turn to a more traditional approach to interpersonal communication—the study of transitions in relational definitions (Altman & Taylor, 1973; Altman, Vinsel, & Brown, 1981; Baxter, 1988; Conville, 1991; Duck, 1986; Knapp, 1984; Masheter & Harris, 1986; Rawlins, 1983a, 1983b; Wilmot, 1987). The goal of this final analysis is to integrate our discourse analysis with a traditional model of movement from one stage of relational definition to another. In effect, the interaction (discourse about relational problems) serves as an anchor point from which to infer a larger unit of analysis (relational transition). In complementary fashion, a model of relational transition fashioned after Conville (1991) is used to embed the particular interaction in a larger social process.

Conville's examination of relational transition hinges on the concept of *dialectical differences* leading to relationship crisis and redefinition. Such differences occur when one or both partners perceive a lack of consensus regarding the definition of their relationship and the terms of that dissensus "stand in contradiction so that they depend upon each other for definition and existence" (p. 11). In the present case, the husband and wife's disagreement about how much time to spend together qualifies as a dialectical difference because being together depends on and is contradicted by their being apart. In addition to *mutuality* (desire to spend time together vs. desire for autonomy), a number of dimensions of dialectical opposition can be seen at work in relationships: *time* (tensions between past–present–future orientations), *intimacy* (openly sharing personal thoughts and feelings vs. holding back or deflecting attempts at disclosure), *validation* (acceptance of other vs. condemnation of other), *affect* (positive liking or caring as an end in itself vs. instrumental use of the relationship as a means to an end), and so on. Tensions in these dimensions appear to produce a patterned sequence of episodes characteristic of relational transitions. Although most models of relationship development try to identify a predetermined set of stages through which most relationships pass, Conville focused on the transition periods between stages. Taking a relatively stable relational definition as a starting point, relational transitions tend to progress through five phases: security, disintegration, alienation, resynthesis, and back to a newly defined level of security. The process reflects two metadialectics: security–alienation and disintegration–resynthesis (see Fig. 1.5).

The initial phase of security depicts a stable state of "comfortable role-action,

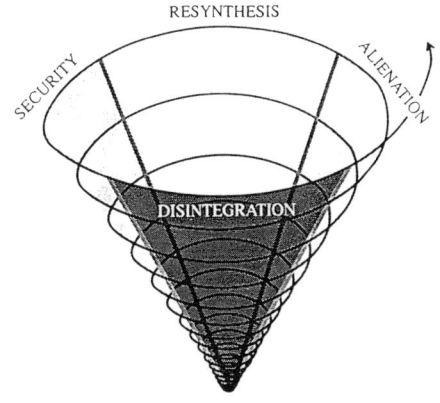

SECURITY$_1$	Comfortable role-action, mutuality of relationship definition, confirmation
DISINTEGRATION	Disruption, events that increase uncertainty, noticing and questioning the relationship
ALIENATION	Withdrawal, separation, nonmutuality, thwarted role-action
RESYNTHESIS	Redefinition, discovery, events that decrease uncertainty, confirmation seeking, coping with dialectical oppositions
SECURITY$_2$	Facilitated role-action, confirming messages, a comfortable redefinition

FIG. 1.5. Structural helical model of relational transition. From Conville (1991).

mutuality of relationship definition, and confirmation" (Conville, 1991, p. 39). Disintegration begins when at least one partner notices a difference in the relationship that disrupts the normal routine, increases uncertainty, and leads him or her to question the relationship in some way. This is followed by a period of alienation in which one or both partners begins to withdraw, rejects the relationship as presently defined, and typically talks explicitly about the relationship with the partner. In some cases, the alienation phase is relatively benign because the partner also desires change (e.g., both want to redefine a friendly relationship as a romantic one). Nonetheless, there is a sense of alienation from the previous definition. Resynthesis is the result of the human tendency to not willingly endure long periods of uncertainty. Partners move the relationship in the direction of redefinition, either to maintain its essential features in the face of change or to transform it to some other type of relationship. The end result is a new sense of security that enables once again comfortable role action and confirmation of their new identities, whether mutually connected or separated.

This model of relational transition shares several features in common with the previous analysis of meanings created through a linear and hierarchical organization of problem-talk. First, the relational transition process is sequential. Each relationship has its own unique history of emergent events and "turning points" comparable to the particular six-episode sequence of problem-talk depicted in the therapy session. But the phases of relational transition also reflect a common temporal pattern that is not unique to individual cases (security–disintegration–alienation–resynthesis). Second, the dialectic tensions and cyclical nature of relational transitions serve as a hierarchical context for making sense of the specific patterns of interaction located in a given episode or sequence of episodes. Although dialectic tensions are often expressed directly in discourse, patterns of security–disintegration–alienation are played out over longer periods of time and are only rarely displayed in the single conversations typically utilized in discourse analytic studies (therapy sessions may be one of the rare exceptions). Finally, the outcomes of relational transitions can be better understood if subjected to the type of hierarchical analysis suggested earlier. For instance, the nature of resynthesis (whether a relationship is maintained or transformed) may well depend on the underlying logic used by each party to frame potential redefinitions of the relationship.

PROBLEM-TALK DISCOURSE AS A REFLECTION OF RELATIONAL TRANSITION

In this section we use the relational transition model to investigate the potential complementary relationship of a discourse analysis with more traditional interpersonal communication concepts. Aspects of the episodes outlined previously are revisited to show how problem-talk simultaneously defines the terms of relational transition and is itself contexted by the relational transition process. The concept of hierarchically organized meanings is central to this understanding.

The contrast between the husband's and wife's telling of the problem exemplifies a typical relational transition process (sequential movement from security to disintegration to alienation) revolving around the specific dialectical oppositions of mutuality, intimacy, validation, affect, and time. Although we have no confirmation in the therapy discourse that the relationship ever achieved a high level of comfort and mutuality (security phase), we can assume that it was somewhat stable prior to the onset of the wife's illness 4 years before entering therapy. Assuming that couples in all close relationships experience frequent and numerous cycles of relational transition, it is likely that each successive cycle in this relationship resulted in what might be called a less stable maintenance of the relationship. Nonetheless, we do find evidence that this most recent cycle harbors the remains of previous ones because the accounts trace events back as far as 4 years. In the discourse available to us, husband and wife recognize differences in their respective relational definitions that indicate phases of disintegration and alienation, but few elements of resynthesis. This is not surprising for a couple in an initial therapy session. More interesting are the specific dialectic tensions exhibited. In fact, it is important to see that the dialectics themselves are subject to hierarchical organization by the participants.

Mutuality and Intimacy. The dialectic of mutuality is defined primarily by contradictory impulses or desires to be connected to one another and yet remain autonomous. In the therapy session, this tension appears interwoven with that of another dialectic, intimacy. We have already shown how the recognition by both husband and wife of a difference in their relationship (i.e. lack of communication or sharing [Episode 1A, lines 21–22; Episode 1B, lines 1–5]) is revealed as a move away from intimacy and toward greater autonomy. Several earlier events such as the wife's religious episode involving the brother-in-law, her being hospitalized, and his failure to visit her frequently in the hospital all clearly contributed to a high level of uncertainty characteristic of relational disintegration. Once couples focus their talk on and mark their differing relational definitions (e.g., the degree of autonomy or intimacy desired) as problems, a process of relational alienation has begun (Conville, 1991). The wife's reasoning that she doesn't "want to share anything with him" (Episode 1B, lines 3–4) and that "it's hard for me to share" (Episode 1B, lines 4–5) because "he's leaving me" (Episode 1B, line 3) reveals the degree to which relational uncertainty has shifted to alienation and also how she connects the tensions of mutuality and intimacy in hierarchical fashion. For her, too much autonomy in the relationship appears not only to threaten the quality of intimacy, but also to negate it. She seems to be saying that an autonomous marriage and a high degree of intimacy are incompatible (Episode 1B, lines 2–5). This suggests that the mutuality dialectic serves as the higher order context for issues regarding intimacy. He also places mutuality as the higher order construct, but values the autonomy end of the spectrum. His need for independence (Episode 1A, lines 4–20) leads him to interpret many of their interactions as a threat to that autonomy. For him, too many of their attempts to be intimate (i.e., to communicate) result in arguments, which prompt him to want to leave (Episode 1A, lines 19–20). Thus, attempting to achieve greater intimacy often has the opposite effect of creating more distance and more relational alienation. Resynthesis appears unlikely to happen as long as both partners maintain their respective hierarchical logics of meaning.

Affect, Intimacy, and Validation. Another misunderstanding surfaces in Episode 5 where the two disagree about the meaning of his visits to her in the hospital. He presents his case as having achieved a level of caring by choosing to visit when he didn't have to (Episode 5, lines 19–23). This he presents as a choice he made, which she should interpret as a validation of herself and the relationship, not as an instrumental obligation. He seems to offer this as an example of an event that should reduce her uncertainty about his commitment to the relationship and forge the beginnings of a positive relational resynthesis (positive in the sense that they might remain together). But she rejects his offer and argues that it is not enough. "Yeah but ya can't live like that honey ya can't live me at my sister's house and you can come up and see me when ya want you can't live a marriage like that. We have to live together" (Episode 5, lines 24–27). Once again, an action presented as positive by one party (i.e., caring, accepting, and expressing mutuality) is interpreted as negative (i.e., instrumental, disconfirming, and autonomous) by the other. There seems to be agreement on the outcome (lack of intimacy), but not on the prescription for solving it (more vs. less togetherness). This repeated inability to resynthesize and stabilize their relationship definition keeps them lingering in an alienation phase, they construct the problem and solution options differently. She seems to place a higher priority on mutuality and intimacy such that togetherness and the degree of intimacy expressed serves as context for issues of validation and affect. Her logic might be expressed as: "if he would spend more time with me (mutuality), then we could communicate more intimately, and then I would know that he values me (validation) and cares about our relationship (affect)." The husband, on the other hand, values his autonomy and seems to give greater credence to the affect dimension that influences how he sees issues regarding intimacy. His hierarchical logic could be expressed as: "I could spend more time with her (mutuality) if we didn't argue and she didn't act the way she does (negative affect), which makes it hard for us to communicate (intimacy) and feel good about our relationship (validation). Until that happens, I frequently have to get away from her (autonomy)." It would seem that a resynthesis that would enable the couple to stay together would have changed the way their respective logics affect each other.

Time. The couple also bring different time perspectives to bear on their telling of the problem. The husband's emphasis seems to be on the past (problematic relational time) as prelude to his present need for independence (Episode 1A). As mentioned previously, he cites the length of their marriage and the long period of her illness as justification for his current need for additional freedom. In contrast, the wife seems to concentrate much more on the present as it will impact the future by discounting the past. In Episode 1B, she phrases his departure as immanent, "he's leaving me" (line 3), "him and I bein' going to be separated" (line 6). She also has difficulty perceiving any positive alternative in the future (no solution). When asked specifically by the therapist to reflect on the past (when her illness began), she discounts the relevance of the event she mentions (her relationship with the brother-in-law). It is not to be taken seriously because either (a) her husband misunderstands it (lines 13–18), or (b) she was manic depressive (lines 5–6, 18–19). Either way, she seems willing to minimize the past and focus on present difficulties such as the lack of communication (Episode 1B, lines 1–7), his "don't give a care attitude" (Episode 5, lines 7–9), or future uncertainties (his leaving, her lack of alternatives). These differences in temporal perspective are not benign. It can be argued that the logic underlying the husband's telling of the problem (Fig. 1.1) is at least partially driven by the time frame he adopts. His need for independence is not a search for self-fulfillment or living up to some social ideal (e.g., "a real man . . . "). It is a highly prefigured reaction to and escape from his perceived circumstances ("I gotta get away," Episode 1A, lines 5–6, 10–11, 17, 20). On the other hand, the wife's temporal emphasis is on the present and future, but she is unable to find a good solution. She would like to be able to do something in order to improve communication and prevent her husband from leaving. Unfortunately, she can't do the former because of the latter. But more significantly, she focuses on his recent (apparently new) behavior (e.g., spending time with friends) while he identifies her current behavior as indicative of a long-term pattern (i.e., all part of the illness?). The differences in time perspective make it doubly difficult for them to make any headway since they cannot agree on where the boundaries should be drawn. Unlike the dialectics of mutuality, intimacy and affect, it does not appear that either party is very aware of the time perspective held by the other.

Dialectic tensions in relationships reflect differences in partner's hierarchical conceptions of meaning. For therapeutic relationships, recognition of these hierarchical dilemmas can serve as a first step in helping clients to see alternative conceptions of their interaction patterns.

DISCUSSION AND IMPLICATIONS

Our project here has been to show that discourse about problems has an underlying hierarchical organization. This notion of the hierarchical organization is important because it provides us with a model to see the turn-by-turn sequencing of talk as oriented toward the construction of "the problem." The presentation of the problem is an object to which participants are oriented. This problem-as-object has an underlying structure that is hierarchically organized. In other words, superordinate meanings provide a frame in which to see subordinate meanings. For instance, in the husband's initial presentation of the problem (Ep. 1A), his talk about problematic relational time and his wife's actions are used to justify his superordinate claim of his need for independence. Likewise, the wife's initial presentation is organized around the claim, husband is leaving, which provides the frame to see the consequences of her not wanting to share with him, as well as the lack of a solution for this problem.

This discourse unit of hierarchical organization is useful, not only for the construction of the problem but also for seeing how responses are made to the problem. Participants typically make their responses (e.g., denials, justifications, excuses, counteraccusations) to others' higher order meanings. In Episode 5, the husband and wife move up levels of the hierarchy in their exchange: from the reason for visiting the wife in the hospital to being with friends versus concern for wife to his need for independence versus her need for mutuality. Also, that the therapist's questions and requests for information are oriented toward superordinate levels of meanings, such as the question in Episode 5 about the husband's decision to stay or go reflects the wife's superordinate level of meaning. The point here is that participants recognize differing levels of importance in talk and will use this recognition to organize their own responses. In other words, participants make their utterances globally coherent by responding to others' higher order meanings.

Hudson (1980) and Agar (1979) questioned the utility of a hierarchical model of discourse. For instance, Hudson argued that hierarchical structure may be found in written discourse, but not in ordinary conversation, due to the latter's tendency to drift from one topic to another, unlike written discourse, which can be highly organized around topics (i.e., chapters, sections, subsections, paragraphs, and sentences). Hudson's criticism is well taken. We need to consider the constraints and logic of the form of discourse, the language game (Wittgenstein, 1953), or the activity type (Levinson, 1979). However, therapy sessions involve a topic-focused discourse around the discussion, analysis, and solution of problems. Also, Hudson's criticism seems to be directed at schematic or formal hierarchical models. Our conception of hierarchical organization is based on the content of discourse; that is, speakers frame their telling of the problem under a superordinate meaning which subsumes subordinate meanings.

Agar's criticism is that a hierarchical organization is an a priori assumption arising from the world view literature in anthropology. Agar found only one case of hierarchical organization in his analysis of themes in ethnographic interviews. In a later work, Agar and Hobbs (1982) developed this notion of themes into a third type of coherence—what they call *themal coherence* based on recurrent themes in a text. We have used recurrence as a criterion for hierarchical organization that is a form of global coherence, while Agar and Hobbs used recurrence as a criterion of themal coherence.

Agar's (1979; Agar & Hobbs, 1982) work suggests the issue of alternative models for the same text and criteria for deciding among them. This issue of competing accounts is a fundamental issue for discourse analysis (Dillon, Coleman, Fahnestock, & Agar, 1985; Levinson, 1983) that can only be touched on here. In the present case of problem-talk in a therapy session, the hierarchical model recommends itself because participants are oriented toward the problem as objects of concern. Problems are presented with a whole–part structure such that the parts are subsumed under the speaker's superordinate meanings. Participants distinguish among higher order and lower order levels of meanings, as we saw in Episode 5 in which the wife and husband moved from the subordinate level of reason for visiting wife in hospital to the superordinate level of independence needs versus mutuality needs. Other arguments on both sides could be marshaled, but perhaps the issue turns on the amount of discourse being analyzed. Agar collected a series of life history interviews from drug users (Agar, 1979; Agar & Hobbs, 1982), while our corpus is part of the first 9 minutes of an initial therapy session.

Different structural devices may be more useful, depending on the quantity of discourse to be simplified and organized. Also, certain types of discourse may lend themselves more readily to a model of hierarchical organization. In any case, whichever of these approaches prove more useful, they both represent a top–down approach to the discourse to complement a bottom–up approach.

We have also seen how partners present alternative conceptions of their relationship through problem-talk, which sets in motion a process of relational transition. We have argued that in dealing with relational problems, partners are implicitly attempting to construct a new relational definition (a resynthesis) by presenting their own preferred hierarchical conceptions of their ideal relationship. From the perspective of systemic family therapy (see the appendix), most people, although adept at explaining their own view of relational problems, are unable to articulate how the relational system operates. Because at least one goal of systemic family therapy (Boscolo, Cecchin, Hoffman, & Penn, 1987) is to help couples see their problems as emanating from the system of interaction (and not from autonomous individual actions), the approach outlined here offers a method for discovering systemic relationships in problem-talk. From this perspective, and consistent with the Milan approach employed by the therapist, a primary goal of therapy could be construed as helping the couple develop "working hypotheses" about the hierarchical logic of their problem-talk. By implication, successful resynthesis would require that problematic issues be dealt with in a way that takes into account each individual's hierarchical logic and how the logics, when intertwined, affect the relationship. In the case discussed here, the hierarchical structures embedded in the dialectic tensions of mutuality and intimacy can be offered as working hypotheses of the problem. In turn, the couple, with the assistance of the team of therapists, set out to construct alternative logical relationships among their actions and the meanings attached to those actions.

Recently researchers have turned to self-critically reflecting on their doing of research studies (R. Brown, 1992; Clifford & Marcus, 1986; Steiner, 1991). In our own case, we have approached these therapy materials as speech communication researchers, not as therapists. For the first author, the therapy setting seemed to offer a rich area for the analysis of accounts, although the study ended up focusing on the related activity of telling problems. Likewise, for the second author, the therapy setting promised to shed light on the nature of relational transitions because in the telling of their problems, partners implicitly comment on the turning points in their relational history.

Being an outsider to the specialized knowledge and practice of therapy seems to be both an advantage and a disadvantage. A disadvantage because we may be blind to the therapeutic strategies and miss the connection or coherence among different segments of the session. An "insider" can more readily see what a practitioner is up to in the course of their work.

However, being an outsider can also be advantageous because it allows for bringing a different array of analytic tools and concepts to examine the setting. Even though therapists may be specialists in family and interpersonal relations, their practice does not allow for the fine-grained analysis of therapeutic talk offered by discourse analysis. In the spirit of cross-disciplinary studies, the describing of structures of problem tellings may aid the therapist in recognizing what clients are "doing with words."

APPENDIX: METHOD

Data Collection

An audiotape recording of a family therapy session is used here for analysis. These family therapists routinely record their therapy sessions. A written transcription of the tape recording was prepared.

Participants

There are three participants in this therapy session: a heterosexual husband and wife and a male therapist. This is the couple's initial therapy session.

The Therapy Session

Our analysis centered on the discourse of the husband, wife, and therapist, and not the therapeutic process itself. However, it is important to note the assumptions underlying the therapeutic process as context for the analysis. The therapeutic team utilized a Milan-style of systemic interviewing as modified by Boscolo et al., (1987). This approach typically includes an initial interview with the couple by one therapist, while one or more members of the therapeutic team observe the session behind a one-way mirror. A telephone allows the therapy team to be in contact with the interviewing therapist, and to make requests, offer suggestions or hypotheses, or validate perceptions of the interviewing therapist. Early Milan-style therapy viewed the client–counselor relationship as a strategic battle of wills and relied on counterparadoxical injunctions ("positive connotations" of both problematic and symptomatic behavior) designed to overcome client resistance. In more recent approaches (as typified by this interview), family resistance to therapeutic interventions is no longer seen as strategic and willful, but simply as additional evidence of how the system operates. Interventions themselves are not directed at specific behavioral changes, but are attempts to "jog the system" and learn more about its structure. Clients are invited to join the therapist in developing "working hypotheses" about how the system works. Consistent with our analysis, this style of Milan therapy takes a meaning-centered stance where the internal cognitive frames employed by clients are of primary interest while actual behavioral change is of secondary interest.

ACKNOWLEDGMENTS

This chapter was begun in 1985 by the first author and was partially supported by a National Endowment for the Humanities Summer Seminar Fellowship on "Discourse Analysis" at the University of Chicago. The first author conducted the primary analysis of the discourse; the second author integrated that analysis with the model of relational transition. Thanks to Jack Lannamann and Joe Williams for their discussions in the early stages of this project.

REFERENCES

Agar, M. (1979). Themes revisited: Some problems in cognitive anthropology. *Discourse Processes, 2*, 11–31.

Agar, M., & Hobbs, J. R. (1982). Interpreting discourse: Coherence and the analysis of ethnographic interviews. *Discourse Processes, 5*, 1–32.

Altman, I., & Taylor, D. A. (1973). *Social penetration: The development of interpersonal relationships.* New York: Holt, Rinehart & Winston.

Altman, I., Vinsel, A., & Brown, B. B. (1981). Dialectic conceptions in social psychology: An application to social penetration and privacy regulation. In L. Berkowitz (Ed.), *Advances in experimental social psychology* (Vol. 14, pp. 107–60). New York: Academic Press.

Baxter, L. A. (1988). A dialectical perspective on communication strategies in relationship development. In S. Duck (Ed.), *Handbook of personal relationship: Theory, research, and interventions* (pp. 257–73). Chichester: Wiley.

Bergmann, J. R. (1992). Veiled morality: Notes on discretion in psychiatry. In P. Drew & J. Heritage (Eds.), *Talk at work* (pp. 137–162). Cambridge: Cambridge University Press.

Bochner, A. P. (1984). The functions of human communication in interpersonal bonding. In C. C. Arnold & J. W. Bowers (Eds.), *Handbook of rhetorical and communication theory* (pp. 554–621). Boston: Allyn & Bacon.

Boscolo, L, Cecchin, G., Hoffman, L. & Penn, P. (1987). *Milan systemic family therapy: Conversations in theory and practice.* New York: Basic Books.

Brown, G., & Yule, G. (1983). *Discourse analysis.* New York: Cambridge University Press.

Brown, R. H. (Ed.). (1992). *Writing the social text: Poetics and politics in social science discourse.* New York: Aldine de Gruyter.

Bruner, J. (1985). Narrative and paradigmatic modes of thought. In E. Eisner (Ed.), *Learning and teaching the ways of knowing: Eighty-fourth yearbook of the national society for the study of education* (pp. 97–115). Chicago: University of Chicago Press.

Buttny, R. (1985). Accounts as a reconstruction of an event's context. *Communication Monographs, 52*, 57–77.

Buttny, R. (1990). Blame-accounts sequences in therapy: The negotiation of relational meanings. *Semiotica, 78*, 219–248.

Buttny, R., & Cohen, J. R. (1991). The uses of goals in therapy. In K. Tracy (Ed.), *Understanding face-to-face interaction* (pp. 63–78). Hillsdale, NJ: Lawrence Erlbaum Associates.

Cantor, N., & Mischel, W. (1979). Prototypes in person perception. In L. Berkowitz (Ed.), *Advances in experimental social psychology* (Vol. 12, pp. 3–52). New York: Academic Press.

Clifford, J., & Marcus, G. E. (1986). *Writing culture: The poetics and politics of ethnography.* Berkeley: University of California Press.

Conville, R. L. (1991). *Relational transitions: The evolution of personal relationships.* New York: Praeger.

Cronen, V. E., Johnson, K. L., & Lannamann, J. W. (1982). Paradoxes, double binds, and reflexive loops: An alternative theoretical perspective. *Family Process, 20*, 91–111.

Dillon, G. L., Coleman, L., Fahnestock, J., & Agar, M. (1985). Review article. *Language, 61*, 446–460.

Duck, S. W. (1986). *Human relationships: An introduction to social psychology.* London: Sage.

Gale, J. (1991). *Conversation analysis of therapeutic discourse: Pursuit of a therapeutic agenda.* Norwood, NJ: Ablex.
Gale, J., & Newfield, N. (1992). A conversation analysis of a solution-focused therapy session. *Journal of Marital and Family Therapy, 18,* 153–65.
Goffman, E. (1976). Replies and responses. *Language in Society, 5,* 257–313.
Halliday, M. A. K., & Hasan, R. (1976). *Cohesion in English.* New York: Longman.
Harré, R., & Secord, P. (1972). *The explanation of social behaviour.* Totowa, NJ: Littlefield Adams.
Heritage, J. C., & Watson, D. R. (1979). Formulations as conversational objects. In G. Psathas (Ed.), *Everyday language: Studies in ethnomethodology* (pp. 123–162). New York: Irvington.
Hewitt, J. P., & Hall, P. M. (1973). Social problems, problematic situations, and quasi-theories. *American Sociological Review, 38,* 367–374.
Hinds, J. (1979). Organizational patterns in discourse. In T. Givon (Ed.), *Syntax and semantics, Vol. 12: Discourse and syntax* (pp. 135–157). New York: Academic Press.
Hobbs, J. R., & Evans, J. J. (1979). Why ask? *Discourse Processes, 2,* 311–318.
Hopper, R. (1981). The taken-for-granted. *Human Communication Research, 7,* 195–211.
Keenan, E. O., & Schieffelin, B. B. (1976). Topic as a discourse notion: A study of topic in the conversations of children and adults. In C. N. Li (Ed.), *Subject and topic* (pp. 335–384). New York: Academic Press.
Knapp, M. (1984). *Interpersonal communication and human relationships.* Boston: Allyn & Bacon.
Labov, W., & Waletsky, J. (1968). Narrative analysis: Oral versions of personal experience. In J. Helm (Ed.), *Essays on the verbal and visual arts* (pp. 12–44). Seattle: University of Washington Press.
Labov, W., & Fanshel, D. (1977). *Therapeutic discourse: Psychotherapy as conversation.* New York: Academic Press.
Lannamann, J. W. (1989). Communication theory applied to relational change: A case study in Milan systems family therapy. *Journal of Applied Communication Research, 17,* 71–91.
Lannamann, J. W., & Buttny, R. (1985). *The counterpoised problem definitions of clients and therapist.* Unpublished manuscript.
Levinson, S. C. (1979). Activity types and language. *Linguistics, 17,* 365–399.
Levinson, S. C. (1983). *Pragmatics.* New York: Cambridge University Press.
Levy, D. M. (1979). Communicative goals and strategies: Between discourse and syntax. In T. Givon (Ed., *Syntax and semantics, Vol. 12: Discourse and syntax* (pp. 183–210). New York: Academic Press.
Longacre, R. E. (1979). The paragraph as a grammatical unit. In T. Givon (Ed.), *Syntax and semantics, Vol. 12: Discourse and syntax* (pp. 115–134). New York: Academic Press.
Masheter, C., & Harris, L. M. (1986). From divorce to friendship: A study of dialectic relationship development. *Journal of Social and Personal Relationships, 3,* 177–89.
McLaughlin, M. L. (1984). *Conversation: How talk is organized.* Beverly Hills, CA: Sage.
Meyer, B. (1975). *The organization of prose and its effect on recall.* New York: North-Holland.
Morris, G. H. (1985). The remedial episode as a negotiation of rules. In R. L. Street & J. N. Cappella (Eds.), *Sequence and pattern in communication behavior* (pp. 70–84). Baltimore: Edward Arnold.
Pearce, W. B., Cronen, V. E., & Conklin, F. (1979). On what to look at when analyzing communication: A hierarchical model of actors' meanings. *Communication, 4,* 195–221.
Peyrot, M. (1987). Circumspection in psycho-therapy: Structures and strategies of client-counselor interaction. *Semiotica, 65,* 249–68.
Rawlins, W. K. (1983a). Negotiating close friendship: The dialectic of conjunctive freedoms. *Human Communication Research, 9,* 255–66.
Rawlins, W. K. (1983b). Openness as problematic in ongoing friendships: Two conversational dilemmas. *Communication Monographs, 50,* 1–13.
Rawlins, W. K. (1992). *Friendship matters: Communication, dialectics, and the life course.* New York: Aldine de Gruyter.
Sacks, H., Schegloff, E. A., & Jefferson, G. (1974). A simplest systematics for the organization of turn-taking in conversation. *Language, 50,* 696–735.

Schank, R. C., & Abelson, R. (1977). *Scripts, plans, goals, and understanding.* Hillsdale, NJ: Lawrence Erlbaum Associates.

Scheff, T. (1968). Negotiating reality: Notes on power in the assessment of responsibility. *Social Problems, 16,* 3–17.

Scott, M. B., & Lyman, S. M. (1968). Accounts. *American Sociological Review, 33,* 46–62.

Semin, G. R., & Manstead, A. S. R. (1983). *The accountability of conduct: A social psychological analysis.* New York: Academic Press.

Steiner, F. (Ed.). (1991). *Research and reflexivity.* London: Sage.

Tracy, K. (1985). Conversational coherence: A cognitively grounded rules approach. In R. L. Street & J. N. Cappella (Eds.), *Sequence and pattern in communicative behavior* (pp. 30–49). Baltimore: Edward Arnold.

Van Dijk, T. A. (1980). *Macrostructures.* Hillsdale, NJ: Lawrence Erlbaum Associates.

Wilmot, W. W. (1987). *Dyadic communication* (3rd ed.). New York: Random House.

Wittgenstein, L. (1953). *Philosophical investigations* (G. E. M. Ascombe, Trans.). New York: Macmillan.

Wodak, R. (1981). How do I put my problem? Problem presentation in therapy and interview. *Text, 1,* 191–213.

2

Therapists' Techniques for Responding to Unsolicited Contributions by Family Members

Charlotte M. Jones
Carroll College

Wayne A. Beach
San Diego State University

OVERVIEW

Therapists' techniques for managing and regulating multi-party conversations are central to the interactional work involved in organizing family therapy sessions. Although clients' freedom of expression and voluntary comments are routinely encouraged in family therapy sessions, therapists must direct and constrain clients' contributions in ways deemed relevant and meaningful to constructive and healthy therapeutic environments. This joint (and at times, seemingly contradictory) task of "*opening up/closing down*" is routinely tailored by therapists as responsive to ways family members attempt to actively structure the session in progress. For example, it is not uncommon for family members to produce overlapping talk when responding to therapists' queries and therapists may impose structure by selecting a particular member to speak next; a family member may interject and attempt to "speak for another," prompting therapists to request cooperation in letting individuals speak for themselves; and/or family members may begin talking to themselves, creating a "schism" from what the therapist is attempting to address with others, and is subsequently treated as a distraction to be eliminated before returning to what therapists orient to as the "main business" at any given moment in the session.

Managing a family therapy session can be challenging conversational work. Therapists organize sessions in order to discuss the functioning status of family interaction. This work includes focusing on and drawing out particular family members' various kinds of information before moving onto other matters, determining whose perspective to solicit currently and whose next, and also when to allow family members to talk together and when to come back into the conversation.

In Exemplar 1, we can observe the therapist's response to one family member attempting to "speak for another" by answering a question directed to another speaker.[1] (Throughout the data presented in this chapter, the following abbreviations are employed for speaker designations: TH = therapist, F = father, M = mother, D = daughter, G = grandmother, RP = romantic partner, and SF = stepfather. See the appendix in the introduction to this volume for transcription symbols.)

```
Exemplar 1— FAM:B2((simplified))
          TH:    Oh you gotta house er somethin?
=>1       RP:    He's gotta property right around the corner he
                 doesn't havta pay rent deposit he doesn't havta pay
                 anything (he owns his own) property
                 [                                                 ]
*=>2      TH:    Let me hear it from him cause he's    gotta deal
                 with the reality
          F:     I'm probably not going ta stay in the area
```

This instance involves talk concerning what a father might do if he and his daughter move out of his romantic partner's home. It begins with a therapist directing a question to F. Notice, however, that RP speaks *for* F by answering the therapist's question (=> 1). In response, the therapist fails to address the issues raised in RP's unsolicited comment, in favor of instructing RP, in essence, to refrain from taking a turn (*=> 2).

This instruction from TH is permissively packaged as a polite request (i.e., "let me"), but minimally so; it is also command-like. Furthermore, even though TH does provide a reason for his instruction, notice that he interactively overlaps RP's turn (at a non-transition relevance place), sequentially deleting the possibility that she will continue.

As in Exemplar 1, the activities we examine display identifiable features of sequential organization. These activities begin with either a two-part or three-part opening, subsequently treated as problematic by therapists. The first turn in both is a question from the therapist specifically directed to a *next* and *selected* speaker, family member 1 (FM1). Speaker selection is accomplished by the current speaker (therapist) selecting the first family member to answer the particular ques-

---

[1]The family therapy data segments are coded in the following manner: A, B, and C correspond with the three therapists whereas 1, 2, and 3 correspond with the families. Therapist A worked with two families (i.e., two sessions were with one family), Therapist B worked with two families, and Therapist C worked with one. The participants included: a single mother and son (Family A1); a divorced family with a mother, father, daughter, son, and grandmother (Family A2 and A3); a mother, father, toddler son, and preschool daughter (Family B1); a father, his live-in romantic partner, and his daughter (Family B2); and a mother, stepfather, and son (Family C1).

tion. This can take one or more of the following forms: addressing the person by name, employing the recipient proterm "you," gazing at the person, or continuing with follow-up questions to the same person (Goodwin, 1980; Lerner, 1993).[2] The simplest, "unproblematic" version would consist of a therapist's question to FM1, followed by an answer from FM1.[3]

Exemplar 2
    TH: Question to FM1
    FM1:   Answer

For instances treated as "problematic" by therapists, the sequential organization of the two-part opening involves a second turn as an *unsolicited* contribution from a nonaddressed family member (FM2).

Exemplar 3
          TH: Question to FM1
          FM2:   Response
*=>   TH: Response

The three-part opening consists of an answer from the addressed family member (FM1) followed by an unsolicited contribution from a nonaddressed family member (FM2).

Exemplar 4
          TH: Question to FM1
          FM1:   Answer
          FM2:   Response
*=>   TH: Response

Regardless of where in the activity the FM2 offers a comment, whether directly after the therapist's question or after the FM1's response, it is *unsolicited* and *self-selected*. This turn by FM2 may be an attempt to be helpful or, to aid in the therapeutic process. However, TH, subsequently, is the one to direct attention to particular matters and away from others.

TH's response to FM2's unsolicited contribution (see *=> in Exemplars 3 and 4 above) is of primary concern for this chapter. We have identified several tech-

---

[2]Unfortunately, in the majority of segments chosen, the therapist happened to be off camera or his or her gaze direction was undetectable. Therefore, the analysis of gaze direction of the therapist as an addressing device was not possible.

[3]For the purposes of this study, we are treating the categories of "question" and "answer" as unproblematic. However, see Schegloff (1984) and ten Have (1991) for discussions of the problematic issues involved in determining what counts as a "question" or an "answer."

niques employed by therapists to manage interactional junctures of this sort: (a) close down the unsolicited contribution, as in Exemplar 1, (b) not respond verbally to the additional comment, (c) briefly acknowledge or confirm the remark but continue with the first family member, (d) redirect the focus to the second family member's unsolicited comment, or (e) allow the family members to collaborate while the therapist remains silent.

These responses seem designed to deal with two issues concerning unsolicited second family member contributions. The first three types of TH responses treat FM2s' contributions as not particularly useful to the current therapeutic moment. For whatever reason, TH wishes to continue the current line of questioning or ongoing narrative with the FM1. Rather than redirect his or her attention to the second member, TH closes down the unsolicited contribution, does not respond to the volunteered contribution, or briefly acknowledges the contribution but continues with FM1.

The last two types of TH responses treat the FM2s' volunteered contributions as helpful or useful to the current therapeutic moment. That is, after an unsolicited comment from a second family member, TH redirects his or her focus to the second member and questions him or her, or allows the two family members to collaborate while remaining silent.

Thus, therapists' responses to unsolicited contributions range from verbally "shutting down" the second family member to "opening up" the talk, letting him or her momentarily direct and control the interaction with the first family member. In between these extremes, therapists can use responses to discourage, acknowledge but discourage, or encourage the second family member.

Routine problems such as this faced by therapists in family therapy sessions are readily apparent when inspecting 8 hours of videorecorded and transcribed family therapy sessions, involving three therapists and five families ranging in size from two to five.[4] As the analysis proceeds, it becomes evident that talk in therapy sessions, like other types of institutional talk (e.g., physician–patient encounters, lawyer–witness interaction), is distinguishable from everyday casual interaction (cf. Drew & Heritage, 1992).[5] Casual conversations are characterized by varying turn order, turn length, turn type, and number of turns and participants, all of which are locally occasioned on a turn-by-turn basis (Sacks, Schegloff, & Jefferson, 1974). Few restrictions are placed "on what can be said and how it should be said" (West, 1983, p. 76). Therapeutic discourse, however, is more constrained than casual conversation in that therapists routinely restrict topics, turn types, turn length, number of turns, and speaker order (Jones, 1988; Viaro &

---

[4]Therapist solicitation was not based on theoretical orientation to study for several reasons: (a) the study was not intended to contrast or compare therapists with varying or similar orientations, and (b) the limited number of therapists and families who both consented to participate.

[5]Family therapy discourse does not seem to be as constrained as other forms of institutional talk. For instance, family members can spontaneously offer a telling as the result of being triggered by a word or thought; this is not usually permitted in witnesses' testimonies (Beach, 1985) or by students in the classroom (Mehan, 1979).

Leonardi, 1983). In the ways therapists are treated as experts and display expertise, they influence the ordering and direction of the interaction at any particular moment.

There has been limited systematic examination and description of the details of therapeutic interaction. In 1977, Labov and Fanshel noted that "very few authors have addressed the question of what is actually done in the therapeutic interview" (p. 3). Several notable exceptions (Davis, 1984; Jones, 1988, 1992a; Labov & Fanshel, 1977; Scheflen, 1973; Siegfried, 1993; Stamp, 1991; Viaro & Leonardi, 1983) do provide extensive detailed analysis of the interaction in therapy.

However, the overall lack of explication is especially problematic for practitioners and students of family therapy (Labov & Fanshel, 1977). Labov and Fanshel remarked that in order for therapeutic practice to develop as a technical skill, focus must be placed on the particular use of language within the therapeutic interview. This chapter is a response to the call for this type of study. Before an in-depth analysis of therapists' techniques for managing unsolicited comments, a brief discussion of therapeutic discourse in general is warranted.

THERAPEUTIC DISCOURSE AS CONSTRAINED TALK

Examinations of therapeutic discourse often focus on how stories or narratives get organized (cf. Jones, 1988; Labov & Fanshel, 1977; Scheflen, 1973). Narratives are themselves considered diagnostic and treatment techniques uniquely adapted to therapeutic purposes (e.g., The Family Interaction Apperception Technique: Elbert, Rosman, Minuchin, & Guerney, 1964; The Mutual Storytelling Technique: Gardner, 1969, 1971, 1975). Family therapy sessions may be understood as diagnostic tools and as methods of therapy aimed at behavioral and/or interactional changes within family systems. Therapists design their talk as a means of discovering *how* family members co-produce potentially dysfunctional communicative patterns, a prerequisite to facilitating and recommending specific solutions to such problems and their consequences.

A good portion of therapists' work involves eliciting from members various narratives regarding past, present, and future events and, by so doing, make available the kinds of everyday experience comprising a family's existence. Such narratives are comprised of general descriptions of family-related events, as well as specific states of mind and/or emotionally relevant issues—concerns ranging from events deemed particularly troublesome and in need of remedy, to unnoticed or taken-for-granted activities pursued by the therapist. Narrative descriptions provide an opportunity for therapists to directly observe how family members interact with one another during the session. By integrating information of externalized events produced through the narrative, and data apparent in the ways family members produce these narratives in real-time therapy sessions, "the raw material for the therapeutic work" (Labov & Fanshel, 1977, p. 35) is made available.

Clearly, a therapist maintains some degree of "control" in order to structure or influence the sequences of interaction and draw out particular stories or information. The ways in which therapists organize narratives is one of the constraining features characterizing therapeutic discourse. For example, a therapist may need to understand specific family members' points of reference or viewpoints on a particular issue or event and, therefore, question individuals one at a time getting each person's perspective before moving onto the next. Alternatively, a therapist may question several members in an alternating or successive fashion, building a more collaboratively produced narrative.[6]

A second set of constraining features characterizing therapeutic talk is its turn-taking organization of question–answer sequences. The therapist asks questions to create a picture of how the family has been, is currently, and will be interacting (e.g., to manage decisions) in the future. MacKinnon and Michels (1971) noted a therapist's questions "may serve to obtain information or to clarify his own or the patient's understanding" (p. 35).[7] Considering the family's desire to receive help,

---

[6] It should be noted that we are using a particular notion of narrative. Past conceptualizations seem a bit limiting. For instance, Labov and Fanshel (1977) defined *narrative* as "one means of representing past experience by a sequence of ordered sentences that present the temporal sequence of those events by that order" (p. 105). Similarly, Scheflen (1973) considered a narrative to be "a series of declarative statements about events which have taken place elsewhere" (p. 85). These conceptualizations identify narratives as past events only, related by a single speaker, and as "occurring in large chunks or periods in time in which the narrator holds the floor and the audience listens" (Beach & Japp, 1983, p. 868). However, we know that family therapy discourse does not only deal with the past but also the future and the present (Friedlander, Highlen, & Lassiter, 1985; Penn, 1982). Furthermore, the end product (story or narrative) of a collaboration of all or some participants seems more generative, fertile, and exponential than a group of individually produced stories. Thus, Beach and Japp's (1983) perspective of storytelling seems more applicable. It considers a story to be a delineation of some event that can be set in the past, present, or future and, is collaboratively produced by participants.

[7] "N"-prefaced queries, as one specific type of question design, have been noted as prevalent within talk comprising institutional settings. The "n" preface includes the conversational tokens of "okay," "and," "so," continuers such as "uh huh" and "mm hm," and assessments. Several authors have described the use of turns that begin with or are prefaced by conversational tokens such as "okay," "and," and/or by assessments and continue with a question (Beach, 1992, this volume; Heritage & Sorjonen, in press; Jones, 1992b; Schiffrin, 1987; Sorjonen & Heritage, 1991). "Okay- what happen:s (.) when you get upset and someone is beating up on yo:u" is an example of a turn that begins initially with an "okay" followed by a question. This feature of question design, "n"-prefacing, is "comparatively prominent in interactional environments characterized by extensive questioning activity in which questions are constructed into one or more series—for example, classrooms, courtrooms, medical settings, and other forms of 'institutional' interaction" (Sorjonen & Heritage, 1991, p. 68).

"N"-prefacing is a way in which "nextness" is achieved in conversation. That is, it treats or acknowledges the prior turn as sufficient and hence, displays a "forward"-looking orientation; it moves "the talk forward either within or across a topical and/or sequence boundary" (Sorjonen & Heritage, 1991, p. 72). In particular, "okay"-prefaced questions can show a readiness for a shift to relevant subsequent matters (Beach, 1992), whereas "and"-prefaced questions can display a serial movement of agenda relevancy (Sorjonen & Heritage, 1991). Both types of these prefaced queries can also tie back to the immediately prior turn to address some problematic facet of it. Assessment-prefaced questions can also show a movement to other matters, but do so with an evaluation of the prior utterance first (Jones, 1992b).

members routinely provide answers. The majority of speaker turns in family therapy sessions are distributed in an alternating style: T–A–T–A–T–B . . . , with T referring to the therapist and A and B referring to two different family members (Jones, 1988; Viaro & Leonardi, 1983).

But *how* do therapists direct and orchestrate family members' contributions (both elicited and volunteered) and lack of contributions to narratives through the primary use of questions? How do therapists reinforce particular behaviors or contributions but not disrupt the overall flow of the current line of talk? Viaro and Leonardi (1983) noted that the *ways* in which a therapist gathers his or her information are important because they determine the quality of the information that he or she obtains from a family.

The specific focus of this chapter is how therapists manage narratives in multiparty therapy sessions when a second family member voluntarily contributes a turn while the therapist is conversing with another. The additional family member may be offering his or her perceptions, contradicting something the other said, or may be adding information/embellishing the telling. Whatever the contribution, the following addresses therapists' responses in these recurring situations.

THERAPISTS' TECHNIQUES FOR MANAGING UNSOLICITED CONTRIBUTIONS

As noted, we identify five responses by therapists to unsolicited contributions by a nonaddressed family member. Attention is now turned to explicating and exemplifying each of these.

Closing Down Unsolicited Contributions

Although family members may voluntarily contribute opinions or feelings concerning an event or topic being discussed, therapists may display greater interest in the prior speaker's contributions. By somehow directing the volunteering family member to relinquish speaking, therapists typically encourage continuance by the initial family member. Just as Viaro and Leonardi (1983) observed that "the therapist has the exclusive right to decide who may speak at any given moment" (pp. 30–31), therapists may essentially sanction particular contributions by family members at specific interactional junctures. Such work may temporarily disrupt the interaction, as illustrated in Exemplar 5.

```
Exemplar 5—FAM:B2 ((simplified))
         TH:   Oh you gotta house er somethin?
  =>1    RP:   He's gotta property right around the corner he
               doesn't havta pay rent deposit he doesn't havta pay
               anything (he owns his own) property
                      [                                    ]
```

*=>2	TH:	Let me hear it from him cause he's gotta deal with the reality
	F:	I'm probably not going ta stay in the area
=>3	RP:	See
=>4	TH:	Oh this was the relocate thing?
	F:	I'm preddy mu<u>ch</u>-decided that I ah if we s- separate I'm going ta leave the area
		[
=>5	RP:	S- he doesn't wanna move twice
		[
*=>6	TH:	Le-leme- let me hear 'im sa you don't wanna move twice I don't understand where would you go like outta state? er
	F:	Yeah quite a ways
	TH:	You have definite kinna:? =
	F:	= Ah yeah I may go down ta Florida ta St. Petersburg

This instance provides an extended version of Exemplar 1. In response to RP's unsolicited comment (=> 1), TH first informs RP of the inappropriateness of her turn-at-talk by re-directing the focus to F, and then accounts for his action by explaining "cause he's gotta deal with the reality." F then states that he will probably not stay in the area if the breakup occurs. At (=> 3), RP again offers an unsolicited comment, "<u>See</u>", a re-do and thus second attempt to explain F's situation. However, in (=> 4), TH does not attend directly to this comment (discussed further later) and continues his questioning of F ("Oh this was the relocate thing"), in response to which F further explains his plans for leaving the area if the separation occurs. In what amounts to a third effort to join in the ongoing talk, RP offers yet another unsolicited explanation for TH's consideration (=> 5). For the second time, TH instructs RP to allow F to speak (*=> 6). Notice, first, that TH's overlapped and then recycled "let me hear" prefaces a restatement of RP's prior "you don't wanna move twice"—a more specific attempt to close down RP's contribution than the deictic "let me hear it" in (*=> 2), but also evidencing that RP's comment was nevertheless heard on its merits by TH. Next, TH addresses two questions to F by employing the address term "you" (again, a more specific speaker selection technique than apparent in (*=> 2)). After this second direction to RP, TH and F continue the narrative about possible future events without further unsolicited comments by RP.

In Exemplar 5, it is evident that TH deals with RP's persistance by first providing a reason in (*=> 2), disattending RP's abbreviated attempt to speak again in (=> 5), and in (*=> 6) by displaying adequate hearing but then moving via "you" to address F even more directly.

Not Responding to Unsolicited Contributions

When a therapist treats a family member's contribution as untimely and not helpful at any given moment, a second and less explicit way to respond (as compared, e.g., to Exemplar 5) is to *not* respond directly to the contribution. In other words, the therapist appears to disregard the remark and simply asks another question to the initially queried family member. Although the family member's unsolicited contribution may disrupt the therapist's line of questioning, the disruption is momentary and does not promote a departure from the therapist's line of questioning. By not responding, the therapist essentially and sequentially deletes the unsolicited comment by treating it as a nonoccurrence as seen in the following exemplar.[8]

```
Exemplar 6—FAM:A2 (simplified))
         TH:    Who does she depend on? fer: Hazel who does
                Hazel depend on?
         M:     I think Hazel depends on Christy en (1.0) Donald
                en Tina? ^those are the people^=
         TH:    =Christy is: who?
         M:     ^Christy^
                [
=>1      D:     M- our aunt our aunt
*=>2     TH:    That's your si-?
         M:     My sister
         TH:    Your sister

         M:     She's still ^at home^
```

Here, TH queries M about who her mother (i.e., Hazel) depends on, and then seeks clarification concerning one of the people that the mother named (i.e., Christy). As M softly says "^Christy^", D volunteers an answer, "M- our aunt our aunt" (=>

---

[8]Ignoring a person's verbal contribution, however, may momentarily deny the value of a speaker's contributions and possibly "disconfirm" the person (Watzlawick, Beavin, & Jackson, 1967; Wilmot, 1987). Satir (1967) argued that disconfirmation functionally undermines a person's confidence. Thus, although this type of response (i.e., nonresponse) may not appear to disrupt the therapist's line of questioning, questions may be raised as to possible and negative consequences of such actions (e.g., when later eliciting comments from a previously ignored speaker).

Based on Watzlawick et al.'s (1967) claim that openly disagreeing with someone still confirms her or him as a person, one might argue that the therapist response of *no* response (second in our list) should instead be placed first in the list (i.e., a disconfirming response is more extreme or "worse" than a direction to refrain from taking another turn). We, however, ordered the therapists' responses based on the therapists' verbal explicitness in "closing down" to "opening up" of the second family member.

1). As an alternative to responding directly to D, TH instead asks for further clarification from M using the recipient proterm "your" ("That's your si-?") (∗=> 2)—one means of attending to M's utterances by indirectly building on what D's volunteered response implied, but also better ensuring M (*not* D) as both recipient and next speaker.

In Exemplar 7, TH is talking with G about her children:

Exemplar 7—FAM:A3

```
           TH:    Let's see you had u::h (0.3)
           G:     Four children
                     (0.4)
           TH:    Four children a::nd what was the other one's
                  Chris and (something)
  => 1     M:     (That's) my sister (.) (Christine)
  *=> 2    TH:    Is that the one that's living with you
                                   [
           M:                    (Yeah)
           G:     Uh huh
                     (0.8)
           G:     ^Christina^
                     (0.8)
           TH:    ^Uh huh^ What's her situation
```

After hearing that she had four children, TH repeats "four children" and then uses an "and"-prefaced question to first ask G for the other daughter's name and then offers a possibility ("Chris and (something)"). Responsive to TH's ambiguity and obvious "search," M then volunteers "That's my sister (.) (Christine)". Here again (∗=> 2), TH does not directly acknowledge M's unsolicited information, opting instead to query and seek G's affirmation that this is the daughter "that's living with you." Although M overlaps and provides an affirmative answer ("yeah"), it is clear that TH continues by relying on "you" to address G but also disattend M's contribution. G then affirms TH's query and provides a specific name, followed by further questioning by TH to G, now unencumbered by further (volunteered, unsolicited) contributions offered by M. As compared to RP's persistance in Exemplar 5, in this case M can be heard and seen as assisting in TH's apparent "search," and not actively seeking the floor. Even though M's "yeah" does affirm the correctness of TH's (∗=> 2), it is not implicative for further talk as the problem (i.e., TH's uncertainty) has now become resolved. And it was this problem to which M's talk was addressed, talk that proposed active involvement, but that was neither pursued by M nor encouraged by TH.

Briefly Acknowledging the Contribution But Continuing With Initially Queried Family Member

Therapists can respond in a slightly confirming vein even when they wish to continue with the first family member. Following an unsolicited remark from a family member, a therapist can briefly acknowledge the remark but continue the questioning with the first family member. Such brief acknowledgments can take the form of acknowledgment tokens such as "okay," "yeah," "ah ha," partial repeats of the prior speaker's contribution, a short question, or a combination of these.

The acknowledgment, however brief, displays some responsiveness, "confirms" (albeit minimally) the family member's unsolicited contribution, and may momentarily validate his or her involvement. Responses of this type are both efficient and sensitive to relational issues (i.e., brief confirmation *en route to* quickly getting "back to business," thus minimal disruption to therapists' lines of questioning).

Work of this type may occur within one conversational turn (Exemplar 8, 9, 10) or across several conversational turns (Exemplar 11).

```
Exemplar 8—FAM:C1 ((simplified))
          TH:   Are you saying that in a way you do want to get
                into a discussion of it yet you're jus so afraid
                that- (1.0) you can't handle it? (2.0) is it kind
                of like (that cold feet)
                     (2.0)
          M:    I'd like to know: ((sniff)) (I dunno I) feel like
                (1.0) I'd like to know what I did wrong (1.0)
                ^that's how I feel^
 => 1     SF:   That's something she stated- (1.0) last week I
                guess it was
 *=> 2    TH:   ^Kay^ an who would you like to know that from?
          M:    From Scott
```

In this instance, TH and M discuss M's thoughts and feelings concerning her son's desire to move in with his father. After one of M's turns, the stepfather (SF) voluntarily offers a comment reinforcing M's contribution (=> 1). In (*=> 2), TH briefly acknowledges his receipt of SF's comment with "^Kay^", then continues with an "and"-prefaced question to the mother. Here TH's "^Kay^" is employed to both acknowledge *and* close down SF's contribution by treating it as sufficient (cf. Beach, 1993b, in press, this volume). Next, TH's "an" prefaces a query tied to a portion of M's turn not yet answered due to SF's contribution, once again relying on "you" to specifically address M. In this sense, just as the "^Kay^" closes down SF's contribution, the "an plus question" builds *across* a series of questions, thus revealing the connectedness of prior/next questions (cf. Heritage & Sorjonen, in press; Sorjonen & Heritage, 1991).

In Exemplar 9 when TH is questioning M concerning the type of work she does and where she does it, TH's "^Okay^" treats information regarding M's work as sufficient, immediately prior to transitioning to home/Hazel.

Exemplar 9—FAM:A2 ((simplified))

```
            TH:   What kind of work do you do?
            M:    Ah food service
            TH:   At?
            M:    Ah post office cafeteria downtown main post
                  office on Redwood
            TH:   ^Okay^ so if you didn't get home ah Hazel?
  => 1     D:    Hazel would watch us
  *=> 2    TH:   ^Would watch us^ an then if you were in the
                  hospital? (1.0) for an accident or something
                  then she would probably call Joe an Joe an Hazel
                  would work out something? (1.0) An if you were
                  dead they'd probably work out something
            M:    Well they'd have to wouldn't they?
            TH:   They'ud have to
```

Here, TH's "okay"-prefaced question turns the talk to the subject of M's nightmares (i.e., having a car accident on the way home from work and not being able to pick up her children). Even though the question is directed to M (i.e., "if you didn't get home"), D answers the question for her mother (=> 1). And while D responds in M's "slot," notice in (*=> 2) how TH offers a *partial repeat* of "^Would watch us^" in the first part of his response, which confirms TH's hearing of D's contribution. TH then continues his turn once again relying on an "and"-prefaced question to re-connect following issues as issues-in-a-series that TH was focusing on/working toward (and also via repeated references to "you" in addressing M).

And in Exemplar 10:

Exemplar 10—FAM:A1 ((simplified))

```
            TH:   Ah:ha Steven you sound like you're a ah good
                  helper (0.5) huh? (1.0) do you help your friends
                  too? any of 'ema come to you when they're in
                  trouble? er unhappy?
            S:    ((Nods head up and down))
            TH:   ^Do you know how to help any of your little
                  friends at school when they're cryin er unhappy?^
            S:    ((Nods head up and down))
```

```
=> 1    M:    He's a very sensitive little boy
*=> 2   TH:   ^Yeah^ tell me a story about somebody you helped
              at school
```

TH questions S about his being a good helper. After S nods affirmatively in response to TH's last question, M offers an unsolicited evaluation of her son (=> 1). In (*=> 2), TH then utters a soft "yeah" that briefly acknowledges, but minimally so (cf. Jefferson, 1993) M's contribution en route to continuing with a direction for S to "tell me a story" about someone he helped at school.

Again, in Exemplar 11 a slightly different variation occurs:

Exemplar 11—FAM:A1 ((simplified))
```
            TH:   Sounds nice an now how did you get up this
                  morning? does your mom wake you up or did
                  you get up by yourself?
            S:    I wake up by myself
=> 1        M:    Yeah he's an early bird
*=> 2       TH:   Ah ha an you sleep a little later?
            M:    Yeah
            TH:   So:
                  [
=> 3        S:    I'm an owl
            TH:   You're an owl?
            S:    A night owl
            TH:   A night owl
=> 4        M:    Ha:(h) ˙hh
*=> 5       TH:   An so a: when you got up was it still dark?
            S:    ((shakes head side to side))
```

Here, TH questions S about how he got up that morning. After S's answer, M offers an unsolicited evaluation in (=> 1). In (*=> 2), TH's newsmark ("Ah ha") and "and"-prefaced query briefly acknowledges M's remark but then (via "you") retains the questioning on M and away from her son. This new focus seems to be a momentary event, as evidenced by TH's next turn which he starts with "so." "So" forecasts a summarizing type of utterance, a "formulation" (Heritage & Watson, 1979). Heritage and Watson claimed that one function formulations serve is to terminate topics. Furthermore, they noted that authority figures in institutional settings (e.g., judges, chairpersons) hold the "rights" to formulate.

However, TH drops his utterance when S offers an unsolicited remark about being an owl (=> 3), and then TH continues with the son. However, at (*=> 5), TH relies on an "and so"-prefaced question to continue the past narrative with S (the relationship between it being "dark" and being a "night" owl is evident), even though M's (=> 4) can be understood as a reaction to S's "owl" description, TH fails to acknowledge it. The "and so"-prefaced query here shows a summarizing and "forward" movement in TH's line of questioning; it displays that TH has a series of questions or an agenda "in mind."

Redirecting Focus to the Second Member

Rather than treat a second family member's unsolicited contribution as unhelpful at that time, a therapist may instead treat it as helpful and useful and want to redirect his or her attention to the second member. That is, a therapist may follow-up on a family member's unsolicited contribution, dropping her or his focus and previous line of questioning with the initially queried family member. For any number of reasons, the therapist may decide his or her redirected attention to the second family member may prove more productive or constructive in the therapeutic process. Considering that interaction is created moment-by-moment, the therapist can clearly redirect his or her attention and utterances back to the initially queried family member (or to another, for that matter) if interaction with the second family member does not seem to be constructive in the therapist's view. Exemplars 12 and 13 are illustrations of redirected attention to the second family member's unsolicited contribution.

Exemplar 12—FAM:C1 ((simplified))
```
           TH:   Is there anything wrong with that? ^to be mad
                 at him?^
           M:    I think so I don't think people should carry grudges
                                  [
           TH:                    He's cheating you
           M:    Er ^ya know^
           TH:   But he's cheating you
                      (1.5)
           TH:   He's takin away yer son
=>1        S:    He's not takin me away he's not cheating her if
                 anybody's doin it it's me I'm takin me away he's
                 ^it wasn't his decision for me to move^
*=>2       TH:   But these are your mom's feelings Scott do you
                 hear that?
           S:    Yeah I know but see she's not getting it through it's
                 me that's doin this so why should she be mad at him?
```

Exemplar 12 involves TH's questioning of M about her feelings towards her ex-husband. In (=> 1), S offers an unsolicited comment. TH then redirects his attention and focus, questioning S (*=> 2).

And in Exemplar 13:

2. RESPONDING TO UNSOLICITED CONTRIBUTIONS   63

Exemplar 13—FAM:A3
        TH: You mean u- when- the kids are sick are upset
                    or (0.8)
        F: Hm hm
                    (0.4)
        TH: And how bout their sleeping in her b*e*d before
                    she goes to (s- sleep)
        F: Yeah that doesn't (.) ^(hurt me)^
=>1   G: They h*a*ve to sleep in one bed or be out in the
                    front room with the T V and that isn't
                    very good either so
                    [   ]   [ ]
*=>2 TH: I see   So they don't have
                    separate beds for ^themselves^
        G: No I have two bedroom apartment

TH and F discuss F's children's sleeping arrangements while being baby-sat at their grandmother's house. After one of the father's answers, G offers an unsolicited explanation for the sleeping arrangements (=> 1). At this moment, TH switches his attention away from F, to G by uttering an acknowledgment token ("I see") while she is talking and then in overlap offering a formulation (Heritage & Watson, 1979) concerning the bed, for G's confirmation (*=> 2).

Letting Family Members Collaborate

After a family member offers an unsolicited comment, the therapist may refrain from taking a turn and instead let the two family members talk together or collaborate on some narrative. The therapist may wish to do this for any number of reasons. For instance, the therapist may want to view the members interacting, may consider their collaboration productive or constructive for them, or may simply be taking advantage of the opportunity to gather information. Whatever the reason, the therapist stops asking questions for a few moments and allows the family members to talk with each other (without questions from him or her). This form of response by the therapist "opens up" the interaction to family members alone, momentarily giving them control of the interaction.

Exemplar 14—FAM:A3
        TH: I see so they remember that you flunked first
                    grade and even though you're in third grade
                    they call you a flunking first grader?
        S: But I don't flunk I didn't flunk Mom didn't
                    want me pass cause I missed too much school
        TH: Oh she wanted you to
                    [

```
            S:                 Right
            TH:       make=
    =>1     M:        =No::
                      (.)
            S:        ·hh But y ou didn't
                              [
            M:                Mom     mom made a trade with the
                      school if they would take you out of handicapped
                      classes (0.8) instead of putting you in the second
                      grade we would leave you in the first grade
            S:        Yeah
                      (1.4)
    =>2     TH:       I see
```

Here, TH questions S about being teased at school. In (=> 1), M interjects negatively concerning a particular part of the story. At this point, TH stops his participation and M and S continue together for several turns. In (=> 2), TH comes back into the conversation by uttering a newsmark ("I see"), displaying his receipt of the information (i.e., the reason behind the son's school status).

And in Exemplar 15:

```
Exemplar 15—FAM:A1 ((simplified))
            TH:       =To think about how he died you mean?
            S:        I dunno
    =>1     M:        I don't think she did go back there after=
            S:        =>>Yeah she did<<
            M:        That sounds strange to me
    =>2     TH:       ^Eh ha^ n- could I ask you ta do some- I'm gunna
                      ask you ta do something that's gunna make you
                      kinna sad (1.5) ^do you think you can handle it?^
```

TH and S discuss S's memories of his grandmother. In (=> 1), M offers an unsolicited comment disagreeing with her son's perceptions of the grandmother's behavior after her husband died. TH allows them to interact for several turns without his participation. In (=> 2), TH re-enters the conversation by uttering a soft acknowledgment token ("Eh ha"), and then begins to say "now" before moving to a new topic. After allowing the family members to interact without his participation, TH uses a "now"-prefaced query to return to the here-and-now and his current agenda for the therapeutic process.[9]

---

[9]It is interesting to note that both the previous segments include the second family member disagreeing with the first family member in front of the therapist. Lerner (1993) noted that this type of event can show association between the two speakers. He argued that the second speaker's disagreeing and attempting to correct demonstrates his or her own involvement and hence, their association. The disagreement and attempt at correction is produced for the recipient, the therapist, by the second family member on behalf of him or herself and the other, as members of a family.

SUMMARY

This chapter describes how therapists work through and accomplish the difficult task of managing unsolicited contributions from nonaddressed family members. The examination of naturally-occurring family therapy sessions enables us to see *how* therapists construct narratives with family members while also resolving routine problems such as unsolicited comments. We explicated the common sequential organization of this event, which begins with a two- or three-part opening involving the unsolicited comment by the nonaddressed family member, and is followed by the therapist's response.

We identified and described the techniques that therapists use at these interactional junctures: (a) close down an unsolicited contribution, (b) not respond verbally to the additional comment, (c) briefly acknowledge or confirm the remark but continue with the first family member, (d) redirect the focus to the second family member's unsolicited comment, or (e) allow the family members to collaborate while remaining silent. We observed how these responses vary in the degree of "closing down/opening up" a particular family member's participation in the interaction.

In particular, responses that "close down" (cf. Beach, 1993b, in press, this volume; Button, 1987, 1990; Schegloff & Sacks, 1973; Vuchinich, 1990) an opening bid of a nonaddressed family member form a continuum. As discussed, this range of responses varies in the degree of sanction and acknowledgment of the nonaddressed family member's contribution, and also in the degree of disruption to the interaction and to the therapist's line of questioning.

This continuum occurs within a larger continuum as we compare therapists' responses to unsolicited contributions in family therapy with those of other "officially designated" participants or authority figures in various institutional settings (e.g., courtroom judges, facilitators in focus groups). At one end of the continuum, for example, are courtroom judges. They can be explicit, and even crude in their directives to those in their courtrooms, for example, by telling them to "shut up" (Beach, 1990b, 1993a).

At the other end of the continuum, Beach (1990a) described a facilitator's responses to a focus group member's volunteered piece of information. The facilitator's response consisted of a positive evaluation (*"Oh grea:t!"*) of the contribution followed by a continuation of her turn in which she moved the focus of the talk to an alternative topic.

Thus, judges', therapists', and group facilitators' responses are similar, but are tailored to the particular requirements of the setting. That is, the basic opportunity to "open up" and "close down" talk is afforded to all authority figures (i.e., illustrating one of the ways in which institutional talk is asymmetrical, cf. Markova & Foppa, 1991), but how the talk is shaped differs with the degree of formal, a priori power associated with particular roles and the tasks to be achieved. Specifically, judges do not depend on the cooperation of the people before them to the same degree as therapists and facilitators and, are not attempting to build possible long-term working relationships with them. Additionally, within the courtroom, judges are empowered with legal authority over those they interact with. Therefore, more crude or explicit commands may be more appropriate for judges.

On the other hand, therapists must maintain working relationships with their clients over the course of the therapy (i.e., possibly years). Similarly, group facilitators must foster participation and enlist the cooperation of group members. Therefore, a more delicate handling of volunteered responses may be helpful and appropriate in comparison to cruder, and more explicit commands.

FUTURE RESEARCH DIRECTIONS

Research studies in the future should examine ways in which authority figures in other institutional settings involving multi-party interaction (e.g., news show interviewers, talk show hosts, pediatricians) manage unsolicited contributions from nonaddressed participants. Responses employed in everyday multi-party conversations (e.g., family discourse) also could be investigated. Research projects of this nature would further expand the continuum of such responses.

The responses of therapists from different theoretical orientations could be compared and contrasted to see if particular types of responses are more or less characteristic of specific therapeutic orientations. Are there differences between therapists from different orientations? Future studies could investigate therapists' responses to unsolicited contributions in group therapy. Do therapists use different techniques with groups of unrelated individuals than they do with families? Potential differences in the responses used by therapists in other cultures (i.e., speaking other languages in addition to English) could be explored. ten Have's (1991) research on medical consultations in the Netherlands suggests that differences across cultures may exist concerning clinical discourse. These are but a few of the possible directions for future research projects.

IMPLICATIONS FOR PRACTITIONERS

Descriptions such as this allow students and practitioners of therapy to observe and examine in detail actual therapists' responses to one type of activity treated as problematic in family therapy sessions. The findings illustrate, at a microscopic level, how the "problematic" activity is displayed by family members and the different ways it can be responded to by therapists. For example, the continuum of responses to "close down" an unsolicited contribution offers clinicians a variety of conversational techniques to use at these interactional junctures. Based on the interactional and therapeutic needs at any given moment (e.g., to disrupt the interaction or not, to complete a line of questioning or not, to confirm or acknowledge a family member or not), a therapist can more clearly enact a specific response.

Being sensitive to the many demands of being a therapist is delicate work. He or she must treat each family member as a valuable and worthwhile person capable of participating in and contributing to the therapeutic process while also managing and directing a meaningful and relevant interaction. Microanalytic studies such as this one can be used to provide insight and practical guidance concerning techniques and behaviors for interaction management that can influence the process of therapeutic care.

REFERENCES

Beach, W. A. (1985). Temporal density in courtroom interaction: Constraints on the recovery of past events in legal discourse. *Communication Monographs, 52,* 1–18.

Beach, W. A. (1990a). Language as and in technology: Facilitating topic organization in a Videotex focus group meeting. In M. J. Medhurst, A. Gonzalez, & T. R. Peterson (Eds.), *Communication and the culture of technology* (pp. 197–220). Pullman, WA: Washington State University Press.

Beach, W. A. (1990b). Orienting to the phenomenon. In J. A. Anderson (Ed.), *Communication Yearbook 13* (pp. 216–244). Newbury Park: Sage.

Beach, W. A. (1992). *"Okay-prefaced" queries and contingent institutional relevancies.* Paper presented at the annual meeting of the Speech Communication Association, Chicago.

Beach, W. A. (1993a). *Judges' sanctions.* Unpublished manuscript.

Beach, W. A. (1993b). Transitional regularities for 'casual' "Okay" usages. *Journal of Pragmatics, 19,* 325–352.

Beach, W. A. (in press). "Okay" as a clue for understanding conversation analysis and "consequentiality." In S. J. Sigman (Ed.), *The consequentiality of communication.* Hillsdale, NJ: Lawrence Erlbaum Associates.

Beach, W. A., & Japp, P. (1983). Storifying as time-traveling: The knowledgeable use of temporally structured discourse. In R. N. Bostrom (Ed.), *Communication Yearbook 7* (pp. 867–889). New Brunswick, NJ: Transaction.

Button, G. (1987). Moving out of closings. In G. Button & J. R. E. Lee (Eds.), *Talk and social organization* (pp. 101–151). Clevedon: Multilingual Matters.

Button, G. (1990). On varieties of closings. In G. Psathas (Ed.), *Interaction competence* (pp. 93–147). New York: Irvington.

Davis, K. (1984). The process of problem (re)formulation in psychotherapy. *Sociology of Health and Illness, 8,* 44–74.

Drew, P., & Heritage, J. (1992). *Talk at work: Interaction in institutional settings.* Cambridge: Cambridge University Press.

Elbert, S., Rosman, B., Minuchin, S., & Guerney, B. (1964). A method for the clinical study of family interaction. *American Journal of Orthopsychiatry, 34,* 885–894.

Friedlander, M. L., Highlen, P. S., & Lassiter, W. L. (1985). Content analytic comparison of four expert counselors' approaches of family treatment: Ackerman, Bowen, Jackson, and Whitaker. *Journal of Counseling Psychology, 32,* 171–180.

Gardner, R. A. (1969). Mutual storytelling as a technique in child psychotherapy. In J. Masserman (Ed.), *Science and psychoanalysis* (Vol. 14, pp. 123–134). New York: Grune & Stratton.

Gardner, R. A. (1971). *Therapeutic communication with children: The mutual storytelling technique.* New York: Jason Aronson.

Gardner, R. A. (1975). Techniques for involving the child with MBD in meaningful psychotherapy. *Journal of Learning Disabilities, 8,* 16–26.

Goodwin, C. (1980). Restarts, pauses, and the achievement of mutual gaze at turn-beginning. *Sociological Inquiry, 50,* 272–302.

Heritage, J., & Sorjonen, M.-L. (in press). Constituting and maintaining activities across sequences: "And"-prefacing as a feature of question design. *Language in Society.*

Heritage, J. C., & Watson, D. R. (1979). Formulations as conversational objects. In G. Psathas (Ed.), *Everyday language: Studies in ethnomethodology* (pp. 123–162). New York: Irvington.

Jefferson, G. (1993). Caveat speaker: Preliminary notes on recipient topic-shift implicature. *Research on Language and Social Interaction, 26,* 1–30.

Jones, C. M. (1988). *An examination of storified discourse in the family therapy context.* Unpublished master's thesis, San Diego State University, San Diego, CA.

Jones, C. M. (1992a). *Chin tuck displays in family therapy interaction.* Paper presented at the annual meeting of the Southern States Communication Association, San Antonio, TX.

Jones, C. M. (1992b). *"That's a good sign": Encouraging assessments as a form of social support in medically-related encounters.* Paper presented at the annual meeting of the Speech Communication Association, Chicago.

Labov, W., & Fanshel, D. (1977). *Therapeutic discourse: Psychotherapy as conversation.* New York: Academic.

Lerner, G. H. (1993). Collectivities in action: Establishing the relevance of conjoined participation in conversation. *Text, 13,* 213–245.

MacKinnon, R. A., & Michels, R. (1971). *The psychiatric interview in clinical practice.* Philadelphia: W. B. Saunders.

Markova, I., & Foppa, K. (1991). *Asymmetries in dialogue.* Hamel Hempstead: Harvester Wheat–sheaf.

Mehan, H. (1979). *Learning lessons: Social organization in the classroom.* Cambridge, MA: Harvard University Press.

Penn, P. (1982). Circular questioning. *Family Process, 21,* 267–280.

Sacks, H., Schegloff, E. A., & Jefferson, G. (1974). A simplest systematics for the organization of turn-taking for conversation. *Language, 50,* 696–735.

Satir, V. (1967). *Conjoint family therapy.* Palo Alto, CA: Science and Behavior Books.

Scheflen, A. E. (1973). *Communication structure: An analysis of a psychotherapy transaction.* Bloomington: Indiana University.

Schegloff, S. (1984). On some questions and ambiguities in conversation. In J. M. Atkinson & J. Heritage (Eds.), *Structures of social action: Studies in conversation analysis* (pp. 28–52). Cambridge: Cambridge University Press.

Schegloff, E., & Sacks, H. (1973). Opening up closings. *Semiotica, 3,* 289–327.

Schiffrin, D. (1987). *Discourse markers.* Cambridge: Cambridge University Press.

Siegfried, J. (Ed.). (1993). *Therapeutic and everyday discourse as behavior change.* Norwood, NJ: Ablex.

Sorjonen, M.-L., & Heritage, J. (1991). And—prefacing as a feature of question design. In L. Laitinen (Ed.), *Asennonvaihtoja [Changes in Footing]: Essays in honor of Auli Hakulinen* (pp. 68–84). Helsinki, Vastapaino.

Stamp, G. H. (1991). Family conversation: Description and interpretation. *Family Process, 30,* 251–263.

ten Have, P. (1991). Talk and institution: A reconsideration of the "asymmetry" of doctor-patient interaction. In D. Boden & D. Zimmerman (Eds.), *Talk and social structure* (pp. 138–163). Cambridge: Polity Press.

Viaro, M., & Leonardi, P. (1983). Getting and giving information: Analysis of a family-interview strategy. *Family Process, 22,* 27–42.

Vuchinich, S. (1990). The sequential organization of closing in verbal family conflict. In A. D.

Grimshaw (Ed.), *Conflict talk: Sociolinguistic investigations of arguments in conversations* (pp. 118–138). Cambridge: Cambridge University Press.

Watzlawick, P., Beavin, J. H., & Jackson, D. D. (1967). *The pragmatics of human communication.* New York: W. W. Norton.

West, C. (1983). "Ask me no questions . . . " An analysis of queries and replies in physician-patient dialogues. In S. Fisher & A. Todd (Eds.), *The social organization of doctor-patient communication* (pp. 75–106). Washington, DC: Center for Applied Linguistics.

Wilmot, W. W. (1987). *Dyadic communication* (3rd ed.). New York: Random House.

3 Resourceful Figures in Therapeutic Conversations

Ronald J. Chenail
Nova Southeastern University

Liana Fortugno
Tressler Clinics of Delaware

Ask psychotherapists (i.e., mental health counselors, family therapists, psychologists, clinical social workers, or psychiatrists) what it is they do when they work with patients or clients and their answers will be varied and usually rich with psychological and sociological theory, pathological diagnoses, and declarations about the therapeutic models that guide their practice, but talk about language will be absent.

> It is a matter for astonishment, when one comes to think of it, how little use linguistics and other sciences of language are to psychiatrists. When one considers that the psychiatrist spends most of his [or her] time listening and talking to patients, one might suppose that there would be such a thing as a basic science of listening-and-talking, as indispensable to psychiatrists as anatomy to surgeons. Surgeons traffic in body structures. Psychiatrists traffic in words. (Percy, 1954/1987, p. 159)

Percy's comment about psychiatrists' talk is fitting for most therapists' descriptions of their work: Despite language being their major resource in their encounters with others in therapeutic relationships, therapists' models of therapy do not appear to be language-based or linguistics-sensitive. This absence of discourse-oriented theory and practice is not unique to therapists, and again Percy (1991) reminds us how human it is to be unaware of living in language because we are

> languaged creatures and see everything through the mirror of language, asking [us] to consider the nature of language is like asking a fish to consider the nature of water. [We] cannot imagine its absence, so [we] cannot consider its presence. (pp. 419–420)

LANGUAGE AS RESOURCE

Although we can never totally remove ourselves from our language environment, we can, from time to time, catch a glimpse of what it is to be in language by experiencing particularities of our everyday patterns of language usage or "languaging" (Becker, 1991) in a slightly different light. Discourse scholars like anthropologists, linguists, and philologists, who undertake extended, cross-cultural interpretation projects, report that translating one language into another allows them a new sensitivity to their native or first language practice (see Becker, 1979).

Juxtaposing these connecting, yet differing, styles and shapes of languaging is one way they become sensitive to a "taken-for-grantedness" attitude toward language. The particularities of one form of languaging (Becker, 1984, 1988), with its ways of saying and not saying (Tyler, 1978), help to bring out said and unsaid particularities of another language practice, and vice versa. These discourse scientists and artists become fish out of water by filling their mouths, lungs, and minds with new language patterns and experiences. By doing so, these language amphibians, or maybe ambilinguals, gain new awareness and appreciation of what it is to be in language.

For therapists, then, one way to become more language sensitive in therapy would be to adopt and adapt theories and techniques from these language scientists and artists in order to put therapeutic languaging in a new perspective and to develop the basic science and artistry of listening-and-talking in therapy that Percy called for in the 1950s. Before this can happen, clinicians have to begin to reflect upon their views of language and the purposes it serves in the therapeutic process.

Predominantly, psychologists, psychiatrists, and other therapists work from a structuralist perspective that limits their interest in their clients' language usually only as a means to an end (see de Saussure, 1959; Harland, 1987; Sarup, 1993). The words of the clients serve only as signs or symptoms for underlying structures of thoughts and feelings in the clients. By stressing the signified, the underlying psychological structures of the clients, over the signifiers, the language of the clients, therapists are not utilizing a very important resource in their interactions with their clients, the language itself.

In contrast to this approach to therapy, some clinicians and researchers are using poststructuralist and social constructionist ideas in their conceptualization and practice of therapy (e.g., Anderson & Goolishian, 1988, de Shazer & Berg, 1992; Edwards & Potter, 1992; Friedman, 1993; McNamee & Gergen, 1992). These therapists and theorists have suggested that the works of thinkers such as Derrida (1976), Lyotard (1984), Deleuze and Guattari (1983), Kristeva (1984), Foucault (1980), and Baudrillard (1988) might be well-suited to the practice of therapy, especially for those who want to explore the possibilities of language in therapy.

According to Best and Kellner (1991):

poststructuralists gave primacy to the signifier over the signified, and thereby signalled the dynamic productivity of language, the instability of meaning, and a break with conventional representational schemes of meaning.... For poststructuralists, ... the signified is only a moment in a never-ending process of signification where meaning is produced not in a stable, referential relation between subject and object, but only within the infinite, intertextual play of signifiers. (p. 21)

With poststructualists and social constructionists, therapy is practiced as a co-evolving, collaborative conversation in which therapist and client attempt to create new meanings with each other. In this chapter, we present a clinical approach that shares much of the language sensitivity found in the poststructuralist and social constructionist models, but with one important difference. Whereas the theorists and therapists discussed earlier are concerned with privileging language (the signifier) over the signified (the underlying structures), we are not interested in taking an "it is all language perspective." Rather, we want to propose a new way for therapists to view their languaging in therapy.

Instead of employing language as a simple, transparent medium for conveying ideas and diagnosing underlying psychological structures, we suggest that therapists consider the possibilities in contemplating language in therapeutic conversations as a vibrant, complex resource in and of itself. We propose a style of therapeutic language practice grounded in a discourse sensitivity that holds that common, everyday language usage, including clinical talk, has figurative qualities heretofore restricted almost entirely to literary and poetic discourse. In such a way, our language itself becomes a medium with a message.

By privileging and working within a conversation at hand, the language itself makes its "own contribution to the meaning" (McLaughlin, 1990, p. 85), and this contribution of language to the particular conversation at hand, be it poetry, prose, or narrative, can be readily understood and practiced from this perspective of configuration in language. With such an orientation to conversation and meaning in talk, language as patterns of figures takes a place in interaction alongside hearer and speaker to complete a triadic configuration of participants in conversation, both configurations of speech and speakers of configurations.

> That is, if even the "proper" meaning of words are in this sense figurative, then the complexity of communication in a poem is not only a product of the poet's inventiveness but also a result of the interaction of tropes built into the language. These tropes bring out possibilities of meaning that pre-exist the poem in language, in the meaning structures that make tropes possible. (McLaughlin, 1990, p. 85)

An emphasis on the particularity of language notifies us that, with all possible meanings words or figures may have, we *create* a particular meaning with a particular someone at a particular place and time through our particularities of configurations with words. We struggle to accomplish this goal by paying close attention to the ways words or figures are used and not used in patterns with other spoken and unspoken words or figures. The ways in which we configure figures with other figures restrict certain possible meanings while encouraging other interpretations to be heard and spoken by conversation participants. Hearing and speaking with a mind to figures in relation to other figures, instead of solitary figures, is

> to think in terms of a complex system of categories and analogies in order to make sense of them; but so does any use of language. How does any word make sense? It makes sense by being part of a system of meanings, a set of contrasts and comparisons. No word has meaning in isolation but only insofar as it relates to and differs from other words in the language system. (McLaughlin, 1990, pp. 85–86)

Our approach to languaging in therapy, *resourceful figures,* asks therapists to work closely with the language our clients and ourselves use in our conversations together. As therapists, we may never know what the language of another in therapy truly signifies, but we do assume that the talk of our clients is significant. Because of this significance, we are interested in working with the talk at hand in therapy. We want to notice how clients put their talk together and how these constructions of words take on meaning or meanings in the process of clients and therapists communicating with each other.

RESOURCEFUL FIGURES: CONCEPTS AND PRACTICES

A resourceful figures' style of therapeutic conversation is based on the almost complete reliance on the other's languaging, with all it's saying and not saying (Tyler, 1978), with all its exuberances and deficiencies (Becker, 1984, 1988, 1991), with all its articulations and silences (Corradi Fiumara, 1990), and with all its figures and tropes (Fernandez, 1991; McLaughlin, 1990; Tannen, 1989). In doing so, we "legitimize the presence of others, and hence help to converse with those we have trouble conversing with" (Becker, 1991, p. 233). In addition, we also privilege a place for listening in this language interaction. "Listening, in this view, is an active not a passive enterprise, requiring interpretation comparable to that required in speaking, and speaking entails simultaneously projecting the act of listening: In Bakhtin's sense, all language use is dialogic" (Tannen, 1989, p. 12; see also Corradi Fiumara, 1990).

One way to foster such a dialogic posture with resourceful figures is for clinicians to organize their work not from a particular preconversational figure, as seen in Freudian approaches (e.g., transference as metaphor), feminist approaches (e.g., power as metaphor), or systemic family therapy approaches (e.g., negative feedback as metaphor), but by listening and speaking to a figurative quality of the talk itself at hand. By doing so, these conversation participants explore figurative constructions in conversations, rather than constructing figures about conversations.

In following such a path, a resourceful figures approach can be said to be based on a metaphor as metaphor orientation, or to be more general, figure as figure. This emphasis on process allows for the construction of unique figures from each conversation's content. Participants become resourceful figures as they co-construct or co-create configurations of words and co-explore new meanings of these words. Therapy then becomes not a search by the therapist for signs of underlying psychological structures, but a co-exploration by therapist and client of almost endless possibilities of using these resourceful figures in therapeutic conversations. If there can be significant changes in the talk, then there can be significant changes in the lives of the participants in that talk.

With resourceful figures, the concern is not so much that participants can literally speak and hear figures such as "metaphor," "irony," "metonymy," and "synecdoche," as in the case of a language teacher asking students to find all the metaphors and ironies in the short story passage, or when a therapist prepares a therapeutic metaphor to be presented to the clients in a session. Instead, a resourceful figures approach asks that hearers and speakers consider dialectical relationships between all words when contemplating meaning in conversation, rather than saving such an analysis just for those special and isolated instances of "true" figurative language.

This perspective allows for an emphasis on configurations or systems of words, that is, how we speak and hear through our unique ways of configuring speech in our speaking and hearing. Configuration helps to remind us that we need to consider how words are juxtaposed in conversation by speakers and hearers as a way toward meaning creation. In such a way, words in pattern can be thought of as being metaphoric (i.e., how meaning of one word is considered from a perspective of another word's meaning), ironic (i.e., how meaning of one word is changed to an opposite when it is juxtaposed with another word), metonymical (i.e., how more complex meanings of words can be reduced to less complex wordings), or synecdochal (i.e., how words for a part of a thing can be used to represent the whole thing). The challenge of resourceful figures is to examine closely our patterns of speech as a way to figure out the many viable and imaginative meanings that are possible when we put words together. The way we choose to carry out this figuring process in a resourceful figures approach is to engage in conversation with others with an understanding that we can only come to know meaning through our play and work with words.

In partnership with language, we, as resourceful figures in conversation, help to relate and differentiate meanings as we configure and reconfigure words. From this perspective, meaning is understood and created by exploring and constructing relationships between patterns of figures of speech, or in other words, meaning through configuration in conversation. In a resourceful figures approach, playing back and forth with meanings of words is called *troping,* from the Greek word for figures—"trope" (McLaughlin, 1990, p. 81), whereas exploring possible patterns of figures is called *configuring.* "Our association of change of meaning with 'trope' follows the common practice that contrasts trope with 'figure,' a device that has to do with changes in formal patterns. Obviously any rhetorical device involves both and its full analysis must account for each type of change" (Sapir, 1977, p. 4).

Most common and recognizable of these patterns of figures and meanings are shapes like metaphor, metonymy, synecdoche, and irony (see Burke, 1945/1969). In each case, these configurations depend on special, dialectical relationships between particular words. For instance, a *metaphor* pattern is where two, previously unconfigured words are juxtaposed for comparison purposes or to bring out similarities, as in a Burkean (1945/1969) sense of "bringing out the thisness of a that, or the thatness of a this" (p. 503). For example, when a husband, commenting on his wife's handling of their daughter's temper tantrums, says, "She dropped the ball on that one," he suggests his sports or business perspective on parenting by his configuring "dropped the ball" with "that one."

A *metonymy* pattern is where previously configured words are reconfigured such that one word is used for another to show a cause and effect association or a container for thing contained relationship. For instance, an observation by a mother concerning her son's recent behavior, "He showed a lot of heart when he helped his little sister" is considered metonymic because it both reduces having feelings and emotions to having "a lot of heart," as in the heart being the container of the emotions, and also suggests a causal relation between having such a condition, "He showed a lot of heart," and doing a good deed, "when he helped his little sister."

Synecdoche would be a configuration of words where a relationship between two words is reconfigured such that a word for a part of thing replaces the word for the whole thing. For example, when a supervisor asks a therapist, "How long have you been seeing the schizophrenic," the question is said to have synecdochal characteristics because the word for a whole, "person or patient," has been replaced by a word for a part of that person, their diagnosis as in "the schizophrenic."

Finally, *irony* would be a configuration of two groups of words brings out a slightly adjusted, or even opposite meaning for one of the word groups. An exemplar of irony would be when a client says, "I'm worried about losing my ex-husband" can be considered ironic because her configuring of "losing" with something already lost, "my ex-husband," suggests a different if not opposite meaning for what "my ex-husband" might mean for her.

Another style of configuration is called *abduction* (Bateson, 1979). According to Tannen (1989)

> the working of tropes is more the norm than the exception in language: Most meaning is communicated in daily language not by the logical processes of induction and deduction but by the "lateral extension of abstract components of description" (pp. 157–158) such that, "We can look at the anatomy of a frog and then look around to find other instances of the same abstract relations recurring in other creatures, including . . . ourselves" (p. 157). (pp. 24–25)

Just as Bateson found abductive patterns in nature by "seeking to put side by side similar chunks of phenomena" (Bateson, 1979/1991, p. 232), therapist and supervisor as resourceful figures can hear and speak similar abductive patterns in and with the talk at hand through juxtaposition of words. To configure words abductively is to declare both figures as "falling under that same rules. In each case, it is assumed that certain formal characteristics of one component will be mirrored in the other" (Bateson, 1979, p. 158).

In other words, a relationship between two figures (A and B) may configure in a pattern or logic similar to a relationship between two other figures (C and D). Abductive configuring can be seen as a configuration of configuration: Figure A is to Figure B as Figure C is to Figure D, or as Bateson (1979) put it, "Every abduction may be seen as a double or multiple description of some object or event or sequence" (p. 158). For example, a father's saying, "I'm worried that I'm going to make the same mistakes with my son as my father made with me" may suggest to a therapist that this man is using a configuration of configurations in his life such that the logic of the relation between him, as father (Figure A) and his son (Figure B) may be the same as the relation between his father (Figure C) and him, as son (Figure D).

From a resourceful figures perspective, one of the reasons people come to therapy is that their patterns or forms of languaging have become rather rigid. This rigidity or repetitiveness of speech is usually associated with a certain degree of tightness of meaning: Participants' tropes have been twisted so tightly that this torque does not allow for flexibility in meaning or action (see Chenail, 1993, for closer examination of the torqued quality of clients' talk in therapy). To help loosen talk, resourceful figures in therapeutic conversation "act always so as to increase the number of choices" by acting in language (von Foerster, 1984, pp. 60–61) through a dialectic process of troping and configuring.

Change can occur by juxtaposing previously unconnected or unconfigured words, or by reconfiguring earlier configured discourse. Conversation participants can discover and create new meanings from formerly stagnant, stale, or torqued talk. By definition then, if participants' meanings can be loosened a bit through conversations over time such that new patterns become possible, then such conversations, from a resourceful figures perspective, are said to be therapeutic. In other words, our goal in engaging in these conversations is to help

> organize the talk of therapy so that it becomes an alternative means of expression for clients and a viable vehicle for articulating solutions to their problematic life situations. If we do not help to loosen up the talk, if the shape of the talk in therapy stays the same as it has been for the clients in their previous interactions, then it is likely that the clients will remain locked in their conflict, and the conversation in therapy will not provide an alternative means of communication for resolving their problems. (Chenail, 1993, p. 28)

For instance, the father mentioned in the abduction example may be having trouble with his relationship with his son and may be limiting or restricting his options for change due to his spoken connection between his fathering style and his own father's way of parenting. In conversation, father and therapist as resourceful figures would use various figures (e.g., "father," "son," "mistakes," etc.) to create new configurations (e.g., "What mistakes has your son made that you never made?") or to work these tropes so to play with their figurative meanings (i.e., "What other father figures have you had besides your father?"). By working tropes or troping in conversation this way, new meanings may emerge from the language and father and therapist may begin to construct new patterns in the speech. Also, new juxtapositions or configurations may help these resourceful figures in therapeutic conversation to create new meanings and possibilities for both therapist and father alike.

A practice of resourceful figures in therapeutic conversation then is based on relationships between, on the one hand, patterns of words, and on the other hand, meanings of these word patterns. Processing the content of discussions in therapy, along these lines, helps to create a rich source of new materials and meanings. Exploration and re-exploration of these words, *clients', therapists', supervisors',* and *team members',* become a practice of resourceful figures that allows for (a) new meanings through troping and (b) new possibilities of speech patterns through configuring for all figures, people, and words. Change in therapeutic conversations is created through attention to both meanings and patterns of words.

A THERAPEUTIC CONVERSATION

With the following transcript, the authors attempt to re-present one such therapeutic conversation, this one between a supervisor (S), a therapist (T), and a therapy team member (M1). The discussion took place during what, in systemic family therapy, is commonly called a *break:* a time when therapists take a break from talking with their client or clients, to converse about the previous conversation with a group of colleagues, the therapy team and/or supervisor, and to plan for subsequent therapist–client interactions. With this particular break, the therapist has joined his group of colleagues, a supervisor and other team members, who have been watching and listening, through a one-way mirror/audiovisual system, to a conversation between the therapist and a mother and her son. In the analysis of their interaction, we attempt to show how the participants, using a resourceful figures approach, were able to reconfigure their talk in such a way as to bring forth new meanings and patterns, and to be therapeutic.

Exemplar 1
501   S: It was funny that uh, that, uh, following about two minutes or a minute after you went and checked out, she went and checked out too.
502   T: Yeah. It's kind of funny.

503	S:	Your uh, your, uh, timer is a little different than her timer as far as how long you would have to be gone before you could check out....
504	T:	Yeah, yeah, that's right. That's the way it works (laughter). You do have that internal clock that only works so long before you make a move.
505	S:	My wife's is about five minutes faster than mine (laughter). What is going on?
506	T:	Well, with the insertion of the grief is, uh, I wanted to just explore that for a second because I knew it was information that you did not know about. The boy's dad died. Uh, that as some of what the original problem was for therapy. But that colors a picture exceedingly black background or whatever you call it, but it colors it real fast. So I did not want to have all that as more information, too fast. Because it may not have anything to do with anything.
507	S:	Yeah, because we could have seen that, uh, his behavior was a symptom of warmth, or . . .
508	T:	Yeah, yeah. I did not want to do that because I knew I have that information and I am already coloring things.
509	S:	Yeah.
510	T:	But I wanted new colors.
511	S:	His is at the Rolling Stone, paint it black right?
512	T:	Yeah, yeah.
513	S:	But, uh, well we kind of got the impression early on that uh, his acting up was more of uh, uh, that it was a symptom because he was a bad boy or something like that. That there was something going on, uh, circumstantially. We probably would not have heard that if you had not talked earlier on that it was, uh, his special way of mourning or something like that.
514	T:	Right

Reflections on Exemplar 1

In Turn 506, the therapist presents talk about a figure, grief, which had remained unsaid for most of the previous conversation, and re-presents one configuration of his conversation with his clients. He juxtaposes grief, the boy, and a dead dad as one system of meaning, or in other words, he configures the preceding talk as follows in Configuration 1:

>   grief   /   boy   /   dead dad

At the same time, the therapist acknowledges that he had been silent about such a reconfiguration of the talk: "So I did not want to have all that as more information, too fast." He expressed such a concern because such a configuring of grief with the rest of the talk in the room would have limited the meaning because "that colors a picture exceedingly black background or whatever you call it but it colors it real fast."

Therapist and supervisor continue to play with the figure, black, as seen in Turns 508–512, and then the supervisor makes his first attempt at participating in the therapist's configuration of the previous therapy talk by juxtaposing "acting up" with "bad boy" (see Configuration 2):

acting up   /   bad boy

Also, the supervisor alludes to the therapist's previous talk as represented in Configuration 1: "his special way of mourning or something like that," but does not say anything as to a possible relationship between the two figures.

Exemplar 2

515 S: You know, his mom does not seem to be too sure right now what, what's uh, what's the, what's the key factor?
516 T: Yeah, see my hypothesis is, see how it fits with whatever is going on the way you all thing about it. Mom is uh . . . , still somewhat perplexed over the loss of her husband, so she is being a, uh . . . , a tentative mom and dad. She is a full fledged mom, but she is still being a tentative dad, and every once in a while, we check with this guy named Bill for some of the dad information that I don't have. And uh, just to make sure that I am doing okay. Something like that, and I just happen to fulfill the surrogate dad role. So she was seen earlier with Jody and, after just a couple of sessions, transferred to me for the benefit of wanting a male figure. It was not me, it is just the male figure.
517 S: There was no one else available and you had to go in. Is that what it was?
518 T: Um, yeah (laughter), yeah, that is kind of luck of the draw.
519 S: I think the word you are looking for was "tentative". That seems to come through for me back here.
520 T: Yeah, she is tentative in her . . . approval of her own skills and she is tentative also in her plan of attack or her reasoning through whatever may be wrong, and concluding that this is a good idea. It was not it is tentatively a good idea.
521 S: Yeah, that was a really nice sequence here at the end where earlier she spoke of, uh, uh, that, that system of the

		nickels seemed to work pretty good and she said I am not sure that that is really what I should be doing.
522	T:	Yeah, that helped because you punctuated it differently. You changed the, the mannerisms and then you changed the, the role to back to the expert role that she is looking for.
523	S:	Yeah, the mature thing role too because you showed how that you, uh, you were the boss and you just put the child down and told him he had his own chair, and that worked very nicely, also, and, uh, I had a nice little chat there, and it seemed, uh, really clear with the way she was kind of of, uh, because you all back here were saying I wonder who else is the expert in the system. And you know, one hypothesis seems to fit you, and because she is really not sure or she, or she is possibly she is sure, or she is not sure she is sure kind of stuff. And I was saying back here it is kind of like that worrying about worrying.
524	T:	Yeah, you know, what I would like to do, and I would just like to rush by you, your filters. Mom is so tentative in her uh, and apprehensive about, following through on her conclusions that she seeks this expert role of either me or this clinic or whatever it is.
525	S:	I think you are God.

Reflections of Exemplar 2

The beginning talk of Exemplar 2 (i.e., Turns 515–520) is displaced around the repetitive use of the figure, tentative, or what Empson (1951/1989; see also Culler, 1989; Miller, 1990) called a *complex word*. In referring to the notion of complex words, Miller (1990) wrote:

> a narrative, even a long multiplotted novel . . . with all its wealth and particularity of character, incident, realistic detail, may be an exploration of the resonances of a single "complex word," to borrow William Empson's term for such words. A complex word is in a special sense a figure. It is the locus of a set of perhaps incompatible meanings, bound together by figurative displacements. . . . In a narrative such a word may be explored by being given contexts or situations in which it may be appropriately used. (p. 77)

As therapist and supervisor work the tentative trope, other talk from previous conversations between therapist and family becomes configured through the troping of tentative (see Configuration 3):

tentative /	mom and dad	(Turn 516)
	in her approval of	
	her own skills	(Turn 520)
	in her plan of attack	(Turn 520)
	her reasoning	(Turn 520)
	a good idea	(Turn 520)
	in her uh and apprehension	
	about following through on	
	her own intentions or on	
	her conclusions that she	
	seeks this expert role of	
	either me or this clinic	
	or whatever it is	(Turn 524)

Exemplar 3

526 T: I would like to (laughter) . . . we are going to bring that up. I would like to tell her that the team concluded that her idea was so good we never even thought of anything "quite like that". Yeah, the nickel thing may not last very long, like most any kind of, any way of punishment, you always have to change different ways because no one way does it.

527 M1: Well, it is broken and it isn't. He has got sixty cents but he is in here.

528 T: Yeah, but it is, see that is where it is a problem for him. And she is just kind of checking up to see whether her problem's solution is working or if it is got somebody higher authority's approval.

529 S: In here, this is what is going on in the room. This is what is happening right here, it is that you are talking about in a sense one side of the issue that, yeah it is working but is is not working. And the next thing you say, yeah, but in that is what right here it seems to be we have it all side by side going here. Is that you have got, yeah, that reward system would work if he was just a bad boy, but it may not work if he is a sad boy.

530 T: Um hum, that is true, she could put the other piece in there.

531 S: Because like you said that when you came back here, you talked about, uh interject the grief in there, and we could look at it that grief contextualizes everything. That this is all a reaction to a very sad situation, or what you may do, and this may fit with her, is that we may not know if this is all a reaction because, you know, he is acting out, those things that are going on to a bad boy, we also don't know how much of this has to do with him being a sad boy. He has rea-

sons for being sad, he has reasons for being bad too. And uh, you know that kind of following what you are saying, talk about that the team thinks that, uh, uh, that is probably good that she, she remain a bit tentative about which theory is the right theory because we may never know which one, it is very difficult to say that is the reason exactly, for why the kid is acting this way. And maybe what what she can do is continue doing what she has been doing and that is, to have different solutions that fit if he is just acting out. That seems that she is doing a very good job in it, ignoring him while he is [ ], putting him in his room, picking up on the things that she knows are bad, like hitting the girl or yelling on the bus, you know, so it looks like she is doing a good job with her own resources that, you know, that is always a problem with single parents, they get stretched too thin. And so, she is reacting with him in those really important things, she has got a better chance because the kid is going to hear it when she gets upset for something she should get upset about rather than everything.

Reflections of Exemplar 3

In Turn 529, the supervisor continues to organize his talk around the figure, tentative, and reflects the unsaid part of the tentative configuration. The therapist, therapy team, and supervisor all share with the mom in the tentative figure: "In here, that is what is going on in the room. This is what is happening right here." The supervisor continues to play with the meaning of being tentative: "it is that you are talking about in sense one side of the issue that, `Yeah it is working, but it is not working'" and begins to suggest ("it seems") that there is another configuration or pattern of meaning: "we have it all side by side going here. Is that you have got, yeah, that reward system would work if he [the boy] was just a bad boy, but it may not work if he is a sad boy." For therapist and supervisor, the mom's so-called tentative behavior starts to make sense to them as they begin to re-configure the talk in a side by side shape (see Configuration 4):

bad boy
sad boy

This configuration takes clearer shape in Turn 531 as the supervisor works the talk in an attempt to abductively shape the talk in a side by side configuration, as in Configuration 5:

acting up / bad boy
grief   / sad boy / dead dad

The saying of the unsaid (i.e., the boy being either sad or bad) helps the therapist and supervisor better understand or configure the mother's position with her son, "And uh, you know that kind of following what you are saying, talk about that 'the team thinks that uh, uh, that it is probably good that she, she remain a bit tentative about which theory is the right theory because we may never know which one [bad boy / sad boy], it is very difficult to say that is the reason exactly, for why the kid is acting this way [bad boy / sad boy]'" (Turn 531). With the use of the trope tentative, therapist and supervisor begin to connect the patterns of figures (i.e., boy talk, dad talk, grief talk, and acting up talk) in an abductive fashion: acting up is to bad boy, as grief is to sad boy, and grief is to sad boy is to dead dad. By doing so, they begin to create a system of meaning from the said, and they also can begin "to hear the unsaid" as they try to complete the distinctions in Exemplar 4 (i.e., If the configuration of grief and sad boy are configured with dead dad, with what figure is the configuration of acting up and sad boy configured?).

Exemplar 4

533	S:	The other thing it might be is, uh, what kind of rituals they [ ] =
534	T:	= The grief again.
535	S:	Remember you said it was just the three of you . . .
536	T:	Yeah, she and the little boy and their minister . . . went to the grave site, this is after the funeral stuff and all that, this is whatever weeks later, because he was still seeing the [ ]. So they went and had a separate private ceremony for him including something that I forget now . . . but releasing balloons and stuff and little things that he wrote and put in the balloons. So he went, this minister, whoever it was, went through a very elaborate ritual that they put together themselves. So that was pretty interesting.
537	S:	I think what they have to balance with the rituals is that, yes the father is dead and they need to remember that. They also need to remember how the father [ ] and how that, uh, the boy looks like dad or acts like dad. So that is the other side of this, is how going to rituals, not just death rituals like funerals and wakes, and life, life rituals and, uh, you know, eventually dad, you know, how can dad still be a part of, uh, because he hasn't lived much of a life. How old is he? Eight?
538	T:	Yeah
539	S:	He is only just a little boy. How many years does he remember? Five? Six? Seven? He was [ ] about a year. And so how much of it when he was with his dad? His dad is so much a part of his life. They need to put, uh, to bury dad. So dad can be buried and be alive. There is different

		ways like planting a tree, or they have a picture of something like that [ ]. So that may be too much to do today, but may, I am just wondering, do you want to see him again?
540	T:	Well, I want, I want to allow where she calls kind of checks in in a couple of weeks to, not necessarily cut it off, but cut it off where she checks in just to let me know because I was curious how he was doing.
541	S:	Yeah, because you know one thing that happens, is if we were to dismiss her quickly here then she could really call the question whether she should even have come in at all.

Reflections of Exemplar 4

Exemplar 4 begins with a bit of repetition from earlier talk, grief (Turns 533 and 534) and continues with the working of another complex word, remember (Turns 535, 537, and 539). The working of the figure, remember, is especially interesting because its usage is a good exemplar of the both/and relationship between literal and figurative usage. In Turn 535, the supervisor is asking the therapist "literally" to recall and then subsequently, the therapist uses remember as a "complex word" or figuratively to configure other talk (see Configuration 6):

remember	/	yes the father is dead and they need to remember that how that, uh the boy looks like dad or acts like dad How much does he remember?	(Turn 537) (Turn 537) (Turn 539)

As the talk is turned around the figure, remember, supervisor and therapist begin to develop the unsaid parts of the side by side configuration (i.e., including talk of an alive dad and rituals to remember dad when he was alive; see Configuration 7):

acting up	/	bad boy	/	alive dad	/	planting a tree
grief	/	sad boy	/	dead dad	/	releasing balloons

The talk of Exemplar 4, as configured in Configuration 7, is a good depiction of how the aforementioned abductive process in therapeutic conversation (i.e., "lateral extension of abstract components of description" Bateson, 1979, pp. 157–158 or "seeking to put side by side similar chunks of phenomena" [Bateson, 1979/1991, p. 232]) works for resourceful figures in therapeutic conversations. The relationship between figures acting up and grief is configured with the relationship between figures bad boy and sad boy, which in turn is configured with the relationship between alive dad and dead dad, and finally, the relationships between alive and dead rituals (i.e., planting a tree and releasing balloons) is also configured.

Following the abductive logic pattern, therapist and supervisor begin to shift their understanding of the relationship between all of the relationships. Previously, their talk seemed to be along the lines that the relationships were of an "either/or" nature, as seen in their talk of the mother's being tentative talk, but as the talk is developed, the nature of the relationship between the relationships becomes more along the lines of "both/and": In Turns 537 and 539, there is talk of the dad being remembered both in death and life, and there is also talk of the family having both death rituals and life rituals. The shift from either/or to both/and with the dad and ritual talk should also allow for a similar shape for the talk about the boy and his behaviors (i.e., both his acting up and his grieving).

CONCLUSIONS: CONVERSATIONS, INTERPRETATIONS, AND IMPLICATIONS

New meanings and patterns created during the break by these resourceful figures are in turn shared with the family as the therapy session resumes and another therapeutic conversation begins. To this interaction, participants contribute only that which they can contribute: their own particular style of saying and not saying with all of its own unique shapes of exuberance and deficiency (Becker, 1979). They reflect upon these words in an attempt to interpret and to create meaning and to engage mutually with each other in conversation to help with this text-building and pattern connecting. The task of all parties in therapeutic conversations is to listen to the said and unsaid, to trope and to play with meaning, to help with configuring and reconfiguring of talk, and to reflect these particularities with a particular someone over time in conversation.

Similarly, an interpretation of a therapeutic conversation, like the one presented in this chapter, shares in the same process: It is both exuberant and deficient because it says more and less than was intended, it has its own pattern of said and unsaid, and it is a particular interpretation at a particular time for a particular someone by a particular someone. It is also intended as an involvement strategy in that its patterns of configurations are meant to engage readers in new therapeutic conversations and to remind them what it means to be in language.

This approach to understanding and practicing therapy helps to create some interesting possibilities for therapists and researchers alike. If therapists take a stance that moves them closer to their language usage in therapy, then they will be able to appreciate and employ research that has been produced by researchers using communication, discourse, and language concepts. At the same time, if therapists can improve their ways of talking about their talk in therapy, researchers will begin to have a clearer sense of therapists' mind operating systems (MOS; G. E. Hernandez, personal communication, September 11, 1993) and will be able to conduct therapist-sensitive research, that is, inquiry which is more useful to practicing therapists.

REFERENCES

Anderson, H., & Goolishian, H. A. (1988). Human systems as linguistic systems: Preliminary and evolving ideas about the implications for clinical theory. *Family Process, 27,* 371–393.

Bateson, G. (1979). *Mind and nature: A necessary unity.* New York: Dutton.

Bateson, G. (1991). The science of knowing. In R. E. Donaldson (Ed.), *A sacred unity: Further steps to an ecology of mind* (pp. 231–233). New York: HarperCollins. (Original work published 1979).

Baudrillard, J. (1988). *The ecstasy of communication.* New York: Semiotext(e).

Becker, A. L. (1979). Text-building, epistemology, and aesthetics in Javanese shadow theatre. In A. L. Becker & A. A. Yengoyan (Eds.), *The imagination of reality: Essays in Southeast Asian coherence systems* (pp. 211–243). Norwood, NJ: Ablex.

Becker, A. L. (1984). The linguistics of particularity: Interpreting superordination in a Javanese text. In *Proceedings of the tenth annual meeting of the Berkeley linguistics society* (pp. 425–436). Berkeley, CA: Linguistics Department, University of California, Berkeley.

Becker, A. L. (1988). Language in particular: A lecture. In D. Tannen (Ed.), *Linguistics in context: Connecting observation and understanding. Lectures from the 1985 LSA/TESOL and NEH institutes* (pp. 17–35). Norwood, NJ: Ablex.

Becker, A. L. (1991). A short essay on languaging. In F. Steier (Ed.), *Research and reflexivity* (pp. 226–234). Newbury Park, CA: Sage.

Best, S., & Kellner, D. (1991). *Postmodern theory: Critical interrogations.* New York: Guilford.

Burke, K. (1969). *A grammar of motives.* Berkeley, CA: University of California. (Original work published 1945).

Chenail, R. J. (1993). Becoming resourceful figures in therapy. In A. H. Rambo, A. Heath, & R. J. Chenail, *Practicing therapy: Exercises for growing therapists* (pp. 225–263). New York: Norton.

Corradi Fiumara, G. (1990). *The other side of language: A philosophy of listening.* New York: Routledge.

Culler, J. (1989). Forward to the 1989 edition. In W. Empson, *The structure of complex words* (pp. v–xiii). Cambridge, MA: Harvard University.

Deleuze, G., & Guattari, F. (1983). *Anti-Oedipus: Capitalism and schizophrenia.* Minneapolis, MN: University of Minnesota Press.

Derrida, J. (1976). *Of grammatology.* Baltimore, MD: Johns Hopkins University Press.

de Saussure, F. (1959). *Course in general linguistics.* New York: Philosophical Library.

de Shazer, S., & Berg, I. K. (1992). Doing therapy: A post-structural revision. *Journal of Marital and Family Therapy, 18,* 71–81.

Edwards, D., & Potter, J. (1992). *Discursive psychology.* Newbury Park, CA: Sage.

Empson, W. (1989). *The structure of complex words.* Cambridge, MA: Harvard University. (Original work published 1951).

Fernandez, J. W. (Ed.). (1991). *Beyond metaphor: The theory of tropes in anthropology.* Stanford, CA: Stanford University Press.

Foucault, M. (1980). *Power/knowledge.* New York: Pantheon Books.

Friedman, S. (Ed.). (1993). *The new language of change: Constructive collaboration in psychotherapy.* New York: Guilford.

Harland, R. (1987). *Superstructuralism: The philosophy of structuralism and post-structuralism.* London: Routledge.

Kristeva, J. (1984). *Revolution in poetic language.* New York: Columbia University Press.

Lyotard, J-F. (1984). *The postmodern condition: A report on knowledge*. Minneapolis: University of Minnesota Press.

McLaughlin, T. (1990). Figurative language. In F. Lentricchia & T. McLaughlin (Eds.), *Critical terms for literary study* (pp. 80–90). Chicago: University of Chicago.

McNamee, S., & Gergen, K. J. (Eds.). (1992). *Therapy as social construction*. Newbury Park, CA: Sage.

Miller, J. H. (1990). Narrative. In F. Lentricchia & T. McLaughlin (Eds.), *Critical terms for literary study* (pp. 66–79). Chicago: University of Chicago.

Percy, W. (1987). *The message in the bottle: How queer man is, how queer language is, and what one has to do with the other*. New York: Farrar, Strauss and Giroux. (Original work published 1954).

Percy, W. (1991). *Signposts in a strange land* (P. Samway, Ed.). New York: Farrar, Strauss and Giroux.

Sapir, J. D. (1977). The anatomy of metaphor. In J. D. Sapir & J. C. Crocker (Eds.), *The social use of metaphor: Essays in the anthropology of rhetoric* (pp. 3–32). Philadelphia: The University of Pennsylvania Press.

Sarup, M. (1993). *An introductory guide to post-structuralism and postmodernism* (2nd ed.). Athens: University of Georgia Press.

Tannen, D. (1989). *Talking voices: Repetition, dialogue, and imagery in conversational discourse*. New York: Cambridge University Press.

Tyler, S. A. (1978). *The said and the unsaid*. New York: Academic Press.

von Foerster, H. (1984). On constructing a reality. In P. Watzlawick (Ed.), *The invented reality: How do we know what we believe we know? (contributions to constructivism)* (pp. 41–61). New York: Norton.

4
Behind the Looking Glass: Tinkering With the Facts on the Other Side of a One-Way Mirror

David A. Todtman
Family Therapy Institute of Vancouver Island

In the book, *Foundations of Family Therapy,* Hoffman (1981) wrote that the field of psychotherapy and especially family therapy was changed when a new tool—the one-way mirror—came into use during the 1960s and 1970s. With the new tool, a therapist could interview clients accompanied by a group of colleagues who could watch and listen from behind the mirror. Whereas previously the conduct of therapy was a solitary activity, a different sensibility evolved. The whole group, rather than the interviewing therapist alone, took on responsibility for the case. By the late 1970s, family therapists who had been working this way routinely wrote about themselves as "the team" (cf. Selvini-Palazzoli, Boscolo, Cecchin, & Prata, 1978).

This chapter is about such a team. I focus on part of the group's work as it struggles on a particularly difficult case. The analysis discusses a clash between members of the team and shows how they achieve consensus and preserve their ability to work together.

SETTING

The setting was a public psychotherapy clinic at a large university in the U.S. southwest. Therapy at the clinic was provided by graduate students working toward doctoral degrees in marriage and family therapy. The therapists were relatively skilled: Each had a master's degree and clinical experience prior to admission to the doctoral program. Also, each had completed at least 2 years of the doctoral program that included course work in family psychotherapy and clinical practica.

In the team approach, clients were interviewed by a single therapist with the other members looking on through a one-way mirror. Clients were informed about the observing team, which was described as a group of consultants who worked with the therapist to help make the therapy more efficient.

The observing team and interviewing therapist were linked across the one-way mirror by a telephone intercom (Todtman, Bobele, & Strano, 1988). The telephone allowed the observing team to call the interviewing therapist at any point to request that the interviewer ask a particular question, pass along a compliment to the client(s), or simply make a statement to the therapist about the progress of the session.

The interview structure used by these therapists was influenced in part by the Milan style (cf. Selvini-Palazzoli, et al., 1978). In the Milan style, interviews are usually structured in five parts. The first part is called the *presession*. The therapists use the presession to recall the previous session, discuss the progress of the case to that point, and plan the impending interview. The discussions may last 5 to 15 minutes.

The next segment is the *main body* of the interview itself. The interviewing therapist meets with the clients in the interview room while the rest of the team observe from behind the mirror. This lasts approximately 45 minutes and is followed by a *midsession break*. During the break the interviewer leaves the interview room to go behind the one-way mirror where the whole team has a consultation. In this break, the team engages in an intense brainstorm and sharing of impressions and ideas. In the vernacular of the Milan style, the end goal of this discussion is to construct a "message" or "therapeutic intervention" for the interviewer to "deliver" to the clients. This midsession discussion may last 5 to 20 minutes, depending on how long it takes the group to reach a consensus.

Next, the interviewer returns to meet again with the clients to deliver the *intervention* message. The purpose of the intervention is to introduce new meanings about interpersonal relationships into the client system; the therapists believe that this new information has the potential to change what the family previously knew about each other's behavior that in turn may alter or eliminate the symptom (Tomm, 1984). The therapy interview is capped by a *postsession* exchange in which the therapists discuss the client's reaction to the intervention and form strategies for the next meeting.

These therapists were also influenced by the Mental Research Institute (MRI; Watzlawick, Weakland, & Fisch, 1974) approach. In particular, the MRI model prescribes that the therapists seek a clear and concrete definition of the problem from their clients. The underlying principle of seeking a clear definition is that it permits a therapist to understand how the problem was established and has been sustained by the social system; "[it] reveals what maintains the situation that is to be changed [by the therapy] and where, therefore, change has to be applied" (p. 111).

THE THERAPY CASE

This case began with a telephone call to the family therapy clinic by Rose,[1] age 29. She was married to Jimmy, age 27, and they lived together in a rural farming and ranching area. They had two children, ages 1 and 3. In the call, she explained she had recently experienced periods of shaking, physical weakness, and shortness of breath that made her "feel like rubber." This had never happened before and her physician had suggested psychotherapy. Eight therapy interviews were conducted over a 10-week period. The outcome was positive: Rose's rubbery feelings disappeared as did serious marital problems that had come to light over the course of therapy.

THE ANALYSIS

In a transcribed text[2] of the team's work, eight episodes were identified as pivotal to the team's eventual declaration that the case was a success. Here, I attend to Episode 2 which took place in the postsession discussion in the minutes after the end of the first meeting with Rose. The episode offers a particularly interesting example of the group's encounter with conflict and disagreement. This section discusses how they resolve their embroilment through tinkering with the facts.

In the text that follows, therapists are identified by numbers. T3 is the interviewing therapist and T1, T2, T4, T5, and T6 are the observing team therapists. In the analysis[3] following the episode transcript, frequent references are made to specific utterances in the transcript text. The referenced lines of discourse have been indicated in the text by their line numbers, which are placed inside of parentheses. In all, eight episodes were identified and analyzed.

EPISODE 2: YOU DID ASK THE RIGHT QUESTION

Context

From the outset, working with Rose was not easy. Her extremely soft-spoken but rapid speech was often accompanied by sobbing, thus making her words difficult to understand. The problem was even more pronounced for the team members behind the mirror who had to try to understand Rose through a microphone and sound system. Furthermore, Rose shifted topics haphazardly, listing problem after

---

[1] Names have been changed to protect the privacy of the people involved.
[2] I am indebted to Rhonda Johnson (Johnson, 1987) for making the data record available.
[3] The analysis method follows Labov and Fanshel (1977).

problem. It was difficult for the therapists to get a handle on the clear problem definition required by them to conduct the therapy.

As the team's postsession discussion dealt with these matters, a pivotal dispute emerged within the group. A position was put forward that Rose's difficult behavior was partly due to errors made by the interviewing therapist. According to this team member, the interviewer had asked the wrong questions of Rose, which had encouraged her lack of focus and contributed to the muddled emotionality. This called the interviewing therapist's competency into question and posed a threat to the ability of the group to work as a team. Another member offered a different position that held that Rose was the sort of client who would behave this difficult way no matter what any interviewer could have done. These issues were debated through several exchanges, but no settlement seemed possible. With tension evoked but unresolved, the episode ended with a topic shift to a less threatening and more agreeable subject.

But soon, the initial dispute erupted again. It happened as T1 made a request for a review of the intervention message delivered to Rose at the end of the session. This question and the complete text of the episode follows.

Text

1	T1:	What did we do at the end?
2	T2:	We essentially said "Look, this is a
3		close of information and your situation
4		is overwhelming. We would like to get
5		more."
6	T1:	Yeah, we said we would like to hear
7		more, but we did hear more and more.
8	T3:	Well, a . . . a client that was more
9		distinctive, she's not, the other kind
10		of client is the one that comes in and
11		after 10 minutes says "Now what do I do?"
12		She never really asked that and so that
13		if we had asked the question ah, "What
14		would you like for us to talk about?"
15		instead of try to focus it, we would not
16		have got a focused answer back.
17	T4:	You, you asked her that.
18	T5:	I thought that was the answer.
19	T4:	And she said. . . .
20	T5:	The answer to that . . .
21	T3:	Yeah, that the you're not going to get a
22		focused response back. The other
23		thing is that she could have rattled.

24	T2:	So, how would we . . .
25	T3:	For shouldn't say rattled, talked.
26	T6:	What might we have done different in
27		this session? How would you change for
28		the next session?
29	T1:	Well, if we are going to focus on the
30		headache, if that's the way we are going
31		to go.
32	T3:	Well, let me tell you what she asked
33		while I was filling out the receipt.
34		She asked if she should, and I said she
35		should, suggested that she talk to her
36		physician and tell him that she was
37		seeing us here and talk to him about
38		that. That may be an agreement that
39		the headaches are prime right now. That
40		would be the first thing to work with.
41	T4:	The thing that she is the most concerned
42		about at this point.
43	T1:	You know that. So that we start
44		focusing on it. This is an area that we
45		think we might be able to make some
46		change in your life, and maybe some of
47		those other things might have some
48		changes in themselves with time.

Analysis

T1 opened this episode with a request for information (Line 1). But, it was not a simple request for information in which Person A wants to know something that Person B may provide. No, in this situation both speakers knew that A had the information that A requested. It was rhetorical and baiting. Baiting questions lure an interlocutor into supplying irrefutable information that may be used by the questioner in a subsequent argument.

Read the following expansion of T1's first turn with baiting questions in mind. First, however, a brief note on expansion should be provided: An expansion begins with the transcription of a conversational turn that is then augmented with the "unsaid" elements, thus producing an elaborated text. For more information on expansion see the appendix.

> T1: What did we do—say to the client—at the end of the session when T3 delivered the intervention our team developed?. (Line 1)

T1 knew the answer; T1 had been present and thus plainly knew what was said not more than 15 minutes previously in final intervention message to the client. The expansion that follows shows how T2 responded to the bait.

> T2: We essentially said to the client: "Look, this ending of the session is a close of our information gathering activity for the day. (Lines 2–3) We have received so much information about your numerous problems that we are unable to decide at this time how we might help you. We would like to express our belief that your situation must seem overwhelming to you. (Lines 3–4) Please return for another therapy session because we would like to get more information from you and at that time we expect to be able to decide how we might specifically help you. (Lines 4–5)

Here, T2 recounted several ideas that were presented to the client: (a) the therapists had received so much information about various problems of the client, that (b) they were unable to decide upon which of the various problems to focus, (c) the client's problems were so numerous as to seem overwhelming and, (d) if the client would return, the therapists would be able to discern a direction for the therapy.

In the subsequent exchange, however, these ideas were less important than the proposition T1 derived from the utterance that closed T2's turn: "We would like to get more." (Lines 4–5) Read the expansion of T1's next turn and notice this.

> T1: Yeah, that is what we said in the intervention at the end: we said that we would like to hear more of the same information in the subsequent session. (Lines 6–7) That is also what we said to her <u>during</u> the session—"Tell us more"—and we did hear more and more and more of the same information. (Line 7) You didn't ask the right questions.

T1 had turned the previous speaker's statement on its ear. T2's statement, "We would like to get more" (Lines 4–5) proposed that the client return so that she could assist in determining a focus for the therapy. But, T1 began the response to this by stating "Yeah" (Line 6). "Yeah" is often an indication that there is agreement between speakers. Here, however, it signaled that a new meaning, a *re*interpretation would be presented. This "yeah" was a shortened version of the common every-day form, "Yeah but . . ." that signals disagreement. The proposition that T1 asserted in this reinterpretation was, "You didn't ask the right questions." Faced with this assertion, T3's competency had again openly been called into question. In the expansion of the next turn you will read a defense:

> T3: Well I don't agree that she told us more and more simply because we asked her to tell us more. (Line 8) Consider the other kind of client that

is more distinctive with respect to the ability to specify what she would want from therapy—she's not this sort, by the way. (Lines 8–9) This other client is the one who comes in to the therapist and after only ten minutes of conversation says: "Now I want you, the therapist, to tell me what do I do?" (Lines 9–11) She never really asked that question because she is different. (Lines 12–13) So, if we had asked her the question: "What, specifically is the problem for which you seek help and thus is the thing you would like for us to talk about?" it wouldn't have worked as a means to get her to focus. (Lines 13–14) Instead of being a successful try at getting her to focus, we would not have been able to get a focused answer back because the type of client she is. (Line 15–16)

How was the defense accomplished? T3 told a very short narrative. It was about a class of clients, the "more distinctive" (lines 8–9) ones who are characteristically able to quickly specify their problem. Embedded within the narrative, T3 asserted that Rose was different from the "more distinctive" ones: ". . . she's not . . ." (Line 9) that kind. T3 backed this assertion by another assertion that Rose failed to speak a key phrase that the other, more distinctive kind of client, would say to the therapist: "Now, what do I do?" (Line 11). "And so" (Line 12) because the client failed to ask her key question T3's argument asserted, the interviewing therapist was put on notice: His key and important question, that would be asked of the more distinctive kind of client, would flounder. That is, T3's argument was that if he had asked his key question of Rose in the absence of the client's key question, a poor result would have ensued. The foundation for this had been laid down in a discussion previous to this episode when principal propositions about Rose were consensually established by the team: Rose was a difficult client, extremely emotional, and vague. Notice also that T3 put forward the proposition that his activity in the session was reasonable, given the type of client Rose was.

So, the therapists were again embroiled in a dispute about a pivotal issue: To what should Rose's difficult behaviour be attributed? T1 reasserted that it should be attributed to T3's mode of interviewing and thus called T3's competency into question. T3 defended his competency and reasserted that Rose was different, special, and could not be subjected to the usual approach; it would not have been possible to productively ask the proper key therapist's question: What specific problem brought you to this clinic?

T3's defense was not the direct object of the next speaker's turn. Instead, a different kind of defense was launched when T4, supported by T5, made a surprising assertion that T3 actually had asked the key question! The following is the expansion of the next four turns:

T4: But T3, I thought you asked her that exact question (Line 17) and she replied something about headaches.

T5: I too, thought that "headaches" was the answer to the question. (Line 18)
T4: And she mentioned she needed help with headaches. (Line 19)
T5: The answer to that question may have been a bit oblique but it was that she wanted to work on headaches. (Line 20)

As an aside, although "headaches" was not in the original text for these lines, we were able to use the word by reading forward to Line 30.

T4's first turn in this series of short exchanges—the assertion that T3 had asked the therapist's key question—was a contradiction to T3's proposition that it was reasonable that he had not asked Rose the question because it would have been unproductive. As noted, this proposition by T3 was a defense of his competency. The contradiction by T4 and T5 was particularly interesting because it spoke directly against T3's proposition yet, it simultaneously defended T3's competency. It was as if T4 had said "You did ask the correct question, but you must have forgotten this detail."

Following T4's turn, T5 joined the conversation with an agreement that the question had been asked and "headaches" was the answer (Line 18). Both T4 and T5 again added support in the next two turns (Lines 19 and 20).

T3 returned to the dialogue with the idea that Rose was vague (Lines 21–22). As you begin to read the following expansion of T3's response, keep in mind that T3 must deal with the new proposition that he had actually asked the key question and Rose had returned an answer about headaches.

T3: Yeah, that vagueness is the significant thing, when you ask her a specific question you're not going to get a focused response back from her. (Lines 21–22) The other thing about asking her that question is that she could have rattled on and on providing an excess of information. (Lines 22–23)

Did T3 contradict or accept the new proposition that he actually had asked the key question and received a response? T3 did neither. Rather, T3 reasserted a previous and relatively noncontroversial proposition—Rose was vague—and *avoided* directly addressing T4's dramatic assertion about getting an answer to the key question.

Then, with the contradiction still hanging in the air T2 asked a question. The expansion follows.

T2: So given that she is a difficult client who responds vaguely, how would we talk with her so that we could get her to focus on a specific problem? (Line 24) What is the correct way to talk with her?

In music, this question would be analogous to a change of key. Prior to this turn, the central topic had been whether the quesion had been asked of Rose. With the turn, however, T2 requested a discussion of strategy that also was an implicit request to change topic. But this was not a request to move away from the dispute, rather it approached the dispute from a different angle—embedded within the turn was the proposition that there were ways to correctly talk with Rose that would influence her to focus on a specific problem. This proposition sharply conflicted with T3's position that the client would not focus on issues (Lines 19, 15–16).

T3's response to the above request was expanded as:

T3: For the purposes of speaking directly with her, we shouldn't say that she "rattled on;" that would not be her description and if we used it in the session she would be offended. Better words, ones that she might have used would be "talked a lot"— it's less prejudicial. (Line 25)

There is a contradiction here by T3 of T4. T3's position was that Rose could not be helped to focus, yet in this turn T3 offered a suggestion regarding how to correctly talk with her to produce a specific problem statement. Had T3 begun to shift his position? Read on.

T6 spoke next, and in the following expansion, addressed T3 directly.

T6: What might we have done differently in this session so as to have gotten her to focus on a specific problem? (Line 26) T3, how do you think you could change the way you interview her for the next session so that she will focus? (Line 38)

This was a request that T3 offer a proposal regarding how to incline Rose toward providing focused answers. Like the previous two turns, it rested on the proposition that Rose could focus if the therapist talked correctly with her. They were now discussing strategy.

Next, T1 entered:

T1: Well, if we have agreed that we are going to focus on the headache problem that Rose mentioned, if that is the way we are going to go in the next interview, then that gives us direction as to how to interview her. (Lines 29–31)

T1 did not respond to T6's request to discuss strategy. Rather, T1 offered a principle at a more abstract level about a disputable event—"the headache problem that Rose mentioned...." Had Rose actually stated (obliquely or otherwise) that headaches was the problem for which she sought help? This had been asserted but, it was potentially disputable especially because T3 had yet to comment directly about the idea and there seemed to be no evidence offered to support the assertion in this episode or other parts of the conversation text.

A disputable assertion takes the form, if Person A makes an assertion about an event or proposition that is considered to be disputable, it is heard as a request that Person B give an evaluation—agreement or disagreement—of the assertion. As noted earlier, T3 had yet to provide an evaluation of this very important assertion. A general principle of the rule for requests states that if B does not respond to a request by A, A is likely to repeat the request: "Didn't you hear me? I want an opinion, 'yes' or 'no' on X." From this perspective, the turn by T1 can be read as a pointed request for T3 to evaluate the assertion that he had asked the key question and Rose had answered.

In the following expansion, T3 answered through a narrative.

T3: Well, let me tell you what question she asked me while she waited as I was filling out the receipt for her. (Lines 32–33) She asked if she should talk to her physician about her coming here, and I said she should; I suggested that she talk to her physician. (Lines 34–35) I suggested that she let him know that she was seeing us here and that she should talk with him about that fact. (Lines 35–37) That question of hers may be an indication and a tacit agreement that physical symptoms—the headaches—are the prime issue for her right now. (Lines 37–38) I find it acceptable that the issue of headaches would be the first thing to focus on, in order to attempt to work with her from a problem perspective. (Lines 39–40)

Narratives are historical accounts with a "point." What was T3's point? It can be found in Line 39: "headaches are prime right now. . . ." In the narrative, T3 recalled that Rose had asked if she should tell her physician about the therapy appointments. Although she had not specifically remarked about headaches in that conversation, T3 constructed a connection that her mention of the medical setting (where her headaches had been treated unsuccessfully) was evidence that Rose's headache difficulty would serve as the problem focus for the therapy. T3's point, then, was a declaration that he had evaluated the assertions about the therapist key question and headaches (Lines 17–20) and had now joined the position of the other members of the team.

With the following two turns, the episode was completed—T4 and T1 provided support for the frame that Rose specified headaches as the problem upon which she wished to work.

T4: I agree, the headache issue is the thing she is most concerned about at this point. (Lines 41–42)
T1: You know that by the evidence: in the session, she talked about headaches as a problem and, while waiting for the receipt she asked if

she should talk with her physician about her visit here. (Line 43) At the next session, we should tell her, "This headache problem is an area that we think we might be able to help you make some change in your life. (Lines 44–46) And, we know that you have a lot of other large worries too—we have heard you. (Lines 47–48) Maybe if we can help you with the headaches some of those other things might have some positive changes in and of themselves with the passage of time. (Lines 46–48) So many things distress you, we can only work on one at a time: the headache thing is a prime problem for you and, it is a problem-type with which we can be of assistance. Therefore, we propose to you that this therapy concentrate on the headache problem for now."

Perhaps the most interesting aspect of these last two turns begins at Line 44 where T1 talked for the first time about a strategy for working with Rose (Lines 44–48). Previous to this, references by T1 to strategy were geared only toward arguing a point: A problem focus must be established with Rose. But here instead of arguing a point, T1 actually offered some lines of discourse for T3 to use in the therapeutic conversation with the client. T1's change was a response to the recent shift by T3. Because it dealt with strategies for how to talk productively with Rose about her headaches, it further underscored the idea that the team should concentrate on headaches as a specified problem focus. It also signaled the dispute had concluded and team cohesion appeared to be intact at this point. They were then ready to get on with the task of how to bring about change.

In the course of the ensuing weeks, the team continued to work with Rose and occasionally, her husband Jimmy attended too. The team had to face and work through other internal disputes. As the therapy progressed Rose's complaints gradually diminished and were replaced by confidence. At the last session, Rose and Jimmy entered the therapy room in a mood the team interpreted as "playful." The couple reported they had no problems and they were both optimistic about the future. In the postsession discussion the therapists expressed confidence too.

REPRISE

From the outset, these therapists believed they were involved in a difficult case. What was the source? Was it the client, a type who was not able to focus her thoughts and could not be productively asked the proper questions to specify a problem? Or was it, as T1 asserted, the interviewer, T3, who had asked the wrong questions and encouraged Rose to be vague and tell "more and more"? This implied that T1 had done a poor job. We may ask: How could the team expect to succeed if the interviewer was construed this way? How could they work together if T1 and T3 disagreed?

With this in the air, a team member made a surprising move. It was asserted that the interviewing therapist had made the request—asked the proper question—and Rose had replied that headaches were a problem. This was a sharp contradiction yet at this point, the team accepted the assertion. Something had crystallized and the group shifted gears from open dispute to a discussion of tactics. The difficulty had been overcome and team cohesion was preserved.

Tinkering With the Facts

As valuable as it was for the group, the conclusion that overcame the dispute was not predetermined. In fact, it is conceivable to imagine several different ends. So, from an inherently open array of possibilities, how did the team reach this particular closure?

We may begin an answer by recognizing that therapists always operate within a social domain and such is no less true for those who work together on teams. This is to say, they operate within contexts of interaction—the sequential string of action and reaction between individuals over time and place (Bateson, 1972).

In contexts of interaction, participants make meaning from resources available from the environment. This is the work of tinkerers. "A tinkerer . . . does not know what he is going to produce but uses whatever he finds around him . . . to produce some workable object" (Jacob, 1977, p. 1162). The objects therapists find around them are ideas that float in out of the conversation like the odds and ends in the basement tinkerer's workshop bins. On the team we investigated, the ideas were assertions about Rose, the interviewer, or what questions had or had not been asked of the client.

This is especially illustrated in Lines 17 through 20 where T4 and T5 together contradicted T1 and T3 by floating the assertion that T3 had asked the key question and got a focused answer about headaches. In what conversational bin did T4 and T5 find this? According to T4, Rose had "mentioned" headaches during the interview.

T3 at first ignored this odd and end. Perhaps it came from a bin that was too obscure to be recognized as a part that could be fitted into a workable object for the team. But tinkering came into full force moments later when T3 suddenly recalled that Rose had made a remark about her physician! With a tinkerer's opportunism, the light bulb had switched on and T3 radically altered his position to one that agreed that the key question had been asked and headaches was the answer. The reasoning was this: Physicians often treat headaches; Rose had mentioned a physician after the session and headaches during the session; and therefore, headaches are what she wants to focus on. Although this argument would never pass muster as proper in formal logic, it is the logic of tinkering.

Specifically, this type of tinkering logic is a backward-looking intention. T3's competency had been questioned because he had not produced a problem focus in the interview. As discussed previously, this had posed problems for T3 and the ability of the team as a whole to conduct its work with Rose. After T4 and T5 had made their assertion about "headaches," all members supported the fact in some way or other. It was as if they had said, "Oh yeah, we recall now that you mentioned it a problem focus had been achieved and 'headaches' was what she wanted to focus on." By recalling after the event in this backward-looking way, they were able to manufacture the fact that the interview had actually evoked the problem specification they required to conduct the therapy.

CONCLUSION

In the transcribed text of the whole case, the author identified several other junctures where similar resolutions to conflicts were constructed through tinkering. Clearly, the therapists' actions toward Rose were influenced by their own social process. The decision to focus on "headaches" was at least partly a result of how they worked through the dispute on the team and not entirely determined by Rose. If this therapy was thus influenced then perhaps other therapies are too. Perhaps they all are. In discussing similar social processes for resolving differences among scientists, Kuhn (1962) wrote, "the parties to a dispute must finally resort to the techniques of persuasion" (p. 93). This precisely what we observed in the team working with Rose.

APPENDIX: THE ORIGIN OF THE DATA RECORD

The data for this investigation were collected as part of a previous project on a team approach to therapy (Johnson, 1987). Audiotape recordings of conversations between therapists were collected and transcribed to assist the Johnson project and later made available to this investigation.

Method of Analysis

The analysis method used in this investigation was adapted from Labov and Fanshel's (1977) work, *Therapeutic discourse: Psychotherapy as conversation.* The steps to this type of analysis include, (a) expanding the text, (b) identifying rules of discourse, and (c) analyzing interactions. These and a discussion of global coherence are outlined here.

Expansion. Expansion involves bolstering a raw text by incorporating the unsaid. The meaning of an utterance can only be decided by "knowing or assuming" something about the context within which the words have been spoken (Garfinkel, 1968, p. 4). Contextual sources used in expanding the text include pronoun referents, factual and other material from other parts of the conversation, and knowledge of the setting in which the conversation takes place. From this perspective, my participation as one of the members of the therapy team was beneficial and helped to enhance the richness of the analysis (Geertz, 1988).

Propositions. With the text expanded, the discourse analyst is able to extract propositions. Propositions are agreements among speakers about the "facts" of their world. According to Labov and Fanshel, "they may be defined as 'what we are talking about,' or what is 'really being talked about'" (p. 52). Propositions may be linked to specific social relationships, role definitions, personal attributes, factual assertions, or norms. They may also be classed as to whether they are local or general.

Rules of Discourse. With expansion and propositions, we have been concerned with what is said in a conversation. The concept of rules begins to "bridge the gap between what is said and . . . the actions performed by those words" (p. 71). Working from the original and expanded texts, Labov and Fanshel identified several rules of discourse, including those that govern how speakers challenged each other, made requests for information, presented narratives, and disputed assertions. They pointed out that rules are like the precepts of sentence construction (syntax) in that they are typically unconscious yet, at times, utterly compelling.

Analysis of Interaction. The final component is an analysis of the interaction between speakers. "We define *interaction* as action which affects (alters or maintains) the relations of the self and others in face-to-face communication" (Labov & Fanshel, 1977, p. 59). This goes beyond blow-by-blow descriptions that rules of discourse provide to an explanation of what people are doing and what they mean when they interact in discourse.

The Unit of Analysis: Episode. Large texts are too complex to analyze the discourse as a whole and hence must be broken down into smaller parts that can be systematically attacked one at a time. The basic unit is the episode, which is a sequence of utterances bounded by shifts in topic (Labov & Fanshel, 1977), structure, or conversational style (Buttny & Lannamann, 1987).

Global Coherence. Why choose specific episodes and not others? The answer to this turns on global coherence (i.e., taking the text as an ecological whole). Global coherence of a text can be taken into account by the intertextual process of linking local portions of discourse with other portions distributed throughout the text. "Utterances scattered through various parts . . . must be brought together to provide the basis for the interpretation of any one [specific utterance]" (Labor & Fanshel, 1977, p. 26). In this way, the process of analysis slowly builds a webwork of linkages that constitutes the global coherence of the text. In essence, the discourse analyst must, ultimately, be a teller of stories.

REFERENCES

Buttny, R., & Lannamann, J. W. (1987). *Framing problems: The hierarchical organization of discourse in a family therapy session.* Unpublished manuscript.

Garfinkel, H. (1968). Discussion. In R. J. Hill & K. S. Crittenden (Eds.), *Proceedings of the Purdue symposium on ethnomethodology.* Purdue: Purdue Foundation—Institute for the Study of Social Change, Department of Sociology Purdue University.

Geertz, C. (1988). *Works and lives: The anthropologist as author.* Stanford, CA: Stanford University Press.

Hoffmann, L. (1981). *Foundations of family therapy: A conceptual framework for systems change.* New York: Basic Books.

Jacob, F. (1977). Evolution and tinkering. *Science, 196,* 1161–1166.

Johnson, R. (1987). *Development of a multiteam/multiperspective model of therapy.* Unpublished master's thesis, Texas Tech University, Lubbock Texas.

Kuhn, T. (1962). *The structure of scientific revolutions.* Chicago: University of Chicago Press.

Labov, W., & Fanshel, D. (1977). *Therapeutic discourse: Psychotherapy as conversation.* New York: Academic Press.

Selvini-Palazzoli, M., Boscolo, L., Cecchin, G., & Prata, G. (1978). *Paradox and counterparadox.* New York: Jason Aronson.

Todtman, D. A., Bobele, M., & Strano, J. D. (1988). An inexpensive system for communicating across the one-way mirror. *Journal of Marital and Family Therapy, 14,* 201–203.

Tomm, K. (1984). One perspective on the milan systemic approach: Part II. Description of session format, interviewing style and interventions. *Journal of Marital and Family therapy, 10,* 253–271.

Watzlawick, P., Weakland, J., & Fisch, R. (1974). *Change: Principles of problem formation and problem resolution.* New York: W. W. Norton.

5 Marital Therapy and Self-Reflexive Research: Research and/as Intervention

Jerry Gale
University of Georgia

Mark Odell
Bowling Green State University

Chandra S. Nagireddy
University of Georgia

In this chapter we describe how utilizing clients as self-reflexive research collaborators can engender therapeutic gain. Our study initially began as an exploratory inquiry examining the benefits of Interpersonal Process Recall (IPR) in marital therapy. As part of the study, a couple was also interviewed after treatment regarding both the IPR interview and their therapy experience in general. What developed from this post-therapy Reflexive Process Analysis (RPA) interview was the clients stating that the research interviews were more "therapeutic" than the marital therapy itself. Although research as intervention has been discussed previously in the literature (Gale, 1992; Gilgun, 1992; Heath, 1992; McNamee, 1989; Rubin & Mitchell, 1976; Steier, 1992a; Wright, 1990), no studies have provided an analysis of how that change process may occur. This chapter presents four key elements of the change process that were developed from analyses of the first session of marital therapy and three research interviews, and the clinical and research implications of these themes.

As IPR may be unfamiliar with many, we first provide an overview. Following that, we present the methods, procedures, and analytic approaches used in the study. A brief description of the couple and a summary of the first session are provided. The next section presents the analysis of the talk that occurred in the four interviews (first session of therapy, IPR with couple, IPR with therapist, and RPA). Exemplars from each of the four interviews are used to demonstrate the four categories. Limitations of the study are presented, and finally, the clinical and research implications of the research are explicated.

BACKGROUND CONTEXT

IPR

Interpersonal Process Recall is the technique of playing back videotape or audiotape recordings to assist clients and therapists in describing their experiences during particular moments in the therapy session. This method, referred to by such names as *stimulated recall, playback, videotape inquiry,* and the *retrospection method* has been independently developed by a number of different researchers (see Elliott, 1986). Kagen (1980) was one of the first to apply IPR to the field of psychotherapy. He used IPR to train and supervise therapists. Following Kagen's pioneering work, others utilized IPR as a research method for studying the psychotherapy process.

Initially, IPR research developed within the events paradigm model that focuses on specific events occurring in the therapeutic process (Elliott, 1984; Mahrer & Nadler, 1986; Rice & Greenberg, 1984; Wiseman, 1992). Early in his research, Elliott (1986, 1989) had the client listen to the entire tape of his or her therapy and both rate and describe experiences that occurred at particular moments. These moments were labeled *significant events*. This early approach followed a hypothesis-testing model. However, after a number of studies, this method evolved into the Comprehensive Process Analysis (CPA) method that is a qualitative, discovery-oriented model (Elliott, 1989; Elliott & Shapiro, 1988, 1992). In this approach, the client selects meaningful events from therapy following the session, but without reviewing the entire tape of the session. Trained clinical observers would then independently observe these significant moments and employ a qualitative methodology to develop models of the change process. Both IPR and CPA focus on individuals.

In conducting our study, we adapted IPR procedures to research marital therapy. Specifically, we used IPR to understand each participant's phenomenological experience of the first session. The following questions guided our initial foray: Could IPR be used in conjoint, not individual therapy? What impact (if any) would the IPR interview have on the couple and therapy? And, were early significant events predictive of the outcome of treatment? (Gale, Odell, & Nagireddy, 1992).

PROCEDURES OF THE RPA STUDY

Departing From IPR Protocol

As noted, one of the original purposes of this study was to examine the utility of using the IPR protocol with couples. Most IPR psychotherapy research conducted previously had been with clients in individual therapy (R. Elliott, personal communication, October 7, 1991; N.I. Kagen, personal communication, October 8, 1991). Another departure from traditional IPR research was in relation to how the research interviews were conducted. Elliott (cited in Rennie, 1992) suggested that IPR interviewers should keep their activity to a minimum in order not to lead the respondent. Rennie, however, adopted a more active role toward assisting the respondent in bringing forth his or her expressions to the surface. Embracing a constructionist epistemology, Rennie stated that his involvement hinges on being as active as necessary to establish a relationship and assist respondents who have difficulty articulating their experience. In our study the interviewer also adopted an active role.

Method

The couple was selected randomly from all couples entering a university marriage and family therapy clinic. They agreed to participate in the study for reimbursement. The clinician (Odell) was a second-year doctoral student in the Marriage and Family Therapy Program. The procedures were explained to the couple prior to their first session.

The IPR interview with the couple was conducted 48 hours after the session. The IPR interview with the therapist occurred 72 hours after the session. The interviews were videotaped and audiotaped. The RPA interview was conducted 4 months after the couple terminated treatment and was audiotaped. The interviews were all conducted by Gale.

The IPR protocol had the couple and interviewer view the videotape of the therapy session together. When either the husband or wife noted an event he or she perceived as meaningful (i.e., significant to the therapy process in either a positive or negative manner), he or she would tell the interviewer to stop the videotape and the person who initiated the event demarcation would state the start and stop time of the event. As needed, the interviewer would replay the event. At that time, both husband and wife would independently describe and rate that event (see the appendix). When both finished the rating sheet the couple were interviewed and asked to explain what the event meant, both at the time of the session and currently, as well as to share any possible implications of that event. When both husband and wife had nothing further to add, they proceeded with viewing the videotape. This procedure was also adopted for the therapist's IPR interview. The couple's interview lasted $2\frac{1}{2}$ hours, and the therapist's interview lasted $1\frac{1}{2}$ hours.

Also, in order to gain perspective on the couple's IPR interview itself as well as the entire therapy process, we conducted another interview with the couple 4 months following therapy termination, and 7 months after the first session. In the RPA interview, the couple were asked to reflect upon their experience of therapy, as well as their experience of the first IPR interview. During this interview, the summary analysis of the first IPR interview (the interview with the couple, not the IPR interview with the therapist) was shared with the couple as well as the transcript of their first session. The entire RPA interview lasted about 2 hours and was audiotaped.

Analysis

The tapes were transcribed by a secretary as well as by the authors. As the transcription process is part of the iterative analysis, each person took turns transcribing the tapes and improving the level of transcript. Discussions and analysis of the IPR transcripts and videotape were conducted by all three authors. Field notes were kept. Occasionally, another faculty person and graduate student joined our discussions. Themes and categories were discussed and evaluated using the constant comparison method of analysis (Glaser & Strauss, 1967).

Our study examined the four interviews in two distinctive manners. One approach was to focus on how the actual talk in the four interviews was managed in a rhetorical/responsive manner. This focus was on discursive themes presented by the participants and utilized the broad strokes of discourse analysis (Edwards & Potter, 1992; Gale & Newfield, 1992; Potter & Wetherell, 1987). This form of sequential analysis examines talk, situated in social sequences, to find the rhetorical and discursive techniques used by the participants in a responsive (back and forth) manner to achieve particular actions and social outcomes. The concern of this approach is not with finding underlying cognitive states nor accessing privileged knowledge about a person's inner experience, but of studying how the talk is managed.

The self-reflexive nature of the IPR and RPA interviews, however, permitted us to consider the talk of these exchanges from a second perspective.[1] That is, these interviews do provide a privileged account of each participant's experience (Elliott & Shapiro, 1992). Both the IPR and RPA interviews allowed each participant to self-reflect, from his or her own metaperspective, about what had been said in prior interviews. The interviews thus provided a spoken text about each person's phenomenological experiences and presented themes that each participant viewed as meaningful. This element of the study introduced the couple and therapist to the project as research collaborators. Together, these two foci of analyses led us to develop four meaningful themes from the data. Before these themes are discussed, a brief summary of the clients and their presenting issues is provided.

A BRIEF DESCRIPTION OF THE FIRST SESSION[2]

The couple, Dan and Sally, are in their mid-40s, have been married 15 years, and have two children. Dan is an accountant and Sally is a legal assistant. Odell is the therapist. Sally states that their problems have been building for 10 years. She feels a lack of control in her life and is angry at Dan as he does not seem to understand

---

[1]As another example of merging research methods, see Moerman (1988), who combined ethnography with conversation analysis.

[2]The names of the clients and pertinent information about them have been changed in order to maintain confidentiality.

5. RESEARCH AND/AS INTERVENTION

her feelings. Dan states that his understanding of the problem is very different. Dan notes that he has always strived to be the primary breadwinner for his family. He finds Sally's concerns surprising as she had never expressed them until recently.

The precipitating issue that led them to come to therapy was Dan's ex-wife's recent demand for back payment of child support. Sally said that Dan had repeatedly assured her that he had taken care of that issue. However, in order to pay the arrears child support, Sally needed to go back to work. Sally said that prior to this, they had sold their house and moved so that she could go back to school. At that time she left a well-paying job, but now, her new job is a "dead end" that is "embarrassing and degrading." During the course of the first session, the therapist suggests that Sally and Dan have two different expectations of what a marriage is, and it is as if they speak two different languages. The therapist states that Dan and Sally are really trying to reach each other, but they just do not know how to speak a common language.

RESULTS

Key Elements of the Change Processes Occurring in the Research Interviews

The analysis of the four interviews (Therapy Session 1, IPR interview with couple, IPR interview with therapist, and RPA interview) was an iterative process. Although the four interviews occurred sequentially in time, the analysis of each interview informed the analysis of the other interviews. As patterns and meaningful categories developed, we would re-examine each of the other interviews to confirm relationships. What emerged from this constant comparative method was the development of four major themes. These themes include (a) the said and the not-yet-said, (b) the couple's expectations, (c) framing talk as research or therapy, and (d) externalizing problems.

The Said and the Not-Yet-Said. One benefit of having meta-reflections about the earlier interviews is that these secondary and tertiary reflections provide us with privileged knowledge from the participants. This privileged knowledge need not be what the person *really* thought during that prior event, but this additional knowledge does expand the said into the not-yet-said. Anderson and Goolishian (1988) stated that "therapy is the process of expanding and saying the unsaid" (p. 381). This section presents how the IPR and RPA interviews helped create a context that moved the said of the therapy session into further reaches of the not-yet-said.

Consider the following exemplar from the therapy session.[3] In this exemplar,

---

[3]The letter with the Exemplar numbers refers to which interview the excerpt is from (A = first session therapy; B = couple's IPR; C = therapist's IPR; and D = RPA with couple). The line numbers refer to line numbers from the original interview. Within the examples, S = Sally, D = Dan, I = interviewer.

which follows Sally's response to the therapist's question of, "Tell me a little bit about yourselves. Just help me get to know you" (A: Lines 1–2), the husband is responding to the therapist's question: "How about you Dan, a little bit about yourself" (A: Line 84).

Exemplar 1A:
```
85   D:   (laughs) I grew up in Georgia, and I guess the only time
86        I've ever lived anywhere else was when I was in the service.
87        And I have both a bachelor's and a master's degree in
88        business from the University. Let's see (.4)
```

In the therapy session, these remarks elicited no verbal responses from either the therapist or wife and the talk shifted to other questions posed by the therapist. However, in the couple's IPR interview, Sally selected Dan's comment and states:

Exemplar 2B:
```
2    S:   He said that the only time we have not lived in Georgia was
3         when he was in the service and that was when he was married
4         before (.) he wasn't married to me (laughs) I've always
5         lived in Georgia.
6    I:   OK, and how is that significant to you?
7    S:   Because he is lumping me in with his vile ex-wife.
8    I:   OK
9    S:   And I have never been able to get him to leave Georgia, so I
10        sort of felt like he was indicating that he's lumping me in
11        with this other woman.
```

As can be observed from Lines 2–5, 7, and 9–11 in Exemplar 2B, Sally has expanded her silence from the session into a meaningful disclosure. Sally understood Dan's comment about not living in Georgia as implying a relationship between herself and his ex-wife. That this element of Sally's not-yet-said was a possibility to Dan can be seen from his comments in this same IPR discussion.

Exemplar 3B:
```
48   D:   Like I knew why she stopped it but she had more in it
49        than I had anticipated because I wasn't responding to a "we"
50        fashion. To me I was only responding to Mark's questions
51        about my background. Since the questions were asked simply.
52   I:   Would it be useful to play back that little segment again
53        for you? It's up to you.
54   D:   I know what I was saying, but I'm not sure (.2) I felt like
55        it was misinterpreted because
56   S:   I thought I heard you say we.
```

57	I:	Well, if you'd like to play it back
58	S:	But it doesn't (.3) I've already gotten this down and
59	I:	This is fine for the purpose of this
60	S:	and if you didn't say we it was probably you know my
61		mistake. Whoops.
62	D:	No, I believe I said you know that I was responding to
63		Mark's question about my background just personally, where I
64		grew up and where I have been exclusive of anybody else is
65		what I was trying to answer. But that has been a (.)
66		regardless of whether it is we or I, that has been a
67		criticism that Sally has directed toward me before.

Thus, that Sally's reaction to Dan's statement is not a complete surprise to Dan can be seen from Lines 48–49 and 65–67 in Exemplar 3B. In this segment, while Dan and Sally discuss if Dan was responding to the therapist's question about both of them ("we"), or just about Dan ("I"), they both acknowledge that Dan's comments regarding where he has lived beforehand is part of a previous and expanded discussion (Line 67).

It is significant too that Sally later notes in the IPR interview that during the session itself, she did not react to Dan's remarks. It was only during the IPR interview, with the playback of the session, that Sally experienced and noted her strong reaction. As can be seen in exemplars 2B & 3B, the IPR interview structure, through having the couple elaborate on their experience in therapy, provides a process whereby the not-yet-said of therapy can be expressed.

In this exemplar Dan was not surprised by Sally's reaction in the IPR interview. There are also incidents where either Dan or Sally are surprised by the other's comments. In the following exemplar Sally is responding to the therapist's question, "Tell me something more about" about your problems (A: Line 174).

Exemplar 4A:
178	S:	I guess it's just something that's been building and been
179		building for I'd say 10 years. I don't know if that's the
180		way he feels.

Dan notes about Sally's comment (4A) in the IPR interview follow:

Exemplar 5B:
99	D:	It was a surprise to me. And I guess that is a measure of
100		communication problems in that that was a surprise to me.
101		That she used a figure of 10 years (5.0) So far as I
102		remember we were really not communicating in the manner that
103		we have over the past year or so is part of our problem of
104		sorts, about 3 or 4 years ago, not close to 10, that figure

```
105             was a surprise to me.
106    I:      ((to wife)) Was this event meaningful to you?
107    S:      No, not really unless you consider something that I just
108            considered truthful to be meaningful. But since I said it (.3)
109    I:      You were just responding to Mark's question
110    S:      Yes, I guess I was trying to put a measure on feelings
111            that have been going way back I guess. And it probably did
112            just pertain to me. I shouldn't have been trying to speak
113            for both of us.
```

In these exemplars it is clear that Sally's comments in the therapy session (Exemplar 4A: Lines 178–180) surprise Dan (Exemplar 5B: Lines 99–105). Sally's IPR comments about her statement in therapy, (Exemplar 5B: Lines 110–113) provide an expansion of her not-yet-said in therapy that are responsive to Dan's concerns.

These are not isolated or rare events. The IPR and RPA interviews readdress and expand many topics expressed in therapy, but that were left unattended at that juncture. In the IPR and RPA interviews, these events open new and meaningful discussions. What also is relevant is how the said is interpreted by each participant.

As Tyler (1978) noted, "from within the infinity of the 'unsaid,' the speaker and the hearer, by a joint act of will, bring into being what was 'said'" (p. 459). However, it can also be added that in this co-creation of the said, each participant acts and responds from his or her own understanding of the infinity of the unsaid and contributes his or her own unique spin to the said. In examining the four interviews, it was noted that there were a number of instances where the therapist glossed an event with his interpretation of the said that was very different from the couple's understanding of the said. In the following example, the therapist (T) is providing his formulation (or interpretation) of the couple's difficulties.

Exemplar 6A:
```
526    T:      Well I think I guess my sense of what's kind of going on
527            in your marriage is that you have always maybe
528            always had very different expectations of what a marriage
529            looks like, what a marriage should function like and how
530            it actually works and I think this is not about money
531            really. Money is the metaphor by which you are talking
532            to each other, cause it seems to be a language that
533            you're both pretty comfortable with. I don't get a sense
534            that other than that that you understand each other's
535            thoughts and feelings real well. I would hazard a guess to
536            say you probably don't you would probably agree with the
537            statement that we do not communicate real real well. I would
```

5. RESEARCH AND/AS INTERVENTION

538		kind of expect you to say yeah that's probably true. And I
539		don't think it's because your skills are poor. I think it
540		instead is because you speak French and you speak Swahili
541		the two of you are speaking completely different languages.

In the therapist's IPR interview, the therapist refers to this segment (6A) as a very positive event as he notes the following:

Exemplar 7C:
167	T:	So I think one of the first things is that they felt
168		validated, they felt understood and hurt. I think it also
169		reframed what is wrong with their relationship away from
170		the surface so much and brought it to a more deeper level.
178		At the time I felt I was cooking with gas, I was doing well.

The therapist's IPR comments indicate that during the therapy session he was perceiving his interpretation (Exemplar 6A: Lines 526–541) as both validating to Sally and Dan (Exemplar 7C: Lines 167–168), as well as successful in bringing their issues to a "deeper level" (Exemplar 7C: Line 170). That the therapist's further actions in the session are influenced by his perception (that his comments and actions are approved by Dan and Sally), can be demonstrated by the therapist's pursuit of this topic during the remainder of the session as well as into his IPR interview (which occurred 3 days later). In the couple's IPR interview, Sally and Dan, regarding this same event (6A) from the session, stated the following:

Exemplar 8B:
679	S:	Umm well as I recall I disagreed with the with what Mark was
670		suggesting was that the problem between us was an issue of
681		communication. I think it goes <u>much</u> further than that.
682		It's not you can't boil it down to that.
. . .		
684		No and I was thinking at the time, I wonder if this is going
685		to do any good.
. . .		
688	D:	I was thinking in terms of what Mark suggested as a starting
689		point rather than a summary of anything what he felt like
690		our problems were. Because we couldn't get anywhere without
691		beginning to communicate. I view it as a little different.
692	S:	See I feel like I have communicated all I possibly could, he
693		<u>hadn't</u> listened, so therefore what more could I do in terms
694		of communication.
. . .		
700		I think I was feeling that Mark sort of had already taken

701		Dan's side
...		
730		I thought well you know if he tries to develop the issue of
731		communication, I'll go along with that. I'll do whatever it
732		it takes but um at the time I thought well maybe it is me,
733		maybe is is <u>MY</u> problem. You know something I'm I'm screwed
734		up up here and maybe I should go to see another
735		therapist for me

As noted in Exemplar 8B, in the IPR interview Sally expresses a very different view from the therapist about this event. Sally disagrees with the therapist's assessment (Lines 679–682) of she and Dan having a communication problem and she did not feel joined with the therapist (Lines 684–685, 700–701, 730–735). Dan does view the therapist's comments differently than Sally, but he sees the issue as a "starting point" (Lines 688–691) rather than the achievement of deeper understanding of their problems as presented by the therapist.

To understand why Sally and Dan do not present disagreement to the therapist about his assessment of their "communication" problem can be understood when we further examine their IPR interview. It can be seen that Dan's and Sally's expectations about the first session influenced their actions during the session.

The Couple's Expectations. The IPR interviews elicited from Sally and Dan clear statements of their expectations about the first session of therapy. These expectations, unexpressed to the therapist, were still an aspect of the therapy session background of the not-yet-said. They articulated three expectations: (a) the first session is a time to present their facts to an "objective referee" (i.e., the therapist); (b) in order to present their facts in a fair manner, they should avoid heated exchanges in the first session; and (c) the first session is not the time to resolve their problems. These three expectations are demonstrated in the following two exemplars:

Exemplar 9B:

135	D:	I think it would have been detrimental to the value of the
136		session. I think it was much more worthwhile to have sort
137		of a third party that we were telling these things to rather
138		than the things we talk to each other about and argue about
139		and never really accomplish anything.
...		
145		Yes, I think it was much more worthwhile to especially in
146		the initial session to respond to Mark's questions rather
147		than trying to have a discussion between us.
...		

155	S:	In fact, I put on the green form and the white form, we need
156		some mediation. We need a mediator because we're both backed
157		into our respective corners and I'm angry and I don't
158		listen to anything he says anymore and vice versa. I need
159		somebody to tell me I'm right and he needs somebody to tell
160		him he's right (.) laughs (.) or I'm wrong and he's wrong.
...		
162	D:	We need somebody there to take an objective (( )) whether
163		I'm right or wrong is irrelevant. It is just to the point
164		that we need somebody else to evaluate our positions and to
165		give us some objective feedback . . .
...		
498		Well the first session, I didn't expect a lot of the
499		problems to be solved.

Near the end of the IPR interview, following Sally's comments disagreeing with some of the therapist's assessments, the interviewer asks Sally if she would have been comfortable telling the therapist that she did not agree with him.

Exemplar 10B:

747	S:	Well you can probably tell that I am rather outspoken, I
748		would probably say something if I if it continued (.)
...		
752		Not this session, but later on.
...		
760	D:	I sort of felt like Sally. The first session I thought the
761		purpose would be you know to get as much as we could into
762		the open and not quibble too much about what the therapist
763		said back to us. That we could get into some things a
764		little more deeper in a future session.

As seen in the Exemplar 9B (Lines 136–139, 155–160, and 162–165) both Dan and Sally viewed the first session as a time to present information to a third person who could be an objective mediator. That they also did not expect to resolve issues in the first session can be seen in Lines 145–147 and 498–499. Finally, that they avoided arguments in the first session can be observed in Lines 145–147 in Exemplar 9B as well as Lines 752, and 760–764 in Exemplar 10B. That the performance of these expectations were achieved in the first session can be demonstrated when we examine how the couple's talk was managed in the session.

One way to demonstrate the achievement of these behaviors is to examine the turn-taking patterns between participants in the therapy session. Sally and Dan directed more than 90% of their comments to the therapist and not to each other. From 258 turn-takings in the first session, 235 turn transitions were between therapist and either wife or husband. There were only 23 turn switches between Sally and Dan. Although the therapist, by the nature of his structured questions, did have a strong influence in this turn-taking pattern, it can still be observed that neither Sally nor Dan challenge this organizational sequence. It is possible that this structure imposed by the therapist accommodated the couple's unexpressed expectations. As can be observed in the following session excerpt, even in those sequences when Dan and Sally's turns were adjacent, their talk was still directed to the therapist.

Exemplar 11A:
```
508   T:   You know what, it sounds almost like a roommate
509        relationship=
510   S:   Yes, that's what (.) in fact (.) that's I tell him
511   T:   =than a marital relationship, a little bit?
512   S:   Well, I'll tell you another thing too. We haven't slept
513        together in probably about a year, so it is a roommate in
514        fact I tell him he's my roommate.
515   D:   Well, one of the reasons we have separate accounts is the
516        year Sally had a pretty good job in ((city)) and we had
517        separate accounts, so she just as long I felt like she
518        should be she was making about the same thing I was for a
519        while there and I didn't see anything wrong with us sharing
520        expenses =
521   S:   No, I didn't either.
522   D:   = and when we moved here and she was not working for a year
523        her spending patterns (.) even though she had zero wasn't
524        working at all (.) just continued on a level plane so that's
525        that really got under my skin.
```

Exemplar 11A, in one of the few instances where Sally's and Dan's turns do follow one another, still demonstrates that their talk is directed to the therapist and achieves the displacement of their facts to the "objective" therapist. In this discussion about their nonsexual relationship, which could easily become a heated exchange of accusations, Sally and Dan construct their talk such that they only speak about the other in the third person (Lines 514, 516, 517, 522, and 523). A symmetrical relationship between Dan and Sally is developed such that they are competing with the other to present the better account to the therapist. When Sally does make a statement in response to Dan's comments and states, "No, I didn't either" (Line 521), her comment, although in agreement with Dan's statement, seems to accomplish more toward providing an account of her position than simply supporting Dan.

The implication of these expectations on the process of therapy come into play when we examine the therapist's expectations. Field notes kept by the therapist state that his "primary goal . . . was joining with both husband and wife" and his second goal was to have "the couple leave the session with a sense that therapy could be helpful." Additionally, in five of the six events selected in the therapist IPR interview, the therapist stresses the importance of providing either an interpretation or reframe of the couple's problems as a way to be "helpful" to the clients.

When we examine the combined performance of these two sets of expectations it can be observed how the couple and therapist interact to achieve a complementary flow of interaction. If a client were wanting to be effective at displaying behaviors that avoided arguments, were unconcerned with resolving issues, and views the therapist as a objective mediator, it is likely that he or she would not be confronting the therapist's actions.

This is indeed the case in the marital therapy session (as noted earlier in Exemplar 6A, 7C, and 8B). The couple's negative feedback remains unexpressed in therapy, and the therapist does not receive any disconfirming feedback of his actions of joining with the couple and striving to make his actions helpful. A complementary relationship is established that finds the couple demurely accepting the therapist's comments without critical objections. However, this complementary relationship leads to the consequence of the therapist perceiving events differently than how the couple perceive the same event (as noted in Exemplar 7C and 8B).

Framing Talk as Research or Therapy. It can be seen that the clients' behavior was different in the therapy and research settings. We suggest that part of this difference is due to the contextual framing of the IPR and RPA interviews as research, rather than therapy. As noted, the couple came to therapy with prior expectations of behaviors and outcomes to achieve. Although they were not asked what they anticipated would happen in a research interview, it is likely that Sally and Dan had a minimal agenda of predetermined behaviors to present in the IPR and RPA research interviews.

Additionally, a rule was evoked for the research interviews that was not present in therapy. Antecedent to the couple's participation in the study they were informed that the research interviews were to collect information about their experiences in therapy and were not for the purpose of doing therapy. Early in their IPR interview, the interviewer again stated, "For the purpose of doing this, I am not doing therapy per se. It is to look at what happens in a therapeutic process" (B: Lines 233–235). That Dan understood this can be seen from the incidents where he interrupted his own talk to state: "No. I don't want to get into therapy here" (B: Line 340) and "Yeah I know this is not a therapy session" (D: Line 450).

We are proposing that imposing the rule of "this is not therapy" into the research context created an opportunity for the couple to interact in a manner different than what they displayed in therapy. A relationship between the participants was created during the research interviews that allowed each to be the expert of his or her own phenomenological experience. It was a rotating parallel relationship such that at different times, each participant could act as the authority in the room.

When there was possibility of their talk escalating into heated conflict, Dan and Sally would either stop the escalation on their own initiation, or the comment "this is not therapy" would be evoked and their conversation would then proceed in a nonargumentive manner. As noted previously, in the first therapy session Dan and Sally were in a symmetrical relationship that diminished the occasions for them to negotiate critical issues. The IPR and RPA interviews developed a context that was conducive for Dan and Sally to discuss problematic issues. In the following example, a different type of exchange between Dan and Sally can be observed.

Exemplar 12D:
```
833   I:   This is interesting. I just want to comment on this for a
884        moment. This goes back to a statement and relational
885        statement. You (Dan) made a statement to maybe going to
886        individual therapy.
887   D:   Uh huh.
888   I:   Sally you said great. Not exactly in those words but that
889        seemed to be what I heard. Then you responded to Sally to
890        clarify what you meant.
891   D:   What she meant, what I think ((Sally laughs)) she meant was
892        great was (.) at last, you'll see things my way.
893   I:   So there is an element I mean this may be a piece that I'm
894        missing that is important. Is that there is both a said and
895        an unsaid. We can take the said and if we simply look at the
896        transcript and you made a statement=
897   D:   Uh huh.
898   I:   =I think of going into individual therapy, summarizing your
899        words (.5) but then going back to you Dan it's like (.5)
900        wait a second it's more than that it's more.
901   D:   Well because she she has encouraged me to do that and it's
902        only I feel like I believe that it's only (.) because I want
903        to come around to her way of thinking.
904   S:   No: It's because I realize I think Dan is a very unhappy
905        person with himself regardless of whether he was married to
906        me or anybody walking on the street. I'm happy and umm I'd
907        like to see him change to have a more positive outlook of
908        life as a whole. Regardless of whether I stick around or
909        whether he decides to stay married to me or what.
910   I:   Were you two ever able to take things at (1.0) face value?
911   D:   I don't know. We really didn't really worry about it until
912        the kids came along. I don't know. We never, when we were
913        dating and when we got married, we never discussed outlooks
914        on life or any the things, I don't recall (1.0) Goals or any
915        of this.
```

916	I:	Can you compliment one another? (( )) That's a nice sweater
917		you are wearing or I like (( )) you're wearing (1.5)
918	D:	We don't do it very often, you know.
919	S:	(( )) Of course in my present physical state, he's very
920		critical of that. So you know ((laughter)) nothing looks
921		good on me. And he quite obs=
922	D:	= wait a second, I was shopping yesterday and said you'd have
923		clothes that fit you right and you looked good=
924	S:	= Yes, OK.
925	I:	And Sally looked what?
926	D:	Just said she'd look nice and not try to wear things that
927		are (.5) *3 sizes (( ))* So that was my specific purpose of
928		hopefully she'd feel better (( )).
929	I:	Are you saying that Sally looks nice?
930	D:	When she wears things that fit her well.
931	I:	Did she last night?
932	D:	(( ))
933	I:	And she looked nice?
934	D:	Yeah ((Sally laughs)). Well she did. I have a hard time
935		(1.5) ((Sally still laughing)) saying that because I get
936		I'm so provoked with her since she weighs probably about
937		100 pounds more than she weighed when we got married and I
938		weigh about 15 pounds more than when we got married . . .

There are a number of features to note in this exemplar. The exemplar begins with the interviewer noting that Sally's response to Dan's statement of "maybe going to individual therapy" is interpreted in two very different ways by Dan and Sally. Dan, using "her" and "you" statements attributes Sally's intentions as being self-motivated (Lines 891–892, 901–903). Sally, however, responds that her intentions were guided out of concern for Dan (Lines 904–909). When the interviewer poses a question (Line 910) to the two of them, Dan's response (Lines 911–915) shifts to a new level of interaction as he uses "we" to discuss shared issues.

The interviewer then asks, "Can you compliment one another?" (Line 916). The exchange that follows has Dan complimenting Sally (Lines 922–923, 934) and Sally enjoying the conversation, as indicated by her laughter (Lines 934 and 935). In this segment, Dan and Sally are interacting in a positive manner and clarifying issues. However, what also stands out in this exemplar are the interviewer's remarks. The interviewer's first remarks can be viewed as points of clarification (Lines 883–886, 888–890, 893–896, 898–900). However, his remarks on Lines 916, 925, and 929 are ambiguous. These comments could be seen as clinical requests for new behaviors rather than simply clarifying questions.

Nevertheless, the couple seems to understand the interviewer's comments as further research type of questions and not clinical intrusion. Although Dan and

Sally were aware of the rule distinction of the research interviews not being for therapy, it can be noted that throughout the research interviews Dan and Sally do not respond to any of the interviewer's comments as if he were violating this rule. Near the end of the IPR interview, when the interviewer asks, "And the purpose of this is not therapeutic to make this better, but that could happen too, and that is why I'm asking the impact of actually doing this" (B: Lines 842–844). Dan replies, "I don't think it was helpful in that light, but it was interesting to see it replayed" (B: Lines 845–846).

Indeed, the one time the interviewer violates this rule, stating near the end of the RPA interview," (6.0) *Well, let me make a recommendation (2.0) as a clinician (1.0)" (D: Line 994), the couple still offer no indication that any of his earlier talk was clinically structured.[4] The only remarks Dan and Sally offer about the therapeutic relevance of the interviews are when they are asked for their social security numbers in order to reimburse them for their time and Sally states, "Well as far as I'm concerned that's not necessary" (D: Line 1070), and Dan adds, "You don't really need to worry about it. I think we should be paying you. (Sally and Dan both laughing). We got something out of this, so don't worry about that" (D: Lines 1071–1073).[5]

Externalizing Problems. Another feature that stands out in the research interviews is the manner in which Dan and Sally were able to discuss some of their problems as if they were external to themselves. White (1989) persuasively described how helping clients objectify problems as external to themselves can be beneficial to therapy. The structure of the research interviews required the couple to examine events that had transpired at an earlier time. Relating to issues in this historical manner created a separation between observer and event, such that Dan and Sally were able to discuss issues without the emotional intensity that could curtail effective communication.

In the IPR and RPA interviews, Dan and Sally were able to discuss their issues from a meta perspective. In the following example Dan and Sally are discussing the transcript of their first session.

---

[4]This is actually a self-reflexive remark that reinforces the "this is research distinction" as it implies that all the previous comments in the interviews were not clinically directed.

[5]It may be that the couple did view the interviewer's actions as being clinically directed. However, if they did, there was tacit agreement to accept that behavior. As noted, when Dan states, "we should be paying you," there is the suggestion that he saw the research interviews as doing more than just research. However, whether this is because he did not know what a research interview really entailed, or because he was OK if the research merged into therapy is a moot point. What is significant is that regardless of their interpretation of the research interviews, there was still a contextual distinction between therapy and research talk such that Sally and Dan's behaviors were different in the two contexts. It is also significant to note that the primary reason the couple chose the university clinic was because of its inexpensive fees. Therefore, refusing reimbursement for participating in the research study further highlights the benefits they perceived.

Exemplar 13D:

```
421   D:   One thing that stands out for me is that one of the things
422        that (1.5) Sally does that puzzles me is that that she
423        always refers things as mine (.) because my children, my
424        this, my furniture, my children. That's one thing that (1.0)
425        she's done for a long time that puzzles me.
426   S:   We're talking about my family furniture here.
427   D:   No no no. But when you said (1.0) twice, you've said my
428        children, *like they're not* ours.
429   D:   You're the one who wanted the who started with my money and
430        your money situation years ago. Anyway
431   D:   What does that have to do with the kids?
432   I:   So the issue here now that you're picking up in these
433        transcripts is the distinction between my and ours?
434   D:   That's what I'm saying that's what jumped out at me, the way
435        Sally says some things all the time.
436   I:   So it's not new but it's
437   D:   Now, but when you see it in the summary like this it sorta
438        jumps out at you because I don't think she's said the word
439        our in the last couple of years.
           ((a long pause here while the husband reads through more of
           the session transcript))
440        Somewhere here is a statement of my you know feelings about
441        the things basically I felt like I was doing the best I can
442        that I'm an imperfect human being and that's what I (( ))
443        That's what I feel like Sally basically said. Because I'm a
444        a CPA I should be making $100,000 a year.
445        ((Sally and Dan both laugh))
```

In this exemplar, Dan is first noting his puzzlement of Sally's use of "mine" in a discussion that occurred in the first session (Lines 421–425). Sally and Dan at first disagree about the significance of this word (Lines 426–431). The interviewer then poses a question "So the issue here now that you're picking up in these transcripts" (Lines 432–433), which indexes this concern to the text and not to their current (real-time) relationship. Dan responds to this temporal shift as he looks through the text for reference to feelings that he expressed in therapy (Lines 440–441). When he cannot find the exact reference, his summary "Because I'm a CPA I should be making $100,000 a year" (Lines 444–445), elicits laughter from both Dan and Sally.

What seems to be happening in Exemplar 13D is that Dan and Sally are able to disengage from their struggle in real time about the meaning of "mine" and "ours" and shift to a self-reflexive discussion about what had been said months earlier. This change of reference allowed them to negotiate issues from a metaperspective without the attachment of the issue to their identified emotional self. This occurs a number of times in the IPR and RPA interviews. As Dan notes at the end of RPA interview, "Yeah, I think in a way it's been more helpful than the sessions ((Sally laughs)) because you're getting to look back at what you said and reflecting on that" (D: Lines 1046–1048).[6]

LIMITATIONS

There are other factors, which were not examined in this study, that may have also had impact on the process differences noted. The first caveat is that only the first session of marital therapy was examined. The other five marital therapy sessions and the wife's individual therapy were not analyzed. Additionally, there is the reactive effect of the interviews occurring sequentially in time. As these interviews (both therapy and research) occurred sequentially, it is impossible to know the impact of prior talk on subsequent talk. The influence that the entire therapy process had on the RPA interview cannot be gauged. However, regardless of that impact, the couple did note differences between their therapy and research interviews.

Another factor is the influence of the self of the therapist and interviewer. Although this study noted the differences between the research and therapy contexts, and the transcripts do highlight differences between therapist's and researcher's behaviors, there are still other aspects of "lived experiences" not represented in the text. A transcript can only convey a limited shadow of the myriad interactions which occur in an interview. The age of the interviewer/therapist, the confidence level of each, their hierarchial position in the clinic (clinician and director), their kinesic behavior, as well as other activities could have contributed to the differences between therapy and research as perceived by the couple. These issues were not explored in this study.

A third factor is the combined unique characteristics of the couple, therapist and interviewer. This population of four individuals may have interacted in a very unique manner such that another case study may reveal different outcomes. These issues do not detract from the conclusions of this study as we are not trying to generalize the results to all situations. We do hope that the distinctions raised are useful conceptual razors that both clinicians and researchers can employ in their own work and provide utility to their efforts.

DISCUSSION AND IMPLICATIONS

This study has presented several key themes that describe how research interviews provided therapeutic benefit to the couple. The four themes developed from our analyses are grounded in the talk of the clinic (both clinical and research talk).

---

[6]This dynamic is similar to White's (1989) historical unique outcomes and Tomm's (1985) use of reflexive questioning.

Three categories (the said and the not-yet-said, framing talk as research or therapy, and externalizing problems) describe how the research talk differed from the therapy talk. The fourth category (the couple's expectations) provided increased understanding of the couple's perspective and how their accounting of their behavior was enacted. To further elaborate on these themes, we propose the following implications. We submit five research implications, six clinical implications, and two teaching and training implications.

Research Implications

Based on the results of this study, we offer the following five suggestions to researchers:

IPR is an Effective Research Protocol for Studying Marital Therapy. Although IPR has been conducted in individual therapy, there is a great deal of potential in using IPR in conjoint therapy.[7] However, in working with couples it is important to consider the interactive effect of interviewing the couple together. Additional analysis indicated that the husband's and wife's responses were moderated by the presence of the other person in the interview (Gale et al., 1992). That is, the IPR interview contributed to the couple achieving a more consensual type of conversation and reaching agreement on various emotional issues. It may be that interviewing the couple separately would have led to a different outcome.

In Employing IPR and RPA Research Protocols, Researchers Need to be Aware of Their Clinical Impact. Many researchers have noted that qualitative research can have an impact on the respondents (Heath, 1992; McNamee, 1989; Steier, 1992a, 1992b; Wright, 1990) and ethical concerns regarding this possibility have been expressed (Gilgun, 1992; Patton, 1990). Although the differing roles between researcher and clinician are not always clear-cut, there is a clear distinction between who is the "customer." In therapy it is the clients who are asking for help, whereas in research the researcher is the one asking for assistance. We suggest that researchers and clinicians have much to learn from each other and would mutually benefit from exchanges. Reflexive research does impact all involved as the observing system becomes part of the second-order cybernetic system (Steier, 1992a, 1992b).

Practitioner-Generated Research is Encouraged (Chenail, 1992). Indeed, the Milan group posited hypothesizing as a research operation engaged in conjointly with the family (Boscolo, Cecchin, Hoffman, & Penn, 1987). Although this study

---

[7]While other researchers and clinicians have noted the benefit of videotape playback (Elliott & Shapiro, 1992; Kagen, 1980; Ray & Sazon, 1992), some researchers do urge caution in the use of playback in marital therapy (see Dowrick & Biggs, 1983).

had a researcher working with the clinician, we also encourage clinicians to conduct their own research.

A caveat to add to this, however, is that the clinician be mindful of his or her goal in doing research or therapy. Although Wright (1990) presented research as an intervention technique, our study suggests that there are key differences in how the research/therapy context is actually created. We propose that research done for the purpose of intervening is a very different process than research conducted from a posture of curiosity (see the following section on clinical implications). We agree with Steier (1992b) who recommended that seeing research as intervention "forces an ethical concern of respect for the 'culture' one is studying" (p. 178).

There are Important Differences in How Relationships are Constructed and Power is Distributed in the Research Context. The discourse between participant and researcher creates particular social realities (and relationships) that will impact the process being studied. The emphasis is on how talk is managed rather then on what is underneath the talk. It is through the discourse that social identities and social institutions are created (see Gale, 1991; Garfinkel, 1967; Heritage, 1984).

Combining Research Methods is Encouraged. Linking discourse analysis with the self-reflexive activities of IPR and RPA provides a description of how performances are achieved with a privileged accounting of behaviors. We do not suggest that one method is better or more accurate than another.[8] In today's postmodern world, information is generated in an ever-increasing fashion (Gergen, 1991) and with the plethora of self-help books, television, and radio programs, there is a place for reflexive research joined with other research methods. Coordinating formal research with practitioner's research can prove to be beneficial to both researchers and clinicians alike.

Clinical Implications

The results of this study support the following six clinical ramifications.

Benefits of Therapeutic Questions. Anderson and Goolishian (1988, 1992) as well as others have advocated the benefits of therapeutic questions developed from a not-knowing position. These types of questions are not presented from the role of expert and do not direct the client to respond in a particular fashion. Rather, these types of "therapeutic questions are impelled by difference in understanding and are drawn from the future by the as-yet unrealized possibility of a community of knowledge" (Anderson & Goolishian, 1992, p. 34). Heath (1992) described this process as being "curious."

---

[8]We can easily imagine a situation where the couples accounting of their activities is very different than what their actions accomplish.

This study has supported this perspective in that the form of questions asked in the research interviews, which proved to be beneficial, followed an organization of collaboration, curiosity, and shared expertise. This type of inquiry, sometimes called *practical knowledge* (Falzer, 1989), advocates that the clinician's actions are better served when focusing on the moment-to-moment experience in the room rather than centering around theoretical premises (Atkinson & Heath, 1990). Amundson, Stewart, and Valentine (1993) stated that "curiosity and empowerment as proper conduct in therapy may seem to be just basic principles of respectful therapy" (p. 120).

Helping Clients Externalize Issues. Through having the videotape and transcripts of prior interviews available, each person is able to index her or his remarks from those documents rather than from an internalized identity. In this way, the couple were able to discuss their issues in a more open manner. Rather than reifying an issue as an integral aspect of their own identity and relationship, the text was used as reference material that helped the couple to disengage from issues and find new ways of solving their differences. Following White's (1989) ideas, the couple were able to develop "retranscriptions of problem definitions . . . to decontextualize problems" (p. 14).

Incorporating Research in One's Clinical Practice is not Just Adding Another Technique to Use With Clients. The research context was created out of a field that embraced curiosity, and was not generated to find solutions or "fix" the clients. The relationships that developed in the research context emerged out of this open, rotating expertise agenda. We suspect that if one were to use research interviews in a formalistic manner to achieve therapeutic benefits, a very different context would be elicited and different outcomes experienced. It is not packaged curiosity. Constructing and defining a context, be it research or therapy (see Goffman, 1974; Keeney, 1990), is predicated on the agendas and actions of all the participants (see Edwards & Potter, 1992; Goffman, 1967).

Clinicians Should Attend to the Discourse of All Participants. How talk is constructed and managed and how questions are forged and presented (see Tomm, 1985) are fundamental elements of the therapeutic process. Clients' actions obviously are not executed in isolation, but are presented in concert with the therapist's actions. Therefore, we urge clinicians to develop and be aware of the rhetorical process.

Clinicians Should Ascertain Clients' Expectations and Views of Therapy. As this study has indicated, the therapist's understanding of the client's experience in therapy was very different than what the couple reported they experienced. Rennie (1992) noted that "what the client says in therapy does not reflect what he or she is actually thinking" (p. 229). Utterances emerge out of prior contexts as well as are connected to what will be said. A client's narrative presents only an aspect of his or her lived experience, as there is much more to an individual's life in the not-yet-said. As Bruner (1986) argued, "life experience is richer than discourse" (p. 143). It is important for clinicians to learn about each clients' phenomenological world and encourage the interplay of each person's phenomenological experience as it is out of this discourse that relationships, meanings and healing narratives are co-constructed and expanded.

Self-Reflexive Activities Provide Beneficial Change. As a healing story is developed, particular discursive threads are tailored, cut, and expanded to flesh out the narrative. Self-reflexive activities are very effective in spinning the not-yet-said into the narrative tapestry. It may be that as participants self-reflect on their actions and interactions, higher levels of learning are achieved (Bateson, 1972). Further inquiry in this area is recommended.

Teaching and Training Implications

Finally, this study offers support for clinical educators and trainers to consider the following two suggestions.

In-Depth Interviewing Should be Taught. In clinical training programs, there may be utility in teaching future clinicians to first do in-depth interviews before they learn how to intervene with clients. In this manner student therapists can learn to listen for and appreciate others' lived phenomenological experience without having a dual agenda of also trying to "help" that person. Doing ethnographic interviews with clients could provide a mechanism for future clinicians to appreciate the lived experience of a client. Incorporating these research skills can also be useful in helping the clinician develop a "narrative lens" for understanding human interactions.

IPR Can be a Very Effective Procedure to Use in Clinical Supervision. Elliott and Shapiro (1992) noted that IPR presents itself as an effective supervision tool. IPR can be used both with the supervisor and clinician, or used by the clinician for his or her own self-supervision. Combining IPR with discourse analysis, and examining brief segments of a session can also be very effective for self-supervision (Gale, Dotson, Lindsey, Nagireddy, & Wilson, 1993).

APPENDIX: PROTOCOL FOR IPR INTERVIEW (CLIENTS FORM)

A meaningful moment is an event in the session where you believe that at least one client member has made some change (positive or negative) in his/her life as resulting from the event. This event could be an insight, the demonstration of a new behavior, or a new understanding of another person. An event could be meaningful for either both of you, or for just one person.

1. Time of meaningful event. (Note time as presented on the bottom of video screen)
   start: end:

2. Brief description of event. In your own words, describe what happened during the meaningful moment event.

3. Brief statement of why you consider this event as meaningful. Include if this event was meaningful to you, to your spouse (significant other) or for both of you.

4. Please rate the significance of this event for the session for both you and your partner.

   For you:

   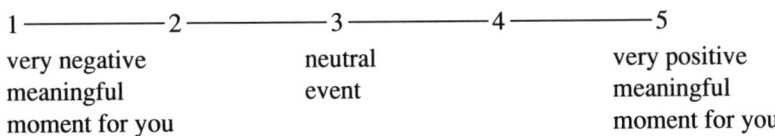

   1 —————— 2 —————— 3 —————— 4 —————— 5
   very negative   neutral   very positive
   meaningful   event   meaningful
   moment for you   moment for you

   For your partner:

   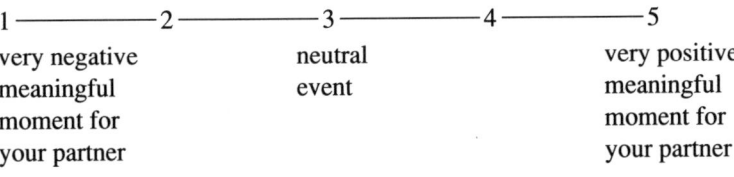

   1 —————— 2 —————— 3 —————— 4 —————— 5
   very negative   neutral   very positive
   meaningful   event   meaningful
   moment for   moment for
   your partner   your partner

ACKNOWLEDGMENTS

We gratefully acknowledge Paul Gallant, Jenny Manders, and Cheryl Williams for their contributions to this study.

REFERENCES

Amundson, J., Stewart, K., & Valentine, L. (1993). Temptations of power and certainty. *Journal of Marital and Family Therapy, 19,*(2), 111–124.
Anderson, H., & Goolishian, H. (1988). Human systems as linguistic systems: Evolving ideas about the implications for theory and practice. *Family Process, 27,* 371–393.
Anderson, H., & Goolishian, H. (1992). The client is the expert: a not-knowing approach to therapy. In S. McNamee & K. J. Gergen (Eds.), *Therapy as social construction* (pp. 25–39). London: Sage.
Atkinson, B. J., & Heath, A. W. (1990). Further thoughts on second-order family therapy—This time it's personal. *Family Process, 29,* 145–155.
Bateson, G. (1972). *Steps to an ecology of mind.* New York: Ballantine Books.
Boscolo, J., Cecchin, G., Hoffman, L., & Penn, P. (1987). *Milan systemic family therapy.* New York: Basic Books.
Bruner, E. (1986). Ethnography as narrative. In V. W. Turner & E. M. Bruner (Eds.), *The anthropology of experience* (pp. 139–155). Chicago: University of Illinois Press.
Chenail, R. J. (1992). A case for clinical qualitative research. *The Qualitative Report, 1,*(4), 1, 3–7.
Dowrick, P. W., & Biggs, S. J. (Eds.). (1983). *Using video: Psychological and social application.* Chichester: Wiley.
Edwards, D., & Potter, J. (1992). *Discursive psychology.* London: Sage.
Elliott, R. (1984). A discovery-oriented approach to significant events in psychotherapy: Interpersonal process recall and comprehensive process analysis. In L. Rick & L. Greenburg (Eds.), *Change episodes* (pp. 249–286). New York: Guilford.
Elliott, R. (1986). Interpersonal process recall (IPR) as a psychotherapy process research method. In L. Greenberg & W. Pinsof (Eds.), *The psychotherapy process: A research handbook* (pp. 503–527). New York: Guilford Press.
Elliott, R. (1989). Comprehensive process analysis: Understanding the change process in significant therapy events. In M. Packer & R. B. Addison (Eds.), *Entering the circle: Hermeneutic investigations in psychology* (pp. 165–184). Albany: SUNY Press.
Elliott, R., & Shapiro, D. A. (1988). Brief structured recall: A more efficient method for identifying and describing significant therapy events. *British Journal of Medial Psychology, 61,* 141–153.
Elliott, R., & Shapiro, D. A. (1992). Client and therapist as analysts of significant events. In S. G. Toukmanian & D. L. Rennie (Eds.), *Psychotherapy process research: Paradigmatic and narrative approaches* (pp. 163–186). Newbury Park, CA: Sage.
Falzer, P. (1989). Epistemology's effect on practical knowledge. *Journal of Family Psychology, 21,* 451–466.
Gale, J. (1991). *Conversation analysis of therapeutic discourse: The pursuit of an agenda.* Norwood, NJ: Ablex.
Gale, J. (1992). When research interviews are more therapeutic than therapy interviews. *The Qualitative Report, 1,* 4, 14–15.
Gale, J., Dotson, D., Lindsey, E., Nagireddy, C., Wilson, R. (1993). Self-supervision through conversation analysis. Unpublished manuscript.
Gale, J., & Newfield, N. (1992). A conversation analysis of a solution-focused marital therapy session. *Journal of Marital and Family Therapy, 18,*(2), 153–165.

Gale, J., Odell, M., & Nagireddy, C. (1992). *Reflexive* process analysis in *marital therapy: The conflation of research and therapy.* Unpublished manuscript.

Garfinkel, H. (1967). *Studies in ethnomethodology.* Englewood. Cliffs, NJ: Prentice-Hall.

Gergen, K. J. (1991). *The saturated self: Dilemmas of identity in contemporary life.* New York: Basic Books.

Gilgun, J. F. (1992). Observations in a clinical setting: Team decision-making in family incest treatment. In J. F. Gilgun, K. Daly, & F. Handel (Eds.), *Qualitative methods in family research* (pp. 236–261). Newbury Park, CA: Sage.

Glaser, B. G., & Strauss, A. L. (1967). *The discovery of grounded theory: Strategies for qualitative research.* New York: Aldine.

Goffman, E. (1967). *Interactional ritual: Essays on face-to-face behavior.* New York: Anchor.

Goffman, E. (1974). *Frame analysis: An essay on the organization of experience.* New York: Harper & Row.

Heath, A. (1992). One thing therapists have learned form qualitative research. *AFTA Newsletter, 47*, 23.

Heritage, J. (1984). *Garfinkel and ethnomethodology.* New York: Polity Press.

Kagen, N. I. (1980). Influencing human interaction: Eighteen years with IPR. In A. K. Hess (Ed.), *Psychotherapy supervision: Theory, research and practice,* (pp. 262–283). New York: Wiley.

Keeney, B. P. (1990). *Improvisational therapy.* St. Paul, MN: Systemic Therapy Press.

Mahrer, A. R., & Nadler, W. P. (1986). Good moments in psychotherapy: A preliminary review, a list, and some promising research avenues. *Journal of Consulting and Clinical Psychology, 54,* 10–16.

McNamee, S. (1989). Challenging the patriarchal vision of social science: Lessons from a family therapy model. In K. Carter & C. Spitzack (Eds.), *Doing research on women's communication: Perspectives on theory and methods* (pp. 95–117). Norwood, NJ: Ablex.

Moerman, M. (1988). *Talking culture: Ethnography and conversation analysis.* Philadelphia: University of Pennsylvania Press.

Patton, M. Q. (1990). Ethnical dimensions of qualitative inquiry: Cultural and research contexts. In M. J. McGee-Brown (Ed.), *Processes, applications and ethics in qualitative research* (pp. 7–38). Athens, GA: College of Education.

Potter, J., & Wetherell, M. (1987). *Discourse and social psychology.* London: Sage.

Ray, W. A., & Saxon, W. W. (1992). Nonconfrontive use of video playback to promote change in brief family therapy. *Journal of Marital and Family Therapy, 18,*(1), 63–69.

Rennie, D. L. (1992). Qualitative analysis of the client's experience of psychotherapy: The unfolding of reflexivity. In S. G. Toukmanian & D. L. Rennie (Eds.), *Psychotherapy process research: Paradigmatic and narrative approaches* (pp. 211–233). Newbury Park, CA: Sage.

Rice, L. N., & Greenburg, L. (Eds.). (1984). *Patterns of change.* New York: Guilford.

Rubin, Z., & Mitchell, C. (1976). Couples research as couples counseling: Some unintended effects of studying close relationships. *American Psychologist, 30,* 1, 17–25.

Steier, F. (Ed.). (1992a). *Research and reflexivity.* London: Sage.

Steier, F. (1992b). Reflexivity and methodology: An ecological constructionism. In F. Steier (Ed.), *Research and reflexivity* (pp. 163–185). London: Sage.

Tomm, K. (1985). Circular interviewing: A multi-faced clinical tool. In D. Campbell & R. Draper (Eds.), *Applications of systemic family therapy: The Milan approach.* London: Grune & Stratton.

Tyler, S. A. (1978). *The said and the unsaid.* New York: Academic Press.

White, M. (1989). The externalizing of the problem and the re-authoring of lives and relationships. *Selected papers* (pp. 5–28). Adelaide: Dulwich Centre Publications.

Wiseman, H. (1992). Conceptually-based interpersonal process recall (IPR) of change events. In S. G. Toukmanian & D. L. Rennie (Eds.), *Psychotherapy process research: Paradigmatic and narrative approaches* (pp. 51–76). Newbury Park, CA: Sage.

Wright, L. (1990). Research as family therapy intervention technique. *Contemporary Family Therapy, 12*(6), 477–484.

6
Telling How to Say It: A Way of Giving Suggestions in Family Therapy Supervision

Dan A. Ratliff
St. Mary's University

G. H. Morris
Texas Tech University

One of the key elements of professional development in most clinical and medical fields is the supervision of clinicians in training by experienced practitioners. Supervision in the field of marriage and family therapy greatly depends on direct observation of clinical interaction either through live or videotape supervision. In live supervision, the supervisor observes the trainee during an actual client session through a one-way mirror or video monitor and can call in suggestions by means of an intercom telephone. In videotape supervision, trainees present videotaped excerpts of a recent clinical session. Then, supervisor and trainee can discuss what is happening with each case to reach a better understanding of the family and possible therapeutic strategies. In this way, videotape supervision can allow the supervisor to focus on the trainee's learning needs to a greater extent than is to be expected under the time pressure of live supervision. The focus of this chapter is on one way masterful supervisors make suggestions to trainees during videotape supervision.

The literature on supervision in marriage and family therapy portrays it as a difficult process in which supervisors must establish a clear hierarchy and set appropriate learning goals for trainees (Fine & Fennell, 1985; Haley, 1976; Liddle & Schwartz, 1983; Mazza, 1988; Montalvo, 1973; Schwartz, 1988; Schwartz, Liddle, & Breunlin, 1988; Tucker, Hart, & Liddle, 1976), yet must preserve trainees' initiative and autonomy, avoid creating dependency, and facilitate growth (Berger & Dammann, 1982; Liddle & Schwartz, 1983; Nichols, 1988; Roberts, 1981; Schwartz et al., 1988). Difficulties in supervision may arise from supervisors' excessive activity or from trainees' responses. Difficulties may come from the trainees' anxiety about how the supervisor may evaluate his or her clinical work (Breunlin, Karrer, McGuire, & Cimmarusti, 1988). Because of the active interventionist style of many family therapists, supervisors may complicate the process by attempting to impress trainees with their skillful suggestions (Schwartz, 1988). In live supervision, supervisors may make suggestions too frequently or in a complex form that may confuse or overwhelm the trainee (Breunlin, Liddle, & Schwartz, 1988; Wright, 1986). Supervisors may also complicate learning by using abstract theoretical concepts that obfuscate what they want trainees to do (Tyler & Tyler, 1985).

Although there is ample guidance available about how not to conduct effective supervision, little is actually known about how effective supervisors conduct supervision in marriage and family therapy. Discovering how experienced and masterful supervisors actually engage in the process can become the foundation for better instruction in supervision, both for family therapy and for other arenas.

Toward that end, we examined transcripts of 23 hours of supervision sessions provided by six supervisors from a master's level program and a doctoral level program at two different universities. All of these are videotape supervision sessions in which a supervisor and trainee reviewed excerpts of a recent clinical session. From this corpus, we chose to examine in detail 12 supervision sessions conducted by three supervisors in a top-ranked doctoral training program in marriage and family therapy. We elected to focus on sessions of these three supervisors because we, along with outside evaluators who examined the transcripts and recorded sessions, concluded that the supervision provided in the doctoral program is extremely masterful in comparison with other supervision. Two of the supervisors possessed over 12 years of supervisory experience. The doctoral trainees being supervised also had extensive clinical and educational experience.

As we commenced analysis of the masterful supervisors' work, we noticed almost immediately that suggestions were very prevalent and that supervisors very often made suggestions in a way we have termed *telling how to say it*. The focus of our analysis became to describe of how supervisors tell how to say it. After a brief overview of the nature of suggestions in the supervision sessions we examined, we offer a description of how supervisors tell how to say it, the circumstances under which they do so, and some of the functions that may be served. We conclude with a few implications of our analysis.

SUGGESTIONS IN SUPERVISION

Supervisors give suggestions in almost every session. We identified 117 examples of supervisory suggestions from 11 of the 12 supervision sessions. The one session with no suggestions was an evaluation of trainee performance conducted at the conclusion of the semester. Most supervision sessions contain, on average, about 10 suggestions about courses of action to take.

This kind of supervision usually has a three-part structure that consists of case summary, problem formulation, and potential actions to take. The case summary deals with past actions of the therapist with a client, which are documented and discussed via the videotape. The case summary leads into the problem formulation, which highlights a difficulty exposed during the case summary. Either party may propose the problem formulation. In the third and final stage, much as in the "treatment phase" of medical encounters, supervisor and trainee determine what should be done in subsequent clinical sessions. Nearly all of the suggestions are made during this phase.

To understand suggestions in supervision, it is instructive to review what has been proposed about suggestions in conversation in general. Someone who is about to make a request often begins by addressing or asking about preconditions of the request being accepted. Determining that these can be met, the speaker then makes the request (Austin, 1975; Levinson, 1983). The last move in the sequence is the recipient's response (e.g., acceptance, weak acceptance, etc.) to the request. A full suggestion sequence, then, would have four moves: preconditioning, go ahead, request, and response. Other sequences are sometimes inserted between these moves (Houtkoop-Steenstra, 1987; Levinson, 1983).

The following is an excerpt from a supervision session that is one of the best "composites" in our data (i.e., this case shows more of the entire process than our other cases). It does, however, diverge from the picture just presented to some degree:

Exemplar 1:
```
1   S:   And, and th-that obviously has an impact on you.
2   A:   Right.
3   S:   hhhhh So  you feel yourself (.) res reacting in some way
4        to her (.5) related to those issues?
5   A:   Uhhuh
6   S:   I'd like you to make at least one process sort of comment-
7        in the session (2.0) I'm feeling confused about this, I'm
8        feeling (.) ((clap)) >like whatever<.
9   A:   I'm feeling >kinda like I'm< hearing two things? or (.)>is
10       that< (.) to:o
11  S:   ^No. I don't want you to tell her what you think I want you
12       to tell her how-what you feel.
13  A:   [Okay.
14  S:   [This makes me feel (.) anxious (.) this makes me feel
15       confused (.) this make-some a:ffecting.
16  A:   Okay (.) Comment (.) affective comment
17  S:   Because, what th- what that's fo:r is uh (.5) I I want you:
18       to do mo:re of (.) incorporating yourself into the therapy
19  A:   Umkay.
```

Lines 1, 3, and 4 describe a precondition, circumstance, or contingency under which the requested action should occur, namely "when you feel yourself reacting in some way to her relating to those issues" (that had previously been identified).

Specifically, the trainee had admitted to some discomfort in dealing with the way the client was being very ambiguous. Stating such contingencies is one of the ways supervisors precondition their requests. In other instances, the trainee's comfort, or ability or availability and so forth serve as preconditions. The trainee's "go-ahead" occurs with Line 5. The request in this instance, comprised of Lines 6 and 7, specifies what is to be done by the trainee, which is "to make a process sort of comment." The trainee's responses to the request occur in Lines 9 and 10, wherein he makes an attempt to emulate the supervisor's saying, and in Line 16 and 19, in which he accepts the request.

Another element of this case of suggestion that is common, both in ordinary conversation (Houtkoop-Steenstra, 1987) and in our supervision data, is the warrant or explanation for the suggestion that occurs in Lines 17 and 18. The supervisor provides a rationale for the request "to make a process sort of statement" that "I want you to do more of incorporating yourself into the therapy."

The request components of suggestions in our corpus look like the following examples:

1. "find out from ((the referring therapist)) what he has in mind besides revenge on the clinic."
2. "This may be one of those cases where you have to drag him into the office and have him call his sister."
3. "Umkay. I think (the couple) split for awhile. It sounds like they're both in pretty much turmoil."
4. "One of the best things that might help is scheduling in this room and using the videotapes from time to time to say 'here's what I see,' 'this is how you might do this better' . . ."
5. "I would just take her aside, and you know just ask her why don't you just ask her to step in ahead of him and then just say 'you know, I I'm aware that because (I) saw your husband that that you may feel like there is some prejudicial information sometimes it just helps to be able to talk one to one'."

Most of the time, supervisors simply request things to be done (as in Examples 1, 2, and 3 just given), relying on trainees to come up with a suitable way to say it. However, a predominant feature of how these masterful supervisors make suggestions is illustrated in Examples 4 and 5, which we term *telling how to say it*. Now only did supervisors suggest what to do in the next session, they often specified precisely how to say it. This type of suggestion occurred in 39% of the examples of supervisory suggestions. When supervisors tell how to say it, supervisors rehearse, model, or script precisely what is needed given a botched, difficult, delicate or otherwise problematic circumstance.

In Example 4, the supervisor suggested using the videotape facilities, which would enable the trainee to ". . .say *'here's what I see,' 'this is how you might do this better'....*" The supervisor in Example 5 tells the trainee precisely what to say to commence the delicate task of "splitting" husband and wife into individual therapy: "... just say *'you know, I I'm aware that because (I) saw your husband that that you may feel like there is some prejudicial information and sometimes it just helps to be able to talk one to one'.*"

In this chapter, we view telling how to say it as a special case of making suggestions. Using this type of suggestion, supervisors rehearse or model how to say something in a coming therapy session. This is one of the ways supervisors share their expertise with trainees. For example:

Exemplar 2:
```
1   S:   Do you feel like you need to take her asi:de . . .
2   F:   And do what?
3   S:   And sa:y um (.) sometimes it feels real unbalanced to be
4        the second person to come into therapy (.) and (.) I'm
5        wondering if-if you would like to see (.) me by myself
6   F:   Uh huh
7   S:   for one session (.) and just offer it that way without a
8        you know, we don't need to do it right now, we don't
9        (need) to keep equal balance, but uh
```

In reply to a question from the trainee about what should be *done,* the supervisor tells how to *say* something (Lines 3–8). The saying includes an invitation, "you would like to see me by yourself," and a warrant for that invitation, "sometimes it feels real unbalanced to be the second person to come into therapy."

We turn now to our analysis of the general and specific circumstances under which how-to-say-its are used in family therapy supervision.

ANALYSIS

Supervisors whose work we examined make suggestions in two ways:

1. by making a request which follows the general requests structure of precondition, go ahead, request, and response,
2. by couching at least a part of their requests as things to be said to clients.

In 39% of the cases, supervisors suggest what to do and tell how to say it. Why do supervisors sometimes elect to tell how to say it?

Generally, supervisors offer how-to-say-its when they sense or anticipate some kind of trouble in the implementation of a course of therapy. For instance, supervisors sometimes detect, by a trainee's failure to display understanding of a technique, that a more precise specification of actions to be performed is necessary.

Such was the case in the first excerpt we examined. In particular, the supervisor commenced telling how to say it after a 2-second pause (Line 7), during which the trainee did not assent to a suggestion. Later, the trainee's unsuccessful attempts to emulate the supervisor's "process comments" prompted further work to tell how to say it—work that eventually succeeded. The trainee offered process comments in a way that invites the supervisor's judgment, as if he knew his tries were inadequate. Put differently, the trainee displays some doubt that his process comments match what the supervisor wants him to say. After giving him a distinction (between thinking and feeling) to follow to construct process comments, the supervisor (Lines 14–15) offers two how-to-say-its.

Parenthetically, to appreciate how-to-say-its as a technique for moving beyond troubles in supervision sessions, consider other alternatives that would be deficient by comparison. One alternative, caricatured in stories of what happens when a U.S. traveler fails to make him or herself understood in an intercultural encounter, is to repeat an utterance more slowly and more loudly. How-to-say-its reveal supervisors' facility in moving to a level of detail appropriate to achieve trainees' understanding.

When supervisors learn that there is something difficult or problematic about how to proceed on a case, they are expected by trainees to be able to propose solutions, or, more generally, to know what to do. The following unsuccessful case of suggestion illustrates what can happen when supervisors do not offer solutions:

Exemplar 3:
1   A: U:h, and I have called CPS a couple of times (.2) in
2   response to that, and she said she was gonna call em and
3   I haven't gotten any call backs and I haven't uh (.3) been
4   lucky enough to catch em there
5   S: It sounds like you need to call ((a particular CPS worker))
6   huh? hhhh
7   A: That's who I called.
8   S: Oh, you can't get ((the CPS Worker)) to (.) respond haha
9   A: Right.
10 S: Gees hhhhh
11   (9.0)
12 S: Okay What's your next step?

There is a 9-second pause after the supervisor learns that what he has suggested has already been attempted, unsuccessfully. Under the circumstances, what would work would be to give the trainee some other way to proceed. Instead, the supervisor only glides past the problem. Another supervisor faced with the identical problem said:

Exemplar 4:
1   S: ...you need to call the supervisor, you say to the
2   supervisor, I've been trying to get a hold of so and so,

```
3                this is what I'm concerned about, if he will leave me a
4                message on the answering machine then I will know what
5                to do.
6      A:        uhhuh
7      S:        Okay. Period. They won't like it, but they can't blame you
8                about trying to reach him.
```

Notice that beginning with Line 2, the supervisor is quoting what he wants the trainee to say. He might just have said "Call the CPS worker's supervisor," but he instead specified very precisely what the trainee could say in the call.

Supervisors need a way of suggesting precisely what is needed at a given time, giving trainees the benefit of their experience without appearing to undervalue the trainee's capabilities. Telling how to say it marks places in which supervisors are giving suggestions about common, yet easily mishandled, clinical situations. These situations are occasions for coaching trainees in "how to say it." Supervisors offer their experience with similar clinical situations as a resource to their trainees. In this way, supervisors are able to be helpful and effective with their trainees.

The kinds of problems that supervisors address by telling how to say it fall into four categories: (a) Because orderly progress is not being made through the course of therapy, the trainee needs to engage in one or more of the "milestone sayings" with which progress in therapy is marked; (b) Cooperation with other institutions and personnel ("the larger system") is breaking down and needs to be restored; (c) Because the therapist is encouraged to do something that might be unseemly, things need to be put delicately; and (d) Therapeutic techniques are not being used optimally. Each of these categories is exemplified here.

Milestone Sayings

A milestone saying is an abbreviated saying that points to a commonly held understanding of the trajectory of therapy. Experienced therapists and supervisors seem to have a sense of the trajectory of therapy that results in a kind of "recipe knowledge" about how to proceed at certain junctures. The milestone saying is voiced in an indexical manner in which only key terms of a saying are voiced to show what is being suggested. In the following example, a milestone saying is suggested (in Line 5) for a case that entails contemplated suicide:

```
Exemplar 5:
1      A:        and she said are you trying to kill yourself? (.2) and he
2                sa:id no I'm just not hungry
3      S:        Severely depressed
4      A:        um huh
5      S:        What would be the worst (.2) have you asked that one?
6      A:        Ut huh
```

We consider this is a case of suggestion because we believe if the trainee had not already asked this question ("What would be the worst. . ."), the supervisor's question would have counted as a request to ask it. That this question has the status of a milestone saying is indicated by the abbreviated/indexical way it is voiced; the supervisor doesn't even need to say the entire saying in order for the trainee to know what he is suggesting. The status as a milestone also is shown in the way it is treated as a routine thing to say under the circumstances ("have you asked *that one?*").

Sometimes the occasion for milestone sayings results from the trainee being stuck or misunderstanding the nature of a case. Supervisors have a sense of the order in which cases unfold, and milestone sayings are sometimes introduced by suggesting the trainee back up to an earlier stage:

Exemplar 6:
```
1    S:    This feels like a case where you really need to back up
2          about 100 steps (.) and talk about (.) assumptions in the
3          marriage (.) and what did you think would happen in the
4          marriage (.) and how have you been pleased about the
5          marriage-and how have you been disappointed=
6    F:    Um huh
7    A:    [Um huh
8    S:    [and        as you look at other peoples' marriages what do
9          you see-is there a thread that kindof-makes marriages go
10         sour?
11   A:    Um huh
12   S:    feels like this one has    [gone sour
13   A:                               [Um huh
14   S:    what about your marriage has has kinda soured
```

We notice that the supervisor in this instance is not content to advise merely "to back up about 100 steps and talk about assumptions in the marriage." Because the trainee failed to do this initially, it may well be something the trainee doesn't know how to do. Accordingly, the supervisor gives several of the milestone sayings by which it can be determined if these spouses have consensus on expectations for their marriage. Starting in Line 3, the supervisor projects the voice of the trainee saying in a coming session "what did you think would happen in the marriage" and "how have you been pleased about the marriage" and "how have you been disappointed." The trainee is thereby being taught how to negotiate a particular, common point in marital therapy with couples.

Larger System Relations

One of the aspects of professional development that therapists in training evidently have difficulty with lies in establishing and maintaining cooperation with personnel of other agencies, such as Child Protective Services (CPS). We looked at such a case—in which the supervisor told the trainee what to say to the CPS supervisor to obtain cooperation from a CPS worker—earlier. Another instance follows. It involves interacting with another therapist:

Exemplar 7:
```
1    S:    I think >that would< be something to work out-to make
2          real clear with ((the other))? is that your you know, I can
3          take this case (.) but only on a hour a week basis? and I
4          (?) will not be, I'll expect you to handle any
5          emergencies? (.2) and, through the psychiatrist (?)
6          treatment? (.2) That that might be possible.
7    A:    That's a good idea.
```

By saying what the supervisor suggests in Lines 2–5, the trainee will be able to contract clearly with the outside therapist. The supervisor treats this as something the trainee does not presently know how to do, an assumption that appears well founded (by the trainee's expressing appreciation in Line 7).

Exemplar 8:
```
1    S:    I think what you >might want to do< is talk through (.)
2          whether you can help them with another referral or what
3          (.2) um we don't really have anybody in in the clinic except
4          ((therapist's name)) who could handle it and ((another
5          therapist's name)) we don't have? anybody that
6          really knows sex therapy...
7    T:    ((Therapist's name)) maybe
8    S:    Okay I would do an assessment on the phone (.) >I
9          don't know< (.) I would follow up with a letter
10   T:    un huh
11   S:    >depending on your phone conversation< and I would (.) I
12         would tend toward saying if you know needs or help or
13         something like that (.) call rather than try and set them
14         up with somebody else.
15   T:    Um huh, kay
16   S:    If they've been (covered) that's one thing (.) but they
17         haven't
18   T:    Allright hhhhh
19   S:    Are you ok with that?
20   T:    Um huh?
```

As in the preceding example, how-to-say-its in this case are for the purpose of finessing a relationship with a representative of another agency. What seems to be required is to ensure that a client can be assisted in an emergency, but to avoid taking on responsibility for a kind of therapy that is beyond the clinic's area of expertise. In part, the how-to-say-its (Lines 5 and 6) give an explanation for not taking on the case of sex therapy. Because turning down a referral could expose the client during an emergency, a way is needed to cover that eventuality. The how-to-say-its given in Lines 12–14 express how to forge the temporary relationship with the clinician who has unsuccessfully sought to refer.

Putting it Delicately

It is very common, given the problems addressed in marriage and family therapy clinics, for issues to arise that call for extreme delicacy in how to speak. The majority of how to say it cases pertain to such delicacies. Acting much like protocol officers, supervisors suggested how to say it in response to such problems as: how to turn down a candidate for therapy; how to urge some family members into therapy and others out; how to get a family to see that merely playing was worth $100 per hour; how to obtain legal advice while maintaining confidentiality; how to mention possible client improprieties (e.g., uncontrolled anger), crimes (e.g., child abuse), or disabilities (e.g., sexual dysfunctions); and how to terminate therapy. These are good candidates for how-to-say-its because they are matters difficult for trainees to do appropriately, which trainees may not yet have encountered, and for which the consequences of error would be severe.

The following instance of necessary delicacy is about possible child abuse:

Exemplar 9:
```
1    S:    U:m (.2) I think in a case like this you should be pretty
2          straight forward and sa:y-you know (.) apparently there
3          have been some problems? and (.2) how do you deal with
4          discipline? and your already been reported? and (.2) I
5          think that-you know the more you can-look in here with
6          parenting stuff, (.2) especially appropriate consequenting
7          so it doesn't hurt the kids (.2) a little bit better off
8          you're gonna be
9    A:    okay
10   S:    And how have you been consequent, you know >but I
11         wouldn't use that word<. How ha:ve you been um (.)
12         correcting ((Child client's name)) in the pa:st. You know,
13         what works, what didn't work (.2) Uh what happened you
14         know all parents get mad at their kids-What would ha'
15         how would you handle it when you got mad (.1) at your
16         kid. What co- well how can you do it differently. And
17         just be real concrete like that (.) around discipline. I
18         would try tha:t.
19   A:    okay, okay
```

Without cataloguing all the how-to-say-its in this instance, we do want to point out that the supervisor tells how to say it in numerous ways, thereby preserving some freedom of choice for the trainee. Moreover, the supervisor says what not to say (i.e., the technical jargon term *consequenting*), and explains the point of all these sayings, namely, to be very concrete (or explicit) about the issue. It is an especially thorough job of educating the trainee.

Ordinarily, supervisors addressed issues requiring delicacy by saying what to say. Following is one of the very few "don't say it like this" cases. It pertains to the problem of how to terminate therapy with an uncooperative or unreliable client:

Exemplar 10:
```
1   S:  OK so that's just a real(.) and you (.) I get (.) I haven't
2       seen any of your letters (.) yes I have. Sometimes people
3       when they write a let- the danger would be if it (.) not
4       do anything blaming.
5   T:  Right...
6   S:  You know what being (blaming) you know what
7       (blaming) I don't think you would (.) >Some people when
8       they get to writing these letters they say things like<
9       well your re:ady, you know its obvious you weren't ready
10      and  ⎡and you yea yea know
11  T:       ⎣uh huh
12  S:  know people don't need (.) that. Be evaluated just cause
13      they call up to get a appointment for therapy
```

What the supervisor does is to urge the trainee not to say certain things that are common faults of such letters. He anticipates a problem and uses telling how (not) to say it as a way of averting the problem.

Optimizing Therapeutic Techniques and Strategies

The last classification of uses for how-to-say-its is perhaps the most tied to this particular kind of supervision. It concerns the ways supervisors get trainees to make full and appropriate use of the therapeutic techniques and strategies that are being taught. Evidently, trainees are thought by supervisors to do an incomplete job with some therapeutic activities. Put differently, supervisors sometimes advise "mining" therapy techniques for all they are worth. For instance, in the following case, the supervisor encourages the trainee to make fuller use of a metaphor, declaring independence, she has used with a couple:

Exemplar 11:
```
1   S:  so you don't have maybe some follow up work with that
2       Declaration of Independence.
```

```
 3   W:   But the last thing I asked them to do in this case, is to
 4        read their declaration of independence at least every
 5        other day, just to to keep abreast of, of what they,
 6        they declare to do.
 7   S:   Uh huh
 8   W:   So, they-that's what their task was.
 9   S:   Now they're gonna have to create a government for
10        themselves, how it operates financially what its
11        geographical location is, how it relates with other
12        independent countries.
13   W:   And, and I think that's another issue like you were talking
14        about the financial stuff cause she writes, she has
15        control of all his money.
16   S:   Well see once you declare independence the uh.
17   W:   you have to have your own money.
18   S:   you have to create your own financial structure as well
19        as, uh you know. .
20   W:   And I think that's another place we need to go, and the
21        transportation and um. .
22   S:   You have to have your own Army and Navy and uh, highway
23        systems, you know, yea.
24   W:   Haaaaaaaaaaaaaaaaaaa
25   S:   I just think you can use the metaphor more.
26   W:   Yea. It's a good one, boy they went for it they loved it,
27        they loved it.
```

This series of how-to-say-its occurred immediately after the supervisor's more abstract suggestion, "follow-up work with that Declaration of Independence," does not receive the kind of uptake the supervisor sought. By follow-up work the supervisor meant work to explore more kinds of agreements the family needs to work out based upon their declaration. The how-to-say-its represent several of the elements of declarations of independence this family should be urged to explore.

As the preceding instance showed, one kind of therapeutic language toward which these supervisors are sensitive is the use of metaphors to describe, understand and explore problems (a topic explored extensively by Chenail & Fortugno, Chapter 3, this volume). Several of the suggestion cases we examined concerned how trainees could delve more fully into how clients' metaphors could be modified. For example:

```
Exemplar 12:
01   S:   Okay, Next time. . . you see her I have a question I want you
02        to ask her
```

```
03    A:    Okay
04    S:    Just work it in somewhere. Doesn't have to be at the
05          beginning, maybe it should be. Doesn't have to be at the
06          end, maybe it could be. I'd like you to ask her if she
07          didn't have this weight as an issue, what would make you
09          cry?
10    A:    Okay.
11    S:    Would you do that? But you know what, what that's
12          for?. . . Within the context of what we've talked about then
13          weight would function as a metaphor for a lot of the
14          problems that she sees or she feels.
15    A:    Metaphor
16    S:    and getting her to talk about something else would be
17          working toward establishing a different metaphor for those
18          things.
19    A:    Umkay.
```

The final instance exemplifies how a trainee is taught to use a new kind of questioning technique. A series of how-to-say-its model how it is to be done:

Exemplar 13:
```
1     S:    And she kindof opened a door there for you (.2) Uh (.) that
2           that would be nice to use (.2) I know you're just
3           information gathering >but some of this-you know you
4           can< (.2)
4     A:    yah=
5     S:    =un, get useful information in lots of different wa:ys. Uh,
6           she likes to (.) probably (.) most people like to tell you
7           behavioral information. This person does >this and this
8           and this< (.2) Uh, and that's a good way of getting
9           information.
10    A:    Uhhuh
11    S:    But another way of getting information (.1) you know in
12          the systemic sense that we talk abo:ut-is their reactions
13          to this person (.2) Or >how they-or how they< feel they've
14          influenced (.) positively or negatively another person.
15    A:    uhhuh
16    S:    And uh (.) and then feed that back into the presenting
17          problem of how she feels about herself-or her weight . . .
```

CONCLUSION AND IMPLICATIONS

Supervising therapists encompasses more than teaching them how to follow abstract models of therapy. Sometimes, it also includes coaching about what to say. Telling how to say it is a common way supervisors make or augment suggestions to trainees in family therapy supervision. Supervisors use this technique, when situations are problematic or novel to trainees, in order to model or rehearse the language to use in therapy. By using how-to-say-its, supervisors specify precise ways to do things while at the same time maintaining a sensitivity to the intricate and unpredictable nature of clinical interaction. The identifying characteristic of telling how to say it is the change of footing, that is, a shift from a supervisor talking with a trainee to a therapist talking with a client.

This chapter explored four circumstances under which this technique is used in family therapy supervision:

1. When supervisors sense something out of order about the trajectory or course of therapy, they may offer milestone sayings, which are indexical expressions that point to common clinical activities which have not, but should occur in the case in question.
2. Larger system relations comprise difficulties trainees have encountered in establishing and maintaining cooperative relations with other therapists, agencies or referral sources.
3. When saying something in a clumsy fashion is likely and this would have severe consequences, supervisors script how to put it delicately.
4. Sometimes trainees need to make fuller use of certain therapeutic activities. Accordingly, supervisors suggest ways of using language that will optimize therapeutic techniques and strategies.

In the remainder of this chapter, we address some of the implications we discern of using how-to-say-its in clinical supervision. First, how-to-say-its seem to be fashioned to help trainees move beyond especially difficult points in therapy. Supervisors offer how-to-say-its when they detect that trainees are somehow at a loss about what to do, or when what trainees plan might have unforeseen negative consequences. These supervisors do not appear to be being too particular about what should happen. They merely use greater specificity as a means of showing how a difficult thing can be done. A process of "zeroing in" on a good way to do things can be observed. Often, trainees' statements about what to do in a coming session are simply endorsed. In other cases, suggestions are made using general action specifications (such as "Bring the husband into therapy"). There being no indication on the part of the trainee that a general suggestion is insufficient, supervisors do not proceed to say tell to say it. When some trouble does become apparent, supervisors model or rehearse ways to say something, and they often offer several alternatives. In some cases, they even give feedback on trainees' practice attempts at how to say it, and give additional options. The common denominator of the uses for how-to-say-its is something amiss in trainees' understanding of how to proceed on a case.

Second, the opportunity to rehearse how to say it arises in other clinical situations than videotape supervision of therapists in training. Therefore, whatever payoff there may be from using this technique might be earned in other talk as well.

Third, this analysis may provide some support for a model of how expertise develops. Based on observations of decision making in complex situations such as those faced by chess players, air traffic controllers and nurses, this model posits that expertise is developed as the professional moves from an awareness of nonsituational rules of action to an ability to readily identify relevant contexts (Thomas, 1993). The expert has encountered enough situations that he or she decides on a course of action based on experience, rather than on rules and models for action. In contrast, the novice bases decisions on abstract rules derived from recognized authorities with little reference to the specifics of a given situation. One with a midrange acquisition of skill, a competent professional, bases decisions and goals on salient aspects of a situation which are illuminated by a particular model (e.g., a model of therapy). The method of telling how to say it described in this chapter reflects at least the competent level of skill acquisition on the part of trainees. Telling how to say it helps trainees to know what to pay attention to and how to do something that is appropriate to that context. In delicate situations or in relationships with other professionals, abstract rules are not sufficient. Supervisors go beyond such rules to show how to avoid common mishandlings of routine problems. Decisions about whether to be persistent with a therapeutic strategy are completely reliant on accurately interpreting the situation.

Fourth, it should be noticed that how-to-say-its were almost never marked by their recipients as problematic or as requiring clarification. One would expect such indications of trouble if telling how to say it were an example of obfuscation that can confuse trainees (Tyler & Tyler, 1985). In our judgment (and considering that one of the authors is not a clinician), these masterful supervisors are being anything but difficult to understand. Part of their masterfulness, we would argue, lies in their reading of problems to gauge when clarity and explicitness is called for and when trainees can be relied upon to act accountably or appropriately with less explicit direction. By telling how to say it, supervisors focus the benefits of their experience on the learning needs of trainees. The point does not appear to be to flaunt supervisors' therapeutic acumen, their status, or their facility with language.

Fifth, to perform how-to-say-its successfully may require considerable clinical experience and also current experience. Because a predominant method for giving suggestions is to adopt the perspective of the therapist talking with a client, it is imperative that the supervisor have considerable experience with a variety of situations. This is what would allow the supervisor to recognize the kinds of problems that recur, the situations that might require more delicacy than usual, etc. Professional standards often do require supervisors to possess considerable clinical experience. Such is the case, for example, of marriage and family therapy supervisors (American Association for Marriage and Family Therapy, 1993), who are also required to be involved continually in clinical practice (Commission on Accreditation for Marriage and Family Therapy Education, 1993). Relatedly, graduates of doctoral training programs who intend to teach in master's programs, need support for their acquisition of clinical experience. Supervisors should maintain a diverse clinical practice for their own professional development, and faculty development policies should recognize and support this aspect of professional development.

Finally, as we see it, how-to-say-its develop the leading edge of trainees' abilities because they tell how to negotiate especially difficult performances or to make full and appropriate use of clinical methods. Perhaps that supervision is best which focuses attention on the leading edge of the trainees' abilities and helps them negotiate new, difficult domains. Good and effective supervision may compel trainees to "push the envelope" of their professional development. The earmark of well trained professionals, and this applies to all professionals whose stock in trade is their use of language, is their knowledge of how to say it.

REFERENCES

American Association for Marriage and Family Therapy. (1993). *Approved supervisor designation: Standards and responsibilities.* Washington, DC: Author.

Austin, J. L. (1975). *How to do things with words.* Cambridge: Harvard University Press.

Berger, M., & Dammann, C. (1982). Live supervision as context, treatment, and training. *Family Process, 21,* 337–344.

Breunlin, D. C., Karrer, B. M., McGuire, D. E., Cimmarusti, R. (1988). Cybernetics of videotape supervision. In H. A. Liddle, D. S. Breunlin, & R. C. Schwartz (Eds.), *Handbook of family therapy training and supervision* (pp. 194–207). New York: Guilford.

Breunlin, D. C., Liddle, H. A., & Schwartz, R. C. (1988). Concurrent training of supervisors and therapists. In H. A. Liddle, D. S. Breunlin, & R. C. Schwartz (Eds.), *Handbook of family therapy training and supervision* (pp. 207–224). New York: Guilford.

Commission on Accreditation for Marriage and Family Therapy Education. (1993). *Manual on accreditation.* Washington, DC: Author.

Fine, J., & Fennell, D. (1985). Supervising the supervisor-of-supervision: A supervision-of-supervision techniques of hierarchical blurring? *Journal of Strategic and Systemic Therapies, 4,* 55–59.

Haley, J. (1976). *Problem solving therapy.* San Francisco: Jossey-Bass.

Houtkoop-Steenstra, H. (1987). *Establishing agreement: An analysis of proposal-acceptance sequences.* Unpublished doctoral dissertation, University of Amsterdam.

Levinson, S. C. (1983). *Pragmatics.* Cambridge: Cambridge University Press.

Liddle, H. A., & Schwartz, R. (1983). Live supervision/consultation: Conceptual and pragmatic guidelines for family therapy training. *Family Process, 22,* 477–490.

Mazza, J. (1988). Training strategic therapists: The use of indirect techniques. In H. A. Liddle, D. S. Breunlin, & R. C. Schwartz (Eds.), *Handbook of family therapy training and supervision* (pp. 93–109). New York: Guilford.

Montalvo, B. (1973). Aspects of live supervision. *Family Process, 12,* 343–359.

Nichols, W. C. (1988). An integrative psychodynamic and systems approach. In H. A. Liddle, D. S.

Breunlin, & R. C. Schwartz (Eds.), *Handbook of family therapy training and supervision* (pp. 110–127). New York: Guilford.

Roberts, J. (1981). The development of a team approach in live supervision. *Journal of Strategic and Systemic Therapy, 1,* 24–35.

Schwartz, R. C. (1988). The trainer-trainee relationship in family therapy training. In H. A. Liddle, D. C. Breunlin, & R. C. Schwartz (Eds.), *Handbook of family therapy training and supervision* (pp. 172–182). New York: Guilford.

Schwartz, R. C., Liddle, H. A., & Breunlin, D. C. (1988). Muddles in live supervision. In H. A. Liddle, D. C. Breunlin, & R. C. Schwartz (Eds.), *Handbook of family therapy training and supervision* (pp. 183–194). New York: Guilford.

Thomas, F. (1993, October). *Solution-focused supervision.* Paper presented at the annual conference of the American Association for Marriage and Family Therapy, Dallas, TX.

Tucker, B., Hart, G., & Liddle, H. (1976). Supervision in family therapy: A developmental perspective. *Journal of Marriage and Family Counseling, 2,* 269–276.

Tyler, A. G., & Tyler, S. G. (1985). The sorcerer's apprentice: The discourse of training in family therapy. *Cultural Anthropologist, 1*(2), 238–256.

Wright, L. (1986). An analysis of live supervision "phone-ins" in family therapy. *Journal of Marriage and Family Therapy, 12,* 187–190.

11 THE DISCOURSE OF MEDICAL CARE

7 Precepting Conversations in a General Medicine Clinic

Anita M. Pomerantz
Temple University

Jack Ende, M.D.
University of Pennsylvania Medical Center

Frederick Erickson
University of Pennsylvania

THE RESEARCH PROBLEM

Medical education in the United States has made effective use of interaction with patients only since the turn of the century. Prior to that, students were taught almost entirely by lecture (Ludmerer, 1983). What little exposure to patients students received came as amphitheater demonstrations. They learned about patients, not from and with patients.

Around the turn of the century, clinical training in medicine began to change. Spurred by several prominent medical educators, but most notably by Osler, clinical training moved into the hospital and the dispensary, forerunner of today's outpatient clinic. In his frequently quoted statement, "The student must see, and hear, and feel for himself the hue of the complexion, the feel of the skin, the luster or languor of the eye, the throbbing of the pulse and the palpitations of the heart. . . Where can these be learned but at the bedside of the sick?" (p. 50) Osler (1903) conveyed his commitment to learning through realistic experiences. The clerkship that he installed at Johns Hopkins in 1896 became the model that would be emulated throughout the country. To this day, it serves as a benchmark for clinical medical training even as medical training, like medical care, shifts from the hospital to the outpatient setting.

Osler's model has endured for good reason. The rationale of clinical training is to encourage house officers to apply knowledge in realistic settings. Applied knowledge, or judgment, must fit the patient and his or her situation—the real world of practice. This is something that must be discovered in the field. But although experience in the field is essential in developing medical reasoning and clinical diagnosis skills, it is not sufficient. There are two reasons why experience alone is insufficient for medical training. First, experience alone, unaided by instruction, will not guarantee learning, at least not the lessons that should be learned. And second, learning in medicine entails real situations, some of which involve life and limb. Schon (1988) spoke of teachers in the professions creating a "virtual world," like the architect's sketch pad, where buildings can be erected and then torn down, all without harm. How much like a stretch pad is the coronary care unit or the inner-city clinic? There is little that is virtual about these worlds.

These concerns, of course, provide an agenda for teachers, whether they are attending physicians responsible for patient care on hospital wards or preceptors who are attending physicians in clinics. The teachers must allow trainees to gain firsthand experience with patients, but they also must provide feedback, particularly correction. With correction, teachers influence the lessons that are learned and ensure that patients are well cared for.

The importance of correcting in clinical teaching cannot be overestimated. In a setting such as the teaching clinic, where the student typically "goes first" and carries out his or her own assessment and then presents the case to the preceptor, almost all that the preceptor does can be thought of as guiding, directing, or correcting. This includes when preceptors make comments regarding data collection, formulation, and therapy; when they react to interns' proposed problem-framing and prioritization; and even when they engage in informational discussions, because these discussions serve to redirect interns' assessments.

Not surprisingly, the topic of correcting has attracted considerable attention in the literature of clinical medical education, considered generally under the rubric of *feedback*. In the early 1980s, Ende (1983) began to think seriously about feedback. The standard recommendations for feedback were reviewed and adapted for use in clinical settings. Among these recommendations are that feedback should be objective, specific, and performance-based; that it should be timely and part of every teaching encounter; and that it should be explicit—not harsh, certainly not punitive, but not so vague that it leaves important clinical lessons to chance.

These recommendations and others like them have found their way into books on medical teaching (Foley & Smilansky, 1980; Schwenk & Whitman, 1987) and are discussed frequently in workshops and courses devoted to clinical teaching. Yet there has been little research on what interactive activities constitute giving feedback nor on how preceptors actually perform these activities, let alone the consequences that are achieved. In this chapter, we attempt to address these questions.

THE SETTING

The setting for this study is a primary care outpatient clinic located in a university teaching hospital in a large urban area. There generally are three to four internal medicine interns (first-year residents) and two preceptors in the clinic during the morning session. Precepting occurs in a room designated for that purpose and begins after an intern has completed his or her medical interview and examination of the patient. When an intern enters the teaching room, he or she finds a preceptor with whom to discuss the case. Interns follow a format that is well learned by this stage of medical training. They "present the patient" by reporting the medical history and physical examination. During this presentation, the preceptor may intervene to elicit, clarify, expand, or refocus information about the patient. Then they discuss diagnoses and/or management plans for the patient.

Following this segment of precepting, the preceptor and intern go to the examination room where the preceptor may interview and examine the patient. When completed, the preceptor and intern return to the teaching room. There they briefly discuss any new data that arose during the preceptor's assessment as well as unresolved matters pertaining to the patient's problem. Following this brief second consultation, the intern returns to the patient to work out the details of the management plan.

This structure—where the intern has examined the patient alone, then consults with the preceptor, and finally returns to the patient to discuss the patient's management plan—is shaped by two guiding beliefs. The first is that clinical training serves as an opportunity for interns to gain experience doing what doctors do, including collecting information, synthesizing it, and developing their own assessments. The second set of guiding beliefs is that interns are inexperienced novices in need of training; therefore the diagnosis and treatment plan must meet with the preceptor's approval. Gaining the preceptor's approval is both a pedagogical and legal imperative.

When preceptors agree with interns' assessments, they can be supportive of their authority and judgments. However, when preceptors disagree with interns' assessments, they are in the position of potentially undermining their self-confidence and authority. In these latter situations, preceptors manage the interactions in ways that reveal their multiple concerns. In this chapter, we analyze how preceptors intervene when they perceive interns' assessments and analyses to be off base.

ANALYSIS

In examining how preceptors correct interns, we found a recurrent pattern: Preceptors correct interns in ways that minimize their exposing the interns' errors. Put another way, when preceptors correct interns, their interventions do not necessarily look like corrections, certainly not blatant ones.

In this section, we discuss four interactional strategies that preceptors use when interns either do not answer questions or offer wrong/inappropriate answers or assessments. Preceptors (a) provide opportunities spaces for revisions; (b) ask subsequent questions containing hints; (c) treat answers as reasonable, then re-ask questions; and (d) treat assessments as possible but in need of further consideration.

Provide Opportunity Spaces for Revisions

When interns make proposals or assessments that seem off base to preceptors, the preceptors routinely do not jump in to point out the problems. Rather they provide opportunities for interns to modify their assessments. They provide opportunities by delaying their responses, by offering short moderately positive acknowledgments, and both. These spaces allow the interns to reflect and reconsider their assessments and to qualify or modify them accordingly (Pomerantz, 1984).

Consider the following illustration of how a preceptor provides multiple opportunity spaces for an intern to modify his assessment. The exemplar reproduced here occurs after the intern and preceptor finished discussing the patient's medical problems. The preceptor has just asked the intern whether there are any issues of health maintenance they should attend to. After reviewing the need for various tests, the intern brings up dietary counseling.

```
[From the corpus 8/24/92:24]
1    Intern:   .tch And she probably: an:d (.) I'm sure she needs:
2              (.) dietary counseling
3              (.)
4    Intern:   Least from me:. .hhh About her weight,
```

As the intern makes his assessment (Line 1), the preceptor does not indicate explicit approval or disapproval. After a micropause (Line 3), the intern adds a clarification (Line 4) that reshapes the initial assessment into one involving a lesser investment (dietary counseling done by the primary physician rather than a formal consultation with a dietitian). The first set of moves (preceptor's response plus intern's response) can be summarized as the preceptor's displaying no immediate reaction and the intern backing off somewhat from his original assessment.

Having now modified his assessment (Line 4), the intern is in the position of waiting for the preceptor's evaluation of it. In response, the preceptor delays responding for about half a second (Line 5), and then responds with a short positive acknowledgment (Line 6). There then follows more than 1 second of silence (Line 7). The preceptor breaks the silence with another acknowledgment, although weaker than the prior one (Line 8).

```
[From the corpus 8/24/92:24]
1    Intern:   .tch And she probably: an:d (.) I'm sure she needs:
2              (.) dietary counseling
3              (.)
4    Intern:   Least from me:. .hhh About her weight,
```

```
5                    (0.4)
6    Precep:   s::Sure.
7                    (1.3)
8    Precep:   ihYa:h uh:m.
```

In delaying their responses and giving short, moderately positive acknowledgments, preceptors can avoid making their lack of support explicit, while at the same time conveying that they are not thoroughly supportive of what was just said. If the interns recognize the preceptors' reservations, they may use the opportunities provided to modify their assessments. In the instance examined here, this is exactly what the intern did (Lines 9–10).

```
[From the corpus 8/24/92:24]
 1   Intern:   .tch And she probably: an:d (.) I'm sure she needs:
 2             (.) dietary counseling
 3                    (.)
 4   Intern:   Least from me:. .hhh About her weight,
 5                    (0.4)
 6   Precep:   s::Sure.
 7                    (1.3)
 8   Precep:   ihYa:h uh:m.
 9   Intern:   I don't know that (.) now's the right (.) time
10             necessarily to do[that (    ) .hhhh
11   Precep:                    [No-ah-I I agree with you.
```

Consistent with an understanding that the preceptor did not support his proposal for dietary counseling, the intern formed a question that raised a possible objection to dietary counseling, namely, that the timing was wrong (Lines 9–10). When the intern raised the objection, the preceptor affirmed the position with no delay (Line 11) and formulated his own position as in agreement with the intern's. In this way, he actually gives credit to the intern for a position arrived at interactionally.

This excerpt illustrates several features of how the preceptors' withholding their evaluations provides opportunities for the interns to revise their assessments.

1. In giving no immediate approval or disapproval of an intern's assessment and/or in giving delayed, short, moderately positive acknowledgments, a preceptor may be read to have some reservations about the intern's assessment.
2. In withholding any explicit disapproval, a preceptor provides an opportunity for an intern to alter, modify, or qualify his or her original assessment. If the intern uses the opportunities successfully, the intern will have modified his or her own assessment rather than having been corrected by the preceptor.

3. When the intern modifies his or her own position, the authorship of (and hence credit for) the new position is attributable to the intern.

Ask Subsequent Questions Containing Hints

Through providing opportunity spaces, preceptors allow interns to modify their initial positions so that they, not the preceptors, articulate the correct answers. Using silences and short acknowledgment tokens as their initial responses, preceptors provide the possibility that the interns' assessments will be right without any interactional record of their having been initially wrong.

A second set of techniques works in a similar way. When interns respond to preceptors' elicitations, they look for the preceptors' evaluations of their responses.[1] When preceptors see the responses as off base, they generally withhold their evaluations.[2] Instead they may reformulate questions, with each reformulation providing more cues to the interns (Billig et al., 1988). The subsequent questions provide opportunities for the interns to articulate correct answers without having the interactional record of having been initially off base.

The following instance illustrates a preceptor's use of cued elicitations. The patient was a 53-year-old woman who came in complaining of a feeling that she needed to urinate frequently plus stinging and burning when she did. After hearing about the case, the preceptor apparently considered the possibility that the bladder infection may have been related to menopause.

The first question the preceptor asked about the bladder problem was, "Well how do you put this together."

```
[From the corpus 1/17/91:2]
 1   Precep:   Wha- how do you put this: together
 2             (0.5)
 3   Intern:   .hhhh I It sou It sounds to me that she may have
 4             another uhhh uhhh y'know cystitis uhh She hasn't
 5             been having fevers or chills at home 'r any other
 6             .hh systemic symptoms that would uh suggest that
 7             she has upper (0.5) uhh urinary infection. ( ) I
 8             think this most likely Uh y'know uh a cystitis
 9             especially with uh uh yknow with uh with uh blood
10             on dip an' uh and micro
11   Precep:   Mm [hm
```

---

[1]Mehan (1979) revealed how the sequential organization of lesson discourse revolves around a three-part unit: teacher elicits, student responds, teacher evaluates.

[2]This is similar to interaction in classrooms. Griffin and Humphrey (1978) examined classroom lesson sequences. They found that although positive evaluations were overtly uttered, negative evaluations were implicitly accomplished.

12	Intern:	[Uh (.) She doesn't have uh (.) uh any other
13		symptoms significant for stones for instance or uh:
14		uh uh I suppose a tumor is uh .hh uh possi
15		possibility but she's a relatively young woman and
16		uh I've uh (1.0) Y'know I think that (an apparent)
17		trial of antibiotics an' to see whether this clears
18		up uh would be more appropriate than cystoscopy er
19		er any further

The preceptor hears out a rather lengthy answer from the intern as to how he "puts this together." In his answer, he addresses why cystitis is the most likely cause of the patient's symptoms but not why she might be having it now in her life. Through a series of questions and comments, he attempts to lead the intern to think about that relationship (see Lines 1, 8, 9, 11, 16, and 19.)

[From the corpus 1/17/91:3]

1	Precep:	...how many episodes has she had all together.
2		(0.5)
3	Intern:	Uh: it looks like uh: this episode last year: in
4		the Emergency Roo[m
5	Precep:	[Right
6	Intern:	And then uh this one which is uh y'know been over
7		(.) the past couple weeks
8	Precep:	So just two:. -in her life
		[Some text omitted]
9	Precep:	And she's fi:fty::: (.) th[ree
10	Intern:	[fifty three
11	Precep:	Uhhh Why is she beginning to get bladder
12		infections (.) now do you suppose
13		(0.5)
14	Intern:	.hhhhhh Uh: that's a good question
15		(0.8)
16	Precep:	Well(ar) are there risk factors that
		[Some text omitted]
17		(0.8)
18	Intern:	U[hh
19	Precep:	[Is she menopausal? intrameno [pausal?
20	Intern:	[She She is yeah

Through a series of questions ("How many episodes has she had all together," "So just two in her life," "And she's 53," "Why is she beginning to get bladder infections now do you suppose?" "Well are there risk factors?"), the preceptor provides clues for the intern to see the patient's cystitis as possibly related to the onset of her menopause. As the intern was not able to use the hints, the preceptor provides the answer he was seeking, although in a question, "Is she menopausal?".

Having now suggested a possible relationship between cystitis and menopause, the preceptor attempts to solicit from the intern the basis of the relationship (Lines 26–28). In response, the intern hesitates and indicates uncertainty (Lines 30–31). The preceptor asks a subsequent question, one that gives hints as to the correct answer (Line 32). He supplies the location and asks the intern to name the change. This hint is sufficient; the intern offers an acceptable answer to the preceptor's latest question (Line 33).

[From the corpus 1/17/91:3]

19	Precep:	[Is she menopausal? intrameno[pausal?
20	Intern:	[She She *is* yeah
21		(.)
22	Precep:	When did she: actually stop having periods
24	Intern:	Uh:: I think she mentioned two years if I recall.
25		Uh
26	Precep:	So what might (.) be happening now in connection
27		with her menopause that might change her (0.8)
28		[susceptibility to
29	Intern:	[((coughs))
30		(0.8)
31	Intern:	Uhh (1.5) uh (0.8) (I'm) really not sure
32	Precep:	What happens to the vaginal and urethral epithelia
33	Intern:	There's some atrophy
34	Precep:	Right yeah.
35	Intern:	post menopausal which I'm not sure if that would
36		predispose us to
37	Precep:	((head nods)) Well I think it can

In this sequence, cued elicitations allowed the intern to produce a correct answer. But during the course of the sequence, the preceptor and intern discovered that the intern was not knowledgeable about the topic. The sequence continued with the intern soliciting and the preceptor giving more information about the relationship between cystitis and menopause.

Treat Answers as Reasonable, Then Re-Ask Questions

Thus far we have discussed two strategies preceptors use when dealing with interns' off-base responses. They use pauses and acknowledgment tokens that serve as opportunity spaces and they ask questions containing hints; these strategies allow interns to arrive at authoring correct answers. Another way preceptors treat off base or unexpected answers is to give them a good hearing. They may treat the interns' assessments not simply as wrong but in terms of the question, "How is this a reasonable answer?". That is, they work at trying to figure out the questions to which the interns' unexpected answers would have been right.

An example of giving a good hearing occurs in a precepting session in which the preceptor is attempting to have the intern synthesize the information about the patient that she (the intern) just presented. Just prior to the start of this fragment, the preceptor asked the intern what her plan was. After several hesitating responses, he prompts her with a more directed question (Line 1).

[From the corpus 5/31/90:8]
```
 1   Precep:   What are his problems in order of priority. Number
 2             one problem.
 3                     (2.5)
 4   Intern:   I 's think at this point hip.
 5   Precep:   Hip.
 6                     (.)
 7   Precep:   [For (him) For him [that's the number one problem.
 8   Intern:   [For him.           [for him.
 9   Precep:   For you what's his number one problem.
10   Intern:   For me his number one problem: i:s:::: (3.5)
11             probably his pressure
12   Precep:   Okay      [good stroke intervention is pri[mary we=
13   Intern:             You [know                       [right
14   Precep:   =don't need him [to stroke out and we don't need a=
15   Intern:                   [right.
16   Precep:   =heart attack.=
17   Intern:   =Right.
18   Precep:   So his problem is the hip (.) your problem is th:e
19             blood pressures.
20   Intern:   [Uh well he's
21   Precep:   [They're very different problems but we have to
22             take care of both of 'em.
23   Intern:   An' I he's a pretty (.) you know he's with it I
24             mean he he's he also I think is recognizes that he
25             needs to take care of his pressure.
26   Precep:   Okay 'h so: let's let's talk about the number one
27             medical problem first. . . .
```

In reviewing this whole segment of interaction, it is evident that the preceptor views the patient's high blood pressure, and not the patient's hip, as the main problem. Our evidence for this assertion is that he was unenthusiastic in his response when the intern named hip, that he re-asked the question, and that he was enthusiastic in his response when she named pressure. Moreover, after acknowledging the importance of both problems, he elects to talk about the blood pressure problem first.

In response to the preceptor's asking for the intern's prioritization (Lines 1–2), the intern delays answering for 2.5 seconds and then tentatively names the hip. The preceptor must now deal with having received the wrong answer. As has been true in the previous examples, the preceptor does not openly disagree with her assessment. Instead he acknowledges the answer through a rather flat repetition (Line 5). After a very brief gap (Line 6), both intern and preceptor simultaneously say, "For him." Our interest is in analyzing the reasoning that enabled the preceptor to say "for him."

Faced with a wrong answer ("the hip"), the preceptor apparently considered how it could have been a right answer. Apparently he reviewed his question to see if there was a way to interpret it such that "the hip" would be right. Indeed, he did locate such an interpretation (Line 7). In adding "For him," he respecified his question; she now had answered correctly what the main problem for the patient was. Thus, the preceptor located an alternative interpretation of his question, an interpretation that made the intern's answer right.

In giving good hearings to interns, preceptors treat the interns as more, rather than less, competent. With bad hearings, interns' unexpected answers would be seen as wrong and the interns could be seen as unknowledgable. With good hearings, their answers would be seen as products of misunderstandings and thus have their competency preserved.

Treat Assessments as Possible But in Need of Further Consideration

Almost by definition, the basic message conveyed when correcting another is that what the other said or did is wrong. In fact, it would seem that if one chooses to correct another, casting the other as wrong is unavoidable. This is not quite the case. Speakers have ways of packaging their corrections that do not cast the others as wrong. Jefferson (1986) described one such technique, called *colligation,* where speakers offer their correction as another item on a list. Instead of correcting in a "Not *X* but *Y*" form, they may offer their alternative as another possibility ("*X* and *Y*" or "*X* or *Y*"). In this way, the item being corrected remains a possibility, at least in form, even though an alternative has been put on the floor.

Similarly, preceptors often correct in ways that treat the interns' proposals as at least possible rather than impossible or totally improbable. The following example illustrates this treatment. The patient in this case returned to the clinic for a follow-up visit. A week before this visit, the patient went to the clinic with symptoms of congestion, coughing, postnasal drip, and sore throat. In addition, she complained about drenching night sweats. During that visit, the intern and the attending (a different one from the current one) decided on an antibiotic and a decongestant in combination to treat the sinus symptoms, hoping that the night sweats would be cured in the process.

During this follow-up visit, the patient reported that she still was experiencing night sweats. In discussing the case with the preceptor, the intern several times mentioned the hope that the medications for sinusitis would have eliminated them. The preceptor clearly takes issue with this proposal, yet in taking issue, he makes efforts to attribute some credibility to it (Lines 7–8, 10–14).

```
[From the corpus 2/16/93-II:31]
1     Intern:    Well I I told her initially: last week that ah::
2                maybe (0.2) you know (0.2) by treating her:: sinus
3                symptoms if it was a:ll: 'cause of (0.2) from that
4                infection .hhhh ahm .p and then (0.4) see how her
5                [night sweat] symptoms went with that. . .
                 [omitted text]. . .
7     Precep:    .t.hhh I think I would be cautious about
8                attributing night sweats to:: (.) chronic sinusitis
9     Intern:    Ok[ay,
10    Precep:      [whi:le (1.3) I'm sure we c'n find cases where
11               that (.) has occurred but I'm just not aware that
12               that's a .hhhh  ih-eh just not automatically write
13               it off as sort of that's the explanation without
14               .hhh thinking more about it.
```

In addressing the intern's assumption that night sweats could be caused by chronic sinusitis, the preceptor does not say it is wrong or even improbable. Rather he cautions her in a modulated form about the assumption (Lines 7–8).[3] The preceptor continues with an acknowledgment of the possibility that such cases may have occurred (Lines 10–11) and reiterates the need to think more about it (Lines 12–14). In acknowledging the possibility, he again treats the intern's assumption as not totally impossible or unreasonable. In the end, then, he communicates his objection to her assumption without telling her in so many words that her assumption is wrong. In fact, he allows that her assumption may be right in some cases but that she needs to think more about it.

DISCUSSION

We found that when preceptors correct, they generally do so in ways in that minimize exposing the wrong answers: They provide opportunities for interns to self-correct, they give hints to assist interns in arriving at appropriate assessments, and

---

[3]Schegloff et al. (1977) proposed that corrections of others are frequently done in modulated form. They suggested that one way of modulating a correction is by including uncertainty markers, for example, "I think." In the instance under discussion (Lines 7–8), the preceptor not only includes "I think" but further mitigates the correction: although he actually is recommending what the intern should do, he forms the statement up as something he would do.

they treat wrong answers as possible and reasonable. In this section, we address two questions: "Why do preceptors avoid exposing interns' errors?", and "what are the consequences for patient care, intern training, and medical accountability?"

Explanations of Preceptors' Correcting Practices

There are different ways of understanding why preceptors correct in such "soft" ways. Here we offer two explanations, one from a conversation analytic perspective and the other from an ideological perspective. Both offer explanations in terms of aspects of our culture.

Much of what we found regarding mitigated corrections comes as no surprise to conversation analysts. In a seminal paper, Schegloff, Jefferson, and Sacks (1977) analyzed the organization of repair in conversation. They showed how interactants often interactionally collaborate to have the speakers of errors correct themselves. Schegloff et al. showed that when corrections are initiated by interactants who are other than those who made the errors, they provide opportunities for the ones making the errors to repair their own errors.

Jefferson (1987) analyzed how interactants embed their corrections in topical talk and thus correct without it looking like they are correcting. She commented that embedded corrections are "a way of doing correction-and-only-correction; of keeping such issues as incompetence and/or impropriety off the conversational surface. In effect, the embedded form provides the opportunity to correct with discretion" (p. 100).

Several researchers have attempted to identify circumstances that would account for when interactants openly and explicitly correct versus when they soften their corrections and allow others to correct themselves. Schegloff et al. proposed that interactants correct others when they assess them as not yet able to self-correct. Similarly, Zahn (1984) argued that when participants assess coparticipants who made errors as not knowing that they are in error, they are likely to correct them. Finally, Norrick (1991) demonstrated that native speakers, parents, and teachers at least some of the time directly and openly correct nonnative speakers, children, and students respectively. He argued that when parties are of equal status and background knowledge, they may perceive corrections as threats to their competency. If, on the other hand, they see an asymmetry between them with respect to familiarity with the topic or the language in use, the threat to competency diminishes or disappears. He suggested that if they see corrections as "friendly help," there will be less threat.

Together, these studies indicate that interactants see correcting others as a potential threat to a sense of competency of those they correct. When viewed as a threatening activity, participants mitigate and embed their corrections and allow coparticipants to correct themselves. When interactants see others as legitimately not knowing the correct versions, they treat correcting as less threatening and tend to correct in unmodulated forms.

In the corpus examined, we found only modulated corrections. We suggest that this way of correcting may be related to a common concern of preceptors of not damaging the interns' sense of competency. During the focus group discussion, preceptors reported that they were concerned with increasing the interns' self-confidence, with providing support and encouragement, and in avoiding humiliating them.

The practices of gently correcting, especially as they may be tied to a concern with protecting the other's face, should be viewed in a cultural context. In contrast to the pattern of modulated corrections that we observed in the clinic, Goodwin (1983) found that urban African American children, ages 4–14, used aggravated corrections, that is, they used formats that displayed, even highlighted, opposition. She discussed how aggravated corrections may be in keeping with the children's activity of contest: They engaged in challenge followed by counter-challenge. Her study suggests that appropriate ways of correcting vary by activity and subculture.

An ideological perspective provides a different, although complementary, answer to the question of why preceptors correct in mitigated ways. Billig et al. (1988) pointed out that people in modern society typically do not live with a unitary and consistent belief system that provides ready-made solutions to the variety of situations in which they find themselves. Rather they (we) live with belief systems that contain contrary themes, where one theme stands in opposition to other themes, and where the satisfaction of one theme often means that others will not be satisfied. Billig et al. analyzed ideological dilemmas in five contexts, two of which are relevant for our analysis: teaching and being an expert.

According to Billig et al., educators in the progressive tradition articulate the value of "learning by doing" or "discovery learning." The philosophy encourages educators to allow pupils to actively try things for themselves and learn from their own experiences. Yet these same educators also recognize that there is a pre-established body of knowledge, thought, and skills that should be taught. They value both discovery learning and transmission-oriented education. The dilemma posed by these contrary themes is: How can educators get novices to discover for themselves precisely what the professionals hold should be discovered? How can they ensure that students "discover" what they are meant to?

Billig et al. described communicative solutions that are responsive to these contrary themes. In general, the practices involve the teacher managing to direct or impose knowledge and understandings while appearing to elicit them.

> What frequently occurs is that teacher and pupils engage in an implicit collusion in which the solutions and answers appear to be elicited, while a close examination of what is happening reveals that the required information, suggestions, observations and conclusions are cued, selected or provided by the teacher. (p. 51)

Specifically, they suggested that teachers use gestural cues and demonstrations while asking questions; they use silence to mark non-acceptance of pupils' contributions and use encouragement to mark welcomed suggestions; they paraphrase pupils' contributions so as to bring them closer to their intended meaning; and they summarize what students had done or said in ways that reconstruct and alter their meanings.

The second dilemma that is relevant to our study involves the contrary themes implicated in being an expert in our society. Experts are assumed to have knowledge that is not possessed by most others, and as such, they have authority. When they display their expertise, they would expect to be respected. Although one's expertise sets one above others, this position may be problematic in a society imbued with democratic norms. Democratic ideology is egalitarian: each person is respected as having opinions valuable enough for an equal say. The dilemma posed by the contrary themes is this: Experts should have more authority and respect than non-experts but all individuals should be on equal ground.

One kind of expert in our society is a teacher vis-a-vis students. In general, teachers' communicative solutions to these contrary themes involve their maintaining authority in a non-authoritarian manner, or what Wetherell, Stiven, and Potter (1987) called *unequal egalitarianism.* Wetherell et al. used the metaphor of a giant attempting to look inconspicuous by bending at the knees and hunching the shoulders. More specifically, teachers restrict their display of authority using delicate semantics and syntax. They may cast a lesson in terms of "we discover things together" instead of "I tell you the already discovered facts." Instead of explicitly telling students to do something, the teacher may merely offer a suggestion and hope that the students will comply.

Goffman (1961) wrote of this as *role distancing*—attempts to mitigate the force of authority in a superordinate position by "making nice" in various ways. Interestingly for our discussion here, Goffman's notion of role distancing arose as he was analyzing the interaction of surgeons and surgical nurses during operations. In spite of the formal position of superordination held by the surgeon in the surgical team, the surgeon is very dependent on the cooperation of the surgical nurse. Accordingly, Goffman reported, the surgeon would mask the force of their requests by such locutions as "If I asked you very nicely would you give me a scalpel?" Role distancing does not change the power relations between superordinate and subordinate. It does lubricate the interaction, easing the face threatening force of unmitigated commands. Erickson and Schultz (1982) also reported this for college academic advisors—they tended to give students academic "bad news" very indirectly and this was sometimes confusing to the students.

In actual interactions, managing these contrary themes around authority is not always easy. There are a variety of ways in which it can go wrong. If an authority is too direct in giving orders, interactants may be offended and react with indignation, hostility, and so on. On the other hand, if an authority phrases a command too hesitantly and indirectly, the respondent may fail to understand the speaker's intention and/or fail to comply. Moreover, sophisticated subordinates (like interns) might sense hypocrisy or insincerity in this "oh so egalitarian" approach.

There are three questions that we would like to further investigate. First, we would like to have comparative data on how supervising physicians correct physicians-in-training in the various disciplines of medicine. In his ethnographic study in a surgery service of a teaching hospital, Bosk (1979) described harsh corrections. The following is an illustration:

> Arthur (the attending) turned to a junior student: "Okay, Larry, what does this lesion suggest to you as your diagnosis?" "Ulcerative colitis?" Larry asked more than he answered. "Absolutely not. Try again." Larry suggests something weird. Arthur answers him: "I've only seen three cases of that in all my clinical experience! C'mon, think will you! What did he get close to—a plane, and a propeller sliced off that portion of his colon? It's a tumor—I'm sure it's a cancer." (p.101)

We clearly need further studies on how corrections currently are performed across the various disciplines of medicine.

Second, in the world of medicine, experienced doctors see themselves as making judgment calls. For them, often there are no definitive answers; rather they must synthesize the evidence and make diagnostic and treatment decisions. We are interested in exploring whether preceptors correct differently when they see a case as clear-cut and straightforward versus when they see one as complicated.

And third, what doctors do affects people's lives, quite literally. We would like to investigate if the consequentiality of medical practice influences correcting strategies, and if so, how. One possibility is that the more life-threatening the case is, the more direct and unmitigated the supervising physician's corrections will be. Another possibility would be the opposite. In a focus group, preceptors said that interns feel the consequentiality of their decisions as a burden. They went on to say there is no need to correct the interns heavy-handedly when people's lives are at stake; a lighter touch may be more appropriate.

Consequences for Patient Care and Training

In the previous section, we attempted to provide a fuller understanding of the preceptors' correcting practices by discussing some circumstances in which members of our culture mitigate corrections and by introducing dilemmas inherent in precepting. In this final section we consider the possible consequences of the preceptors' correcting practices. We discuss the benefits and risks for patient care and training.

If preceptors hesitate to tell interns when they are off base, allowing inadequate diagnoses and inappropriate management plans to stand, patient care could be compromised. We saw none of that; at no point in any of the recorded interaction did any preceptor appear to compromise the medical care of patients. Rather, preceptors pursued their points even when the interns did not initially understand

and/or agree. While it may take more time to arrive *collaboratively* at diagnoses and management plans, we noticed no costs regarding the quality of care.

It is difficult to evaluate the consequences upon learning of a training environment in which "no one is ever wrong." It seems likely that interns remember having arrived at good assessments and judgments but forget that they had different initial inclinations and leanings. Is it consequential for the learning process if interns credit themselves with having arrived at preceptor-endorsed reasoning and judgments without being aware of just how much leading and assistance they received along the way? How does being led to good reasoning and judgment bear on the interns' capability to use those lessons in the future?

We believe that when interns modify their initial analyses and assessments via opportunity spaces, cued elicitations, and so on, they learn the medical reasoning that they are led through, especially if the preceptors discuss the bases for their judgments. An intern's ability to handle similar situations in the future does not seem to be impaired when preceptor and intern collaboratively arrive at the decisions and both parties understand the rationale. We generally see benefits of the preceptors' attempts to minimize laying open the errors of interns who are inexperienced and in the early stages of their clinical training. While we *generally* see benefits of using these methods with interns, we have not explored the circumstances in which other methods may be more effective. For example, if an intern displays a particular *pattern* of problematical reasoning or judgment, we do not know whether or not explicitly addressing the problematical reasoning would be pedagogically better. Further research is required to answer these questions.

Learning can be conceptualized in various ways. For situations such as the General Medicine Clinic where the overarching goal is to have the interns develop expertise as future office-based professionals, learning is more than acquisition of knowledge. Lave and Wenger (1991), in their exploration of situated learning in apprenticeships, conceptualized learning as ever-increasing participation in a community of practice. Under that conceptualization, whenever the intern moves from the periphery, where he or she functions more as an observer than participant, to the center where he or she gains agency, then learning has occurred. In that formulation of learning, direct corrections might serve to reinforce the interns' status as student, rather than colleague, while more mitigated corrections would have the opposite effect. They would imply that the intern is capable of assuming responsibility for patient care; that he or she has learned.

A risk of the preceptors' avoiding exposing errors is that interns may develop inappropriate or skewed self-evaluations. Interns form self-evaluations on the bases of both their own assessments of their performances and assessments of others gleaned though interaction. When viewing the videotapes of their interaction with the preceptors, interns picked out and expressed concern over instances they recognized as errors in data collection. Usually with some discomfort, they identified interaction which revealed that they had neglected either to ask patients for important information or to perform relevant tests during the physical examinations. Additionally, they were quite sensitive to occasions in which patients told preceptors information that was discrepant with their own presentations. Generally, it seems that interns monitor for whether they do a good job in data collection and presentation. The kinds of pedagogical interventions that the preceptors made were often of a different sort; they were designed to develop medical reasoning and judgment. For example, when an intern prioritized the medical problems in a way that seemed inappropriate, the preceptor guided the intern to rethink the prioritization. Or when an intern was ready to discuss a management plan prior to adequately exploring the diagnosis, the preceptor redirected the discussion back to the diagnosis. We suggest that the interns' self-evaluations may be impacted more by their data collection and presentation performances, and the preceptors' attention and pedagogical focus are directed more on medical reasoning and judgment. It follows then that if preceptors correct in ways that allow interns to take credit for their collaboratively arrived at judgments and decisions, interns may feel an inappropriate sense of mastery with respect to medical reasoning and judgments.

Mitigated corrections, probably more so than explicitly stated corrections, run the risk of being passed over or dismissed by interns. Bucher and Stelling (1977) observed that medical trainees either received very little, or if they did receive, they then recalled very little feedback. To their astonishment they found that trainees, in assessing their own performance, relied almost exclusively on their own judgments—a pattern the authors speculated would influence their receptivity to criticism long after their training was completed. These findings were corroborated by Mizrahi (1984) who also reported that housestaffers discounted to varying degrees the judgments of teaching faculty and peers.

To conclude our discussion, we highlight two aspects of professional life that seem to involve contradictory ways of correcting and disagreeing. One aspect is clinical training which involves encouraging young professionals to assume greater agency and responsibility. We argued that an effective way to do this is to use a nearly invisible hand in correcting and directing. Another aspect of professional life involves collegial exchanges. Such exchanges can be especially valuable when colleagues expose their differences of opinion. This apparent contradiction in modes of correcting and disagreeing is resolved by considering the career of professionals. During training, interns are helped along to correct themselves, acquiring in the process both medical reasoning and a professional identity. As trainees progress, their interactions become more collegial. Part of collegiality should include a greater willingness to state openly one's contrary assessments and judgments. We think this combination of mitigated corrections to encourage agency in trainees and more open disagreements between colleagues would well serve the medical community.

APPENDIX

Methods

The primary data for this study are videotapes and transcripts of 11 cases. The management of each case involves five stages:

Stage 1: The intern takes the patient's history and examines the patient in the examining room.
Stage 2: The intern presents the case to the preceptor in the teaching room and they discuss possible diagnoses and treatment plans.
Stage 3: The preceptor gathers information directly from the patient in the examining room with the intern co-present.
Stage 4: The preceptor and intern briefly confer again in the teaching room or in the hall.
Stage 5: The intern informs and discusses the diagnosis and treatment with the patient in the examining room.

We collected videorecordings of all stages (with the exception of the physical examination in Stage 1, which was audiotaped instead of videotaped). We analyzed in detail Stages 2 and 4, the stages in which the preceptor and intern discuss the case. In addition to the primary data indicated earlier, we collected and analyzed two other sets of data: (a) self-reports from preceptors and interns audiotaped immediately after they dealt with the medical case (in about half our sample), and (b) discourse from a focus group of preceptors.

In the analysis, we combined an ethnographic and conversation analytic approach. On the ethnographic side, we attempted to grasp the reality of the participants during the precepting sessions, their concerns, relevancies, problems, and so forth; on the conversation-analytic side, we aimed at identifying the activities the participants performed in the sessions and at analyzing the strategies they used. We find ethnographic and conversation-analytic approaches not only compatible but mutually informing.

This project was thoroughly collaborative. The authors and a research assistant met every 2 or 3 weeks for work sessions. In preparation for the work sessions, we individually viewed the videotapes and wrote memos on our observations. We then compared and reconciled our analyses in the work sessions.

ACKNOWLEDGMENTS

We are grateful to the preceptors and interns who agreed to be studied and who contributed their ideas about medical training. Additionally, we thank Frances Reimer for videotaping and transcribing most of the precepting sessions and for her participation in the work sessions. We thank Gail Jefferson for the transcripts she produced and her comments on them. Finally, we appreciate the editors' patience and feedback.

REFERENCES

Billig, M., Condor, S., Edwards, D., Gane, M., Middleton, D., & Radley, A. (1988). *Ideological dilemmas.* London: Sage.
Bosk, C. L. (1979). *Forgive and remember: Managing medical failure.* Chicago: University of Chicago Press.
Bucher, R., & Stelling, R. G. (1977). *Becoming professional.* Beverly Hills, CA: Sage.
Ende, J. (1983). Feedback in clinical medical education. *Journal of the American Medical Association, 250*(6), 777–781.
Erickson, F., & Schultz, J. (1982). *The counselor as gatekeeper: Social interaction in interviews.* New York: Academic Press.
Foley, R. P., & Smilansky, J. (1980). *Teaching techniques: A handbook for health professionals.* New York: McGraw-Hill.
Goffman, E. (1961). *Encounters: Two studies on the sociology of interaction.* Indianapolis: Bobbs-Merrill.
Goodwin, M. H. (1983). Aggravated correction and disagreement in children's conversations. *Journal of Pragmatics, 7,* 657–677.
Griffin, P., & Humphrey, F. (1978) *Task and talk at lesson time* (P. Griffin & R. Shuy, Eds.). Children's Functional Language and Education in the early Years. Washington D.C.: Center for Applied Linguistics.
Jefferson, G. (1986). *Colligation as a device for minimizing repair or disagreement.* Unpublished manuscript.
Jefferson, G. (1987). On exposed and embedded correction in conversation. In G. Button & R. E. Lee (Eds.), *Talk and social organisation* (pp. 86–100). Clevedon: Multilingual Matters Ltd.
Lave, J., & Wenger, E. (1991). *Situated learning: Legitimate peripheral participation.* Cambridge: Cambridge University Press.
Ludmerer, K. (1983). The rise of the teaching hospital in America. *Bulletin of the History of Medicine, 57,* 218–229.
Mizrahi, T. (1984). Managing Medical Mistakes: Ideology, Insularity and Accountability among Internists-in-training. *Social Science and Medicine, 19*(2), 135–146.
Mehan, H. (1979). *Learning lessons.* Cambridge, MA: Harvard University Press.
Norrick, N. R. (1991). On the organization of corrective exchanges in conversation. *Journal of Pragmatics, 16,* 59–83.
Osler, W. (1903). On the need of a radical reform in our methods of teaching senior students. *The Medical News, 82,* 50.
Pomerantz, A. (1984). Pursuing a response. In (J. M. Atkinson & J. Heritage (Eds.), *Structures of social action* (pp. 152–163). Cambridge: Cambridge University Press.
Schegloff, E. A., Jefferson, G., & Sacks, H. (1977). The preference for self-correction in the organization of repair in conversation. *Language, 53*(2), 361–382.
Schon, D. A. (1988). *Educating the reflective practitioner: Toward a new design for teaching and learning in the professions.* San Francisco: Jossey-Bass.
Schwenk, T. L., & Whitman, N. (1987). *The physician as teacher.* Baltimore, MD: Williams & Wilkins.
Wetherell, M., Stiven, H., & Potter, J. (1987). Unequal egalitarianism: A preliminary study of discourses concerning gender and employment opportunities. *British Journal of Social Psychology, 26,* 59–71.
Zahn, C. J. (1984, March). A reexamination of conversational repair. *Communication Monographs, 51,* 56–66.

8 Two Types of Institutional Disclaimers at the Cancer Information Service

Robert Hopper
University of Texas, Austin

Jo Ann Ward
University of Texas M. D. Anderson Cancer Center

W. Ray Thomason
Tennessee State University

Patricia M. Sias
Washington State University

Studies of disclaimers rarely report data from naturally occurring speech. In this chapter we describe some hedging disclaimers that occurred in telephone encounters at one office of the National Cancer Institute's Cancer Information Service (CIS). We compare these with hedging disclaimers in other settings.

In CIS telephone encounters, we find two somewhat distinctive clusters of disclaimers that are labeled *early* disclaimers and *embedded* disclaimers. The latter are most similar to disclaimers that occur throughout ordinary conversation—they are richly grounded close to the information and claims that they qualify. Early disclaimers seem less richly grounded in the local occasion—and more like *pro forma* institutional responses. Health-care professionals should consider that an institutional requirement to disclaim medical expertise may produce both types of disclaimers.

CIS TELEPHONE ENCOUNTERS

The National Cancer Institute's CIS has been a leader in the establishment of medical helplines. At the time when we collected these data (1989) there were six to eight information specialists on duty each weekday to receive citizen requests for information. These requests occurred at a steady pace from 9 A.M.. to 4 P.M. A call-sequencer was used to minimize how long each caller had to wait for attention, but

CIS health information specialists made sincere efforts to discuss each caller's concern for as long as necessary.

CIS health information specialists provide a number of services, including using computer and print databases to help callers seek medical care, and related support, near their home; and looking up printed information about cancer concerns, and dispensing this information to callers by phone and mail.

Hopper visited the M.D. Anderson CIS location about a dozen times between 1987 and 1990. He initiated this contact to study telephone practices among helping professionals. He offered informal instructional sessions on telephone speaking during this period, including an on-site quarterly training workshop in 1989. He also produced an audiotape of medical terms, and a sample tape of CIS calls for training. Since that time, he has maintained contact with Ward who is director of Public Education for CIS, and shared the writing of several reports about CIS telephone speaking practices. Each of these reports has treated some aspect of an ongoing dialectic between monologic information giving (and gathering) and dialogic practices for maintaining alignment on the caller's concerns.

Hopper, Ward, and Handy Bosma (1992) described how health information specialists teach medical terminology to callers. CIS information specialists accumulate considerable expertise with medical terms, and they must routinely check for callers' comprehension of these terms. CIS phone calls include frequent impromptu tutorials on medical terms. We studied the use of dialogic practices to teach small packets of content, then to check for comprehension. Health information specialists can help callers by brief informings that accompany checking for comprehension. Informing, on this view, is conceptualized as dialogic interaction, not just information transfer.

Hopper, Ward, and Thomason (1993) studied an information-gathering portion of CIS phone calls. After satisfying all patient concerns, CIS information specialists have asked first-time callers a brief series of demographic questions. We compared these demographic questions both to other questions asked in CIS phone calls, and to demographic questions asked by health professionals in other settings. We argued that this set of questions carries some subtle costs within the informative purposes of CIS calls. We recommended a cost–benefits analysis of information-gathering add-ons to health information telephone encounters. (CIS has since improved some procedures for gathering demographic information.)

The present investigation, like the study of demographic questions and answers, examines a particular moment that is characteristic of many CIS phone calls: the delivery of a "medical disclaimer" by the health information specialist.

CIS MEDICAL DISCLAIMERS

When the CIS began operating a toll-free telephone health information service, some physicians groups expressed concerns regarding the appropriateness of laypersons' dispensing medical information—even health information specialists specially trained for this role. We agree that callers must not mistake information distributed by CIS information specialists for the detailed, personalized information available from physicians. CIS policy is that during each telephone encounter in which medical information is transmitted, information specialists should state a medical disclaimer.

Medical disclaimers hold a stable place in CIS organizational culture. There was a specific operational policy regarding the use of medical disclaimers as printed on the Call Record Form (CRF) completed for each CIS phone conversation. This form contained a space for the health information specialist to record whether a "medical disclaimer" had been given. At the time these data were gathered, the suggested wording for the disclaimer was printed on the CRF, with quote marks:

> "I have given you our most accurate and up-to-date information. However, you should keep in mind that I am not a medical doctor. If you have requested this information because of your own medical condition or for someone you know, the information I have given you should be discussed with your physician. Only a physician, who has a complete medical history of a person can determine what is advisable in that particular case."

We did not observe this full statement to occur in any CIS telephone encounter, and at the present writing, a shorter form of printed disclaimer has been proposed. However, we did observe health information specialists at University of Texas M. D. Anderson Hospital saying something like this (see appendix to introduction for transcript conventions):

CIS\253
I'm not a doctor and I can't—I can't tell you that is (0.2) that's what caused the problem or is- you know ·hhhh has caused your arm and your breast to feel sore but ·hhhh you know certainly that could a side effect.

CIS health information specialists call this statement a *medical disclaimer*. The term *disclaimer* seems an apt description of this exemplar's clausal units: a disclaim clause ("we're not doctors"), the conjunction "but," and a claim.

We describe some uses of CIS medical disclaimers, and the forms in which they occur. We review sociolinguistic literature about disclaimers as speech features, then we describe hedging disclaimers that occur in CIS telephone encounters. We compare CIS hedging disclaimers with those that occur in other settings. We conclude with recommendations for researchers and for practitioners.

HEDGING DISCLAIMERS AS ALIGNING ACTIONS

Several writers describe disclaimers as a class of verbal aligning actions targeted toward problematic situations. This literature stresses the hedging (or responsibility-reducing) features of disclaimers. According to Hewitt and Stokes (1975), the disclaimer is "employed by actors faced with upcoming events or acts which threaten to disrupt emergent meanings or discredit cathected situational identities (e.g., 'I know this is against the rules, but. . .')" (p. 1). Hewitt and Stokes argued that speakers use disclaimers "to present others with cues that will lead to desirable typifications of them—to present themselves in ways that will lead others to grant their situated identity claims" (p. 3). CIS health information specialists wish to represent information as accurate without typifying themselves as medical experts.

Hewitt and Stokes (1975) argued that aligning actions can be used retrospectively or prospectively—that is, they may occur after a problematic event or before it. In contrast to most accounts (Scott & Lyman, 1968) that function retrospectively, disclaimers function prospectively to "ward off and defeat in advance doubts and negative typification which may result from intended conduct" (Hewitt & Stokes, 1975, p. 3); see also Morris & Hopper, 1980). Alternatively, Aijmer (1986) argued that hedging (one function of disclaimers) may be prospective or retrospective. We examined CIS disclaimers' locations in terms of their locations relative to associated claims.

Hewitt and Stokes (1975) proffered an intuitive taxonomy of five categories of disclaimers. Their examples are hypothetical constructions, and the categories blur into one another.[1] *Hedging disclaimers,* our main concern here,

> preface statements of fact or opinion, positions in arguments or expressions of belief with disclaimers of the following kind: "I'm no expert, of course, but, . . ." "I could be wrong on my facts, but I think, . . ." etc. (p. 4)

Hewitt and Stokes argued that most disclaimers are hedges. Because virtually all CIS disclaimers are hedges, the rest of this chapter concentrates only on hedging functions of disclaimers.[2]

Prince, Frader, and Bosk (1982), who defined a *hedge* as: "a word or phrase whose job it is to make things fuzzier" (p. 84)[3] distinguish between: (a) the ap-

---

[1] Hewitt and Stokes' (1975) other categories are as follow: the *credentialing* disclaimer and *appeals to suspend judgment* are invoked when the user is certain that his or her intended act will be discrediting: "Don't get me wrong, but. . . ." The *sin license* disclaimer stipulates "that an act to follow might be violate a rule. . . "I realize you might think this is the wrong thing to do, but. . . ." *Cognitive* disclaimers occur before claims that may be interpreted as lacking sense: "I know this sounds crazy, but I think. . ." (pp. 5–6). We do not review these definitions in more detail because we found virtually no clear instances of them in our data.

[2] Hewitt and Stokes (1975) argued that hedges indicate that the user is (a) minimally committed to the impending act or utterance, and/or (b) uncertain about responses to the act. Some researchers use a broader definition stating that hedges "make it possible to comment on one's message while one is producing it" (Aijmer, 1986, p. 14) This view does not limit hedges to disclaimers.

[3] Prince et al. do not limit the hedge to disclaimer forms. Their term *hedge* includes varieties of uncertainty displays. CIS data (which the participants call *disclaimers*) seem to be disclaiming hedges, as described by Hewitt and Stokes. Prince et al. alert us to possible hedging functions of various qualifying particles in the CIS materials. In line with Prince et al.'s connection between disclaiming hedges and other qualifying particles (e.g., "I think") we asked whether CIS medical disclaimers occurred in the environment of other "qualifying" particles such as "I think," "perhaps," or various dysfluencies. This notion received little support.

proximator (i.e., "sort of"), which mitigates the truth conditions of a claim; and (b) the *shield* (i.e., "I'm not sure"), which indicates speaker uncertainty. Prince et al. identified two types of shields; plausibility shields (expressions of uncertain reasoning) and attribution shields (citing a source). They would label many CIS disclaimers as attribution shields; one of their examples of an attribution shield is: "According to Dr. Smith, there was a dramatic response after medication" (p. 91) The Prince et al. definition describes the CIS practice of citing print sources from which information is taken.[4]

Although alignment researchers emphasize that disclaimers portray the speaker in a positive light, speech evaluation researchers described some vulnerabilities in disclaimer use (Bradley, 1981; Erickson, Lind, Johnson, & O'Barr, 1978). On this view, "disclaimers are powerless, deferential linguistic forms. The individual who uses disclaimers does so at a risk to his or her social image" (Bell, Zahn, & Hopper, 1984, p. 29). That is, use of disclaimers may damage, rather than enhance, the user's identity.[5]

In the present research, we inquire about both the assets and liabilities of institutional hedging disclaimers. May we detect in discourse any communicative advantages (as the alignment theorists claim) or disadvantages (as the evaluation theorists claim) attached to disclaimer use?

Hewitt and Stokes (1975) briefly discussed listeners' responses to disclaimers, noting that disclaiming speakers use a disclaim and a claim. A successful disclaimer is one in which a listener accepts both the disclaim and the claim. A disclaimer may still be partially successful if the disclaim is accepted but the embedded material is rejected.[6]

The disclaimers literature does not address their impact on the claims to which they attach. Does a CIS caller find information more credible, or useful, when disclaimers are used; or do disclaimers exact some evaluative price? May we find evidence of callers responses to disclaimers (and their associated claims) in subsequent speaking turns?

We collected a sample of disclaimers, including several prior and succeeding

---

[4]The Prince et al. treatment of hedging, like that of Hewitt and Stokes, stresses hedging's functions of communicating uncertainty and expressing minimal commitment to a claim. They differ, however, with regard to the type of uncertainty involved in hedging. Hewitt and Stokes describe uncertainty regarding the *response* to the proposition; Prince et al. address the user's uncertainty regarding his or her own *knowledge* regarding the proposition.

[5]Bell et al. actually argued against this claim. They argued that speech style subjects face unrealistically a large numbers of disclaimers in experimental manipulations, and therefore these manipulations fail to achieve ecological validity. Bell et al. found no effects on speech evaluation until they exposed subjects to four disclaimers within a 12-turn dialogue.

Speech evaluation studies measure listeners' responses to artificially constructed data. The present research examines data from naturally occurring telephone encounters of health information specialists at the CIS.

[6]Hewitt and Stokes (1975) argued that listeners rarely address the disclaim (i.e., "I realize you are no expert") let alone challenge it (i.e., "You should be an expert in this area"). CIS callers never countered in these ways, but sometimes said "oh I know," or "of course"—apparently to align with the disclaim (and parenthetically to show that this disclaimer was not surprising to them).

turns. We searched for the format described in the literature: disclaim + but + claim. In non-CIS settings we also restricted ourselves to disclaimers that performed hedging functions.

We addressed the following questions in our collections of CIS disclaiming hedges and those from other settings.

1. What are the similarities and differences between CIS disclaimers and those in other settings?
2. What is the location in discourse of disclaimers, at CIS and elsewhere?
3. How do recipients respond to disclaimers?

We have not yet determined satisfactory answers to these questions, however, our investigations yielded descriptions of two disclaimer profiles in CIS data: embedded disclaimers and early disclaimers. Embedded disclaimers are worded much like disclaimers in nonmedical settings, they occur in the process of giving information, and their claims elicit responses. Early disclaimers introduce stock phrasing, occur near the beginning of an encounter, and elicit less uptake.

CIS DISCLAIMERS COMPARED TO THOSE IN OTHER SETTINGS

To compare CIS disclaimers to those in other conversational settings, we identified hedging disclaimers from archives of naturally occurring conversation.[7] We compare these to CIS medical hedging disclaimers.

Non-CIS hedging disclaimers' wording resembles that described by Hewitt and Stokes: a disclaim clause, but, and a claim. Here are two examples:

---

[7]Procedures for identifying disclaimers outside CIS recordings included searching tape recordings and transcripts for the word "but," and testing for each instance the appropriateness of the descriptive terms disclaimer or hedge. We identified 27 disclaimers by this procedure, 13 of which were hedges. This procedure, of course, bypassed any disclaimers not using the word "but." We compared these to 16 CIS disclaimers.

The sample provided a tentative verification of Hewitt and Stokes' claim that most disclaimers perform hedging functions. Two other observations about this sample of disclaimers: First, the disclaimers in ordinary conversation are far from randomly distributed. Most conversations included none at all, and others showed several. Two environments, discussions between executives (1 hour) and calls to a radio talk show (20 minutes) showed more disclaimers than did the other 25 hours of recordings and transcripts that we searched.

Second, except for the category of hedges, the Hewitt and Stokes taxonomy fared poorly as description of actual occurrences. Only 2 of 12 nonhedges bore even remote resemblance to any of the other Hewitt and Stokes' types.

J10.8 ((government purchasing office))
    T: I'm u- I'm not th<u>a</u>t familiar with the pro<u>ce</u>dures but that's just what the rules state

M2 ((radio talk show; political discussion))
    AL: I don't know what Mr. Mullen had to say on y<u>o</u>ur show or anything <u>e</u>lse but I think they been a little bell<u>i</u>gerent on the ones that h<u>a</u>ve voted

These hedging disclaimers, which we term *embedded* disclaimers, use first person singular pronouns and display a claim–disclaimer relationship. Here are two examples of embedded hedging disclaimers in CIS telephone encounters (in CIS instances C= caller and IS = CIS information specialist):

CIS\253
    IS: I'm not a doctor and I can't- I can't tell you what that is what caused the problem . . . but you know certainly that- that could be a side effect

CIS\213
    IS: [S]ince I'm n<u>o</u>t a physician it would be very difficult for me to (0.5) to make a recommendation one way or another bu:t certainly you are within your right to discuss that with him,

Standing in contrast to the above, just over half of CIS disclaimers use a rather stereotyped wording that does not show any special claim–disclaim relevance. These disclaiming hedges use the first person plural pronoun: "we." Here is an example of an early disclaimer:

CIS\B3
    IS: Okay well you know that we're not doctors here but we have a lot of informa:tion

The information specialists who speak these early disclaimers use the somewhat *pro forma* claim: "we have a lot of information" to follow the medical disclaimer.

Compared to other disclaimers (CIS embedded disclaimers and those in non-CIS settings):

1. early disclaimers make a plural self-typification ("we") and speakers of disclaimers in other settings use "I."
2. early disclaimers precede stock phrases (e.g., "we have a lot of information"), whereas others occur embedded before-and-within information and/or claims.[8]

This difference in wording co-occurs with differences in the location of the two types of CIS disclaimers.

LOCATION OF DISCLAIMERS

Hewitt and Stokes argued that disclaimers precede the claims they qualify. We add to this description that the claims themselves are embedded in conversational episodes in progress. That is, users of disclaimers choose carefully the occasions of their placement, and proffer rich sets of orientation within the moment of the disclaimer.

Many everyday disclaimers occur in the contexts of arguments and disputes. In the following exemplar, a radio talk show host (O) and caller (AL) are wrangling over causes for low voter turnout in city elections. AL wants to blame the current mayor (Mr. Mullen), whereas O has claimed the mayor is doing his best to combat the problem:

M2:14

```
         AL:   But they didn't really come out and express
               (0.7) the issues w- the way I thought they
               should.
         O:    Yeah.
                     (0.3)
==>      AL:   I don't know what Mr. Mullen had to say
               on your show or anything else but I
               think they been a little belligerent on
               the ones that have voted
                     (1.0)
         AL:   And the reason that people do not vote cause
               they don't trust the politicians no how
                     (1.1)
```

---

[8]The point is not to argue a hard-and-fast distinction between these two types, but to argue that there seem to be available to persons uttering disclaimers a range of forms from extremely preliminary ritually stated disclaimers to in the course of dialogic co-construction, richly occasioned in the moment disclaimers. Presumably, each of these is most relevant in its proper occasion. However, the situational constraints orienting to consumers' concerns and those most relevant to the worries of medical practitioners may not always match.

O: Yeah but you know Mullen has- has said u:h
that uh (0.5) if they don't find some wa:y to
increase the voter turnout ((discussion
continues))

In the context of an ongoing discussion, AL introduces a hedging disclaimer (see ==>). The turn that includes the disclaimer gets a silent response. AL, apparently reading the silence as disagreement-relevant, expands his indictment to claim that people do not vote because they: "don't trust the politicians no how." The show's host, O, responds with disagreement that defends the mayor. The disclaimer occurs in the context of this ongoing disagreement, which continues afterward. The recipient of the disclaimer continues the discussion in which it occurs.

Such argument rarely occurs in the information-sharing context of CIS encounters. But some CIS disclaimers do occur at moments when the caller's concerns have become quite specific, and when the health information specialist's talk could be taken as medical advice.

CIS health information specialists package these embedded disclaimers in ways that orient to the problem—and put the disclaimer close to substantive concerns or information. In Exemplar 222 the information specialist begins a speaking turn that prefaces information, and then she self-interrups to insert the hedge. The information specialist thereby sandwiches the disclaimer between an information preview and the information itself:

CIS\222

IS: I ha:ve a book that's put out by
the (.) National Cancer Institute
˙hhhh that talks about (.) um skin
cancer=
C: =Uh huh=
IS: =and melanoma s'let me (.) read to you
C: Uh huh
IS: what it sa:ys (.) about what it looks
like
==> u:m (0.4) ˙hhh bearing in mind of auh
course (.) I'm no:t a do:ctor
((continues))

In the next exemplar, the information specialist has been giving information about side effects of the patient's chemotherapy treatment. The information specialist has periodically checked for understanding while reading this information aloud. She concludes by summarizing some drug-protocol changes that might relieve side effects of medication—and sandwiches the disclaimer just before delivering a focal formulation in the exchange:

CIS\213
```
    IS:    ... they can- adjust the dosage ˙hhhhh
           uh adjust the period of time between the
           treatments ˙hh or perhaps put you on an
           other antineoplastic agent
    C:     Mm hm:
==> IS:    Uh- this would be something- since I'm
           not a physician it would be very
           difficult for me to: ˙hhh (0.2) to: u-
           make a recommendation one way or another
           bu:t certainly you- are within your
           right to discuss that with him,
```

This disclaimer is placed after medical information, yet immediately before the information specialist's encouraging the caller to discuss options with a physician. This disclaimer shows specially occasioned fit into the local situation.

In contrast to the artful placement of embedded disclaimers, CIS early disclaimers usually occur within the first few seconds of the call, at the caller's first tentative identification of a concern.

CIS\282 ((simplified))
```
    IS:    Cancer Information Service may I help
           you
                  (0.4)
    C:     Uh- yes I have a book Chemotherapy and
           You: and it tells me in here if I have
           questions (0.4) uh as a family member
           u:h that I could call this number and
           get some-uh have some questions
           answer⎡ed could I-
    IS:          ⎣Ri:, we'll try to answer them
           we're not physicians but
           ⎡we do have a lot of information
    C:     ⎣Yes
```

This information specialist inserts a medical disclaimer into her second speaking turn of this encounter. At this point, the information specialist only knows that the caller has "some questions." This information specialist seems motivated to get the medical disclaimer introduced into the conversation quite early. This orientation may minimize the disclaiming moment's special fit into the local occasion.

The early appearance of these CIS disclaimers may be, in part, prompted by the design of the Call Record Form (CRF) that information specialists complete for each encounter. The CRF asks on its first page for affirmation that a disclaimer has been delivered to the caller. Filling out the CRF may motivate the information specialist to deliver this disclaimer early in the call so she may complete the relevant part of the form, or check one item off the list of tasks to be done.

To summarize, CIS embedded disclaimers (using "I," and showing detailed relevance to the local occasion) occur proximate to (sandwiched into) the giving of medical information. Early disclaimers (using "we" and a stock phrase) occur in the opening moments of the encounter. These two formats for disclaimers attain different responses from callers.

RESPONSES TO CIS DISCLAIMERS

Whatever the explanation for the timing of CIS early disclaimers, they elicit little uptake from callers:

```
CIS\B3
         C:     I'm not (2.0) I'm not fam(h)iliar with
                it or what- what goes on
==>      A:    Okay well you know that we're not
                doctors here but we have a lot of
                informa:tion
                   (0.4)
         A:    And we ha:ve (0.2) specific information
                about breast cancer, let me (.) pull a
                book for you called
                (( continues ))
```

Following the early disclaimer and a stock phrase, there is a transition-relevance place, but the caller does not self-select to speak. The information specialist resumes talking, and continues for some time—in a way that shows no relevance to the disclaimer or its claim. The caller never orients to the utterance containing the early disclaimer.

Like this one, most CIS early disclaimer–claims carry little argumentative load. Most information specialists continue speaking after early disclaimers.[9]

---

[9]The one possible exception to this generalization is the only early disclaimer in which the information specialist referred to herself as "I."

```
         B1 (( beginning with IS' second turn))
IS:      [I'm not a]doctor sir but I'd be happy dtry
         duh- answer your ques⌈tions
C:                             ⌊Well - what I'm u::h
         concerned about is muh- for the las two or
         three months my bowels uv- have changed.
```

Although this caller does respond, he does not orient specifically either to the claim or to the disclaim.

In non-CIS encounters, and in CIS calls that include an embedded disclaimer, the episode continues beyond the disclaiming turn. In the next instance the information specialist empowers the caller by suggesting options, and the caller expresses an intention to follow up these options.

```
CIS\213
==>  IS:     Uh- this would be something- since I'm
             not a physician it would be very
             difficult for me to: ˙hhh (0.2) to: u-
             make a recommendation one way or another
             bu:t certainly you- are within your
             right to discuss that with him, and
             ˙hhhh uh there's- if there's i- of- the
             likelihood that- (0.2) your discomfort
             could be:-made less by (0.4) changing
             your- medication or- or adjusting the
             dosage ˙hhh certainly it's- more than
             worth a try
     C:      Mm hm? pt ˙hhhh Well I certainly will
             discuss those with him
```

In this instance the caller responds directly to the health information specialist's advice.

CONCLUSIONS

CIS embedded disclaimers are somewhat similar to those in other environments. They use "I," as most other disclaimers do, and they occur proximate to the information they qualify. These disclaimers often occur between an information preview and the actual information. The information so given is ordinarily acknowledged.

CIS early disclaimers contrast with disclaimers in other environments. They appear early in an encounter, rather than proximate to information delivery. These hedges typify the disclaiming party as "we," and set up a stock phrase like "we have a lot of information." Callers do little to acknowledge these early disclaimers or the speaking turns in which they occur. Callers rarely respond to these disclaimers, and perhaps there is no reason for them to.

Perhaps use of the term *disclaimer* exaggerates similarities between CIS early disclaimers and those that occur elsewhere in CIS encounters—and elsewhere. One explanation for contrasts between CIS early disclaimers and those that carry more richly occasioned substantive weight: The actual targeted recipient of the CIS disclaimers may not be the co-participant in the phone conversation, but (non-present) members of the professional medical community. By performing medical disclaimers, CIS health information specialists protect their organization from criticism. The early disclaimers may perform no consistent function within the encounters in which they occur.

Is the early disclaimer simply an interactional palliative; or does it have side-effects on the credibility of a health care professional? CIS practices may overemphasize the necessity of giving a disclaimer in every single call, leading health information specialists to do the disclaimer early in telephone encounters and to complete the blank on the front side of the CRF. It may be helpful to move the disclaimer record on the CRF to the back side of the form, so that disclaiming becomes the focus of attention later in the call, proximate to the giving of information and advice. We recommend to CIS health information specialists that they sometimes reserve medical disclaimers until they actually are in the process of giving advice, rather than stating early disclaimers at the first plausible moment in an encounter.

Researchers and communicators should attend to the dangers of discussing speech features detached from the circumstances of their occurrence. To researchers, dangers arise from uncritical consideration of a speech form—expletives, or disclaimers, or powerless speech particles, without attending carefully to ways that partners in interaction embed these features into each singular occasion. Data-reduction techniques in certain discourse analysis traditions may treat all disclaimers in terms of a pre-argued similarity. Such studies might make language use seem like simple aggregating of component parts. The reality of language use is that each speaking turn is best considered as a work of art carefully crafted in the special circumstances of its occurrence.

Practitioners of delicate professions, such as medicine or law, should beware the belief that responsibilities to citizens can be discharged by the simple prescription to use a speech feature—such as a medical disclaimer, or the uttering of Miranda rights to a criminal suspect. We cannot improve human interaction by simplifying practices of local occasioning. These practices, as much as the shape of any lexicon, statement, or utterance format, do the work of human communication. Speech acts, taken in isolation, lose much of their function as well as much of their locally occasioned artistry.

REFERENCES

Aijmer, K. (1986). Discourse variation and hedging. In J. Aarts & W. Meijs (Eds.), *Corpus linguistics II: New studies in the analysis and exploitation of computer corpora.* Amsterdam: Rodopi.
Bell, R., Zahn, C., & Hopper, R. (1984). Disclaiming. *Communication Quarterly, 32,* 28–36.
Bradley, P. H. (1981). The folk-linguistics of women's speech: An empirical examination. *Communication Monographs, 48,* 73–90.
Erickson, B., Lind, E. A., Johnson, B. C., & O'Barr, W. M. (1978). Speech style and impression formation in a court setting: The effects of "powerful" and "powerless" speech. *Journal of Experimental Social Psychology, 14,* 266–279.

Hewitt, J. P., & Stokes, R. (1975). Disclaimer. *American Sociological Review, 40,* 1–11.
Hopper, R., Ward, J. A., & Handy Bosma, J. E. (1992). Dialogic teaching of medical terminology at the cancer information service. *Journal of Language and Social Psychology, 11,* 63–74.
Hopper, R., Ward, J. A., & Thomason, R. (1993). Demographic questions in telephone calls to the Cancer Information Service. *Southern Journal of Communication, 58,* 115–127.
Morris, G. H., & Hopper, R. (1980). Remediation and legislation in everyday talk. *Quarterly Journal of Speech, 66,* 266–274.
Prince, E. F., Frader, J., & Bosk, C. (1982). On hedging in physician-physician discourse. In R. DiPerto (Ed.), *Linguistics and the professions.* Norwood, NJ: Ablex.
Ragan, S., & Hopper, R. (1981). Alignment talk in the job interview. *Journal of Applied Communication Research, 9,* 85–103.
Scott, M., & Lyman, S. (1968). Accounts. *American Sociological Review, 33* 46–62.
Stokes, R., & Hewitt, J. P. (1976). Aligning actions. *American Sociological Review, 41,* 383–849.

9 Educating the Patient: Interactive Learning in an OB–GYN Context

Sandra L. Ragan
University of Oklahoma

Christina S. Beck
Ohio University

Martha D. White
Oklahoma City Community College

```
1   P:    kk kk (.2)
2   NP:   >if ya< want me to <(.) I can > give you sa uh < mild
3         cough medicine (.) if >you think< that would help (.2)
4         I'd rather give .it to ya< (.) than >have you< take
5         someone else's=
6   P:    =ha ha=
7   NP:   =okay? (.1)>not uh< good ide:a to take >other people's<
8         medicine (.1) especially >if it's< prescribed=
9   P:    =mmhmm (.)
```

In the exemplar just presented, the nurse practitioner (NP) offers a specific injunctive against taking medicine prescribed to someone else (Lines 7–8); she softens it, however, by a prior acknowledgment of the patient's (P) cough (Line 1) that incorporates the patient's wishes into her treatment plan (i.e., in Lines 2–5, the NP asserts that she will prescribe a cough medicine if the patient wants her to and if the patient thinks that would help. She follows up this assertion that she will prescribe a cough medicine, if the patient so wishes, with the "lesson" in Lines 4–5, which implicitly suggest that one should not take another's prescribed medicine.) To the patient's brief response of (guilty?) laughter in Line 6, the NP further drives the lesson home in Lines 7–8 with a direct, explicit statement of the inappropriateness of this patient's prior remedy for her cough.

Such a conversational stratagem, although perhaps unwitting, permits the patient's participation in her treatment and her concurrence with the NP's diagnosis and treatment plan. While facilitating the patient's education, it also functions to promote rapport and to preserve the patient's face needs. In the analysis that follows, we discuss an interactive pedagogical style that appears to serve both the information-dispensing and the interpersonal goals of medical encounters.

The analysis presented here utilizes data collected by a Native American researcher who was granted access to an urban health-care facility for women funded by Indian Health service, The Oklahoma Department of Human Services, the Bureau of Indian Affairs, and other nonprofit organizations. In this setting, Glenn (1990) conducted an ethnographic study of the Native American clinic; she also observed and taperecorded many of the interactions between women patients and their White, male physicians as well as their White, female nurse practitioner. This chapter analyzes the health-care interactions between 22 pregnant Native American women, who have come to the clinic for routine pregnancy examinations, and their health-care provider (a female, White nurse practitioner). The transcripts produced from these taperecorded interactions are the data set for this study.

THE EDUCATIONAL FUNCTION OF HEALTH-CARE INTERACTIONS

One of the expected and, frequently, critical outcomes of a successful medical interaction is patient education. Both caretakers and patients believe that a primary function of the health-care practitioner is information giving. Some literature indicates, moreover, that attention to patient education increases both patient satisfaction with the health-care interaction as well as compliance with a prescribed medical regime (see, e.g., a discussion of education in the gynecologic exam context in Leserman & Luke, 1982, and McBride & McBride, 1981). Particularly in Western medicine, patients have been socialized to view their medical caregivers as omniscient dispensers of both medication and medical wisdom.

Yet the educational role of the medical caregiver is a delicate one that must be balanced alongside the patient's complementary needs to appear competent in the health-care interaction and to preserve personal dignity; the doctor is called on to educate, but she or he must achieve patient education while also serving the more primary medical goals of the interaction (e.g., diagnosing, examining, prescribing) in addition to promoting rapport and protecting face. The educational role of medical caregiver is further complicated by the inherent difficulty of achieving patient understanding of complex medical terms, issues, procedures, and treatments. Miscommunication and misunderstandings remain the source of much patient frustration and discontent with their medical care (Korsch & Negrete, 1972; Silver, 1979; West, 1984; West & Frankel, 1991). Not only does the disparity exist between patient and practitioner knowledge about health-care issues, but the patient's relative ignorance is abetted by a cultural phenomenon that proscribes patients' question-asking. Particularly in women's health-care interactions, practitioners may construe the very act of asking a question as challenging to their authority as credible health-care providers (Fisher, 1984). In fact, "by bringing up a topic... normally reserved for the doctor's initiation and by challenging the doctor's medical knowledge abut the topic, the patient appears to be talking inappropriately" (Fisher, 1984, p. 215). Although some practitioners may reinforce patient perception that questions constitute "inappropriate" role behavior through their responses to patient questions, the very expectation that practitioners would construe questions as challenges may inhibit patients' asking for needed clarification. As Smith (1992) asserted in his recent book about women's medical treatment and mistreatment, "the overwhelming picture of the physician–patient relationship, one which doctors have created, is of an authoritative, not-to-be-questioned, powerful doctor and a dependent, passive, not-as-important-as-the-doctor patient" (p. 148)—a relationship that would forcefully inhibit a patient's asking questions of her "not-to-be-questioned" doctor. Ironically, however, women's health-care scholars note that patients in gynecologic examinations desire more information than they are given about procedures, diagnoses, and treatments (e.g., Billings & Stoeckle, 1977; Corea, 1985, Domar, 1985–1986) and that attention to patient education by the practitioner increases patient satisfaction with the encounter (see, e.g., Leserman & Luke, 1982).

Two key reasons may be advanced for the link between patient education and patient satisfaction. First, participants in the gynecologic examination who cooperatively achieve patient education must overcome institutional barriers to the successful transfer of information; second, attention to patient education may minimize an inherently face-threatening situation.

Institutional Barriers to Patient Education

As practitioners and patients communicate during health-care encounters, they must somehow bridge gaps in understanding of essential medical terminology, diagnoses, and recommended treatment. As several scholars observed, such gaps result frequently in misunderstandings during health-care interactions (see e.g., Korsch & Negrete, 1972; Ley & Spelman, 1967; McKinley, 1975; Silver, 1979; West, 1984; West & Frankel, 1991). Practitioners who possess a more academic comprehension of the meaning of symptoms and possible remedies must relate that information to their patients in an understandable, accessible, yet uncondescending manner. To do so, practitioners face the challenge of using language that can accurately and effectively educate patients. For example, a practitioner's use of specific medical terminology to depict a diagnosis to a patient contributes little to that patient's understanding when the patient cannot accurately interpret the medical jargon (Korsch & Negrete, 1972; Ley & Spelman, 1967; West & Frankel, 1991).

The pedagogical role of caregiver is thus complex and worthy of analysis: How does patient education transpire in the medical interaction? How do caregivers and patients collaborate in a process that necessarily places them in a teacher–student role, one that, if it adheres to the traditional medical model of provider as demigod, may be inimical to some of the interpersonal goals of health care (e.g., being empathic and patient-centered)? In short, health-care participants face the interactional challenges of communicating/seeking possible symptoms and explaining/understanding diagnoses and recommended treatments, tests, and prescribed behavior. To do so, they must somehow interactionally align their understanding of shared information throughout the health-care encounter.

The Consequential Nature of Education in the OB–GYN Exam

Whereas patient education is efficacious to the subsequent treatment of patients in a variety of health-care contexts, the uniquely problematic nature of the obstetrical–gynecologic examination makes education during the exam particularly critical, both to the success of the exam and to patient compliance with practitioner recommendations. Specifically, the practitioner's effective dissemination of accurate and clear information to the patient may facilitate the performance of necessary, albeit difficult, examination procedures while also enhancing the patient's ability to follow recommendations that impact both her and, is she is pregnant, her unborn child.

Although an OB–GYN patient likely realizes the medical necessity of prenatal pelvic examinations that permit health-care workers to monitor pregnancy and to detect any possible problems with the growth or delivery of the unborn child, women's health-care researchers contend that many participants in gynecologic examinations—patient and practitioner alike—feel discomfort and anxiety about the exam (Alexander & McCullough, 1981; Domar, 1985–1986; Emerson, 1970; Fang, Hillard, Lindsay, & Underwood, 1984; Leserman & Luke, 1982; Olson, 1981; Ragan & Glenn, 1990; Summey & Hurst, 1986). Such negative feelings are likely the result of the exam procedures themselves, which violate cultural and personal norms of keeping the pelvic area private.

Thus, the performance of the gynecologic exam constitutes a potentially face-threatening experience for the patient as well as a potentially embarrassing encounter for the health-care practitioner (see, e.g., Beck & Ragan, 1992a, 1992b, in press; Ragan, 1990). Ragan explained that face needs become particularly relevant during a "procedure which possibly is seen by both interactants as invasive, intruding on one's personal space and privacy, and culturally taboo" (p. 70).

Although Goffman (1955, 1959) and Brown and Levinson (1987) stressed that social actors attempt to behave in a manner that will preserve their "face" as well as the "face" of their co-interactants, these researchers also suggest that face threats may be warranted if the risks of not threatening face outweigh the actual face threat. In this case, the risk of not participating in the gynecologic exam (particularly during pregnancy) can be far greater than the potential discomfort or embarrassment of the examination. If the participants in the gynecologic exam do not find ways to minimize its potentially face-threatening aspects, then the exam, in and of itself, may be difficult to perform. As the next section details, the integration of education into the examination may actually facilitate the examination as well as subsequent patient behavior (see, e.g., Billings & Stoeckle, 1977; Corea, 1985; Domar, 1985–1986).

Although the achievement of patient education could greatly impact the success of gynecologic examinations and the physical well-being of the patient and the unborn child, the interactional resources enabling patients and practitioners to cooperate mutually in the patient's education are largely unexplored by extant literature. Thus, a sound rationale exists for the empirical analysis of patient education in this vital health context.

ANALYSIS OF HEALTH-CARE INTERACTIONS

In her ethnographic study of the practitioners and patients at the urban Native American health-care clinic, Glenn (1990) explained that practitioners at the facility view patient education as a priority and as a challenge. Patients who seek medical care at the facility generally lack both the financial resources and the educational backgrounds to be effective health-care consumers. Despite the patients' need for knowledge about their bodies and appropriate health-care practices, practitioners at the facility must overcome cultural taboos held by their Native American patients against discussing such personal topics as pregnancy, birth control, breast feeding, and gynecologic care.

Several studies in health-care communication, in fact, suggest that lower class and less educated patients are less knowledgeable about preventive health care (Coope & Metcalfe, 1979), less familiar with medical terminology (Samora, Saunders, & Larson, 1961), and less likely to listen to their physicians (Bochner, 1983; Pendleton & Bochner, 1980)—all of which contribute to problems of miscommunication in health-care interactions (West & Frankel, 1991). Other studies have contradicted such findings, however, noting no significant relation between education, age, gender, or ethnicity and understanding of information in the health-care encounter (Korsch & Negrete, 1972; Plaja, Cohen, & Samora, 1968; Steele & McBroom, 1972). According to West and Frankel (1991), studies by Davis (1963) and Roth (1963) may help explain the apparent inconsistency in the literature regarding the relationship between patients' socioeconomic status (SES) and their health-related behaviors: Davis found that physicians' perceptions of patients' SES (and other attributes) helped to determine what they were told; Roth found that the ways patients presented themselves influenced the kinds of information they received. These findings suggest, then, that practitioners' images of their patients may have affected their health-care interactions at least as much as the patients' actual characteristics. Moreover, such findings undermine a previously fundamental assumption that miscommunication in medical encounters is a function of the characteristics of senders and receivers, rather than of the interaction itself. As West and Frankel (1991) noted, the studies of the relationship between process and outcome variables (e.g., patient education correlated with patient satisfaction) have been somewhat useful in analyzing basic parameters of miscommunication between practitioners and patients; yet this research focus has neglected the issues of context, sequence, and interpretation. As West and Frankel (1991) asserted, "the most fruitful alternative to the variable approach is research that focuses on miscommunication in the context of its occurrence" (p. 178).

It is our belief, then, that as with the studies of miscommunication in health-care contexts, the study of patient education is best conducted through an inspection of the health-care interactions themselves rather than relying on patients' ethnicity, educational level, and so on as predictor variables. In the transcripts analyzed for this study, the nurse practitioner and her patients are seemingly able to transcend some of their cultural and educational differences by utilizing the interactive resources available to dyadic participants. Throughout these audiotaped interactions, the nurse practitioner attempts to elicit information, to relate the significance of that information, and to impress preferred health-care practices on her patients. As she integrates patient education into the health-care encounter, this practitioner interactionally assumes a "teaching" persona (e.g., she asks questions, she issues directives, she offers advice). Further, the practitioner facilitates the achievement of patient education by interactionally creating an environment that preserves the patient's "face" as a person with choice (through phrasing recommendations as suggestions and providing non-threatening rationales to support these suggestions). In this way, the practitioner treats the patient holistically; she is not merely a "presenting symptom" (i.e., a pregnancy), but rather a complex composite of physical and emotional needs, the most effective satisfaction of which requires interactive attendance by both patient and practitioner.

The Facilitative Nature of Face Preservation

As previously noted, the very nature of the gynecologic exam poses threats to the face of patients (and, occasionally, to practitioners) and often prompts attitudes about the exam that can serve as barriers to its successful completion as well as to subsequent patient compliance. In the case of the Native American health-care clinic, the cultural proclivity of Native American women to preserve their privacy can possibly hinder their willingness to attend to the suggestions of the practitioner and to provide the necessary details about their physical and psychological conditions. Although Ragan (1990) and Beck and Ragan (1992a, 1992b, in press) provided empirical examples of the functions of humor, empathy, and relational asides in reducing face threats in the gynecologic exam, the ways in which practitioners present recommendations to patients may also alleviate the face-threatening nature of the encounter while simultaneously enhancing the process of patient education. In this set of transcripts, the nurse practitioner recurrently offers advice about preferred patient behavior in a manner that infers patient ability to reason and to choose. In so doing, the practitioner reflexively attends to both the educational and the face needs of her patients.

PHRASING RECOMMENDATIONS AS SUGGESTIONS

Many health-care practitioners possess a perceived institutional "right" to direct the encounter, to prescribe patient treatment, and to ensure provider control. However, this female nurse practitioner, (as well as another female nurse practitioner whose interactions were analyzed in a series of studies; see Beck & Ragan, 1992a, 1992b, in press; Ragan, 1990; Ragan & Glenn, 1990; Ragan & Pagano, 1987) tempers control by framing her recommendations as suggestions, not as directives. As exemplars 1, 2, and 3 indicate, such suggestions infer patient ability to reason and offer patients an opportunity to participate in the decision-making process about their treatment. This participative, holistic approach to patient education enables the patient to maintain her "face" as a person capable of reasoning and selecting from treatment options and provider recommendations. By engaging the patient's participation in the education process (and preserving the patient's face), the practitioner facilitates patient understanding of information and commitment to behaving in the preferred manner; whereas the practitioner clearly articulates preferences, she nonetheless phrases them as proposals rather than as directives.

```
Exemplar 1
 1   NP:   you might >think about< (.) out[side counseling]
 2   P                                    [well yah] (.)
 3   NP:   >have you< done that? (.)
 4   P:    yah (.) we've been um (.1) working (.) >tryin ta< work
 5         things out>for tha< past three months (.) we've been (.)
 6         >trying ta< get back together=
 7   NP:   =uh uh (.4) cause >often times< (.1) those things
 8         >don't resolve< themselves >until they're< ta:lked
 9         abo:ut (.)
10   P:    yah (.)
11   NP:   >an you< can >talk about< your feelings (.) >and your<
12         rage (.) and >what you< expect from hi:m uh (.) hhh an
13         he >needs ta: (.)>ya know< (.) be >able ta< fulfill
14         your needs and you >need ta be< able ta hhh fulfill hi:s
15         hhh otherwise (.) just be >gettin'back< together hhh (.)
16         >if you< don't resolve those pro: blems (.) they'll all
17         come back (.) >an they< (.) >need ta be< talked about
18         (.) an ya >need ta< (.) >be able ta< (.) really (.) have=
```

19   those >out in tha< open hhh (.) now I don't ask people
20   >to reveal< a:ll feelings about themselves (.) >but
21   they< (.)>need ta< talk about >some of< them.

The immediate context for this exemplar is that the NP has been questioning the P about how she's feeling about her pregnancy. In response to the NP's asking her whether she ever feels depressed, the patient reveals that she does feel some stress and depression about her husband (who is also her unborn child's father). They have been separated for about 8 months but are trying to get back together, and the patient is living temporarily with her grandparents. The NP asks whether the depression has ever been severe enough for the patient to consider suicide, and the patient concedes that she's thought once or twice about taking her life. As the NP begins the exam, she asks if the patient and her husband are "working on getting the relationship back together," and the patient responds that they plan to remarry, but that her husband currently doesn't have a job, that money is a problem for them.

In Line 1, the NP suggests that the patient "might think about outside counseling." This suggestion serves as both a subtle recommendation and a feeler to discover any attempts by P and her husband to obtain professional marriage counseling. After P's equivocal response in Line 2, NP asks specifically whether any counseling has yet occurred (Line 3). P responds (Lines 4–6) that she and her estranged husband have been "trying to work things out." Instead of directly stating that the patient "needs to get counseling" or that "talking between yourselves won't work," the practitioner reiterates her subtle suggestion by offering a lengthy, highly personal rationale for her suggestion (Lines 7–9, and 11–21). Notably, NP never tells P that she must seek counseling; she does describe what P "needs" to be able to do with her husband if she wants her reconciliation to work. In short, NP provides P with an end goal (i.e., effective communication with her separated husband), offers a suggestion for how to accomplish that goal (i.e., counseling), and enables P to decide whether to act on the suggestion or not.

In these few lines, the NP has broadened the patient's options about working on her marriage. She has accomplished this objective without chastising the patient for not having considered the counseling option herself and without inducing guilt or anxiety if the patient does not choose this course. But, clearly the nurse believes that her patients need to talk about their feelings and that they need to seek professional help, particularly if they have suicidal thoughts. She communicates these beliefs unequivocally, yet still leaves the patient with options. This is again the strategy followed in the opening exemplar in which the nurse practitioner suggests that she prescribe the patient her own cough medication rather than her using another's prescription medication.

Exemplar 2
1   NP: >do you< (.) >check your< breasts (.) >every month< ?(.)
2   P: n:ot a:lways (.)

```
3    NP:    okay (.2) I'm gonna t:o (.) >check you< (.1) before I
4           >let ya< (.) now (.)
5    P:     mmkay (.)
6    NP:    >check your< breasts (.1) h:hhh >tauh< good idea >ta
7           check your >breasts (.) mo:nth^ (.1) after you >have
8           your >pe:riod^ (.) that's >when your< breasts are most
9           tender (.2) >you've got< nice soft breasts >are easy<
10          >ta examine< (.) some women have real no:dular breasts
11          (.) hhan they're >hard to< check (.2) >let me< just
12          listen >to your< heart (.)
```

As does Exemplar 1, this dialogue exemplifies how practitioners in the Native American health-care facility frame recommendations for treatment as suggestions to the patient. In this excerpt, NP asks P whether she checks her breasts monthly (Line 1). P answers with "not always" (Line 2). NP responds somewhat hesitantly (Lines 3 and 4); she says "okay," then pauses and adds, "I'm gonna check you before I let ya now."

Although NP does not immediately comment on P's admission that she fails to examine her breasts on a monthly basis, NP incorporates a suggestion for future behavior into her examination of P's breasts. NP informs P that she is going to check her breasts (Line 6) and, after hesitating, notes that it is a "good idea to check your breasts" monthly after "you have your period." NP does not reprimand P for not doing the self-exams; instead, she provides her reasoning for the suggested timing of the exam. NP further notes that P has the type of breasts that may be easily examined. Such an observation educates P about her own breasts in comparison with those women's breasts that are harder to examine, perhaps helping to alleviate any anxiety or discomfort that P might feel about self-examination.

Phrasing recommendations as suggestions, as the first three exemplars demonstrate, implicitly incorporates the patient into the health-care decision-making process and makes her responsible for her own health care, and at the same time, educates her about her body and about appropriate health-care practices. Treating the patient as an active participant, rather than as a passive attendant, in healthcare situations may also facilitate retention of shared information and reduce the face-threatening nature of the encounter. Despite their cultural and educational disparities, this nurse practitioner appears to see her patients as responsible, adult, decision makers, capable of making appropriate health-care decisions if given reasonable information and options. Through her questions and her suggestions, she constitutes her role as a health-care educator, one whose responsibility does not end with examining the patient; moreover, rather than limiting her medical observations to the patient's presenting symptom (i.e., her pregnancy), this nurse practitioner treats the whole patient.

The Nonthreatening Nature of Practitioner Reasoning

As the previous subsection indicates, phrasing recommendations as suggestions serves to empower the patient regarding her own health care and ensuing decisions about it. Similarly, the nurse practitioner in this study frequently follows a suggestion for treatment with a detailed explanation that provides the patient with a rationale for the suggestion. Just as a nurse practitioner could opt to give orders instead of suggestions to patients, she could easily choose not to offer any explanation; she could also give reasons for her recommendations in a face-threatening, condescending manner. During these audiotaped encounters, rationales for suggestions accompany almost all of the suggestions offered by the nurse practitioner; these rationales contain information designed to enable the patient to decide on the value of the suggestion for herself.

```
Exemplar 3
1    NP:    >do ya< write (.) your periods down (.) >on uh< calendar
2           (.) >at home< ?
3    P:     u:m no:o (.)
4    NP:    Oka:y (.) it's really best >if ya< try (.) >to do< that-
5           (.) hhh an make a hhh dal note uh >you know< >monthly
6           habit< (.)
7    P:     mmhmm=
8    NP:    =an then hhh when >something like this< happens (.) we
9           >have a< better id[ea]
10   P:                       [ha] ha yah=
11   NP:    =>ya know< >of what's< going on (.) sometimes we really
12          rely on these pe:riods for (.) hhh a lot of things (.)
13          >not just< pregnancy=
14   P:     =mmhmm=
15   NP:    =if you >start having< abnormal ble:eding (.) hhh
16          something (.) >went wrong< with your reproductive sy
17          (.) track (.) hhh we'd need to know=
18   P:     =mmhmm=
19   NP:    =so it's real important=
20   P:     =mmhmm=
21   NP:    =it's uh >and most women don't remember (.) >I mean < (.)
22          they're so: busy...
```

As NP prepares to examine P (who may or may not be pregnant), NP asks P whether or not she regularly keeps track of her monthly periods (Lines 1–2). Upon P's response that she does not do this, NP acknowledges P's answer with "okay" and then notes that "it's really best if ya try to do that an make a dal note uh you know monthly habit." By phrasing her recommendation as a suggestion, NP enables P to preserve face by not labeling her as ignorant, lazy, and so forth, because she has not recorded her periods. Rather, NP focuses on what P should do in the future.

NP follows this suggestion with the reasoning behind it (Lines 8–9, 11–13, 15–17, 19). Although P came to the medical encounter with complaints about irregular bleeding, she could not provide NP with exact details about her medical condition. NP opts not to dwell on P's inability to supply essential information, yet the rationale that she offers for her suggestion stresses why such information would be helpful in the treatment of future problems.

Throughout NP's explanation, P interjects brief indications of agreement (see Lines 7, 10, 14, 18, and 20). By responding affirmatively to the idea of recording her periods in the future, P, at least symbolically, acknowledges the value of the information and implies that she might comply with NP's suggestions. She also displays that NP has the credibility and the institutional prerogative to make this suggestion. The nature of NP's suggestion and its rationale enable P to behave as an active, responsible participant in her health care and to preserve her face (despite her acknowledged failure to maintain important records).

Exemplar 4:

```
 1   NP:   hhh we'd like >you to< (.) hhh >how many iron< tablets
 2         >are you< taking uh day? (.)
 3   P:    two=
 4   NP:   =two (.) mm okay (.) I'd like >you ta< increase >it ta<
 5         thre:e (.) >every other< day=
 6   P:    =ohaka:y he he (.)
 7   NP:   the reason is (.) if they have to section you (.) you're
 8         gonna lose more blood (.) hhh than you would (.) if you
 9         deliver vaginally=
10   P:    =that's true=
11   NP:   = you only lose like (.) uh >cup and uh< half vaginally
12         (.) which is (.) ve:ry insignificant (.) and most
13         women >that are< healthy (.) can hhh re (.) restore
14         that >pretty soon< =
15   P:    =right (.) pretty soon=
16   NP:   =yah (.) but >if you have uh< Caesarean section (.)
17         there >is uh< chance that you can >lose uh< little bit
18         more blood (.) hhh an we don't want you to > come off
19         of tha< surg=
20   P:    =anemic=
21   NP:   =really anemic (.) an going home (.) hhh you're >gonna
22         be< tired if you >have uh< C section a:ny way>because
23         of< it's major surgery (.)
24   P:    yah
```

In Exemplar 4, NP requests that P increase her intake of iron tablets, as opposed to earlier excerpts in which NP frames her recommendations as suggestions. NP begins this exchange by stating, "we'd like you to" (Line 1); however, NP hesitates and checks with P about her present behavior before recommending a change in behavior to P (Lines 1–2).

NP acknowledges P's response that she takes two iron tablets per day (Line 3) by repeating "two," hesitating, and then stating, "I'd like you to increase it ta three every other day" (Lines 4–5). P agrees to comply with NP's recommendation (Line 6); however, NP launches into a rationale for why P should take an additional tablet every other day (Lines 7–9, 11–14, 16–19, 21–23). By providing P with reasons that are salient to her future well-being, NP implies that P retains the choice to comply or not to comply; she further informs her of the possible ramifications of not following NP's recommendation (i.e., anemia following a Caesarean section).

As in Exemplar 3, the patient interjects brief statements of agreement throughout NP's explanation for the increase in iron tablets. In this case, the patient advances some degree of knowledge about her health-care situation (Line 10) by responding, "that's true," after NP contrasts blood loss in a Caesarean section with a vaginal birth, and (Line 20) by offering "anemic" as a definition for the condition described by NP (Lines 16–19). NP acknowledges P's correct use of the medical term *anemic* by stressing that P could be "really anemic" without more iron. In short, the way that NP frames these in-depth rationales encourages patient participation in the medical encounter and facilitates the interactive process of patient education.

Reinforcement of Specific Information

Within this interactional context, the practitioner and patient dispense and seek information. Extending from the practitioner's treatment of the patient as an active participant in the health-care process, specific information may be advanced—and reinforced through repetition—by the practitioner. Further, as Exemplar 5 shows, the way in which the practitioner provides the information enables, even prompts, a dialogue with and not a monologue to the patient. As the patient offers more examples and asks questions, NP gains valuable insight into the patient's real understanding of the directions as well as the importance of those directions.

```
Exemplar 5:
1    NP:    I want you to re:st (.) re:st (.) re:st (.) as much as you can do (.)
2           is just re:st (.) hhh when >you go< home (.) >you tell< your
3           husband you make dinner honey (.) hhh you take care of me
            (.) ... I
4           need >to set=< down (.) I need >to rest< (.)
5    P:     mmkay (.)
6    NP:    and >get down< (.) watch your sodium (.) the salt=
```

7	P:	=right=
8	NP:	=potato chips (.) hhh hidden salt (.) ketchup (.) mustard (.)
9		pickles (.) >pickle relish< (.) all that stuff is lo:aded with sodium
		(.)
10	P:	che:ese (.)
11	NP:	che:ese (.)
12	P:	Calcium (.) >I know<
13	NP:	Right (.) Calcium (.) but milk ?(.)
14	P:	I know (.) [I've been drink] in milk=
15	NP:	[that's the better] that's the better alternative (.) yah
16		(.) we just want uh (.) healthy healthy baby (.) >and we want < you
17		healthy too (.) hhh your hematocrit^ are you taking your iron tablets
18		now
19	P:	hhh ye:s (.) ha ha (.)
20	NP:	Okay (.) your hematocrit >is up< a little bit (.) at >thirty five< percent (.)
21	P:	which (.) I don't under?=
22	NP:	=okay (.) well (.) the numbers (.) okay (.) >let's see< the last time
23		we >did a< hematocrit >on you< (.) it was >forty percent< (.) and
24		that was in January (.)
25	P:	o:h (.) >for the< diabetes?=
26	NP:	=no, no (.) that's >for the< for the red blood cell count (.)
27	P:	Oh (.)
28	NP:	Okay(.) >so it's gone< down (.) okay (.) anemia (.) okay=
29	P:	=mmhmm=
30	NP:	=women develop anemia (.) hhh >often times< (.) when they get
31		pregnant (.) because (.) hh they don't have enough ir:on (.)
32		for their red blood cells (.) because your body's (.) making red
33		blood cells hhh (.) >for the< baby=
34	P:	=right=
35	NP:	=>the baby's< (.) making its blood cells really (.) but (.) >the baby<
36		takes iron from you (.)
37	P:	right

In Lines 1–4, the NP uses repetition (i.e., "rest") in directing the patient to take good care of herself during her pregnancy; she personalizes this directive by also instructing the patient in how she should approach her husband in order to get the rest that she needs: "when you go home, you tell your husband, you make dinner honey, you take care of me." It is interesting, too, that the nurse gives this advice in conversational form—again, a warmer, more personal approach than merely instructing the patient that she should tell her husband that she requires more rest during her pregnancy. In Line 6, the NP advises the patient to watch her sodium intake and in Lines 8–9 begins a litany of high sodium foods that the patient should avoid. Note, however, that the NP never gives an explicit instruction to avoid ingesting these foods; instead, she appears to rely on a common sense understanding that the patient is getting the message. Line 10 displays this alignment: The patient offers "cheese" to the list of high sodium foods, and the nurse affirms the "correctness" of the offering by repeating "cheese" in the next utterance. Further evidence that the "lesson" is being understood is the patient's volunteering (Line 12) that "calcium," on the other hand, is a nutrient that she should be ingesting more of during her pregnancy. Apparently, the NP both confirms that calcium is desirable and that milk is the best source for it (Line 13), because the patient quickly volunteers (Line 14) that she realizes this and has been drinking milk, which, again, the NP confirms as the "better alternative" (Line 15). These lines (6–15) are revealing of the aligned relationship between the practitioner and her patient, in that each is able to complete the other's utterance; each confirms the other's prior suggestion.

Lines 17–37 display even more clearly the value of this aligned relationship as an educational tool. At this point, the NP herself is somewhat confused because she asks the patient whether she is taking her iron tablets and then mistakenly notes that the hematocrit is "up a little bit at thirty-five percent." Later, she corrects herself when she discovers that the level is actually down from 40% in January. What is interesting, however, is that both the NP and the patient seem comfortable enough to work through the misunderstanding without anyone's losing face, as partners in the transaction.

For example, in Line 21, the patient alerts the NP that she does not "understand" something, and the NP begins to explain the hematocrit. As she does so, the patient indicates that she thinks the test is "for the diabetes," so the NP is able to correct that misunderstanding (the hematocrit measures red blood count) and move on to link her original question about iron tablets to the possibility of anemia and the pregnant woman's need to ingest extra iron. The NP treats both her own mistake and the patient's misconception matter-of-factly, suggesting that she feels no need to be infallible in the patient's eyes. Further, she does not exaggerate the patient's misunderstanding, which might threaten the patient's self-esteem and discourage questions and comments. The patient remains a participant whose contributions are valued as an integral part of the health care encounter, and both NP and patient have learned from the transaction.

In this exemplar, the nurse practitioner again offers specific directives to the patient in that she clearly states her preferences that the patient get enough rest, that she watch her sodium intake, and that she take her iron tablets. As in her encounters with other patients, the NP softens these directives by interactively involving the patient in her instruction giving for healthy prenatal care. In this way, the patient actively participates in her own health-care learning: She contributes to the list of high-sodium, forbidden foods; she receives reinforcement for volunteering the appropriate nutrients; she displays a willingness to ask questions when she is confused. In short, she assumes responsibility for her own health in that instruction is interactive rather than merely didactic.

Asymmetry in Provider–Patient Interaction

At this point, it might be helpful to note the contrast between the dialogue of the previous conversations and some examples of assymetrical exchanges between patients and health-care providers. The intent is not to indict the more traditional question–answer format, but to sharpen the focus on the educational possibilities of a more balanced discourse.

As the following exemplar from Todd (1984, p. 181) demonstrates, health-care providers often hold the floor and manage the health-care encounter. In so doing, they may limit patient participation and encourage passivity.

Exemplar 6:
```
 1   MD:   Now, look what I want to do, you understand now, all
 2         right, you have X number of tablets, then you finish
 3         finish the package, right?
 4   P:    Right.
 5   MD:   Right. Finish them wait four to five days. If you
 6         flow, come in then while you're flowing and I'll, uh,
 7         uh, and I'll give you more pills. (long pause)
 8   P:    Okay
 9   MD:   I won't charge you. If you don't flow, call me, then
10         I will give you an injection, don't take any more
11         tablets then.
12   P:    Uh hum
13   MD:   I'll give you an injection and I'll, uh, get you
14         started with your menstruation and I'll give you
15         a different type of pill. (long pause)
16   P:    Okay
17   MD:   Okay?
18   P:    All right.
19   MD:   But meanwhile, stay on the pills. Don't you get
20         into trouble.
21   P:    Right.
```

This exchange between a woman suffering from amennorrhea (cessation of menstruation) and her male physician is typical of Todd's (1984) data set. The physician begins by instructing the patient to "finish [the tablets]," and then prompts the patient to reply (Line 3) when he says, "Right?" The patient repeats, "Right," and the doctor continues with several lines of directives. Again (Line 7), he apparently solicits a reply with a long pause because the patient says, "Okay." Near the end of the conversation, the physician pauses again, and the patient replies, "Okay." The doctor immediately prompts her again (Line 17) with "Okay?," and she responds, "All right."

One significant aspect of this excerpt is that the patient speaks only a few words, two of which are specifically dictated by the physician. He does not solicit any information, and the patient asks no questions, so the physician must assume both assent and understanding on the basis of some seven words, of which he explicitly prompted over half. Between those few patient utterances are seven specific, detailed directives that the patient must remember in order: "finish the package," "wait four to five days," "If you flow, come in," "If you don't flow, call me," and so forth. The physician finishes by admonishing the patient not to "get into trouble." That seems ironic considering that we have no indication that these instructions are in written form so that the patient can review them at some later time; her primary "trouble" may well be in remembering them.

Another crucial facet of this discourse is that the physician offers no rationale for any of the directives. He seems to presume that the patient understands why each step of the process is important because he never asks, and the patient shows no particular interest, or at least does not verbalize it. Among educational formats, this most resembles a lecture in which the teacher speaks, and the student listens, recalling the information later in order to assimilate and retain it. But as good students know, that process requires good class notes, a period of review, and possibly a textbook, tools that are not applicable to most health-care encounters. Patient "testing" and accountability depend on active compliance with instructions, which may be unlikely in this case.

In some health-care exchanges, the patient does offer information, but the provider is nonresponsive for some reason. As the following exemplar from a conversation between a female NP and her patient demonstrates, the NP controls the topic for discussion, does not respond to the patient's concerns, and perhaps loses an opportunity to engage the patient in a real dialogue.

Exemplar 7
1   NP: Okay (.1) every time you come (.) you should hh bring
2   that with you (.1) mmkay?=
3   P: =mmhmm (.4) She told me (.) u:m (.2) >to tell< you (.)
4   >about the cold (.) that I've had (.)> I've had it
5   almost thre:e weeks (.) now.
6   NP: Okay.

7	P:	started >coughing< up <uh >little blood< (.) last
8		ni:ght.=
9	NP:	=Okay. (.6) birthdate?
10	P:	one (.) six (.) >sixty-eight<

Apparently, the NP is filling out a form or an identification card because she tells the patient to "bring that" (Line 1) with her every time she comes. NP also ignores the patient's concern about her cold and the bleeding to ask for the patient's birthdate (Line 9). The patient is obviously distressed about her physical condition because she indicates that she has mentioned her cold to someone else and that "she told me to tell you" about it (Line 3). The NP seems unperturbed, which may be medically appropriate under these conditions, but the patient is not knowledgeable enough to infer that her bleeding may not signal a serious condition, and the practitioner does nothing to reassure her or to explain her own lack of concern. This appears to be an opportunity for the NP to show interest, to educate her patient about the nature of her illness, and to let her know that she should always bring such problems to the NP's attention. What seems to happen is that the form to be filled in takes precedence over the patient's needs; that is a risky message to the patient. If she "learns" that she can safely ignore bleeding, the results may be serious at some time in the future.

Exemplars 6 and 7 contrast dramatically with Exemplars 1–5 in that they are primarily didactic and practitioner-focused rather than interactive and patient-focused (i.e., asymmetrical in quantity as well as in quality). The balance of power rests with the practitioner, making the patient an attendant in the health-care encounter, not an active participant and ultimately not responsible for what occurs. This pattern of communication seems ineffective and inefficient if patient involvement and education are among the providers' desired outcomes.

PRACTICAL IMPLICATIONS OF THE ANALYSIS

In the exemplars analyzed for this chapter, we illustrate a model of interactive learning that we purport to be an enviable model for any teacher–learner interaction. Because the NP utilized for this chapter routinely communicates with patients in ways that facilitate dialogue and active learning, these conversational excerpts are representative of an interactive style that appears to evoke patient response and ensure patient understanding. Particularly in the medical setting, and more particularly in the context of women's prenatal health care where information dissemination and patient compliance affect critical health outcomes, such a model appears desirable. This teacher–learner model is characterized by several features: It is interactive—both practitioner and patient ask and answer questions; it is personal and holistic—without addressing the patient by name, the nurse practitioner, nonetheless, discovers the status of her psychological as well as her physical health through her probing, follow-up questions and her permitting the patient to answer and to ask questions; it is efficient—these interactions and the others reviewed for this study interweave examining, reading charts, interviewing, and diagnosing with disseminating information and giving advice.

Yet this model is not the one believed to be in widespread practice in the medical community, particularly in women's health-care contexts, according to Corea (1985), Todd (1984), West (1984), and Smith (1992). These researchers, instead, concluded that the more typical woman's health-care interaction involves a passive patient and a not-to-be-questioned physician.

What is the desirability of the model described in this study and what are the pragmatic constraints that impede its use? Because the present analysis does not attempt to measure health-care outcomes, because we cannot address whether, in fact, the Native American women treated by this White, female nurse practitioner do comply with her health-care instruction, there is little basis for judging the efficacy of this model. Overt, behavioral changes in patients would require measuring to attest whether the interactive instructional environment created by this nurse practitioner and her patients had, indeed, produced learning or had affected patient compliance with desired health-care practices.

It is not within the purview of this chapter to make such claims but rather to demonstrate the possibility of health-care interaction that involves patients and that appears, at least, to warm the chilly climate of women's health-care encounters heretofore analyzed. Too, given education's predilection for incorporating an interactive learning model into current instructional practices, it appears reasonable that patient "students" would benefit from such pedagogy in many of the same ways that traditional classroom students do. Hence, we offer the model as an option, and probably a desirable option, particularly in the context of women's health care.

Toward a Paradigm of Interactive Learning

Finally, we wish to advance and further explicate a belief that interactive learning is beneficial in health-care interactions, especially in the women's health-care context described in this chapter. Proposing such a "model" assumes certain caveats, not the least of which is that no such model can accommodate every individual practitioner's unique style of communication, nor can it account for the differences that inhere in individual patient–practitioner relationships as developed over a period of time. Such a communication pattern need not unnecessarily prolong the health-care encounter (a primary concern of many providers), and it offers a qualitatively better use of time than directives and instructions that require considerable repetition. Thus, what follows is a discussion of attitudes, expectations, and philosophical considerations that, when adapted by the concerned practitioner, should engender more effective and productive communication.

If we accept, ideally, that education is a process that empowers students, then it follows that education is an active process rather than a passive one. Teaching is only a part of education, and without active learning, it is virtually useless. The very word "education," from the Latin educere (to lead or draw out), connotes the development of possibilities, of what is already within the student; to reduce it to imparting information is facile. Thus, the communication process that makes learning–education possible must, by definition, be interactive, not reactive.

Whether in a health-care context or any other teaching–learning situation, the teacher-practitioner's awareness of her own communication style is requisite to effective education. Fisher (1984) noted that doctor–patient discourse is usually asymmetrical and that doctors are "active and dominant," whereas patients are "passive and dependent" (p. 201). She likened this imbalance of power to the asymmetrical communication between teacher and student in which the teacher controls the choice of topic as well as access to the floor. If this analogy is accurate, then health-care professionals and teachers alike should reflect on the sorts of language, questioning, and "power plays" that lead to such communication imbalances. The student who remains passive and dependent is less likely to learn than the one who develops as a partner in the educational process. Practitioners already know, in most cases, what patients should do to enhance their health or recover from disease, but that information is useless if patients cannot assimilate it, synthesize it, and develop a fund of general health information for future use. It is crucial, then, for the patient to be an active participant, and for the practitioner to focus on the patient in the communication process.

To facilitate self-awareness, the practitioner might note which questions and/or comments elicit patient response that is more than monosyllabic. Even a glance at the practitioner–patient conversations and the doctor–patient discourse reported earlier reveals a contrast between the longer and more thoughtful patient response usually evoked by the NP and the "right," or "okay" that the doctor gets. To assume that the monosyllabic response indicates either assent or understanding is risky; however, if the practitioner remains focused on her own needs to transfer or receive information quickly, she may make this mistake. In addition, extended patient response provides opportunities for broadening patient understanding, correcting misunderstanding, and adding to a patient's general fund of health knowledge. In this context, nonverbal cues are important as well. The more the patient speaks and questions, the more she provides the practitioner with significant information through facial expressions and body movements that indicate whether or not she understands the necessity of carrying out the practitioner's suggestions or instructions.

Such compliance with appropriate, if not life-saving, health practices is critical to positive health-care outcomes, but if the practitioner/teacher retains focus on herself, she may limit the patient's actions to that which "pleases" the practitioner. The NP's approval may sometimes reinforce desired behavior, but only as a function of her own action, not as a function of the patient as agent or partner. This subtle form of compulsion relieves the patient of responsibility for his or her actions, whether positive or negative; on the other hand, if patients are responsible for their actions, they must "learn" in order to survive. Enabling the patient/student to learn, then, suggests impulsion, not compulsion. Motivation is mythical if it connotes one person's ability to compel action in another; moreover, directives, instructions, or orders without patient understanding are anathema to developing cognitive skills. They promote an insidious kind of passivity that bypasses the student's mind in favor of muscle movement. Conversely, interactive communication cultivates the patient's ability to use information and ideas, to synthesize, to infer relationships, because the patient is ultimately responsible for what she does.

Practitioners may promote this kind of responsibility in several ways. In addition to patient focused communication, expectation is key. Educators have long acknowledged that students tend to meet teachers' expectations, so in the context of health care, the practitioner should "expect" that patients will comply with positive health practices if they understand the desirability of doing so. By way of negative example, if the NP lectures the patient on nutrition during pregnancy—the value of iron and calcium, avoiding sodium, and so on—and approves of the patient's positive verbal response, the communication is more self-congratulatory than patient focused. The expectation is for the patient to "pay attention," not to learn. The practitioner in the present study, however, discusses the need for iron, yet allows the patient to add that calcium is important. She corrects only when the patient inaccurately links diabetes to her red blood count. The correction is matter-of-fact, almost casual, rather than a stern admonition (e.g., "You have to remember what I've told you about your hematocrit. It has nothing to do with diabetes!"). The practitioner's casual manner suggests, perhaps, that she expects the patient to assimilate the correction without feeling the need to threaten her. It also seems reasonable to suggest that if the practitioner maintains focus on patient action (rather than on what the patient "remembers" of what the practitioner has told her), then she encourages the patient to infer the relationship of the same nutritional information to the suckling process as well as to gestation and even to overall health. When the focus is on remembering (and "regurgitating"), on the other hand, the patient is encouraged only to pay more attention to the practitioner's superior knowledge; the responsibility remains with the practitioner.

One further note about partnership and responsibility: This practitioner's use of the pronoun "we" is worth emulating. Her usage is not the condescending "Did we take our pill today?" usage. In Exemplar 3 (Line 15) the NP says, " . . . if you start having abnormal bleeding, something went wrong with your reproductive track. . . *we'd* need to know. . ." (italics added). Here, the focus is clearly on the kind of information that only the patient can provide, and the practitioner's use of "we" connotes a real partnership that places responsibility squarely on the patient. Again, the practitioner expects the patient to contribute to her own health care as well as her learning process.

Thus, whereas we would readily acknowledge that practitioner directives or instructions are efficient for the short term, they produce less real learning for the patient. In view of clinical time constraints for health-care providers, directives and other didactic forms of disseminating information are tempting time-savers; their drawbacks are that they only work to the extent that the provider can monitor the patient's actions to ensure compliance. There is little probability of producing a continuing behavioral pattern, either overt or covert. Interactive education, on the other hand, represents a qualitatively better use of clinical time because it promotes a patient's understanding of alternatives in order to make decisions. In the case of the Native American health-care clinic, an interactive learning environment would seem particularly critical because of high turnover rates in personnel and the resulting lack of continuity in patient–provider relationships. If the interactive learning process promotes patient accountability and engenders trust, then these can be transferred to another practitioner–patient relationship.

Although the pragmatic value of this pattern of interactive learning for practitioners during examinations is clear, the impacts of this model on patient learning and compliance and other health outcomes remain unknown and require empirical testing. Thus, we offer this paradigm to practitioners and health communication researchers as one to be tested and adapted in a variety of health-care situations, not just women's health-care encounters. The interactional resources detailed in this method of interactive learning in health-care encounters transcend one particular genre of health care and are available to practitioners regardless of gender, degree, or specialty. The important issue of patient education is not a women's issue; it is a critical (albeit unexamined) patient issue.

REFERENCES

Alexander, K., & McCullough, J. (1981). Women's preference for gynecological examiners: Sex versus role. *Women and Health, 6,* 123–134.

Beck, C., & Ragan, S. L. (1992a). Negotiating relational and medical talk: Frame shifts in the gynecologic exam. *Journal of Language and Social Psychology, 11*(1), 47–61.

Beck, C., & Ragan, S. L. (1992b). *The co-production of roles in the gynecologic exam.* Paper presented at the annual meeting of the Western Speech Communication Association, Boise, ID.

Beck, C., & Ragan, S. L. (in press). The impact of relational activities on the accomplishment of practitioner and patient goals in the gynecologic examination. In G. Kreps & D. O'Hair (Eds.), *Relational communication and health outcomes.* Cresskill, NH: Hampton Press.

Billings, J., & Stoeckle, J. (1977). Pelvic examination instruction and the doctor-patient relationship. *Journal of Medical Education, 52,* 834–839.

Bochner, S. (1983). Doctors, patients, and their cultures. In D. Pendleton & J. Hasler (Eds.), *Doctor–patient communication* (pp. 127–138). London: Academic Press.

Brown, P., & Levinson, S. C. (1987). *Politeness: Some universals in language use.* Cambridge: Cambridge University Press.

Coope, J., & Metcalf, D. (1979). How much do patients know? A MCQ paper for patients in the waiting room. *Journal of the Royal College of General Practitioners, 29,* 482–488.

Corea, G. (1985). *The hidden malpractice: How American medicine mistreats women.* New York: Harper & Row.

Davis, F. (1963). *Passage through crisis.* Indianapolis: Bobbs-Merrill.

Domar, A. (1985–1986). Psychological aspects of the pelvic exam: Individual needs and physician involvement. *Women and Health, 10,* 75–90.

Emerson, J. (1970). Behavior in private places: Sustaining definitions of reality in gynecological examinations. In H. P. Dreitzel (Ed.), *Recent sociology, No. 2: Patterns of communicative behavior.* New York: Macmillan.

Fang, W., Hillard, P., Lindsay, R., & Underwood, P. (1984). Evaluation of students' clinical and communication skills in performing a gynecologic examination. *Journal of Medical Education, 59,* 758–760.

Fisher, S. (1984). Institutional authority and the structure of discourse. *Discourse Processes, 7,* 201–224.

Glenn, L. D. (1990). *Health care communication between American Indian women and a White male doctor: A study of interaction at a public health care facility.* Unpublished doctoral dissertation, The University of Oklahoma, Norman.

Goffman, E. (1955). On face-work: An analysis of ritual elements in social interaction. *Psychiatry, 18,* 213–231.

Goffman, E. (1959). *The presentation of self in everyday life.* Garden City, NY: Doubleday Anchor Books.

Korsch, B. M., & Negrete, V. F. (1972). Doctor-patient communication. *Scientific American, 227,* 66–74.

Ley, P., & Spelman, M. (1967). *Communicating with the patient.* St. Louis, MO: Warren H. Green.

Lesserman, L., & Luke, S. (1982). An evaluation of an innovative approach to teaching the pelvic examination to medical students. *Women and Health, 7,* 31–42.

McBride, G. B., & McBride, W. L. (1981). Theoretical underpinnings for women's health. *Women and Health, 6,* 37–55.

McKinley, J. (1975). Who is really ignorant?—Physician or patient. *Journal of Health and Social Behavior, 16,* 3–11.

Olson, B. (1981). Patient comfort during pelvic examination: New foot supports vs. metal stirrup. *JOGN - Nursing, 10,* 104–107.

Pendleton, D. A., & Bochner, S. (1980). The communication of medical information in general practice consultation as a function of patients' social class. *Social Science and Medicine, 14A,* 669–673.

Plaja, A. D., Cohen, L. M., & Samora, J. (1968). Communication between physicians and patients in outpatient clinics, social and cultural factors. *Milbank Memorial Fund Quarterly, 46,* 161–214.

Ragan, S. L. (1990). Verbal play and multiple goals in the gynecologic exam interaction. *Journal of Language and Social Psychology, 9,* 67–84.

Ragan, S. L., & Glenn, L. D. (1990). Communication and gynecologic health care. In D. O'Hair & G. Kreps (Eds.), *Applied communication theory and research* (pp. 313–330). Hillsdale, NJ: Lawrence Erlbaum Associates.

Ragan, S. L., & Pagano, M. (1987). Communicating with female patients: Affective interaction during contraceptive counseling and gynecologic exams. *Women's Studies in Communication, 10,* 45–57.

Roth, J. A. (1963). Information and the control of treatment in tuberculosis hospitals. In E. Freidson (Ed.), *The hospital in modern society* (pp. 293–317). New York: The Free Press.

Samora, J., Saunders, L., & Larson, R. (1961). Medical vocabulary knowledge among hospital patients. *Journal of Health and Human Behavior, 2,* 83–89.

Silver, J. (1979). Medical terms—a two-way block? *Colloquy, Journal of Physician–Patient Communications,* 4–10.

Smith, J. M. (1992). *Women and doctors.* New York: Atlantic Monthly Press.

Steele, J. L., & McBroom, W. H. (1972). Conceptual and empirical dimensions of health behavior. *Journal of Health and Social Behavior, 13,* 382–292.

Summey, P., & Hurst, M. (1986). Ob/gyn on the rise: The evolution of professional ideology in the twentieth century—part 2. *Women and Health, 11*(2), 103–122.

Todd, A. D. (1984). The prescription of contraception: Negotiations between doctors and patients. *Discourse Processes, 7,* 171–200.

West, C. (1984). Medical misfires: Mishearings, misgivings, and misunderstandings in physician–patient dialogues. *Discourse Processes, 7,* 107–134.

West, C., & Frankel, R. M. (1991). Miscommunication in medicine. In N. Coupland, H. Giles, & J. M. Wiemann (Eds.), *"Miscommunication" and problematic talk.* (pp. 166–194). Newbury Park, CA: Sage.

10 Discussing Health-Related Quality of Life in Prenatal Consultations

Richard L. Street, Jr.
Texas A&M University

William R. Gold
Texas A&M University Health Science Center

Tony McDowell
Scott & White Clinic and Hospital

Since the 1980s, there has been a growing recognition among clinicians, policy makers, and researchers that the evaluation of medical care effectiveness should expand beyond the traditional standards of mortality and morbidity. Medical care also should improve the patient's health-related quality of life (Lohr, 1992). Generally speaking, health-related quality of life (also referred to as health status) represents the patient's perceptions of physical and emotional well-being, overall health, and health-related limitations in daily activities (e.g., with work or family). To date, most of the research has focused on the creation and validation of instruments measuring health status and on how these measures can be used to assess the status of patients suffering from chronic diseases (Kaplan, 1987; Rost, Flavin, Cole, & McGill, 1991; Wasson et al., 1990) or receiving certain medical treatments (e.g., type of surgery, drug; Fowler et al., 1988; Kiebert, de Haes, & van de Velde, 1991). Interestingly, although improvement in the patient's health status is considered an important medical objective, there is very little research examining how issues related to health-related quality of life are actually discussed and managed during the consultation itself.

Prior to elaborating on the purposes of this research, we should provide a brief overview of health status as a theoretical construct. There are several approaches to the study of this topic, most of which agree that health (functional) status is multidimensional and represents the patient's views of health in general, of emotional well-being, and of how health affects daily living. Authors differ, however, in their specific definitions of and methods of measuring individual health status dimensions (see, e.g., Moinpour, Hayden, Thompson, Feigl, & Metch, 1990; Nelson, Landgraf, Hays, Wasson, & Kirk, 1990; Parkerson, Broadhead, & Tse, 1991).

We adopted Ware and Sherbourne's (1992) conception that health status consists of eight distinctive dimensions. Five represent patients' perceptions of problems with the health of their bodies and health in general. These include bodily pain, physical functioning (i.e., routine physical activities such as bending, walking, and lifting), role limitations due to physical problems, vitality (i.e., pep and energy), and health in general. Another three aspects of health status address the patient's perceptions of social and psychological problems. These include social functioning (i.e., relationships with family and friends), mental health (i.e., emotional well-being and psychological distress), and role limitations (e.g., work, chores, and other daily activities) due to emotional problems. For two reasons, we adopted Ware and Sherbourne's (1992) perspective on health status. First, their health concepts and SF-36 Health Status Questionnaire are arguably the most widely used approaches to the study of health status. Second, as is discussed later, the eight health status dimensions provide a convenient and diverse category system for classifying topics of physician–patient communication.

The purpose of this research was to examine two issues pertaining to physician–patient communication about health-related quality of life, patients' preferences for physician inquiry into these matters and how discussion of the patient's health status is introduced, managed, and terminated during medical encounters. We anticipate that patients' preferences for physician inquiry into health status and the extent to which physicians and patients discuss these issues will vary depending on the degree to which the health status dimension relates to physical health versus psychological and social aspects of health. This claim is grounded in the premise that, although physicians and patients have different orientations toward health, it is the physician's perspective that dominates the encounter.

Perspective and Power in Medical Encounters

When conducting medical consultations, physicians typically adhere to the "biomedical model," the view that health consists primarily of bodily functions and that the important forces impinging upon health are organic (e.g., disease, muscle trauma) and behavioral (e.g., diet, alcohol consumption) in nature (McWhinney, 1989; Smith & Hoppe, 1991). Due to their training and the need to diagnose and remedy medical problems, physicians tackle medical problems in a reductionistic manner by taking a medical history, conducting the physical examination, identifying deviations from normal bodily functioning, and offering or recommending treatment (Todd, 1989; Waitzkin, 1991). From the physician's perspective, the patients's health-related quality of life improves to the extent that the doctor is able to find solutions to a specific organic (e.g., infection, cigarette smoke) cause of the patient's distress.

On the other hand, the patient's personal experience with health is highly subjective and inherently linked to contextual and psychological concerns. For example, not only do patients have their own unique understanding of and worries about health and illness, they also evaluate health in relation to its effects on work, family, recreation, and other daily activities; (Kleinman, Eisenberg, & Good, 1978; Levenstein et al., 1989). As are doctors, patients are concerned about bodily functions. However, whereas social and psychological aspects of health may be a secondary concern (if a concern at all) to the doctor, they are the principal reasons for the patient's interest in seeing the physician.

Although patients and doctors bring different perspectives into medical encounters, it is the physician's agenda that tends to dominate the consultation. For a variety of reasons (e.g., the doctor's social status and medical expertise), physicians and patients typically assume that communicative control in the consultation primarily rests with the doctor (Stiles, 1993; Street, 1992a, 1992b). In other words, although patients may ask questions and express their concerns, doctors typically control (and are allowed to control) the visit by initiating most of the discussion topics, interrupting to ask questions, offering opinions, directing the patient through the physical examination, and prescribing a course of action for the patient to follow. However, although the doctor tends to be the more dominant interactant, physicians who ignore the patient's beliefs about health or fail to address the patient's concerns often have dissatisfied and noncompliant patients (Frankel & Beckman, 1989; Stewart, 1984), achieve poorer health outcomes (Kaplan, Greenfield, & Ware, 1989; Street et al., 1993), make incomplete or erroneous diagnoses (Beckman & Frankel, 1984), and may produce malpractice litigation (Sommers, 1985).

Patients' Preferences for Physician Inquiry into Health Status

We anticipate that most patients want physicians to be concerned about physical dimensions of health status such as physical functioning, pain, and health in general. These features of health are important to patients and, importantly, are topics often addressed by doctors during medical encounters. However, patients may vary considerably in their desires for physicians to ask about psychosocial aspects of health such as role limitations due to emotional problems, social functioning, and mental health. The available evidence suggests that some patients will want doctors to ask about these issues and others will not.

For example, patients in Nelson et al.'s (1990) study wanted doctors to be aware of their overall well-being. Other studies also have reported that patients express more satisfaction with care when physicians make a point to discuss the patient's feelings, family, and work (Campbell, Neikirk, & Hosokawa, 1990; Weinberger, Greene, & Mamlin, 1981). However, Hyatt (1980) found that more than 50% of the patients in his study believed that primary care providers should not handle issues related to emotional problems, marital problems, and social matters without referral. In summary, then, we expect that the degree to which patients want physicians to ask about health status will vary for different health status dimensions.

Physician-Patient Communication About Health-Related Quality of Life

In light of the information just presented, it is likely that individual health status dimensions will not receive equal treatment during medical encounters. On the one hand, we might expect physicians and patients to communicate openly and for extended periods about physical aspects of health because these issues concern patients and fit within the doctor's primary focus on bodily functions (Todd, 1989; McWhinney, 1989). On the other hand, physician–patient discussion of psychosocial aspects of health status may vary considerably depending on whether the patient wishes to discuss these matters and on whether the physician is interested in exploring them.

For example, some patients may think that their psychosocial concerns fall outside the purview of medical doctors. Patients holding such beliefs may be reluctant to discuss emotional and social aspects of their lives even if physicians openly express an interest in these matters. Another possibility is that physicians may seek to avoid or downplay psychosocial issues and redirect the discussion to physical or medical matters. For example, Waitzkin (1991) argued that physicians often "marginalize" the patient's attempts to discuss personal and social issues. Doctors achieve this by using conversational devices such as interruptions, topic changes, and de-emphasis. Relatedly, because they are medical "experts," physicians may "medicalize" psychosocial issues by advocating medical solutions to nonmedical problems. For example, a physician may prescribe an antidepressant for the patient's anxiety about a marital relationship. Marginalization and medicalization typically shift the focus away from the social and psychological context of the patient's health to the physician's agenda of discussing biomedical aspects of health.

Research Questions

We investigated three research questions: Do prenatal patients want physicians to ask about some aspects of health status (e.g., pain) more than others (e.g., social functioning)? Are patients more satisfied when they perceive their physicians as having asked about health status? How often and to what extent do physicians and prenatal patients talk about health-related quality of life? Specifically, we were interested in how physicians and patients introduced, extended, and terminated discussion of health-related quality of life, particularly those aspects of health status with which the patient was reporting problems. Thus, for the third research question, we examined only those episodes where doctors and patients discussed a health status issue regarding which the patient indicated limitations. Limiting our analysis to this subset of the sample also had the advantage of reducing the rather large number of possible interaction sequences to analyze.

Prenatal visits in an outpatient clinic were chosen as the research context for two reasons. First, the medical tasks of these visits are generally consistent across encounters. Thus, variability in the communicative content of a prenatal visit may be related to a woman's experiences with pregnancy. As Inui and Carter (1985) observed, studying physician–patient interaction within relatively homogeneous settings minimizes confounding influences due to differences in medical conditions and type of practice. Second, prenatal patients may vary considerably with respect to their health status. For some patients, the pregnancy has little effect on their health and daily functioning, whereas other patients may experience anxiety, decreased vitality, and limitations with social, family, and work activities.

RESEARCH DESIGN AND METHODS

Research Setting and Participants

Research participants were solicited over a 4-month period from prenatal patients in the Department of Obstetrics and Gynecology at Scott and White Clinic in Temple, Texas. New prenatal patients who were being cared for by residents were asked to participate in this study. The decision to include only new prenatal patients was based on the fact that these visits are usually longer than follow-up visits and may allow more opportunities for discussing a variety of topics. Patients were excluded only if they were non-English speaking, could not be reached by telephone, or previously had seen a physician regarding the current pregnancy. Over the 4-month period, 67 patients were invited to participate and of these, 58 were enrolled in the study. Table 10.1 presents the sample's characteristics. The patients were ethnically diverse (59% White, 17% Hispanic, and 24% African American) and were between 17 and 37 years of age. Patients varied considerably with respect to number of previous pregnancies and gestational age of the current pregnancy.

TABLE 10.1
Patients' Characteristics (N = 58)

Patient Characteristic	M	SD	Range
Age (years)	21.93	3.83	17-37
Number of pregnancies	2.69	1.57	0-8
Gestational age (weeks)	23.90	8.70	8.5-35.0
Health status[a]			
Health perceptions	70.44	15.47	28-100
Physical functioning	85.36	11.43	43-100
Social functioning	82.12	18.34	27-100
Role limitations/physical	58.31	37.29	0-100
Role limitations/emotional	62.24	40.55	0-100
Pain	73.45	16.07	36-100
Vitality	54.12	16.02	17-92
Mental health	72.28	18.58	27-100

[a]Health status scores were standardized on a scale of 0 to 100. The higher the score, the less the limitation.

Seven resident physicians volunteered to participate in this project. These doctors (three females, four males) were first ($n = 3$), second ($n = 1$), and third ($n = 3$) year residents in obstetrics–gynecology. Each doctor consulted with at least 5 and no more than 12 patients.

Procedure[1]

A research assistant contacted patients by phone 1 or 2 days before their visits. If a patient was willing to participate in the study, the SF-36 Health Status Questionnaire was administered over the telephone. On the day of the appointment, the research assistant met the patient in the examination room prior to the arrival of the doctor. At this time, written informed consent was obtained, the preferences measure was completed, and the taperecorder turned on. After the consultation ended, the research assistant re-entered the room and administered the perceptions and satisfaction measures.

Scoring Health Status

The range of possible scores for each health status dimension varies considerably with a minimum range of 0–3 (e.g., role limitations due to emotional problems) to a maximum of 5–30 (e.g., mental health). Thus, the patient's scores were standardized on a scale of 0–100. We arbitrarily chose 63 or below to be scores indicative of limitations. Using this criteria, 26% of the patients ($n = 15$) perceived problems with health in general, 26% ($n = 15$) reported problems with mental health, 5% ($n = 3$) had difficulties with physical functioning, 41% ($n = 24$) reported role limitations due to physical problems, 34% ($n = 20$) experienced role limitations due to emotional problems, 10% ($n = 6$) had difficulties with social relations, 21% ($n = 12$) reported bodily pain, and 67% ($n = 39$) had problems with vitality. All but 7 patients reported at least one health status limitation.

Measures Assessing Patients' Preferences, Perceptions, and Satisfaction

Table 10.2 includes the instrument assessing patients' preferences for and perceptions of physician inquiries into health status. Each instrument contained a single-item scale for each of the eight health concepts. The items were formulated directly

---

[1] A more detailed description of the methods is presented elsewhere (Street, Gold, & McDowell, 1994) where some of these results have been reported. This research actually included an experimental manipulation where doctors received health status information prior to consultations with half of their clients and no health status reports on the other half. For the sake of space, we chose not to provide the complete description of the experiment because the manipulation had no noticeable effect on patient's preferences, perceptions, satisfaction, and on any linguistic evidence of communication about health-related quality of life.

TABLE 10.2
Statements Used to Assess Patients' Preferences[a] and Perceptions[b]

1. The doctor asks your opinion about your health. (Health Perceptions)
2. The doctor asks about any problems related to daily activities such as bending, walking, running, working, etc. (Physical Functioning)
3. The doctor asks if your physical health is causing any problems with work or other daily activities. (Role Limitations due to Physical Problems)
4. The doctor asks if you're having any emotional problems which interfere with work or other daily activities. (Role Limitations due to Emotional Problems)
5. The doctor asks if you're having any physical or emotional problems that interfere with your social activities with family, friends, neighbors, or groups. (Social Functioning)
6. The doctor asks if you have been experiencing any pain. (Pain)
7. The doctor asks about how much pep and energy you've been having. (Vitality)
8. The doctor asks about your mental health such as whether or not you've been happy, nervous, depressed, etc. (Mental Health)

[a]For the "preferences" measure, the response options included: "I definitely would like this," "I probably would like this," "It doesn't matter," "I probably would not like this," and "I definitely would not like this."
[b]For perceptions measure, statements were worded in past tense and the response options included: "This definitely happened," "I think this happened," "I'm not sure if this happened," "I don't think this happened," and "This definitely did not happen."

from Ware and Sherbourne's (1992) conceptualization of each health concept and from the SF-36 items themselves. For example, for patient's vitality, the statement was "The doctor asks about how much pep and energy I've been having." For physical functioning, the item was "The doctor asks about any problems related to daily activities such as bending, walking, running, lifting, etc." The same statements were used for each of the two measures although for patients' perceptions the verbs were in past as opposed to present tense.

The two self-report instruments differed from one another with respect to their response options. For the preferences measure, each item had the following options: "I definitely would like this," "I probably would like this," "It doesn't matter," "I probably would not like this," and "I definitely would not like this." The following response options were used for the perceptions measure: "This definitely happened," "I think this happened," "I'm not sure if this happened," "I don't think this happened," and "This definitely did not happen."

Patients' satisfaction with care was assessed using a measure developed by Street and Buller (1987). This measure contains four items tapping into patients' global evaluations of health care received: very dissatisfied–very satisfied, not very well cared for–very well cared for, very ineffective–very effective, and very low quality–very high quality. Patients reported their responses on a scale of 1 to 10. Although there are various dimensions of patients' satisfaction with care (e.g., cognitive, affective), a global measure was chosen to prevent a long response form and because global measures tend to correlate highly with specific dimensions of satisfaction (Roter, Hall, & Katz, 1987). Alpha reliability for this measure was .81.

Coding of Discourse

The first step in coding the discourse was to identify episodes in which health status was discussed. Two coders, blind to the purpose of the research, participated in three 2-hour training sessions. Codes reviewed definitions of the eight health status dimensions and specific items representing these dimensions in the SF-36 questionnaire. In addition, examples of physician–patient discussion of these topics were provided. Coders were then instructed to listen to seven randomly chosen recordings of consultations, find episodes in which health status issues were a topic, and identify the specific health status dimension being discussed. Admittedly, some episodes may contain "multiple" health status issues (e.g., vitality, pain, and general health). For these episodes, coders were to decide whether there was a predominant health status issue and, if so, to place the episode in that category. If there was not a predominant issue, coders placed the episode in a ninth category for multiple issues.

Both coders worked separately to code the seven consultations and achieved a rate of agreement of 72%. Street worked with the coders to resolve the differences and refine interpretive rules for categorizing. Once their differences were satisfactorily resolved, each coder then coded the entire sample of encounters searching for episodes where the doctor and patient discussed a health status issue regarding which the patient indicated limitations. Overall rate of agreement on coding was 86%. For further analysis, we included only those episodes ($n = 43$) that both reviewers agreed on in their coding.

The second step of the analysis was to identify whether there were particular patterns of communication that repeatedly emerged in the episodes. After transcribing the 43 episodes verbatim, the coders and Street reviewed and discussed similarities and differences in the various episodes with respect to how the health status issues were managed communicatively. It was finally decided that each of the 43 episodes could be placed into one of five categories:

1. extended discussion, which includes those episodes in which the health status issue was discussed for some length of time. In these exchanges, each interactant produced five or more conversational turns.
2. physician marginalizes, which occurs in those episodes where the doctor deemphasized or ignored the patient's complaint.
3. patient complaint–physician provides solution–next topic, which represents those exchanges where, soon after the patient's complaint, the doctor offered a solution and then moved on to the next topic. In these situations, the doctor did not investigate the complaint, explain the condition, or provide a rationale for the proposed remedy.
4. patient avoids, which consists of those episodes where the patient avoided the topic or where the patient chose not to talk about an issue even when the doctor asked about it.

5. other, which is a category for those episodes not falling within the other four categories.

Using this coding scheme, the coders agreed in their categorization on all but five episodes (agreement = 88%). The coders worked together and resolved their differences for the remaining five.

RESULTS

Patients' Preferences and Perceptions

Table 10.3 presents the distribution of scores on the individual items of the preferences and perceptions measures. To answer the question of whether patients' preferences and perceptions differed for one health status dimension (e.g., social functioning) relative to another (e.g., physical functioning), analyses of variance were conducted using the eight health concepts as categorical levels of a single variable. Given the data presented in Table 10.3, it is not surprising that significant effects due to health status category were observed on both patients' preferences [F (7,456) = 14.84, $p < .001$] and perceptions [F (7,456) = 25.59, $p < .001$]. These findings can be placed roughly into three groups. First, most patients wanted physicians to ask about some health status issues and, generally speaking, perceived doctors as inquiring into these matters. These included pain and health perceptions. Second, there were aspects of health status that most patients wanted physicians to discuss yet more than half of the patients either believed these issues were not addressed or were unsure whether the physician had asked about them. These included physical functioning, vitality, and role limitations due to physical problems. Finally, patients varied considerably in their preferences for physician inquiries into social functioning, mental health, and role limitations due to emotional problems. Approximately half of the patients wanted these topics discussed, whereas the remainder either did not care or preferred that physicians not ask about these matters. However, patients uniformly perceived physicians as not asking about these aspects of health status (see Table 10.3).[2]

---

[2] It would be reasonable to assume that patients' functional limitations would be related to their preferences for physicians to ask about health status. However, none of the correlations between individual health status scores and patients' preferences reached statistical significance. There was some evidence indicating that the more patients experienced limitations with respect to vitality, mental health, and role limitations due to physical problems, the more physicians were perceived as inquiring into these issues ($r = -.32$, $p < .05$ for vitality; $r = -.23$, $p < .08$ for mental health; $r = -.30$, $p < .05$ for role limitations due to physical problems). This is an interesting finding and worthy of future research. Perhaps the more limitations a patient experiences with respect to a particular aspect of health status, the more critically he or she evaluates whether or not the physician indeed addressed this issue.

TABLE 10.3
Number and Percentage of Patients Responding to Each Item on the Measures Assessing Patients' Expectations, Preferences, and Perceptions

Measure	Responses (N and %) for Each Health Status Dimension Doctor Asks About							
	HP	PF	R/Ph	R/Em	SF	P	Vit	MH

Preferences

Would like this	36	31	31	18	13	52	31	22
	62%	53%	53%	31%	22%	90%	53%	38%
Might like this	12	17	16	15	13	6	21	14
	21%	29%	28%	26%	22%	10%	36%	24%
Don't care	10	9	9	18	24	0	5	19
	17%	15%	15%	31%	41%		9%	33%
Might not like this	0	0	0	3	4	0	1	2
				5%	7%		2%	3%
Would not like this	0	1	2	4	4	0	0	1
		2%	3%	7%	7%			2%

Perceptions

Definitely happened	36	16	16	10	5	48	17	9
	62%	28%	28%	17%	9%	83%	29%	15%
Probably happened	7	6	6	3	4	3	4	4
	12%	10%	10%	5%	7%	5%	7%	7%
Not sure	8	7	7	1	0	0	6	0
	14%	12%	12%	3%			10%	
Probably did not happen	0	6	5	6	5	0	2	7
		10%	9%	10%	9%		3%	12%
Definitely did not happen	7	23	24	38	44	7	29	38
	12%	40%	41%	66%	76%	12%	50%	66%

Note. Key to abbreviations: HP = Patients' health perceptions, PF = Physical functioning, R/Ph = Role limitations due to physical problems, R/Em = Role limitations due to emotional problems, SF = Social functioning, P = Pain, Vit = Vitality, MH = Mental health

Patients' Satisfaction and Physicians' Inquiries Into Health Status

Patients' perceptions of physician inquiry into individual health status issues were not equally predictive of satisfaction. Specifically, satisfaction was greater when patients thought physicians had asked about health perceptions ($r = .51, p < .001$), pain ($r = .39, p < .01$), vitality ($r = .33, p < .05$), and (to some extent) role limitations due to physical problems ($r = .23, p < .08$). Although the correlations were positive, patients' satisfaction was not predicted by whether physicians had inquired into physical functioning ($r = .19$), role limitations due to emotional problems ($r = .21$), mental health ($r = .13$), or social functioning ($r = .19$).

Physician–Patient Discussion of Health Status

Overview. Table 10.4 presents descriptive results from the coding of physician–patient discussion of health status. There were four instances in which coders believed multiple issues were discussed. Because a common theme in each of these episodes involved the patient's perceptions of health in general, these four episodes were grouped within the category of general health perceptions. Of the 43 episodes, 34 (79%) addressed physical dimensions of health status including general health, pain, physical functioning, vitality, and role limitations due to physical problems. Nine (21%) episodes addressed strictly psychosocial aspects of health such as mental health, role limitations due to emotional problems, and social functioning.

Another way of looking at these data is to examine whether particular health status issues were discussed in those encounters involving patients reporting lim-

TABLE 10.4
Patterns of Physician-Patient Communication About Health Status

	Health Status Dimension							
	HP	PF	R/Ph	R/Em	SF	P	Vit	MH
General Information								
Number of encounters with patients reporting limitations	15	3	24	20	6	12	39	15
Number of above encounters in which the health issue was discussed	10	1	1	1	1	10	7	6
Number of eposides in which the health status issue was discussed[a]	11	1	1	1	1	13	8	7
Patterns of communication								
Extended discussion	8	0	1	1	1	3	2	2
Physician marginalizes	1	1	0	0	0	3	3	1
Patient complaint-Dr. Solution-Topic change	0	0	0	0	0	5	3	0
Patient avoids	1	0	0	0	0	0	0	4
Other	1	0	0	0	0	2	0	0

Note. Key to abbreviations: HP = Patients' health perceptions, PF = Physical functioning, R/PH = Role limitations due to physical problems, R/Em = Role limitations due to emotional problems, SF = Social functioning, P = Pain, Vit = Vitality, MH = Mental health

[a]There are more episodes of specific health status dimensions being discussed than there are number of encounters in which a specific health status issues was mentioned because some encounters contained more than one episode.

itations in that area. Of 23 patients reporting problems with health in general, pain, and/or physical functioning, one or more of these issues were discussed in 17 of the encounters. Forty-six patients reported low vitality and/or role limitations due to physical problems. These issues were discussed in only 9 (20%) of these encounters. Finally, 28 patients reported limitations in mental health, role limitations due to emotional problems, and social functioning. These issues were mentioned in 8 (29%) of these encounters.

Approximately 70% of these topics were introduced by the patient (see Table 10.4). In the vast majority of cases, the patient raised the issue after the physician asked whether the patient had any problems or complaints. This general pattern held for all health status categories with the exception of mental health. In six of the seven episodes in which mental health was mentioned, the physician raised the issue by asking whether the patient was happy about the pregnancy.

Finally, Table 10.4 also presents information on the number of episodes placed within the categories of extended discussion, physician marginalizes, patient complaint–physician offers solution–next topic, patient avoids, and other. However, these frequencies are rather small and, in and of themselves, are not particularly enlightening. Greater insight may be gained by discussing specific exemplars within these categories.

Physician Marginalizes the Patient's Concern. There were several exchanges ($n = 9$) in which doctor (D) marginalized the patient's concern by ignoring the complaint or de-emphasizing its significance. These instances occurred most often when the patient (P) complained of either fatigue or pain.

Exemplar 1
D: Let me go ahead and give you a quick once over. You've been feeling healthy everyday?
P: Tired all the time.
D: Well, that should get better.
P: I hope so.
D: At the very latest when you have the baby! (Laugh) I'm going to start by listening to your lungs real quick.

In the following example, the patient clearly wants to discuss the issue in greater detail than does the doctor who ultimately prevails.

Exemplar 2
D: Are you having any other problems right now?
P: Yeah, shortness of breath. Pretty bad.
D: That can be pretty normal.
P: It gets pretty bad though at times.

D: You have to set up to breathe or what?
P: Yeah, I have to sit way up.
D: Ok, any loss of fluid? Contractions or bleeding? Cough?
P: No.
(There is no further discussion of shortness of breath.)

Patient's Complaint–Physician's Solution–Physician Raises Next Topic. A second type of exchange was characterized by the following sequence of events—patient's complaint, doctor's solution (often given after interrupting the patient), doctor introduces next topic. In these situations, the doctor offered little information that explained the patient's problem or the proposed remedy. Once again, this communicative pattern was most likely to occur when doctor and patient were discussing problems of physical discomfort or fatigue.

Exemplar 3
D: Are you having any problems? Any labor pains?
P: No, I, uh, the last time when I was pregnant I had nosebleeds all the time. It's come back.
D: It's back again? Keep the lining of your nose as moist as you can. You can use a little coat of vaseline in your nose, and sometimes the humidity will help. You can use a humidifier at night if it gets real bad. You had this problem with your previous pregnancy, right?
P: Yeah.
D: Ok, what do you think this is, a boy or a girl?

In the following encounter with a patient complaining of severe headaches, the doctor presented the solution with a condescending tone of voice perhaps because he wanted to terminate the consultation.

Exemplar 4
P: Um . . . I've been . . . I've run out of Tylenol. I need to know if I can take Ibuprofin?
D: No, not Ibuprofin. Tylenol.
P: Just Tylenol?
D: Even extra-strength Tylenol. But not Ibuprofin.
P: Ok, also my back's been killing me . . .
D: (Interrupts) Local heat. Local heat and Tylenol. Get your husband to give you some back rubs.
P: He's pretty good about that. Oh God, my back hurts so bad somedays.
D: There's one cure for that and that's delivery of the baby.
P: (Laughs) Amazing, isn't it?
D: Call me if you need anything. We'll see you back in three weeks.

In one case, the patient questions the adequacy of the physician's suggestion for pain relief. Her comment did not noticeably alter the doctor's conviction in the proposed solution.

Exemplar 5
D: Do you take anything for them?
P: I've taken ( ) that prescription and those work, or my mother would take me to the hospital and I would get a shot. But other than that nothing . . .
D: (Interrupts) Do you ever try Tylenol?
P: Yeah
D: And that doesn't work at all?
P: No, I've tried a bunch a bunch of Tylenol. Handfuls-not at one time- but in general it doesn't work.
D: Ok. . . . So what do you think about this pregnancy?
(The problem of headaches is not mentioned again)

Patient Avoids the Issue. There were several instances in which the patient chose not to introduce her concerns or to elaborate on health status limitations. Part of the reason may be that the doctor did not specifically ask about these issues or, if he or she did, it was in the form of closed-ended questions. In turn, the patient did not attempt to raise the issue or elaborate after her brief answer. This patient's scores on the SF-36 indicated problems with both pain and health in general.

Exemplar 6
D: You have any headaches, visual changes, any problems like that?
P: No.
D: You having any problems urinating?
P: No.
D: OK

The topic of the patient's emotional well-being most often was introduced by the physician, typically in the form of "how do you feel about having this baby?" However, in four of the encounters the patient does not elaborate on her feelings even though her health status scores indicated some problems in this domain. The physicians often considered the patients' nonresponsiveness to be acceptable. The following exemplars are two examples.

Exemplar 7
D: So are you pretty happy about being pregnant?
P: Yeah.
D: Huh?

P: Yeah.
D: Ok, good. Let's see there is no speculum in this room.

Exemplar 8
D: You pretty excited?
P: uh huh.
D: Yeah, you look happy. Today is a lot of paperwork.

In these episodes, one cannot be sure whether the patient's nonresponsiveness is due to patient's discomfort discussing the topic or the belief that the doctor is not really interested in discussing her emotional well-being. Exemplar 9 certainly suggests the former explanation and highlights the awkwardness sometimes experienced when discussing emotional issues in supposedly routine consultations. The doctor initially encourages the patient to discuss her feelings. The patient then briefly expresses discomfort with the doctor's queries. The doctor is taken aback by this, offers an account, and then quickly shifts the discussion to the presumably "safer" biomedical topics.

Exemplar 9
D: Have you felt just real depressed? Really hopeless? How are you feeling now?
P: I don't know. Sometimes I get depressed a lot. Lately, a lot.
D: Lately a lot? Because of the pregnancy? Or?
P: Yeah, I guess. I don't know. Just everything.
D: Just everything. Are you by yourself? Do you have family down here?
P: No, I have my boyfriend. But, you're making me nervous.
D: Oh, I'm sorry. We don't need to discuss these things. I just wanted to be sure you hadn't been taking any medication and that you're feeling relatively well yourself. You have another being to be taking care of and be thinking about.

Extensive Discussion of Issue. The longer discussions of health status occurred because the physician used one or more of the following communicative strategies—probing to gain more information on the patient's complaint, encouraging the patient to express her concerns, allowing and not interrupting the patient's floorholding. In turn, the patient was relatively responsive. The following was one of the "multiple issues" excerpts and contains several of the conversational moves previously listed.

Exemplar 10
D: Anything you have questions about, or concerns?
P: Yeah.
D: What's that?

P: Why do I always feel so sleepy? I'm tired all the time.
D: Are you really?
P: I have no energy whatsoever.
D: How much do you sleep a day?
P: During the daytime ( ).
D: How much do you sleep at night?
P: I go to sleep about 9:00, then I wake up anywhere between 4:30 and 5:00.
D: 4:30 or 5:00? Is that long enough for you?
P: No.
D: That's unusual. What do you do when you wake up? Do you ever go back to sleep?
P: Sometimes. Sometimes I don't.
(Doctor and patient discuss headaches as a reason she cannot sleep)
D: Is there something else in you're worried about or concerned about?
P: Life.
D: In general, huh?
P: Yeah.
D: What do you think is the best way to resolve that? I mean you're tired a little bit because you're pregnant, but you shouldn't be drained. Waking up in the morning like that is sometimes an indication that you're worried about something more than you realize or admit to.
P: I know what I'm going to do about it.
D: What's that?
P: I'm going to live with my mom.
(Doctor and patient briefly discuss patient's problems with her fiance and his mother. The doctor shifts the talk back to physical issues such as fatigue and weight loss. Patient ultimately mentions that her depression might be due to the death of her first child. The doctor and patient close the episode with a brief discussion of Sudden Infant Death Syndrome.)

Extensive discussion does not necessarily indicate that doctor and patient had a "happy" exchange or that doctor and patient shared the same views of how to resolve the patient's difficulties. This patient is in her 15th week of pregnancy.

Exemplar 11
D: Any other problems?
P: Not really other than I wanted to ask about my work.
D: Uh huh
P: I stand on my feet all day long and I only get a 20 minute break to sit down. And my feet is already starting swelling and they're hassling me at work.

D: Uh huh
P: And I mean, we have a job that bags and belts where we have to take and fill, you know, the big bins and bags. You have to take 'em and open 'em and fill 'em and everything. And after I get through bending and everything a lot my back hurts.
D: Uh huh. Well its probably not hurting because of the pregnancy. That kind of work will tend to make it hurt.
P: No! It didn't hurt before I was
D: (Interrupts) Being pregnant is not a contraindication to working. OK? Uh, there are lots of women who work right up until the time they deliver. What we might advise here is there, what else, are there other things you can do at work that don't involve heavy lifting?
P: Not really. Not really because I check groceries out and they have dog food and, you know, stuff like that. So not really.

The doctor and patient continue this discussion for the next several minutes. The doctor initially offers suggestions for changing the work environment (e.g., getting a helper, talking to her manager, etc.), which the patient rejects as not possible. The patient complains that she is not treated fairly and that her physical discomfort is getting worse. Finally, the patient asks for a medical excuse saying she cannot work because of the pregnancy. The doctor refuses but says that this is perhaps a possibility later in the pregnancy.

DISCUSSION

Health-related quality of life is a multidimensional phenomenon representing the patient's perceptions of problems and limitations related to physical, social, and psychological functioning (Ware & Sherbourne, 1992). This research examined two issues related to physician–patient communication about the patient's health status, patients' preferences for physician inquiry into these matters and the manner in which doctors and patients talked about health status. Although this was a study of prenatal patients and residents specializing in obstetrics and gynecology, several of our findings are noteworthy and have implications for both research and clinical practice.

Patients' Preferences for Discussing Health Status During Medical Consultations

Considered collectively, our findings of what doctors and patients chose to discuss and of what patients wanted physicians to ask about indicate that the interactants share an understanding that the health of the body is inherently linked to the health of the person. Patients uniformly wanted physicians to ask about pain, health in general, and physical functioning and (with the exception of physical functioning) were more satisfied with care when doctors fulfilled these desires. In turn, consistent with the biomedical perspective, pain and general health were the issues most often discussed by doctors (see Tables 10.3 and 10.4).

Where their perspectives differ, however, centers on whether the discussion of health needs to address issues related to the patient's emotional well-being and performance of daily activities. The discrepancy between what patients wanted physicians to address and what physicians did discuss was most noticeable for health status domains where the patient's physical limitations interfered with daily activity and function. For example, most patients wanted physicians to ask about vitality and role limitations due to physical problems and expressed greater satisfaction with physicians who were perceived to have addressed these issues. However, both patients and researchers observed little evidence indicating that physicians as a whole pursued these issues at length.

Although most patients wanted doctors to ask about pain, general health, vitality, and role limitations due to physical problems, preferences for physician inquiry into primarily psychosocial matters varied among the patients. Approximately 50% of these prenatal patients wanted physicians to ask about emotional problems and social functioning, whereas the remainder either did not care or preferred that doctors not ask about these matters. As can be seen in Table 10.4, some patients even actively avoided discussing these issues. As was the case with vitality and role limitations due to physical problems, physicians rarely examined social and psychological issues.

In summary, whether due to training and/or to institutional constraints, these residents investigated the patient's health in a manner rarely extending beyond the context of the body. Patients, however, understand that the health of the body is not independent of everyday activities and thus wish physicians would show interest in the body as it relates to matters of daily living such as vitality and role limitations. In turn, a considerable number of patients also believe that their health-related quality of life generally, and not just problems of physical dysfunction, should be of interest and concern to physicians.

Discussing Health Status in Prenatal Visits

When health status was discussed during the encounters, one of several patterns of communication tended to emerge. In a few episodes, primarily those involving talk of pain and general health, doctors and patients spent considerable time discussing the matter. In these longer discussions, the doctor would inquire into the issue with a series of questions or the doctor would avoid interruptions and encourage the patient to elaborate on her concerns. In turn, patients were willing to discuss the issue at some length. In these episodes, both parties seemed to be engaged in the issue although not necessarily in agreement. For example, in Exemplar 11, the patient complained that her pregnancy was interfering with work. Both the doctor and patient talked extensively about the matter although the parties could not reach agreement on a solution to her problems.

The remaining patterns of communication were characterized by much less discussion of health status. "Physician marginalization" and "patient complaint–doctor solution–next topic" are two types of exchanges that typically involved the patient's problems with pain and vitality. In addition, both types of exchanges were characterized by physicians who spent little (if any) time discussing the nature of the patient's problems or who moved to another topic shortly after the patient presented the complaint. Consider first the exchanges characterized by "patient complaint–doctor solution–next topic." For pain, the typical solution was Tylenol even for a patient (Exemplar 5) who said Tylenol was not effective in alleviating her headaches. For vitality, the typical solution was to take vitamins and improve diet. For lack of a better phrase, the doctor's solution–next topic ploy could be labeled the *hypodermic* approach to the patient's problem. The doctor "injects" the solution conversationally and then moves on to the next topic believing that the previous complaint is now resolved. This strategy may stem from medicine's traditional approach of isolating and resolving problems or from institutional values to provide services quickly and efficiently.

Physicians who marginalized the patient's concerns seemed to take-for-granted the view that lower vitality, headaches, stomach pain, and swollen feet were "normal" features of pregnancy (to quote a doctor in this study, "just part of being pregnant"). Although a normal complication of pregnancy, physical discomfort and a lack of energy are nevertheless of great concern to patients, yet these issues were rarely discussed and, when they were, often received only superficial attention.

Finally, there were five episodes in which health status, mental health in particular, was not discussed at great length because the patient was relatively nonresponsive and chose not to elaborate or discuss her concerns even when the physician expressed an interest in the matter. These findings are consistent with evidence indicating that some patients either did not care or preferred that doctors not ask about social and emotional issues. Speculatively, perhaps those patients expressing indifference or reluctance to discuss these issues believed there was no need to discuss their social and psychological concerns, perceived such topics as beyond the expertise and responsibility of the medical doctor, or thought the doctor had neither the time nor the interest in extensively discussing the matter.

In summary, our evidence suggests that health status issues are rarely discussed and, when they are, often receive limited attention. Doctors tend not to pursue these matters; patients typically follow the doctor's lead and choose not to force discussion of health-related quality of life. Future research should examine whether there is a need to make health status a more prominent focus of medical encounters. For example, will patients express more satisfaction, take a more active role in their care, or experience better health outcomes if doctors and patients spend more time discussing particular aspects of health-related quality of life? Relatedly, if some patients are reluctant to discuss certain topics, such as emotional well-being and social relationships, is it because of their perceived powerlessness as communicators or their belief that some health status issues fall outside the domain of the doctor's role and responsibility?

Clinical Suggestions

First, the fact that some patients were either indifferent toward or preferred physicians not to ask about certain psychosocial topics should not be taken as an argument against using a "patient-centered" approach in the consultation or against discussing personal matters with patients. As Shapiro (1990) observed, physician management of the patient's psychosocial concerns is a multifaceted process that includes listening skills, rapport with the patients, respect for the patient's perspective, attention to the patient's worries about health, as well as interest in the patient's social relations, work, and emotional well-being. Our findings suggest that patients generally respond favorably to patient-centered physicians who show a sincere interest in the patient's health and concerns about the body such as pain, vitality, physical functioning, and role limitations due to physical problems.

Doctors may think matters of bodily functioning are part of the normal investigative routine. However, a distinction should be made between attention to the patient's physical health per se (reviewing symptoms, conducting the physical exam) and attention to the patient's perspective on these issues. The latter is very important to patients. One could argue, for example, that by marginalizing or offering the "quick fix" solution for the patient's problems, some of these physicians failed to appreciate and address the patient's concerns about health, particularly vitality and pain. The patients, in turn, expressed less satisfaction with care received. Although the complications created by pregnancy may be routine and normal to the physician, they are often quite unique and problematic to the patient.

We would recommend that physicians listen attentively and allow (even encourage) patients to elaborate on their concerns. Such a move reveals the physician's interest in the patient's perspective. Also, by allowing the patient uninterrupted floortime, information may be gained that is important for diagnosis and for formulating management plans suited to the patient's individual needs and circumstances and that would not have emerged had the physician used a series of close-ended questions on a symptoms checklist (Beckman & Frankel, 1984).

Second, for a variety of reasons, physicians may wish to uncover information about the patient's mental state, family, and work activities. As mentioned earlier, some patients actively avoided talking about these issues, and approximately half of these patients expressed indifference or a desire for physicians not to pursue these matters. One strategy for encouraging the patient's responsiveness on these topics is to use an open-ended interviewing style coupled with nonverbal attentiveness (e.g., eye contact, facial expressiveness). Questions like "Anything stressing you these days?" or "Everything going OK at home and work?" offer windows of opportunity (Branch & Malik, 1993) for patients to discuss personal, emotional, and social matters. Open-ended questions also allow patients freedom to structure their response in a manner comfortable to them. Research indicates that patients indeed are more responsive when physicians use utterances encouraging patients to elaborate on their concerns (Cox, 1989; Street, 1992b).

Finally, some physicians may argue that they have a great deal of interest in promoting the patient's health-related quality of life but that the limited time allowed for consultations and the medical tasks required during these visits provide little opportunity to discuss these matters at length. However, there is evidence indicating that consultations are not appreciably longer when doctors allow patients uninterrupted floortime (Beckman & Frankel, 1984; Branch & Malik, 1993). In addition, our results suggest that patients often perceived physicians as inquiring into health status (Table 10.3) although the researchers observed that physicians and patients infrequently discussed these issues (Table 10.4). It appears that patients give doctors considerably more credit for showing interest in health-related quality of life than do the researchers. This may be because patients expect doctors to examine factors affecting the body. However, doctors who verbally or nonverbally reveal their concern about the patient's well-being, even if briefly, are perceived to be interpersonally sensitive (Street, 1992b) and interested in the patient's health status.

Perhaps the best way to conclude this essay is to compare two hypothetical exchanges between doctor and patient on the subject of vitality.

P: I've just been feeling so tired. I have so little energy.
D: (Looking at the medical chart) Yeah, that's part of being pregnant. Ok, the next thing we need to do. . . .

In contrast to the previous example where the physician marginalizes the patient's concern, consider the following:

P: I've just been feeling so tired. I have so little energy.
D: (looking at the patient) Yeah? In what way?
P: I just don't have any get up and go. I wake up and it seems I just want to sit down and not get up. Just veg and look at the TV all day. But, you know, I have all these things I have to do. Go to work, pick up the kids, do the laundry.
D: No time to be tired, huh? Well, it should get better over the next few weeks. There are a couple of things you can do now that might help. You're feeling tired in part because your body is changing and providing nutrients to both you and the baby. Taking vitamins will provide more of the nutrients that your body needs. And, you know, it's like any other time when you're feeling tired. It always helps to get as much rest as you can and eat good, healthy meals. Does that make sense?

In this example, we simply wanted to demonstrate that in less than 60 seconds, a doctor's verbal and nonverbal communication legitimized the patient's concern, was sensitive to the patient's feelings, offered an explanation for the patient's condition, and provided reasonable suggestions for helping the patient. Of course, there are other "patient-centered" ways of handling this complaint by discussing how the situation could be changed to accommodate the patient's condition (e.g., have the husband help with the laundry, do different tasks at work) or simply allow time for the patient to vent her frustrations (Waitzkin, 1991).

In conclusion, we believe physicians and patients may benefit if doctors were to use a biopsychosocial approach to the medical encounter. This perspective advocates that physicians attend to medical and technical matters, understand and display sensitivity to the patient's feelings, legitimize patient-initiated complaints, and negotiate medical solutions suitable to the patient's personal situation (Ben-Sira, 1990). Our suggestions are not intended to discredit current medical practice. Rather, they are aimed toward helping physicians achieve what Levenstein et al. (1989) referred to as the "patient-centered, clinical interview," where both the doctor's and patient's perspectives are integrated in the medical encounter.

REFERENCES

Ben-Sira, Z. (1990). Primary care practitioners' likelihood to engage in a biopsychosocial approach: An additional perspective on the doctor-patient relationship. *Social Science and Medicine, 31,* 565–576.

Beckman, H. B., & Frankel, R. M. (1984). The effect of physician behavior on the collection of data. *Annals of Internal Medicine, 101,* 692–696.

Branch, W. T., & Malik, T. K. (1993). Using "windows of opportunity" in brief interviews to understand patients' concerns. *Journal of the American Association, 269,* 1667–1668.

Campbell, J. D., Neikirk, H. J., & Hosokawa, M. C. (1990). Development of a psychosocial concern index from videotaped interviews of nurse practitioners and family physicians. *Journal of Family Practice, 30,* 321–326.

Cox, A. (1989). Eliciting patients' feelings. In M. Stewart & D. Roter (Eds.), *Communicating with medical patients* (pp. 99–106). Newbury Park, CA: Sage.

Fowler, F. J., Wennberg, J. E., Timothy, R. P., Barry, M. J., Mulley, A. G., & Hanley, D. (1988). Symptom status and quality of life following prostatectomy. *Journal of the American Medical Association, 259,* 3018–3022.

Frankel, R. M., & Beckman, H. B. (1989). Conversation and compliance with treatment recommendations: An application of micro-interactional analysis of medicine. In B. Dervin, L. Grossberg, B. J. O'Keefe, & E. Wartella (Eds.), *Rethinking communication: Paradigm exemplars* (Vol. 2, pp. 60–74). Newbury Park, CA: Sage.

Hyatt, J. D. (1980). Perceptions of the family physician by patients and family physicians. *Journal of Family Practice, 10,* 295–300.

Inui, T. S., & Carter, W. B. (1985). Problems and prospects for health services research on provider-patient communication. *Medical Care, 23,* 521–538.

Kaplan, S. (1987). Patient reports of quality of health status as predictors of physiologic health measures in chronic disease. *Journal of Chronic Disorders, 40* (Suppl), 27S–35S.

Kaplan, S., Greenfield, S., & Ware, J. E., Jr. (1989). Assessing the effects of physician-patient interactions on the outcomes of chronic disease. *Medical Care, 27* (Suppl), S110–S127.

Kiebert, G. M., de Haes, J. C. J., & van de Velde, C. J. H. (1991). The impact of breast conserving treatment and mastectomy on the quality of life of early-stage breast cancer patients: A review. *Journal of Clinical Oncology, 9,* 1059–1070.

Kleinman, A., Eisenberg, L., & Good, B. (1978). Culture, illness, and care: Clinical lesson from anthropologic and cross-cultural research. *Annals of Internal Medicine, 88,* 251–258.

Levenstein, J. H., Brown, J. B., Weston, W. W., Stewart, M., McCracken, E. C., & McWhinney, I. (1989). Patient-centered clinical interviewing. In M. Stewart & D. Roter (Eds.), *Communicating with medical patients* (pp. 107–120). Newbury Park, CA: Sage.

Lohr, K. N. (1992). Applications of health status assessment measures in clinical practice. *Medical Care, 30*(suppl), MS1–MS14.

McWhinney, I. (1989). The need for a transformed clinical method. In M. Stewart & D. Roter (Eds). *Communicating with medical patients* (pp. 25–40). Newbury Park, CA: Sage.

Moinpour, C. M., Hayden, K. A., Thompson, I. M., Feigl, P., & Metch, B. (1990). Quality of life assessment in Southwest Oncology Group trials. *Oncology, 4,* 79–84.

Nelson, E. C., Landgraf, J. M., Hays, R. D., Wasson, J. H., & Kirk, J. W. (1990). The functional status of patients: how can it be measured in physicians' offices? *Medical Care, 28,* 1111–1126.

Parkerson, G. R., Broadhead, W. E., & Tse, C. J. (1991). Comparison of the Duke Health Profile and the MOS Short-Form in healthy young adults. *Medical Care, 29,* 679–683.

Rost, K. M., Flavin, K. S., Cole, K., & McGill, J. B. (1991). Change in metabolic control and functional status after hospitalization: Impact of patient activation intervention in diabetic patients. *Diabetes Care, 14,* 881–889.

Roter, D. L., Hall, J. A., & Katz, N. R. (1987). Relations between physicians' behaviors and analogue patients' satisfaction, recall, and impressions. *Medical Care, 25,* 437–451.

Shapiro, J. (1990). Patterns of psychosocial performance in the doctor-patient encounter: a study of family practice residents. *Social Science and Medicine, 31,* 1035–1041.

Smith, R. C., & Hoppe, R. B. (1991). The patient's story: Integrating the patient- and physician-centered approaches to interviewing. *Annals of Internal Medicine, 115,* 470–477.

Sommers, P. A. (1985). Malpractice risk and patient relations. *Journal of Family Practice, 20,* 299–301.

Stewart, M. (1984). What is a successful doctor-patient interview? A study of interactions and outcomes. *Social Science and Medicine, 19,* 167–175.

Stiles, W. B. (1993). The process-outcome correlation problem and the uses of verbal interaction process coding. *Southern Communication Journal, 58,* 91–102.

Street, R. L., Jr. (1992a). Communicative styles and adaptations in physician-parent consultations. *Social Science and Medicine, 34,* 1155–1163.

Street, R. L., Jr. (1992b). Analyzing communication in medical consultations: Do behavioral measures correspond to patients' perceptions? *Medical Care, 30,* 976–988.

Street, R. L., Jr., & Buller, D. B. (1987). Nonverbal response patterns in physician-patient interactions: A functional analysis. *Journal of Nonverbal Behavior, 11,* 234–253.

Street, R. L., Jr., Gold, W. R., Jr., & McDowell, A. D. (1994). Using health status surveys in medical consultations. *Medical Care, 32,* 732–744.

Street, R. L., Jr., Piziak, V. K., Carpentier, W., Herzog, J., Hejl, J., Skinner, G., & McLelland, L. (1993). Provider-patient communication and metabolic control. *Diabetes Care, 16,* 714–721.

Todd, A. D. (1989). *Intimate adversaries: Cultural conflict between doctors and women patients.* Philadelphia: University of Pennsylvania Press.

Waitzkin, H. (1991). *The politics of medical encounters.* New Haven, CT: Yale University Press.

Ware, J. E., Jr., & Sherbourne, C. D. (1992). The SF-36 Short-Form Health Survey (SF-36): I. Conceptual framework and item selection. *Medical Care, 30,* 473–483.

Wasson, J. H., Gall, V., McDonald, R., & Liang, M. H. (1990). The prescription of assistive devices for the elderly: practical considerations. *Journal of General Internal Medicine, 5,* 46–53.

Weinberger, M., Greene, J., & Mamlin, J. J. (1981). The impact of clinical encounter events on patient and physician satisfaction. *Social Science and Medicine, 15E,* 239–244.

11 Some Answers About Questions in Clinical Interviews

Richard M. Frankel
University of Rochester School of Medicine and Dentistry

Perhaps the single most important tool available to clinicians and social science researchers is the interview. Although interviewing methods and practice have been a central concern for scholars from such diverse fields as medicine, anthropology, psychology, sociology, and history for more than 50 years, it is only recently that interviews per se have been studied as a type of social occasion governed by discourse rules (Mishler, 1984; Stoeckle & Billings, 1987; Waitzkin, 1990, Maynard, Schaeffer, & Craddock, 1993). This chapter has three goals. The first is to provide a brief history of the interview while developing a focus on the distinctive features of clinical interviews. The second is to examine the role of interaction structure and social context in understanding how clinical interviews work. The third is to offer some case studies that illustrate the practical benefits and limitations of current theoretical approaches to the clinical interview.

No one knows when the first interview was conducted, who its participants were, or what its focus was. According to the Oxford English Dictionary (Compact Edition, 1971) the earliest recorded definition of the interview (1514), comes from the French *entre voire* (literally, to be in sight of), and refers to a "meeting of persons face-to-face, especially one sought or arranged for the purpose of formal conference on some point" (p. 1740). Such meetings were generally held between persons of high status and might actually represent the first contact between the parties. However, being of high status, each individual involved in the interview likely had prior knowledge about the other.

A more modern definition of the interview (1869) is "To talk with or question so as to elicit statements or facts for a publication, particularly in response to a member of the press." In its modern guise, the interview is treated more as a *technique* used by one person to obtain information from another. It is not so much the face to face character of the meeting that makes the modern interview distinctive so much as it is conveying information to an interested, but distant public. This definition of the interview is well summarized as "An instance of the division of labor. The interviewee supplies the matter, the interviewer supplies the form."

Modern social science has supplied its own definitions of the interview. Although many different types of social science interviews exist (see Merriam, 1988, for a review) most would agree with Patton (1980) that,

> We interview people to find out from them those things we cannot directly observe ... we cannot observe feelings, thoughts, and intentions. We cannot observe behaviors that took place at some previous point in time. We cannot observe situations that preclude the presence of an observer. We cannot observe how people have organized the world and the meanings they attach to what goes on in the world–we have to ask people questions about those things. (p. 196)

Interviews in social science then, may be described as a technique for one person (the interviewer) to elicit specialized information from another (the interviewee) using questions and the answers they elicit as a mode of relating.

Although similar in structure, social science and clinical interviews differ in a number of respects. For instance, social scientists gather information from one or many individuals with the goal of reporting or describing their results to a scientific or lay audience. Careseekers, on the other hand, seek out persons who, by legal authority, reputation or community consensus can be consulted for their responses. In addition to their consultative function, clinical interviews are private and confidential, may extend over years during which deep personal relationships may develop and, in addition to information gathering, involve the delivery of diagnostic and prognostic information. In this respect, a major difference between questions asked in a survey as compared with a clinical interview is the extent to which the information provided at the beginning of an encounter is contingent (i.e., will be treated by the interviewer as a problem to be assessed and solved over the course of one, several, or many encounters.) The division of labor in a clinical interview requires some form of evaluation and response in addition to the interviewee supplying the matter and the interviewer supplying the form.

The differences between survey and clinical interviews are not trivial. In my own training as a social scientist, I was taught that the burden of obligation in survey interviewing fell on me. That is, when a respondent shared information that was "high quality" or self-disclosing, I should feel grateful. Clinicians, on the other hand, learn that the burden of obligation focuses on the patient. Patients feel grateful when they have an opportunity to be heard and listened to.

I recall vividly the cognitive dissonance I experienced when, as part of a collaborative study of the experiences of Irritable Bowel Syndrome patients, I did a series of 50 clinical interviews. I was overwhelmed by the amount of personal information patients offered without my having to do anything more than listen attentively. More surprising to me was the fact that the patients, in general, seemed surprised at my expressions of genuine appreciation for their deep, personal sharing. When I presented my perplexity to my co-investigator, Howard Beckman, an internist, he responded by saying that, in general, he felt grateful when patients could limit their discussions and be succinct. In retrospect, I realize that much of my early work on doctor–patient communication was based on my perspective as a survey interviewer, and not as a clinician.

It is also interesting to note that despite the considerable differences in definition offered in a literature that is vast and contains thousands of articles, books, and manuals, there is characteristically very little attention paid to the spectrum of interview types and the theories of speech exchange (either implicit or explicit) that underlie them. When theoretical discussions do appear, they frequently contain global statements about interviewing based on anecdote, retrospection, or made up examples. Several excellent reviews and criticisms of research on interviewing have appeared recently and underscore the lack of direct empirical studies on which a theory of interviewing could be based (see especially, Erickson & Shultz, 1982; Inui & Carter, 1985; Labov & Fanshel, 1977; Maynard, Schaeffer, & Craddock, 1993; Mishler, 1979, 1984; Waitzkin, 1991).

ABOUT QUESTIONS

An obvious fact about clinical interviews is that they unfold largely through exchanges composed of questions and answers. Unlike casual conversations in which the type, length, and content of speaking terms is, in principle unrestricted, speech exchange in clinical interviews is characterized by a relative invariance of speakers and the types of utterances they use (Frankel, 1990; West, 1983). As a rule, clinicians ask, and clients or careseekers respond to questions. Although obvious, there has been relatively little investigation of this property of the clinical interview. More generally, there is as yet no comprehensive theory of questions and how they operate within and across clinical contexts.

Questions have been of considerable interest to linguists in terms of their syntactic, phonological, and semantic properties (see, e.g., Bolinger, 1958). But the theory of interrogative structures generated from traditional linguistic analysis has been of limited value in describing the actual use of questions in the context of the clinical interview. This is so for several reasons. First, the unit of analysis employed in traditional linguistic studies is the single sentence isolated from its context of use and more importantly from the response it engenders from a listener. Second, because the rules of grammar and syntax operate at the sentential level only, it is impossible to judge the effects of being a questioner or an answerer over long stretches of discourse. Finally, single sentence analysis reveals little of the background knowledge speakers must assume of one another in order to communicate intelligibly. Clearly, what is needed is a theory that will link both questions and responses together over time and space.

THE PROBLEM OF INTERACTION CONTEXT

One attempt to put forward a general theory of questions comes from Goody (1978), who claimed that questions may best be understood in terms of the constraints of syntax and usage. At the syntactic level, following Searle (1969), questions may be broken down into two types: yes–no questions that are complete propositions and differ from statements only in the inversion of word order; and questions that are incomplete propositions for which the answer provides the missing clue. At the pragmatic or interactional level, questions have the force of obliging or demanding a response. Schegloff and Sacks (1973) viewed questions as an initial element of a two-part sequence related by timing and content. Timing rules control the relationship of utterances, one to the next, whereas content rules control the coherence or appropriateness of responses to the question that precedes them.

Goody's theory, although it does direct analytic attention to the pragmatic aspects of questioning, is not without its limitations. First, there is no systematic account of how questions constrain or influence responses in everyday or clinical contexts. This limitation points out the need for a discourse-based theory to address the problem of rules that relate the force of the question to the type of response produced, and not merely to internal properties of the question itself. The second problem is related. Although various question types are asserted to exert their force based on syntactic and institutional characteristics, there is no methodological criteria or proof procedure to demonstrate how the properties are actually oriented to or detected. This is really a dual problem because it involves the issue of proof at two different levels: assertions by the analyst that X is true (or false) of Y property; and the practical task of speakers to demonstrate knowledge and understanding of each other's actions in an ongoing way.

The difficulty of connecting questions and responses, plus a lack of criteria for demonstrating pragmatic effects, leads to the problem of fit between utterance and effect. Without a source of individual or comparative data illustrating the range of effects a particular type of question or sequential location may have on a response, it is impossible to discuss the rules that bind discourse elements such as questions and answers together. Similarly, it is impossible to discuss the problem of "normal troubles," for example, mishearings, misunderstandings, clarifications, and so forth, that occur in clinical interviews (see, e.g., West & Frankel, 1991). Indeed, to study questions without a theory of action that links questions and answers at the level of individual exchanges and beyond that within larger structural arrangements such as topics and entire encounters is to miss their instrumental and social significance in clinical encounters.

SOME AMBIGUITIES ABOUT QUESTIONS

Sacks (1966) proposed that questions and answers are one type of base sequential pair whose elements are both time- and type-related. He proposed that speakers attend to the timing of utterances, one to the next, by orienting to a feature of interactive discourse he termed *conditional relevance*. In addition to the general requirement for second pair parts to follow as rapidly after the completion of the first as possible, the rule of conditional relevance states that the absence of a response becomes increasingly noticeable as time elapses. It is not the case that the force of a question is insured simply by its having been spoken at some point in time and responded to at another. Rather, the timing of speech actions in discourse is critical to understanding the force or effect of a particular type of utterance such as a question (Frankel, 1984).

In addition to time order considerations, the force or effect of questions may be viewed in terms of the type relationships which obtain between discourse elements in sequence. Sacks (1966), Mishler (1979), and others, including Garvey (1977), Keenan, Schieffelin, and Platt (1978), and Cicourel (1982) argued that the pragmatic force of a question does not reside in the question itself, but rather in its analysis as displayed in a listener's response. In this view, both the meaning and function of utterances such as questions are contingent, and cannot be specified in advance of those discourse situations in which they actually occur. Additionally, this means that sentences and the actions they perform, following Austin (1965), are essentially incomplete, not simply in the sense that questions are propositions with inverted word order for which the answer provides the missing clause (see Searle, 1969), but that the pragmatic effect of a question cannot be understood without reference to the response of its recipient. From an interactional perspective, form and function do not precede or stand independent of meaning, they constitute it. As such, action on the individual level becomes meaningful only in the sense that it occurs and produces effects in the shared context of communication.

I present three case studies to illustrate the limitations of traditional linguistic analysis and the need for a discourse-based theory of questions. The first focus is on a structural ambiguity created by a particular type of opening to the clinical encounter; the second on the orderly properties of chains of questions and answers; and the third on contingent relations between questions and answers during the assessment and reporting phases of the encounter.

Case Study 1: Opening Questions in the Clinical Encounter

It is by now well established that the basic functions of greetings for initiating casual conversation are: (a) establishing identity, and (b) aligning or realigning speakers' states of knowledge relative to the encounter at hand (Schegloff, 1968). In characterizing the operation of greetings, Sacks (1975), in a paper entitled "Everyone has to Lie," argued that the position of an utterance in the overall structure of an encounter can and does systematically influence the hearing or force that it will be given by a listener. Such is the case for the question "How are you?" and the response it engenders. Sacks demonstrated that where it follows a greeting, "How are you?" is heard not as a literal inquiry about the recipient but as an extension of the greetings. In casual conversation the conventional response to "How are you?" is neutral, "Fine," "Good," "Okay," and so on. The initial question is also conventionally reciprocated in kind with "How are *you?*" Although both parties may have news to the contrary (i.e., that they are not fine), Sacks demonstrated that such announcements are generally "held off" until the entire greeting sequence is completed and at least a first topic is underway. It is in this sense of conventional appropriateness to the location of a question occurring at the beginning of a conversation that Sacks argued, "everyone has to lie." And it is only by reference to the sequential properties of talk in context that such an appreciation can be derived.

In casual conversation, utterance positioning within greetings/alignment sequences is unambiguous. The "How are you?" that follows an exchange of hello's between friends or acquaintances is clearly an affiliate of the greetings, and is typically not a topic-initiating utterance. On the other hand, the same question when it is used to begin the assessment phase of a clinical interview solicits or obliges a topically relevant response, a chief complaint, or reason for the visit. Although many text books on clinical interviewing in medicine stress the importance of the greeting exchange and the use of the open-ended questions such as, "How are you?" to solicit clinical information from the patient, little empirical description or advice on where to begin the assessment phase are provided.

To test the possible confounding effects of sequential location on the response to queries such as, "How are you?" I reviewed transcripts from 74 routine medical encounters, 30 of which began with a greeting exchange followed by the physician (D) initiating a "How are you?" type question. Using the model of conversational sequencing, one would expect patients (P) to respond neutrally, treating the question as a continuation of the greeting exchange. This was not the case. In 15 of the encounters in which a "How are you?" type question followed greetings, a complaint or trouble was eventually named in the patient's response. Data Set 1 ("How Are You?" heard as clinically relevant) illustrates:

Exemplar 1 (from Encounter 11)
D: Mr. Freeman, How're y' doin' t'day.
               (0.3)
P: I am so- tired from- from- walkin'.

Exemplar 2 (from Encounter 50)
D: Hi. How y' doin.
               (0.3)
P: Not so we:ll

Exemplar 3 (from Encounter 23)
D: How are yih
P: Terrible

Given its sequential location immediately following the greeting exchange and the fact that it is also the occasion for an instrumental task (taking care of the medical business at hand) the physician's query, "How are you?" can be heard to relate to two distinct possibilities. One is that the "How are you?" question is meant sociably; the other is that it is meant clinically. The class of responses illustrated in data set 1 indicates an orientation to the question's clinical potential.

By contrast, half ($N = 15$) the sample of responses to "How are you's?" were neutral and extended the greeting sequence. Three illustrations follow. ("How are You?" heard as socially relevant):

Exemplar 1 (from Encounter 23)
D: How are y'?
P: Fine How're you?
D: Just fi:ne. Any trouble getting here today

Exemplar 2 (from Encounter 51)
D: How are y'doin' toda:y.
P: Oh pretty goo:d and yo:u?
D: Ver:y well=what- what brings you in t'see us t'day

Exemplar 3 (from Encounter 18)
D: How are you?
P: Oh fine.
D: I mean how are your medical problems
P: Not so good

Exemplar 1 (Data Set 2) illustrates a sociable response to the physician's inquiry that is followed by an acknowledgment and continuation of nonclinical discourse. Exemplar 2, illustrates a similar orientation on the patient's part to the sociable nature of the physician's inquiry. It is followed by a sociable response from the physician and an initiation of a clinical inquiry "What brings you in to see us today." In the third example, the physician's initial inquiry is responded to socially by the patient. The physician immediately reframes the nature of the question as having been clinical rather than social at which point the patient responds clinically with "Not so good." It is in this set of exchanges that one can readily see the sort of phenomenon Sacks was referring to in terms of structural organization and conventional appropriateness for responses. It is also here that one can see the additional complexity of the intersection of two types of discourse organization, one relating to casual conversation, the other to clinical encounters.

Data Sets 1 and 2 illustrate the fact that two independent potentials exist for how the query "How are you?" can be heard and interpreted in the clinical encounter. In cases where the physician's desire for sociable chit chat is met by a neutral response from the patient, the conversational orientation of the encounter is preserved and casual talk is facilitated. Similarly, where the physician's interest is more narrowly focused on the clinical business at hand, patient responses that provide a complaint or trouble facilitate early entry into a clinical mode. It follows that if sociable and clinical modes of talk are equally appropriate as responses to the physician's initial inquiry, there should also be cases in which the sense intended by the physician and the response provided by the patient are mismatched. This is indeed the case. Data Set 3 ("How Are You" heard as both socially and clinically relevant) illustrates:

Exemplar 1 (from Encounter 6)
D: How's everything
　　　　(0.9)
P: Pretty goo:d ( ) no- no- they ain't pretty goo:d. my feet swole last week and uhm I had dizziness . . .

Exemplar 2 (from Encounter 5)
D: How y' feelin'
P: Oh pretty goo:d n- I- n- I- no I- I_had a (0.3) lotta stuff- when I was comin' down here I didn't feel too good .hhh felt like uh I could feel my heart beatin'

Two of the cases in which a complaint or trouble was eventually named contained evidence of a shift of understanding produced in the course of constructing the response. In both cases, the first part of the patient's response is neutral, indicating an orientation toward a sociable format. The utterances under construction in both cases are then reorganized, reformulating the neutral responses into ones that contain clinically relevant complaints or troubles. Others, notably Goodwin (1979) and Goffman (1981), noted that such midcourse reformulations are a systematic possibility as turn construction progresses. When viewed syntactically, these patients' responses might appear idiosyncratic and disorganized; perhaps the product of poor memory. When viewed sequentially, however, both examples clearly contain material which reflects an orientation to both sociable and clinical possibilities. Given the finding in related research that, once interrupted, patients rarely raise additional concerns at the beginning of the visit (Beckman & Frankel, 1984), the patients in data Set 3 seem to be taking no chances by addressing both possible hearings.

In the previous examples, the burden of a possible ambiguity falls to the patient in considering whether to respond sociably or clinically to the question "How are you?". Data Set 4 contains examples in which patient responses are heard as ambiguous. Data Set 4 (ambiguous hearings and understanding of "How are you?") illustrates:

Exemplar 1 (from Encounter 13)
D: How y' doin'
P: (hh) Okay. (hhh)
D: Not super, just okay, humm.=
P: = Just oka(h)y. I:: have hay fever an' my sinuses are botherin' me (0.5) an'

Exemplar 2 (from Encounter 15)
D: So how y' doin' today misses Jo//nes
P: Pretty good
D: That's good to hea:r. (0.4) Anything been bothering you lately?
P: Mmh hmh
D: No? Haven't had an back pai:ns or anything like that?
P: No.
D: Well that's good t'// hea:r.

Exemplar 3 (from Encounter 33)
D: Ho y' doin'
P: Good
D: Okay w'll if yer good then why are y' here t'day?

In the first example the patient's response to the physician's initial inquiry suggests a sociable orientation. The physician, in response, attempts to clarify whether the patient's response is indeed sociable or clinical. The patient responds by providing clinical information. Exemplar 2 involves a similar problem. In response to the patient's neutral response "Pretty good" the physician provides an assessment, "Well, that's good to hear" followed by an open-ended inquiry about the patient's clinical condition, "Anything been bothering you lately?" The patient responds negatively at which point the physician identifies a more specific candidate problem (back pain), which is arrived at by reading from the patient's chart. Again the patient rejects the physician's suggestion of a candidate clinical problem. In this case we can see that the patient's response to the physician's initial inquiry stands as appropriate despite the physician's attempt to locate a clinical problem.

It is worth noting that this was a first visit between a long-term clinic patient and a resident new to the practice. In fact, the patient had made an appointment simply to have a prescription filled before leaving on a trip and was not currently experiencing any problems. We came to define this type of visit as a "transition visit" (Beckman & Frankel, 1986), and noted that it carries with it an increased risk for misunderstanding based on the different assumptions that each party brings to the encounter.

In the final example of ambiguity, the physician simply rejects the patient's response out of hand. Here, the patient's potentially sociable response is met by the physician's outright rejection of the response and request for clinical information to the question. This is both the most highly marked response and also the one that seems least sensitive to the timing of the initial inquiry creating the potential for ambiguity.

In summary, the opening moments of the clinical encounter provide an ideal location to observe the differential effects questions can have depending on structural location and the orientation displayed in a response. The clinical encounter represents an additional complexity since the queries used to begin it often occur at the same location that they would in a casual conversation. The fact that 22% of the clinical encounters in which "How are yous" followed greetings evidenced problems in getting started suggests that this feature of clinical discourse is worth attention. To the suggestions text books on medical interviewing make about asking open-ended questions, I would add the importance of using questions other than "How are you?" to begin the assessment phase of the encounter. Questions such as "How can I help you?" following greetings make a much clearer transition to the clinical business of the encounter.

Case Study 2: Combining Question–Answer Sequences into Larger Units

It has been suggested that interviews are composed primarily of question–answer sequences whose generalized properties include conditional relations between sequence elements and sensitivity of the pragmatic force of utterances to their overall placement in a conversational structure. Although useful for dealing with the combination of discourse elements at the level of the single sequence, the rules thus far described do not specify how individual sequences are combined into larger strings.

In an early discussion of how sequences relate one to the next, Sacks (1966) developed the concept of a "chain maxim" for questions and answers. The chain maxim states, "When you are asked a question, respond with a direct answer and then give the floor back to the questioner." As applied to interviews, the chain maxim describes a turn taking rule in which speakers alternate in an ABABAB fashion and a rule of recursive enumeration that repetitively relates questions and answers together in a QAQAQA format. Combining the two rules of the chain maxim produces the following abstract design for interviews:

A: Q
B: A

A: Q
B: A

Churchill (1978), using Sacks' chain maxim as the basis for his study of questioning in interview and interviewlike situations, found that the chain maxim was strictly followed in a relatively small percentage of the cases (approximately 24%). He also found that the type of questioning situation affected rates of compliance with the maxim. In the least formal setting of a casual conversation, the maxim performed worst, describing only about 12% of the cases. In the most formal setting studied—direct examination during a legal trial—compliance was much higher, accounting for 54% of the cases.

Churchill went a step further and analyzed the nonconforming cases to determine how they might be related to the chain maxim. He found that in some exchanges questions followed questions. He also found that some speaking turns contained multiple speech acts. Churchill and others, notably Schegloff (1968), and Jefferson (1972), showed that complete exchanges and activities can warrantably be interposed between an initial question and its eventual response. These sequences are normal variants of the chain maxim. Similarly, Shuy (1976) and more recently Frankel (1984, 1990), demonstrated that turns containing multiple speech acts can also be treated as normal variations of the chain maxim. With the expansion of the original rule set to include nonadjacently placed utterances and those containing multiple speech acts, 84.1% of the sequences coded by Churchill could be explained by reference to the maxim.

In addition to sequence types built on or by reference to the chain maxim, Frankel (1990) identified an additional characteristic of question–answer chains in clinical encounters. One type is composed of a full question initiated by the physician, followed by a series of items or particles that, by reference to the initiating utterance, tie the items of the chain together as a series of affiliated actions. For example (from Frankel, 1990, p. 239):

A: Does anybody have Tuberculosis?
B: No, not that I know of.
A: Heart disease?
B: No.
A: Diabetes?
B: No.
A: High blood pressure?
B: My father had that.
A: Did you ever have whooping cough?
B: Yes.
A: Scarlet fever?
B: No.

The chains created in the manner just shown may be likened to topical divisions in casual conversation. Here, they function more as segment initiators followed by checklist items. The feature of note in the use of question particles following full questions is the limitation they place on the hearer to respond in a yes–no fashion. Thus, although it is a QA chain, its overall structural organization does additional work in shaping and limiting patient response. The chain maxim in this case is instructive in describing a recursive pattern of questions and answers. It fails, however, to locate how the large sequential pattern operates interactionally.

Another example that the chain maxim fails to explain is what Branch and Malik (1993) called *windows of opportunity* in the clinical encounter. The authors studied 20 videotaped encounters of senior clinicians identified as outstanding according to colleagues and polls. They observed that despite great differences in interviewing style the physicians they studied used selected moments in their encounters to enter into and explore patients' psychological and social concerns. Branch and Malik concluded that skilled practitioners develop an intuitive sense for the pace and content of the interview and strategically select points in its ongoing development to enter and explore.

In a related context, Markakis, Suchman, Beckman, and Frankel (1993) described what they term *empathic opportunities*. These are defined as physician responses to any patient expression of moderate to strong negative affect. Two examples follow. In the first, an empathic opportunity arises and is not pursued; in the second a similar opportunity arises and is pursued.

Exemplar 1

	D:	How long have you been having trouble feeling dizzy?
	P:	Around - I started back I would say about a week ago.
	D:	When do you notice that - that you feel dizzy? (pause)
	P:	I think it was last Friday or Saturday (morning)// I forgot what day it was.
	D:	What were you doing?
	D:	What were you doing at the time?
Empathic → Opportunity	P:	I (don't know) I just went to getting dizzy and I started crying, I told Bobby I wanted to go to the hospital or somewhere so - I finally felt a little better and I just got into bed and went to sleep.
Nonempathic → Response	D:	Okay. Tell me a little more about the itching.

In this example, the patient in describing dizziness relates an incident in which she felt sick enough to ask her partner to take her to the hospital. She reports the episode in terms of strong affect, "I started crying" followed by gradual relief after which she went to sleep. The patient's affective statement creates an opportunity for empathy. However, the doctor's response minimally acknowledges the affective state or experience of the patient and is followed immediately by a change of topic. (See Beach, chapter 12, this volume, for a discussion of such uses of "okay.") Markakis et al. would characterize this sequence as a "missed empathic opportunity," that is, a nonempathic response.

Exemplar 2

	D:	And you just had your six-month checkup//in December.
	P:	Yes, but Im wondering about something because he (laugh) instructed me to come back in four months, and that's unusual.
	D:	Hmmh.
Empathic Opportunity	P:	But I think he might have noticed something, I don't know (he didn't want to say) when I was there in December which was the first week, cause they had to schedule me for the mammogram about a week later. But anyway, about the first week. . . . Well, it was the exact date fi-five years ago that I had the operation — four years ago. I must have looked worried because he said, "Mrs. Fuller don't worry about a thing, enjoy the holiday." These are things I have to do you know to keep check on you so, uh - but when he was examining me it was . . . sort of, you know, tender there. But, it was alright, I mean, I'm okay. (laugh)
Empathic Response →	D:	You look fine. Uh - how do you feel about . . . uh . . . the cancer and the possibility of it coming back.
Empathic Opportunity	P:	Well, it bothers me sometime, but I don't dwell on it, I don't (uh) . . . here of late though, I don't know what it is, but I'm not as cheerful about it as I was when I first had it. I just had, I don't know, look like I just had very good feelings that everything was going to be alright, you know. I think it's because I dread another operation.
Empathic Response →	D:	You seem a little upset, you seem a little teary-eyed talking about it.
Empathic Opportunity	P:	Yeah, well, it gets to you. You know sometimes . . . you know uh its the first time we've had a little session like this, see where you really are talking to someone about it. But uh . . . I'm doing . . .

		I - I think I'm blessed, I'm really - because so many people I've know had to have the uh - because I had a very dear friend who passed . . . uh and she had . . . but she waited too long and she had to have chemotherapy. Dr. Vaughn was her doctor and then uh but - I haven't had to and I should be thankful and I am you know, I guess that's why I'm crying . . . I don't know.
Empathic Response →	D:	That's right, it's frightening//it's frightening.
Empathic Opportunity	P:	It is because see, uh, you just hear so much about and everything and uh, but I always say if I don't have to endure so much pain I mean, but I imagine when - when the time comes for any pain to, you know, to endure that you can go through that too, you know.
Empathic Response →	D:	What's your greatest fear . . . uh . . . for the rest of your life, do you have any fears?
	P:	Yes the fear of the uhm you know, the therapy if I have to go through any and uh the pain involved you know I think about all that but I don't dwell on that too much either. I read a lot and I look at TV, I try to take little trips and things like that. And then my mother encourages me you know she's - she's great.

The first empathic opportunity in this example is provided in the patient's description of a visit to her surgical oncologist two months earlier than normal and one that took place on the fourth anniversary date of her surgery. The patient describes the surgeon's response to her as being reassuring because "I must have looked worried." She then adds that during the physical examination, she felt tender. She completes her statement, somewhat ironically, by reassuring the doctor that she is really "okay." The doctor, at this point, responds empathically first by observing that she looks fine and then addressing her affect directly by asking, "Uh. how do you feel about . . . uh . . . the cancer and the possibility of it coming back." The patient acknowledges that in fact it bothers her and that lately she's been feeling down ". . . because I dread another operation." The patient's strong affect in describing her situation creates another empathic opportunity which the doctor responds to by direct observation, "You seem a little upset, you seem a little teary-eyed talking about it." The patient responds to the doctor's direct observation by providing a rationale for her response by describing the passing of a very dear friend who ". . . waited too long and had to have chemotherapy." She then returns to her own situation and mentions some doubt or confusion over the source of her affect, "... I guess that's why I'm crying ... I don't know." This statement creates yet another empathic opportunity which the doctor responds to by generalizing his inquiry and asking, "What's your greatest fear ... uh ... for the rest of your life ... " The patient responds once more focusing on the pain involved in therapy. She then begins to shift the topic to describe what she does to cope with her situation.

This entire exchange took less than three minutes to complete. In that amount of time the patient moved from laughter and an assertion that she was fine to becoming teary-eyed and visibly moved. Once having displayed her emotional concerns the patient rapidly returned to a less affect-laden style. The doctor in this exchange used a combination of skills including: hypothesis-testing "You look fine how do you feel ...", direct observation, "You seem a little upset, you seem a little teary-eyed;" support, "It's frightening ....;" and generalization, "What's your greatest fear ..." in response to the patient's expressions of negative affect.

What I wish to bring forward in providing these two examples is the limitation of a sequential theory of questions that operates at the level of single exchanges only. What we have in these two examples are ways of dealing with patients' expressions of moderate to strong negative affect. In one case the response to affect is to close it off and shift rapidly to another topic. In the second case the display or description of the affect is utilized to enter into a discussion of the patient's fears and concerns. In order to understand how affect is managed in the clinical encounter it is necessary to understand the relationship between the doctor and patient both historically and in terms of its local management. It is also worth noting from a clinical perspective that the examples also illustrate two styles of managing patient affect: in the first case it is basically ignored; in the second case it is explored. Although there is some time cost in pursuing empathic opportunities, recent research by Stewart, Brown, and Weston (1989) suggests that, on average, the cost may be as little as one extra minute.

Case Study 3: Questions, Answers, and the Delivery of Diagnostic Information

The argument I just advanced is that only some of what occurs in a clinical encounter can be understood by reference to discourse rules at the level of the individual question–answer sequences. In addition to the mechanics of sequencing, I have suggested that a theory of questions must also account for the timing or dynamics of certain types of clinician responses, particularly in the environment of patient affect. One unaddressed issue that remains is the relationship between concerns or problems elicited at the beginning of the clinical encounter, and the activities that intervene between the identification of the problem and the clinician's response in terms of diagnosis and treatment.

I argue that unlike the survey interview in which questions and answers are designed to cover a range of topics that may or may not be related, the focus in clinical encounters is organized around solving one or more problems. As such, much of the questioning that occurs in a clinical encounter is designed to elicit information that is complete and accurate enough for the clinician to arrive at a conclusion. Two distinctive features of clinical discourse flow from this observation. The first is that a variety of problem assessment activities, including the possibility of multiple visits to multiple providers, can and often do occur between the point at which a patient identifies a problem and the clinician proposes a solution. The second is that the various phases that make up a clinical encounter, that is, problem identification, assessment (including physical exam), and conclusion are regulated not only in terms of local sequencing arrangements, but also in terms of the larger organizational tasks of the encounter.

To illustrate, suppose a patient comes to a physician concerned about chest pain and during the course of the encounter the physician asks a lot of questions about lifestyle that seem unrelated. I would argue that the physician's specialized knowledge and the contingent nature of the activities that occur between the problem identification and the proposed solution provide a warrant for the patient to continue to answer what may seem like unrelated questions. By contrast, suppose that the same patient comes to a physician concerned not only about chest pain but about committing suicide. If the physician inadvertently focuses on the patient's first problem to the exclusion of the second (as happens frequently according to our research, Beckman & Frankel, 1984) then the clinical activities that follow as well as the proposed solution may be inadequate to the overall task of developing a complete data base. My point is that the various activities that make up the clinical encounter are "nested." Delivering an accurate diagnosis and effective treatment plan depends on establishing a therapeutic relationship with the patient, and prior to that, finding out all of the reasons they are seeking health care. The analysis of local question–answer sequences is inadequate to understanding how the various activities in the clinical encounter relate to one another as well as to the outcome of care.

I use two case examples to illustrate this point. Both involve patients seeking care for chronic pain problems, one for headache, the other neck and shoulder pain. They are both first visits and included time for a physical examination. Both physicians delivered their findings immediately following the physical exam and both patients rejected the conclusions reached. The puzzle in these two cases is to understand why the patients rejected the physician's conclusions. Initially I present each of the patient's opening statements and the physician's conclusions, leaving aside the intervening clinical activities. I then consider the two cases again in light of those activities.

Exemplar 1
Problem Statement   D: Now what's the - what's the main problem that brings you in today?
(0.4)

	P:	I have a headache.
	D:	A headache.
	P:	Uh-huh.

.
.
.

Diagnostic Conclusion		D:	I don't think there's anything serious - <u>disease</u> that's causing your headaches (0.3) okay.
		P:	Mmm-hmm.
		D:	Do you understand that?
		P:	Yeah.
		D:	I think that your headaches are (1.2) related to tension and stress (0.8) that when you get upset - when you feel anxious this (0.6) many times causes headaches (0.3) do you understand what I'm saying?
Rejection	→	P:	Yeah. Sometimes I feel the headache without uh//feeling any sadness or s//tress.
		D:	Wh-
		D:	I see.
		P:	Like now I feel it start//a headache.
		D:	Mm-hmm.
		D:	I see.

Exemplar 2 Problem Statement	D:	What brings you here today?
	P:	Uhm spasms in my neck (0.4) and shoulders (0.6) . . . its gotten so bad that (0.4) it's giving me headaches, makes me nauseous vomiting//uhm last week I just massaged here and it felt like lumps of the muscles just rigid hhh uhm two weeks ago I was so tense in here that it was - the throat felt like I was choking to death the thro-like my throat muscles were actually involved in this stuff hhh uhm and it's just painful my head-and now it's gotten to the point that it makes my head hurt again hhh.
	D:	Mm-hmh.
	D:	Mm-hmh.

.
.
.

Diagnostic	D:	Alright, first of all//as far as your physical exam

Conclusion		goes (0.8) a fairly normal physical exam I r-(1.0) I found only one abnormality (0.4) and that was the tenderness that your experiencing (0.4) over some of your spinous processes of your upper vertebrae.
	P:	((clears throat))
		(1.2)
	D:	Uh your (smo-) muscle strength and (0.3) nerve exam all within normal limits.
		(0.4)
	P:	Okay.
	D:	So that's good.
		(1.0)
	D:	Uh the other thing-I've managed to review laboratory results that they obtained from the emergency room and again everything seems to be within normal limits.
	D:	I want to get an X-ray (0.6) of your cervical spine.
	P:	Okay.
		(0.4)
	D:	If you didn't have the tenderness I wouldn't even bother with the x-ray (0.4) but the tenderness is significant.
		(1.2)
	P:	Okay.
	D:	Uh there's probably a few more blood test we can get (0.3) as well.
		(1.0)
	P:	Okay.
	D:	And we'll wait to see what those tests show and we'll take it from there.
Rejection →	P:	Okay what will (we do) with the pain in the mean time. What do I do for my head and my nausea and my numbness?

It is worth noting that in both exemplars the physicians' responses are topically relevant (i.e., each proposes a solution that relates to the identified problem). However, it is also worth noting that both physician responses take the form of ruling out underlying biomedical disease as an explanation for the patient's symptoms. In the face of the diagnostic news delivered by each of the physicians, the patients immediately raise objections. In Exemplar 1 the patient disagrees with the physician's diagnosis and, in fact, produces the symptom (a headache) in the encounter itself. In Exemplar 2, the patient complains about the fit between the diagnostic and assessment information provided by the physician and the symptoms she described at the beginning of the encounter. A clue to the problems experienced by each of the patients can be gained by looking at some of the intermediate exchanges that occurred between the problem identification and problem solution in each encounter. At approximately 2 minutes into the first encounter the physician initiates the following inquiry about the patient's headaches.

	D:	Is there anything that seems to bring it on?
		(1.4)
	P:	Sadness and-
→	D:	Sadness?
→	P:	And studying too much sometimes//or
	D:	And what too much?
	P:	Studying too much.
	D:	Studying too much.
	P:	Right.
	D:	Two years ago did this come on all of a sudden or had you had these before two years ago?
	P:	No I didn't have it.
	D:	You didn't have it.
→	P:	No but I had a problem uh at the beginning of this headache uh that uh hhh uhm when I got my results at school it wasn't eh as good as I wanted//so I became upset too much.
	D:	Uh-huh.
	D:	I see.
	P:	From that day until now I have the headache.
	D:	I see.

.
.
.

	D:	How's your appetite been?
	P:	Hmm?
	D:	How's your appetite-are you eating okay?
		(0.4)
	P:	Yeah.
	D:	Mm-hmh.
	D:	You're not losing weight (0.5) weights the same?
→	P:	I think I lost uh-five pounds//uhm si-about two months from two months til now I lost//five pounds.
	D:	Mm-hmh.
	D:	Mm-hmh.
	D:	Have you been trying to lose weight?

P: No.
D: No.

.
.
.

D: Do you have anything in your life that's upsetting you (0.8) other than getting uh-getting uhm (1.2) other than school occasionally uhm making you uh (0.8) feel tense.
P: You mean something make me thinking too much.
D: Yeah, do you-are you having any family problems or any//problems?
P: No I don't have-
D: Financial problems?
→ P: No I don't have those problems ( )I mean that uh because they are all overseas I'm thinking of them all the time.
D: Uh-huh

By including some of the intermediate exchanges that occurred between the problem identification and problem solution in Exemplar 1, several things become apparent. First, in his assessment, the physician has questioned the patient about his thoughts and explanation for the symptoms he has been experiencing. The patient in turn states that he has been losing weight, is unable to concentrate, and has done poorly at school. These developments are associated in the patient's view with his headaches and, more centrally, with the fact that he is living away from home and misses his family. The patient's thoughts about these matters seem very clear. What is less clear, is how the information provided by the patient during the assessment phase fits to the delivery of diagnostic information. The second striking feature is the physician's apparent insensitivity to the context of patient experience at least as it relates to the proposed problem/solution. Here we can begin to appreciate how the contingent nature of the physician's questioning appears to be, in retrospect, mismatched to the diagnostic conclusion. A third related feature is the physician's framing of the diagnostic conclusion in terms of ruling out significant organic disease. This is especially striking in light of the patient's very vivid description of his experience. From the physician's point of view the delivery of diagnosis is "good news." That is, the problem is nothing "more serious" than tension headaches. The difficulty is that the physician's approach to summarizing the patient's problem is that it introduces a perspective that essentially goes beyond the patient's description, and perhaps expectations. This clash of perspectives is similar to what Mishler (1984) called the "voice of medicine" and "the voice of the life world." Its effect in this case is both striking and immediate.

Exemplar 2 illustrates a similar but less direct outcome. During the family history segment of the encounter the physician in Exemplar 2, elicited the following information.

11. QUESTIONS IN CLINICAL INTERVIEWS   253

D: Uh I don't need dates really//I just need to know the kind of things you were hospitalized for in the past.
P: Okay.
(0.6)
P: Before this (0.4) bleeding colon. Before that (0.4) '70 uhm '71 '72//viral meningitis by then they called it recurring because in '69 I had what they told me was viral meningitis and I would never get it again.
D: Mm-hmh.
P: Before that I had an ectopic pregnancy and the left ovary removed . . . I know the dates are getting screwy now because I've got to put a hospitalization in here that doesn't fit the scheme of things//but it was for hh infectious hepatitis.
D: Well what was that for?
D: Mmm
P: And oh and the nephritis we can't forget that//that's my most recent one so
D: That's the one I just referred to (-uh)
D: Yeah October.
P: Right.

.
.
.

D: You said your father passed away when he was 50-
(0.4)
→ P: Oh he was about 30//I would say 33 I really-I don't know how old my father'd be if he were alive but he (0.3) died when I was- I'm almost 40-so its-he's been dead 35 years.
D: Okay.
D: Okay and your mother's in good health now?
(0.6)
→ P: Yeah she's (mostly) in good health . . . I have uhm-no broth-my brothers were both killed in a car accident in 1979 (1.6) and my one sister died (0.8) in a sickle crisis in 1980.
D: Okay.
D: You have children, you have two children//that aren't in real good health.
P: ( )
→ P: Yes (0.5) uhm I have a 20 year old daughter who's an uncontrolled epileptic (0.4) she's been diagnosed epileptic since 1970- but they've never been able to control her seizures (0.4) uhm and I have a 9 year old (0.5) who has epilepsy and rheumatoid arthritis

In eliciting the patient's family and social history the physician in Exemplar 2 either discovers or has reconfirmed the fact that the patient has had significant medical problems in the past and has a family history that is significant for both psychosocial and stress-related issues. Although perhaps not causally related to the patient's presenting problem, they almost certainly exacerbate it. The physician's response to the patient's problem description, past medical history, and family and social history uses a similar rule-out format. There is nothing abnormal in any of the lab tests or physical examination save some tenderness in the patient's upper vertebrae. Rather than reaching a firm diagnostic conclusion, the physician proposes to extend the assessment by ordering x-ray and other laboratory tests. From the transcript it appears that the doctor's level of diagnostic certainty is high but not complete and that additional testing will complete the picture of "normal physical findings." Again, from the physician's point of view there is good news—no abnormal findings. However, from the patient's point of view, both the news and its narrow focus on physical symptoms are inadequate to the problem initially described. Recall the patient's opening statement and her assertion that "I was so tense in here that it was—the throat felt like I was choking to death the thro-like my throat muscles were actually involved in this stuff hhh uhm and it's just painful my head-and now it's gotten to the point that it makes my head hurt again hhh." The physician's delivery of diagnostic information in Exemplar 2 illustrates the potential danger in rule-out diagnoses that fail to take into account the active nature of the patient's suffering. The physician in this case has answered a diagnostic question about the etiology of the patient's pain. However, he has failed to address her reason for seeking care, that is, for relief of her symptoms.

CONCLUSION

My overall goal in this chapter has been to show that there is currently a lack of theoretical grounding for analyzing clinical discourse. Early work on questions was based primarily on linguistic analysis that proved too limited in terms of describing interactional or pragmatic features of clinical exchanges. An initial step in developing a theory of clinical interviewing comes from work in discourse analysis and conversation analysis focusing on the relative invariance of question–answer sequences (i.e., doctors ask, and patients answer questions), and the observation that some larger sequential patterns can be explained as normal variants of questions and answers as a base sequential pair. The first case study illustrated how local sequential analysis provides a framework for understanding some, but not all, features of clinical discourse.

In Case Studies 2 and 3, I outlined some new directions for a theory of clinical discourse. Although useful in describing the mechanics of clinical interviewing, local sequential analysis is insensitive to the broader context and problem-solving objectives of clinical interviews. One new direction in research is to look at particular moments in clinical encounters that represent windows of opportunity. These might include systematic opportunities created, for example, by patient's expression of affect, or individual opportunities created by the unique intersection of illness and mutual biography. A second new direction is to describe how various tasks or segments of clinical encounters relate to one another. In particular, looking at how problem identification, assessment, and conclusion "nest" together will permit a more dynamic theory of clinical discourse to be developed. Finally, it will be useful to compare and contrast results from analyzing a variety of types of interviews: clinical, personal, survey, mass media, and so on.

There is little doubt that interviews are an important form of social organization. In terms of theory, it will be important in the future to increase our understanding of both the structure and dynamics of clinical talk. For now, a useful framing of the issues is captured by Engel (1988), who asserted that "To know and understand is obviously a dimension of being scientific. To be known and understood is a dimension of caring and being cared for" (p. 124). Perhaps it is no accident, that in our eagerness to be scientific in developing a theory of clinical discourse, we have focused on structure to the exclusion of what may be the most fundamental dynamic feature of interviews, the act of caring and the feeling of being cared for. It is in the integration of both ways of knowing and ways of being that the real potential for an integrated theory of clinical interviews lies.

REFERENCES

Austin, J. L. (1965). *How to do things with words* (J. O. Urmson, Ed.). New York: Oxford University Press.
Beckman, H. B., & Frankel, R. M. (1984). The effect of physician behavior on the collection of data. *Annals of Internal Medicine, 101,* 692–696.
Beckman, H. B., & Frankel, R. M. (1986). Hello I'm your new doctor. *Journal of the American Medical Association, 256,* 1446.
Beckman, H. B., Frankel, R. M., & Darnley, J. (1985). Soliciting the patient's complete agenda: A relationship to the distribution of concerns. *Clinical Research, 33,* 714A.
Bolinger, D. (1958). *Interrogative structures of American English.* Montgomery: University of Alabama Press.
Branch, W. T., & Malik, T. K. (1993). Using windows of opportunities in brief interviews to understand patients' concerns. *Journal of the American Medical Association, 269,* 1667–1668.
Churchill, L. (1978). Questioning strategies in sociolinguistics. Rowley, MA: Newbury House.
Cicourel, A. (1982). Language and belief in a medical setting. In H. Byrnes (Ed.), *Georgetown University Roundtable on Languages and Linguistics. Contemporary perceptions of language: Interdisciplinary dimensions* (pp. 48–47). Washington, DC: Georgetown University Press.
Engel, G. L. (1988). How much longer must medicine's science be bound by a 17th century world view? In K. L. White (Ed.), *The task of medicine: Dialogue at Wickenburg* (pp. 113–136). Menlo Park, CA: Kaiser Family Foundation.
Erickson, F., & Shultz, J. (1982). *The counselor as gatekeeper.* New York: Academic Press.
Frankel, R. M. (1984). From sentence to sequence: Understanding the medical encounter through microinteractional analysis. *Discourse Processes, 7,* 135–170.
Frankel, R. M. (1990). Talking in interviews: A dispreference for patient-initiated questions in

physician-patient encounters. In G. Psathas (Ed.), *Studies in ethnomethodology and conversation analysis No. 1: Interaction, competence* (pp. 231–262). Washington, DC: The International Institute for Ethnomethodology and conversation Analysis and University Press of America.

Garvey, C. (1977). The contingent query: A dependent act in conversation. In M. Lewis & L. Rosenblum (Eds.), *Interaction conversation and the development of language: The origin of behavior* (Vol. 5, pp. 63–93). New York: Wiley.

Goffman, E. (1981). *Forms of talk.* Philadelphia: University of Pennsylvania Press.

Goodwin, C. (1979). The interactive construction of a sentence in natural conversation. In G. Psathas (Ed.), *Everyday language: Studies in ethnomethodology* (pp. 97–122). New York: Irvington Publishers.

Goody, E. (1978). Towards a theory of questions. In E. Goody (Ed.), *Questions and politeness: Strategies in social interaction* (pp. 231–260). Cambridge: University Press.

Inui, T. S., & Carter, W. B. (1985). Problems and prospects for health services research in provider-patient communication. *Medical Care, 23,* 521–538.

Jefferson, G. (1972). Side sequences. In D. Sudnow (Ed.), *Studies in social interaction* (pp. 294–338). New York: The Free Press.

Keenan, E. O., Schieffelin, B. B., & Platt, M. (1978). Questions of immediate concern. In E. N. Goody (Ed.), *Questions and politeness: Strategies in social interaction* (pp. 44–55). Cambridge: Cambridge University Press.

Labov, W., & Franshel, D. (1977). *Therapeutic discourse: Psychotherapy as conversation.* New York: Academic Press.

Markakis, K., Suchman, A. L., Beckman, H. B., & Frankel, R. M. (1993, May). *Coming to terms with empathy: Rater's of the lost art.* Paper presented at the annual meeting of the Society of General Internal Medicine, Washington, DC.

Maynard, D. W., Schaeffer, N. C., & Cradock, R. M. (1993, August) *Declinations of the request to participate in the survey interview.* Report submitted to The Bureau of the Census, Center for survey Methods, Washington, DC.

Merriam, S. (1988). *Case study research in education: A qualitative approach.* San Francisco: Jossey Bass.

Mishler, E. G. (1975). Studies in dialogue and discourse II: Types of discourse initiated by and sustained through questioning. *Journal of Psycholinguistic Research, 4,* 99–121.

Mishler, E. G. (1979). Meaning in context: Is there any other kind? *Harvard Educational Review, 49*(1), 1–19.

Mishler, E. G. (1984). *The discourse of medicine: Dialectics of medical interviews.* Norwood, NJ: Ablex.

Patton, M. Q. (1980). *Qualitative evaluation methods.* Beverly Hills, CA: Sage.

Sacks, H. (1966). [Unpublished lecture notes]. Department of Sociology, University of California, Los Angeles.

Sacks, H. (1975). Everyone has to lie. In B. Blount & M. Sanchez (Eds.), *Sociocultural dimensions of language use* (pp. 57–80). New York: Academic Press.

Schegloff, A. E. (1968). Sequencing in conversational openings. *American Anthropologist, 70,* 1075–1098.

Schegloff, A. E., & Sacks, H. (1973). Opening up closings. *Semiotica, 8,* 289–327.

Searle, J. (1969). *Speech acts: An essay in the philosophy of language.* Cambridge: University Press.

Shuy, R. (1976). The medical interview: Problems in communication. *Primary Care, 3,* 365–386.

Stewart, M., Brown, J. B., & Weston, W. V. (1989). Patient-centered interviewing, part III: Five provocative questions. *Canadian Family Physician, 35,* 159–161.

Stoeckle, J. D., & Billings, J. A. (1987). A history of history-taking: The medical interview. *Journal of General Internal Medicine, 2,* 119–127.

Waitzkin, H. (1990). On studying the discourse of medical encounters: A critique of quantitative and qualitative methods and a proposal for a reasonable compromise. *Medical Care, 28,* 473–488.

West, C. (1983). Ask me no questions: An analysis of queries and replies in physician–patient dialogues. In S. Fisher & A. Todd (Eds.), *The social organization of doctor–patient communication* (pp. 75–106). Washington, DC: Center for Applied Linguistics.

West, C., & Frankel, R. M. (1991). Miscommunication in medicine. In N. Coupland, H. Giles, & J. M. Wiemann (Eds.), *Miscommunication and problematic talk* (pp. 166–194). Beverly Hills, CA: Sage.

12
Preserving and Constraining Options: "Okays" and 'Official' Priorities in Medical Interviews

Wayne A. Beach
San Diego State University

This analysis of medical interviews begins with what physicians themselves have identified as a recurring problem in need of resolution by means of elimination: the use of "Okays" in clinical interactions. Physicians' claims have not emerged solely or even predominantly from self-reported intuitions based on interview experience. Rather, observations regarding the problematic nature of "Okays" are drawn from actual examinations and reviews of videorecorded interviews involving third-year medical students. As will be discussed, the patterns identified and findings put forth are rooted in an educational mission designed to minimize dysfunctional while maximizing appropriate clinical behaviors; the ultimate concern rests with enhancing the quality of doctor–patient communication and thus the possibility of positive healing outcomes.

Beginning an analysis with an initial consideration of physician-identified problems is a somewhat unique point of departure for researchers attempting to understand the practical organization of institutional conduct (e.g., Boden & Zimmerman, 1991; Drew & Heritage, 1992). Yet such a move seems particularly warranted for purposes of this study. First, considering the wide spectrum of interactions comprising work settings, it is indeed rare for professionals to rely on the details of interactional involvements as resources for understanding (and attempting to improve the daily operations) of the very bureaucracies in which they are integrally involved. Second, and relatedly, it is also uncommon for social scientists concerned with everyday language use to be in a position to contrast their observations with those institutional members treat as significant—and to do so by relying on similar methodologies (i.e., recordings and transcriptions) for gaining access to naturally occurring interactions.

On the contrary, the daily work of physicians routinely involved in conducting interviews with patients is typically distinct from analysts' procedures for making sense of how interviews get organized (e.g., by examining relationships among "questions" and "answers"). But throughout the interactional materials addressed here, it becomes possible to reveal both similar and noticeably different concerns held by clinicians and analysts alike. And perhaps even more importantly, systematic attention can be given to a routinely taken for granted, seemingly small and inconsequential feature of talk-in-interaction: the use of "Okay" in clinical settings.

In one very important sense, it is shown that although "Okays" are barometers indicating just what activities are treated as relevant by and for participants, recurrently designed to resolve emergent and contingent problems, "Okays" nevertheless index only partial solutions to ongoing problems. It becomes increasingly clear that "Okays" are meaningless by themselves because removing "Okays" from their immediate and surrounding environments delimits the possibility of understanding the work providers and patients are collaboratively producing and negotiating. Best understood as interactional resources for organizing not just any, but recognizable and particular kinds of activities, "Okays" are decidedly not isolated discourse "tokens" but display precise orientations to more encompassing involvements: generally speaking, with the kinds of activities constituting the routine organization and achievement of what are typically referred to as *topics, agendas/goals,* and *identities/roles* in casual as well as institutional discourse.

More specifically, the following interactional materials reveal how "Okays" document, by their very placements and constructions throughout the discursive question–answer organization of interviews, a remarkable and subtle variation of discourse functions. Of particular interest, however, is how "Okays" are recruited by physicians to guide, direct, and otherwise control the initiation and elaboration of topics: often and simultaneously *toward* matters deemed relevant for achieving "official" clinical business, and *away* from what patients may be pursuing that may be treated by clinicians as less relevant and important; systematically closing down/moving away from nonclinical concerns while opening up/getting back to/working toward the underlying clinical focus of an interview.

As becomes evident, the very fact that it is physicians who overwhelmingly employ "Okays" reflects, in the vast majority of cases, what has become a well recognized set of findings (cf. Drew & Heritage, 1992; Markova & Foppa, 1991) regarding the "asymmetry" of resources involving interactions between institutional authorities and lay persons: Given the predominance of questions and answers (and, more specifically, "prefaced" questions, cf. Heritage & Sorjonen (in press); Sorjonen & Heritage, 1991), institutional incumbents routinely engage in such activities as relying on "next question" to selectively determine what or if some portion of a prior answer counts as an adequate response, what issues may or not be elaborated upon, and (particularly in medical interviews) even whether or for what duration patients' experiences will be talked about (cf. Byrne & Long, 1976; Frankel, 1990; Heritage & Greatbatch, 1991; Mishler, 1984; Silverman, 1987).

These and related contingencies are apparent in the interactions examined here, reflecting varying degrees of difficulties—from little or no troubles marking adequacy of response, to putting on hold and even disattending patients' contributions altogether. Yet in all cases it is shown that "Okays" are relied on to facilitate the likelihood that specific kinds of "official" actions will be accomplished, at once preserving physicians' options while essentially constraining patients' behaviors. Also apparent are ways patients are responsive to physicians' "Okay" usages as attempts to impose interactional structure. Throughout the negotiation of these types of moments, however, clinicians and lay persons alike display careful recognition that "Okays," regardless of placement and construction, are of practical importance and thus are consequential throughout the organization of clinical interviews.

Analysis begins with a brief overview of the teaching–learning mission in clinical settings, including descriptive–prescriptive consequences for clinical practice. Next, a summary is provided of the rationale underlying just how a case has been made that "Okays" should be eliminated altogether in interviewing. By re-examining a single interactional segment, initially provided as evidence of physicians' claims regarding the dysfunctional nature of "Okays," a foundation is laid for contrasting physicians' claims with those emerging from social scientific concerns with naturally occurring institutional discourse. This creates a basis for describing how "Okays" are implicated in "topic organization," but also stresses why analytic concerns with "topic" per se ultimately limit understandings of how and what "activities" are being co-constructed in medical interviews. By examining alternative usages of "Okays" in the context of their usage, and by tracing cross-situational "Okay" usages in terms of how they arise within and are recruited to achieve numerous clinical tasks, attention can be drawn to similar yet arguably distinct usages of what might otherwise appear (and wrongly so) to be an unimportant or even constant interactional resource for physicians.

RECORDINGS AS RESOURCES IN CLINICAL SETTINGS

Recordings of provider–patient interactions are routinely employed as a teaching–learning resource for understanding how clinical relationships become interactionally created and sustained. Not atypically, focus rests with how specific kinds of behaviors are consequential for such interrelated and key activities as building trust, asking and answering questions, eliciting complete disclosures and histories, making efficient and accurate diagnoses, seeking compliance for prescribed regimens (i.e., as remedies for ongoing troubles), offering specific and constructive advice, and in general promoting "healthy" interactional environments wherein "healing" is collaboratively yet optimally attained over time.

In medical schools, for example, faculty and practicing clinicians increasingly rely on video review sessions to facilitate and refine interviewing techniques displayed by medical students, residents in training, and in some cases patients and family members as well. Basic procedures are relatively straightforward: Following actual and/or role-playing medical interviews, participants review their recordings with trained and experienced faculty/clinicians. Throughout several hours of repeated observations, technologically aided by options such as freeze-framing and slow-motion replayings of selected interactional moments, attention is drawn to a wide variety of behavioral displays and interactional contingencies. On a case-by-case basis, ensuing discussion may address and reinforce positive and arguably effective interviewing techniques. Similarly, the identification and elimination of otherwise negative, more or less dysfunctional behaviors or patterns is also a top priority. As noted, the overriding concern, and understandably so, is to minimize interactional behaviors leading to problematic understandings and conflicting relationships constraining positive healing outcomes.

The reliance on directed, interactionally grounded review sessions is both innovative and indispensable for generating real-time and situated explanations of communication in and through medical encounters. No source of data better reveals the details of interactional conduct than audio- and videorecordings of actual events (and, when appropriate, transcriptions as well).

Yet there are inherent problems in work of this sort, many of which are not easily remedied. In practice, quite the contrary may be the case. One central problem may be stated as follows: Do explanations offered accurately depict the interactional organization of provider–patient encounters on their own merits?

Numerous issues underly why such difficulties should neither be overlooked nor prematurely discounted as untimely or peripheral to the teaching–learning mission. Consider, first, the inherent density and thus complexity of the interactional materials under investigation. It is no small matter to identify, recognize, and substantiate the basic existence of some interactional "phenomenon." Such work efforts essentially amount to generating empirical claims about how participants, in the first instance by and for themselves and in these ways made available for analysts' inspection, actually "brought off" the activities claimed to have occurred: What resources were employed, what particular orientations and thus understandings were displayed by participants in the course of achieving specific kinds of situated actions, and just how does such talk-in-interaction progressively shape the unfolding character of medical interviews?

Second, these and related questions only begin to address the fact that just as any given interactional behavior is consequential for shaping real-time interaction (i.e., in the first instance), so do analytic claims offered about the organizing features of such actions impact the kinds of understandings generated regarding "medical interviewing" as a social, practical accomplishment. Relationships among descriptions and explanations of actions-in-context are inherently problematic. The move to prescription (i.e., how clinicians *should* behave) appears all the more troubling. This is not to say, of course, that attempts to refine and improve clinical practice should be avoided. However, to prescribe the enactment of certain behaviors while eliminating others does presuppose some sense of *dis-*

cernment between "positive" and "negative" (and versions thereof, i.e., "good from bad," "productive from unproductive," "healthy from unhealthy," "trusting from untrusting," "warm from cold," "healing from nonhealing," and so on). And this begs yet further questions: How accurate are prescriptive discernments? By what criteria are such critical judgments made, reasoned, and subsequently implemented into clinical practice? What are the practical consequences of "prescribing" courses of action in clinical settings? Ultimately, what reflexive understandings might be generated by attempting to systematically address "description → explanation → prescription" interrelationships?

For all practical purposes these concerns are, no doubt, sufficiently broad and encompassing so as to face the danger of being unanswerable. Perhaps such danger can be put on hold, however momentarily, by considering one set of conclusions (generated by physicians) regarding "okay" usages in medical diagnostic interviews, and then contrasting these findings with inspections of a wider variety of clinical interactions.

WHEN AND HOW "OKAY" IS DETERMINED "NOT OKAY"

Reliance on videotaped interviews to refine techniques for relating to patients and family members has been an integral part of the Rural Physician Associate Program (RPAP), created in 1971 at the University of Minnesota Medical School by Dr. John Verby. Throughout rural communities in Minnesota, it is reported that more than 500 rural physicians have worked with some 600 third-year medical students as a means of grounding and thus facilitating their medical education in practical situations of choice and action. Videotaping and reviews (lasting from 1 to 2 hours) with RPAP faculty occur within the first 2 months and are repeated within months 4 or 5 and 7 or 8. In an article entitled "Ok is Sometimes Not Ok", Verby (1991) reported that reviews and analyses of these interviews revealed:

> a remarkably repetitive and inappropriate use of the word ok (defined in *Webster's Dictionary* as approval or endorsement) . . . This encourages the RPAP student to be sensitive to and aware of the destructiveness of using the word ok as a response . . . approximately 50% of the students recognize they are inadvertently reinforcing some harmful behaviors and the inappropriateness of this phenomenon . . . Given the use of ok as a response to patient answers, the patient may think the doctor believes smoking, drinking, or other potentially harmful behaviors are acceptable. Additionally, an ok response also conditions and prepares patients to wait for the doctor's next question, forcing the student to work and interrogate harder to obtain necessary personal information. RPAP faculty use direct confrontation and suggestion to eliminate the use of the word ok in interviewing. This is done simply and requires little explanation to the student physician.

As evidence for these dysfunctional claims of "Ok," and corollary attempts to alleviate usages in interviews, Verby provided the following "typical scenario" (S = student; PJ = patient Jones):

Exemplar 1 (Verby: "Ok is sometimes not ok")
S: "Mr. Jones, I'd like to find out about your habits and lifestyle. Can you give me an idea of how much alcohol you use in a week?"
PJ: "Oh, about a six-pack of beer."
S: "Ok. What about tobacco?"
PJ: "About two packs a day."
S: "Ok. For how long?"
PJ: "About twenty-five years."
S: "Ok. Now I want to ask you about drugs."

As readers are not explicitly informed that this is a transcription of an actual interview, one where the patient's anonymity was protected by reference to the generic "Jones," we must infer that the "typical scenario" provided is, in fact, typified: A general, reconstructed instance invoked by Verby to provide sufficient evidence of claims offered (i.e., that "This style of questioning ordinarily continues throughout the interview").

From these data it may be useful to consider five sets of issues emerging from the source and nature of multiple claims made by Verby (1991) and, apparently, agreed upon by RPAP faculty and students:

1. "Okay" usages are "remarkably repetitive" in medical interviews.

First, why "remarkably"? Data reveal that "Okays" are routine features in both everyday casual conversations and across a wide variety of institutional interactions (cf. Beach, 1993a; Jensen, 1987), they are frequently used and relied on, although almost exclusively by medical authorities and only in specific cases by patients (as apparent in following sections). Yet just how frequently they are employed, and in what kinds of interactional environments, raises a surprisingly complex set of issues not yet fully addressed. Clearly, "okays" are recruited as resources to achieve particular kinds of tasks, but typically (as is also shown) not following each patient response. Following Exemplar 1, it would be easy to conclude that "okays" are nearly mandatory prefaces to physicians' next questions (i.e., "Okay-prefaced questions"). And although this is by no means the case in naturally occurring interviews, the frequency and apparent foci of "Okay" usages are revealing when determining what is "at stake" in speech exchange comprising discursive medical interactions.

2. *Webster's Dictionary* defines "Okay" as "approval or endorsement," thus usages in interviews are "inappropriate . . . [destructive] as a response . . . inadvertently reinforcing some harmful behaviors."

For analysts of language and social interaction it should come as no surprise that dictionary listings of words and their literal or figurative "meanings" (as well as spellings, pronunciations, origins, semantic groupings, and the like) not only fail to capture utterances and their situated force, but, in these ways, social actions achieved through language. The long-standing attention given to manifold distinctions between what "what words *mean*" versus "what words *do*," initially put forth in speech act theory (cf. Austin, 1962; Searle, 1969), began to reveal how words amount to actions having communicative impact (e.g., requesting, advising, suggesting, correcting, directing, complimenting, complaining, teasing, and so on). Yet the "theory" guiding understandings of "speech acts" has also been shown to be problematic, not due to overreliance on dictionaries to specify inherent meanings of words, but for similar reasons: An overreliance on isolated "sentences" (often contrived) to determine utterance force, situational definitions, a proclivity toward intentional and/or mentalistic explanations of behavioral/scenic displays of social order, and thus an inherent tendency to gloss or underspecify the systematic and salient features of conversational interaction (cf. Atkinson & Heritage, 1984; Beach, 1990b; Levinson, 1983, 1992; Schegloff, 1984, 1987a, 1987b, 1990; Searle, 1987; Streeck, 1980).[1] It is particularly in regard to this latter concern (i.e., a failure to take into account both the *temporal* and *sequential* features impacting, but also being shaped by, participants' orientations to moment-by-moment contingencies of interaction), that the clearest distinction between *conceptual/philosophical* and *empirical* inquires is revealed: The former turns to resources (e.g., dictionaries, contrived sentences) external to the talk itself as a means of attributing consequences and thus imposing meaning and order onto social contexts; the latter attends to context (via recordings and transcriptions of naturally occurring interactions) by directly examining how actions-in-a-series are organized as participants themselves detect and display orientations to prior and subsequent turns-at-talk (cf. Duranti & Goodwin, 1992).

3. "Given the use of ok as a response to patient answers, the patient may think the doctor believes smoking, drinking, or other potentially harmful behaviors are acceptable."

In light of the prior discussion, it should be clear that these claims give rise to yet further questions and issues. First, how do reviews of "Okays" in videorecordings provide access to what "the patient may think the doctor believes"? What is the empirical status of "thinking" in medical interactions? Although there are no doubt times when patients explicitly disclose or inform the doctor about what they are "thinking," regarding a doctor's belief or otherwise, the analytic task

---

[1]This description does, of course, itself underspecify both the tenets of speech act theory and conversation analysts' rejection of such a "theory" as a viable resource for explicating the organizing details of social interaction. No attempt is being made here to cover ground readily available in cited sources. Rather, the kinds of claims made by speech act theorists, and the methods employed to generate these conclusions, are not altogether foreign to the instance and analysis provided by Verby in attempting to better understand the organization and practical consequences of medical interviews.

remains to interactionally reveal just how or if patients treat doctor's "Okays" as doing the work of "accepting or approving" harmful behaviors. Stated somewhat differently, how might doctors practically achieve "rewarding patients" (via "Okay" and by other means), and in what ways might patients orient to having excessive drinking and/or smoking accepted and approved by doctors? However relevant and interesting these questions and their potential answers might be, they address different interactional phenomena than those available by reinspecting three "Okay" usages in Student and Patient Jones. Although seemingly not a naturally occurring instance but a reconstructed and typified example, as noted earlier, it may nevertheless prove useful to consider how each of the three "Okay" usages are accomplishing different tasks (and, in so doing, also reveal the "typified" rather than "naturalistic" sense of these data):

Exemplar 2 (Verby, "Ok is sometimes not ok")
    S: "Mr. Jones, I'd like to find out about your habits and lifestyle. Can you give me an idea of how much alcohol you use in a week?"
    PJ: "Oh, about a six-pack of beer."
1→ S: "Ok. What about tobacco?"

Student's first "Ok." (1→), for example, can be seen as marking adequate receipt of PJ's answer regarding alcohol, not atypically in *third turn position* following response to prior query (i.e., Question → Answer → Receipt (Ok) + Next Question) (cf. Beach, 1993a; Drew & Heritage, 1992; Frankel, 1990; Jensen, 1987; Mehan, 1979; Schegloff, 1991a, 1991b). It is important to note that the work involved in employing "Okay" to display adequate receipt involves attempts to close down some or all feature(s) of prior turn before opening the possibility for moving onto next matter (cf. Beach, 1990a, 1993a). At least in terms of everyday "casual" talk this altogether routine, transitional, and dual-implicative work of attempting to close down prior before moving to next is not "institutionally" synonymous with approving nor accepting of such alcoholic consumption (e.g., as with "That's okay" or "Okay good" as forms of acceptance and/or positive assessment of some behavior or set of behaviors). In this typified case, the severity of drinking "about a six pack of beer" may or may not be indicative of alcoholic tendencies depending, of course, on PJ's history.

Yet notice that S does not, for example, provide a follow-up question pursuing additional information about PJ's drinking, or in any noticeable way treat PJ's response as problematic and thus deserving of further inquiry. Rather, S moves next and immediately to "tobacco" en route to related habits and lifestyle issues (e.g., drinking, smoking, drugs, eating, exercise, etc.):

Exemplar 3 (Verby, "Ok is sometimes not ok")
1→   S: "Ok. What about tobacco?"

	PJ:	"About two packs a day."
2→	S:	"Ok. For how long?"

Here S's (2→) appears again in third turn position, marking adequate receipt of PJ's prior response, but in so doing does not attempt to close "tobacco" as an issue of inquiry. The alternative employed here is "Ok. + [follow-up question]," designed to seek additional information regarding "how long" PJ had been smoking "two packs a day,"

Exemplar 4 (Verby, "Ok is sometimes not ok")

2→	S:	"Ok. For how long?"
	PJ:	"About twenty-five years."
3→	S:	"Ok. Now I want to ask you about drugs."

to which PJ responds with "twenty-five years." But again in (3→), as with (1→)—although unlike the follow-up question in (2→)—S marks receipt and moves to some next and related matter. But here S's "Now I want to ask you" re-formulates that an interview is in fact underway, at once informing PJ of what is coming next and more explicitly marking a shift toward "drugs" and away from "tobacco." As a result of the manner in which S achieves such a shift, there is more of a sense of finality to S's "Ok" in (3→). Perhaps S's marked shift to "drugs" is somehow responsive to PJ's "twenty-five years" reporting? This is clearly an excessive amount of smoking, and S again comes off even more visibly in (3→) as achieving some action *other* than "accepting or approving" via "Ok."

To summarize, from even these brief analyses it can be seen that "Okays" are accomplice to similar kinds of actions but variably so. In each of the instances shown here, S employed "Okays" as third turn receipt objects (i.e., Question →Answer→ Receipt/Response) yet closed down prior and moved to next in recognizably different ways: In (1→) S offered a no-problem response to PJ's prior response and moved directly to next question; In (2→) S employed "Ok" pivotally to generate a follow-up question tied to PJ's "two packs a day" response. In (3→) S's shift to "drugs" was particularly marked, possibly as responsive to the excessive nature of "twenty-five years." And in none of these instances can S be seen and understood to be achieving the work of "accepting and improving" PJ's harmful behaviors via "Ok", nor does PJ display an orientation to having been rewarded for such lifestyle habits.

4. "Additionally, an ok response also conditions and prepares patients to wait for the doctor's next question, forcing the student to work and interrogate harder to obtain necessary personal information."

Basic analytic concerns with such claims rest, of course, with what "waiting" and "work[ing] and interrogat[ing] harder" look like (i.e., how might they be identified as practical achievements and what is their interactional character?). However, neither is argued as relevant to the interview segment provided earlier, even though it is apparent that PJ consistently withholds from producing fuller and more elaborated turns-at-talk. And further specific examples are not provided by Verby. At least on the surface, therefore, these two claims appear minimally as underdeveloped and, perhaps, contradictory to the very work of "approving and accepting" attributed by Verby and discussed previously: *if* patients treat doctor's (student's) "ok responses" as somehow segmenting and imposing boundaries on a series of question–answer paired actions, conditioning and preparing them to wait for next questions (which, as is addressed later, is not in certain environments an entirely inaccurate claim), then why is it more difficult to "obtain necessary personal information"?

At least one reasonable answer could be generated to such a query, en route to describing and explaining certain "hypothetical" consequences noted by Verby. On one hand, patients orienting to "ok responses" as doctor's attempts to "condition/prepare" patients' behaviors (e.g., when they talk, what they talk about, and in what detail they address certain topics/issues/concerns) may come to treat "ok responses" as attempts to constrain, regulate, and otherwise close-down patient-initiated actions. Over the course of an interview one consequence may be eventual and purposive withholdings by patients, making providers' work of eliciting patients' disclosures increasingly difficult. Another involves elaborated speaking and thus continued bids for the floor by patients; a basic display of unwillingness to refrain from talking about matters they deem relevant and important (see Jones & Beach, chapter 2, this volume). As is seen here, such matters often appear to not be anticipated by providers, and in many cases patients respond to providers' "Okay" placements as premature attempts to constrain information they move next to volunteer.

Now it is by no means out of the ordinary to suggest that there are inherent and recurring problems in establishing, coordinating, and maintaining mutual involvements in professional–client interactions. Heath (1984, 1986, 1992), for example, has amply demonstrated how both speakers and recipients rely on vocal and nonvocal resources (e.g., gaze, gesture, postural shifts, kicks) as recruited components for designing particular courses of action, including the work of eliciting another's attention and response. Similarly, Frankel (1990) identified various ways in which physicians display dispreference for patient-initiated questions, impacting how patient's design their talk in ways sensitive to speaker's rights and obligations in medical encounters (i.e., interactional constraints shaping the unfolding character of physician–patient dialogue).

And, indeed, a wide variety of instances examined in this chapter qualify as types of "troubles talk" (cf. Jefferson, 1980, 1984a, 1984b), replete with momentary interactional "asynchronies." However, the interactions examined do not generally involve the kinds of troubles as when speakers telling a trouble receive displays lacking alignment and/or affiliation from recipients (cf. Beach, 1993b; Drew & Holt, 1988; Jefferson & Lee, 1981, 1992). Rather, in the data included herein, physicians come off as trouble recipients who attempt to keep troubles-telling patients aligned with official tasks and purposes for meeting in the first instance.

Thus, in light of present concerns with what Verby described as "ok responses," the task remains to evidence whether or if patients respond to "Okays" by such actions as withholding and/or providing additional disclosures, thus influencing how providers may or may not work toward eliciting personal information. And if these sorts of actions fail to constitute the medical interviews examined, what alternative action sequences are implicated in and built-up around interactional environments involving "Okay" usages?

5. "RPAP faculty use direct confrontation and suggestion to eliminate the use of the word ok in interviewing. This is done simply and requires little explanation to the student physician."

The surety and definitiveness of this prescriptive posture is unmistakable. Verby reported that RPAP faculty have collaboratively identified the interactional work of "Okay" as harmful, seek to exorcise its presence in medical encounters, and are not inclined to substantiate their position to student physicians (a set of positions revisited in the conclusion of this chapter).

The subsequent discussion offers detailed consideration of these and related issues, providing an opportunity to assess positions taken by RPAP faculty and the prescriptive advice arising from such positions.

"OKAY" AS A RESOURCE FOR ORGANIZING TOPICS AND ACTIVITIES

Across a variety of casual conversations (cf. Beach, 1993a, in press; Button, 1987, 1990; Schegloff & Sacks, 1973; Schiffrin, 1987), within medical diagnostic interviews (Jensen, 1987), and across a wider variety of institutional settings (e.g., courts, 911 emergency calls, therapy sessions, classrooms, corporate meetings; cf. Beach, 1990a, 1991), preliminary efforts have begun to identify "Okays" as one type of acknowledgment token signaling and thus evidencing speakers' attempts to shift topics and/or activities. That "Okays" are frequently recruited by speakers to simultaneously close down some prior activity (e.g., by treating prior speakers' contributions as having sufficiently answered and/or elaborated upon a given issue), while also transitioning to some next-positioned matters, highlights an altogether pivotal and routine (though by no means exclusive) set of interactional usages.

The basic work and thus interactional significance of "Okays" may be grounded in and contrasted with Jefferson's (1981, 1993) empirical demonstrations revealing how "Yeahs" often function as recruited components for topic shift. As one predominant yet minimalized acknowledgment token, "Yeahs" commonly precede not only immediate shifts in topic but also such actions as brief assessments (as well as commentaries) leading to such shifts (e.g., "Y<u>e</u>h that's goo:d. u-How <u>is</u> your arthr<u>i</u>tis, you st<u>ill</u> t<u>a</u>king <u>s</u>ho:ts?"; Jefferson, 1993, p. 10).[2] However, although such "Yeahs" repeatedly come off as exhibiting attention to what speaker was projecting in prior utterance, and doing so in the very course of shifting to some next matters, it is also a clear display of a "recipient working to disengage from a topic in progress in order to introduce some other matters" (Jefferson, 1993, pp. 27–28) — efforts toward topic *attrition* in attempting to bring to a close whatever trajectory or topical line is being pursued, thus underway and in progress, by current speaker.

Attempts to understand these kinds of topical activities (cf. Redeker, 1990; Schiffrin, 1987) also emerged from classifications of "okays", among other discourse *markers* or *particles* (e.g., well, now, so), as devices employed to manage episodic boundaries and to *bracket* defining units of talk: for example, beginnings, endings, and/or more subtle movements toward topic shift (cf. Goffman, 1981), including facilitating the "cadence and pulsing activity" of various classroom tasks (cf. Sinclair & Coulthard, 1975). Of particular relevance to the ensuing analysis, however, is what appears to be the only inspection of "okays" in clinical settings: Jensen's (1987) examination of "Okays" in 12 diagnostic medical interviews (across six physicians). Describing "Okays" as "bracketing devices" marking beginnings and endings of tasks in the specialized context of diagnostic interviews, attention was given to how "Okays" reflect physicians' techniques for "pacing and punctuating" (p. 53) interviews by their placements within and across question-answer sequences; "Okays" were found to routinely separate both individual questions and answers, and in other cases mark boundaries among clusters of topically related questions comprising interactional segments of varying lengths.

One key concern raised by Jensen regarded the *generalizability* of results within a larger collection of medical diagnostic interviews.[3] The analysis proceeds by overviewing and elaborating on several of Jensen's findings, and also by offering comparisons with other interviews.

---

[2]See also the "colloquy" on attempts to quantify these shift-implicative features of "yeah" in *Research on Language and Social Interaction, 26,* 1993, pp. 151–226.

[3]Concerns with *generalizability* may also be raised across different, although related kinds of clinical involvements (e.g., family therapy, behavioral therapy, and pregnancy counseling sessions). Such comparative work is ongoing, and provides useful contrasts with role- and task-specific activities of professionals other than physicians as they proactively structure medical interviews (cf. Beach, 1994). In fact, examinations of how therapists and counselors engage in such activities as "preserving and constraining options" while working to maintain an "official" focus through sessions reveals, and quite clearly so, just how formal and discursive most medical interviews actually are.

Beginnings, Endings, and Recognizable Junctures

An understanding of how "Okays" are adapted to achieve particular and larger topical tasks in clinical settings can begin by noticing that an "Okay" can indicate attempts to officially begin and terminate medical encounters (as with phone openings and closings in casual encounters, cf. Beach, 1993a). Two straightforward "opening" instances, drawn from separate medical diagnostic interviews, appear here (D = doctor; P = patient):

Exemplar 5 (CP-014; Jensen, 1987, p. 35; arrow mine)
  D: why 'ncha sit over here Mr. B— (an its gonna
    be a little ( ) .hhhh (.) closer ((cough))
    ( ) to this machine ( ) .hhhhhhhhh ((cough))
    an we'll jes kinda ignore it hhh.
    ((sound of turning pages))
→ D: ok what can I do ya hhh. ( ) what's happening

Exemplar 6 (Street 2.5; arrows mine)
  D: Hello?
  P: Hi =
  D: =I'm Doctor Wilkensen
  P: My name's (Dawn)
  D: Pleased ta meecha
  P: °Me too°
→ D: Ya visited the E R en- (0.8) they said no
    we- wanna send you over here
  P: Yeah
    [ ]
  ?: Huh huh huh
→ D: O:kay.
  ?: Uhuh
→ D: What's happenin to you

In Exemplar 5, D brings to a close the work of getting situated for the interview: where the patient sits, what appears to be explaining the necessity to sit closer to the "machine" (a recorder to be ignored), and turning to appropriate pages for creating a medical record of the event. Once completed, D then relies on "ok" in transition to the official business—"what can I do ya hhh. ( ) what's happening=" — two separate, although related queries, the first revealing D's recognition that the patient has a medical reason for visiting, which D can hopefully assist with, the second a general invitation for the patient to describe the nature of the problem(s) to be addressed. And in Exemplar 6 notice that once the doctor and patient finalize greetings, D moves immediately to explain how "the E R" sent P to visit. Following P's brief acknowledgment ("Yeah"), D's "O:kay. What's happenin to you" solicits P's reasons for the visit.

In both exemplars, then, the doctor relies on "Okay" as one component for achieving the task of shifting orientation from preliminary matters to official business: describing what medical troubles the patient is experiencing that will shape the nature and eventual focus of subsequent interaction.

For purposes of contrast and with regularity, so are "Okays" recruited for purposes of beginning to terminate a wider variety of clinical exchanges, similar to forms of "pre-closings" (cf. Schegloff & Sacks, 1973; but also see Beach, 1993a) in phone conversations as individuals collaborate in bringing talk to a close. The following example terminates a behavioral therapy session involving a client's problems with finding and retaining employment. (Th = therapist; C = client):

Exemplar 7 (SDCL:BT/JD:1A)
```
           Th:    Try that in the mornings. .hh certainly when you
                  get home from school. (1.2) that should be your
                  time to be:: compressed (0.5) get your- (0.6)
    1→            ↓ take the pressure off yourself okay?
    →      C:     °(O)kay° ((whispered))
    2→     Th:    Allright
    →      C:     Oka y
                      [ ]
    2→     Th:         We'll see you o:n (.) Tuesday
    →      C:     Okay
                        ((End of Session))
```

Three observations might be made regarding "Okay" usages in this instance. First, in (1→) the therapist relies on a *tag-positioned,* upward intoned "okay?" which is quietly receipted (°(O)kay°) by C in next turn. Such utterance pairs are common when first speaker seeks some form of agreement and/or alignment from next speaker. But in this case it is important to not overlook how Th moves toward "beginning to end" the session by offering therapeutic advice: "take the pressure off yourself okay?". And via the next receipted °(O)kay° C not only displays a willingness to accept Th's advice, but also refrains from speaking further. By repeatedly passing on fuller turns, C makes possible the unproblematic movement toward closure that Th's "Allright + [We'll see you o:n (.) Tuesday" ("Allright" often functioning in ways similar to "Okay" in the process of terminating exchanges) in (2→) further advances by also looking forward to their next appointment.

However, "Okays" (and/or "allrights") can appear at a wider variety of moments other than beginning and terminating clinical encounters, including precise junctures marking movement from "diagnosis" to "physical examination":

Exemplar 8 (CO-002: #2; Jensen, 1987; arrows mine)
```
        D:   have you found anything more difficult to do in
             the last six months
             (  )
        P:   you mean physically or what
        D:   anything at all
        P:   Ya (  ) no not really
  →     D:   ok. (  ) all right why don't we go ahead n:
             check you over
  →     P:   sure ok
```

Although Jensen (1987) proposed an "apparent equivalency" between "okays" and "allrights," with the possibility that "allright" offered a stronger signal and/or marked more major transitions, here it might be observed that a distinction is merited due to how D's "ok" is decidedly local and backward-looking: invoked to acknowledge and treat P's immediately prior response as having sufficiently answered D's query. Once achieved, D's "all right" officially moves to close the more encompassing activity—the diagnostic medical history—while also transitioning and setting-up the next-positioned physical examination. And as P's "sure ok" displays alignment and thus a willingness to accommodate the suggestion D has made, a suggestion built into a question and receiving an answer from P, yet another usage of "okay" becomes evident: signalling not just adequate receipt but also a "no problem" orientation to the actions D is proposing (similar to P's free-standing and "passing" "okays" in Exemplar 7). Involved less with the official initiation of shifting via closing down/opening up topics and activities (which is decidedly D's work, providing D the opportunity to utilize the expertise associated with medical authorities), and more with what approaches but is not quite "granting D permission" for a physical examination (which is nevertheless expected and procedurally routine in most cases), P's "sure ok" doubly facilitates and indicates involvement in switching from one phase of the medical encounter to another.

PRESERVING AND CONSTRAINING OPTIONS: CONTINGENT PROBLEMS AND SOLUTIONS FOR TOPIC SHIFTS

It is clear, then, that just as clinicians are institutionally responsible for an occasion's focus and purpose (cf. Beach, 1990a, 1994), so must they guide and direct discussion through a variety of topics. As noted previously, attempts to acknowledge, close down, shift, and move to next matter may be situated on a continuum reflecting no or minor problems on one hand, to degrees of troubles in achieving such shifts on the other. These activities are dependent on both the kinds of understandings and activities physicians and patients may simultaneously be *working toward*.

It is not uncommon, particularly in medical diagnostic interviews, for topic shifts to be achieved without a hitch. The basic three-part sequence described earlier as involving "third turn receipts" and comprised of "Question → Answer → ["Okay" + Topic Shift], is easily recognizable:

Exemplar 9 (Street: 2:5:4; arrow mine)
    Dr: When did you first start having your
             periods (0.2) °how old were you°
             (1.3)
    P: Think I was thirteen
→   Dr: "Okay° an when did they get regular

Exemplar 10 (Street 2.5:5; arrow mine)
    Dr: How many days in between yer periods
             (5.0)
    P: °Oh probably° (1.4) they usually la:st
             four days
             (0.2)
→   Dr: °Kay° ya have a heavy flow?

In both exemplars the doctor treats the patient as having been responsive to the original question (or as in Exemplar 9, *two* questions), adequately answering and providing information being solicited. In third turn the doctors' "°Okay°/°Kay°" display such prior orientations while also making way for next-positioned query. This appears to be the case even in Exemplar 10, where P's answer is *not* directly responsive to Dr's question (although the amount of days between periods may nevertheless be deduced from P's answer).

Variations from this basic three-part sequence do occur, however, as when clarifications are employed to elicit not-yet-adequate understandings that, apparently, are prerequisites to topical shifts. In the following instance, where prior to Exemplars 9 and 10 the patient's presenting complaint involved abdominal contractions and pains, in Line (1→) Dr treats P's prior answer as insufficient—partially repeating and seeking clarification by upgrading his original question from "usually" to "always regular";

Exemplar 11 (Street: 2:5:2-3; arrows mine)
    Dr: Er- are your periods usually regular?
             (1.0)
             ((door opens))
    P: Wh- dis the firs time in a long time
             (1.2)

```
1→   Dr:   They're always regular?
             (1.6)
     P:    Ever since I had ma las baby
           [
           ((door closes))
2→   Dr:   °Since ya had yer last baby° (0.3)
           okay now you're seventeen
     P:    Mm hm
             (2.2)
3→   Dr:   °O:kay° you s:tarted bleedin Sunday (0.4)
           now Monday what happened
```

Following what amounts to P's second yet qualified answer, Dr essentially repeats P's prior response in (2→) as one means of displaying and confirming reception and understanding of the gist of P's answer (cf. Sinclair & Coulthard, 1975). In this way Dr builds on and comes to treat P's answer as not equivocal, but rather a qualified and adequate "yes" (i.e., "always regular → ever since I had my last baby"), thereby reducing the ambiguity arising from Dr's first question and P's initial response (cf. Schegloff, 1984). Once achieved, momentary topic shift is then initiated via "okay now you're seventeen." And as responsive to P's unequivocal "Mm hm," Dr's (3→) once again receipts with "Okay + [next (prefaced) question/topic shift]," an activity re-establishing prior focus on symptoms of the presenting complaint ("periods") with a related medical problem ("bleedin").

In Exemplar 11, then, Dr's refocusing in (3→) emerged as a consequence of prior work designed to insure that sufficient understandings had been obtained. It is only following partial repeats in (1→ and 2→) that Dr moves next to confirm P's age and, once completed, to move "back" yet "onto" next official matter—generating a history of events assumed to have direct relevance to the presenting complaints of "abdominal contractions and pains." In this environment, Dr's "Okays" added closure to understandings now refined, and in these ways remedied, via repeated clarification and confirmation; they also made possible the decided shift back/onto matters deemed relevant *by* Dr. In so doing, Dr preserved the opportunity to treat a particular answer as insufficient, remedy the problem in satisfactory fashion, and then (but only then) re-initiate a trajectory of questions addressing symptoms and complaints. Thus, in Exemplar 11 we see that before shifting and moving forward in a diagnostic interview, Dr relies on such devices as partial repeats to seek clarification and display confirmation of prior answer provided by P. Within these environments, "Okays" are recruited by Dr to display that some or all portions of P's answers are not only adequately responsive, but that certain unspoken implications are understood and agreed upon in what appears to be a prerequisite for topical movement.

When "Okays" appear as third turn receipts employed by doctors, however, they do not always preface immediate topical shift and forward movement (e.g., as with 3→ in Exemplar 11). In Exemplar 12 Dr's "Okay"-prefaced query in (1→) emerges, and delicately so, as a consequence of both P's prior answer to the original question ("Yes maam") and the subsequent explanation offered by P ("but u:h . . ."). This utterance essentially *partitions* the two components of P's answer and handles each differently:

Exemplar 12 (Street:2.6:3; arrows mine)

```
         Dr:   Did you realize at that time that you
               had hurt yourself?
         P:    Yes maam but u:h (0.6) I still had two
               hours before I was off
  1→     Dr:   ↑ Okay  so you went ahead and worked?
                      [
  2→     P:            So
  3→     P:    Yes ma'am
               (0.8)
  4→     Dr:   What- < what did you notice hurt after >
               (0.2) the accident
```

In (1→) a decided backward-looking focus can be observed: Although Dr's "↑ Okay" treats P's "Yes maam" as sufficient, it simultaneously enforces closure upon and thus constrains further elaboration by P (commentary that at this point remains incomplete, as is readily apparent with P's "So" in (2→). Next, in lieu of and thus as a replacement *for* P's talking, Dr's "so you went ahead and worked?" addresses what was implied yet unspoken in P's prior elaboration. Of interest here is how Dr provides a sense of what P may very well have specified had Dr not moved to constrain further talking by P. Notice, for example, the overlapping and simultaneous production of "So" by both Dr and P. Moreover, P's turn-initial "So" is placed immediately following Dr's "↑ Okay." Yet in recognition of Dr's imposed closure and obvious continuation, P withholds speaking further until Dr's utterance completion. And only then does P in (3→) answer Dr's query with a terminal "Yes ma'am."

Dr's query in (1→) can now be seen and understood as an effective substitution for the very point P was working toward. But additional work is being achieved here by Dr, namely, the employment of a delicate and precisely timed device for pre-empting P's continuation and insuring that a minimal yet sufficient answer has been obtained. Dr not only retains speakership but, via the query in (1→), obligates a particular kind of minimal answer from P. And having now received two unequivocal answers from P, Dr is in a position (in 4→) to shift and move forward to related "official" business involving what P noticed that "hurt after (0.2) the accident": a position generated and preserved by not just constraining P's options to continue, but also soliciting from P what Dr treats as a suitable response, one making possible forward movement in the interview.

There is also a hint of another emergent problem in Exemplar 12; (see also Exemplars 13–16) involving P's overlapped "So," namely, simultaneous and overlapped speaking by both Dr and P.[4] In this instance the problem of determining who is to speak, for how long, and on what topic is immediately resolved due to both P's discontinued speaking and (in 4→) Dr's movement to the next question. Yet this fleeting moment is nevertheless reflective of the collaborative work necessary between Dr and P in jointly managing floor access and, ultimately, ways in which topics get raised, elaborated upon and/or brought to a close (and, of course, by whom).

In Exemplar 13, for example, Dr and P are addressing P's recent and painful back problems:

Exemplar 13 (Street:2.6:5; arrows mine)
```
         Dr:   You kept thinking it'd get better
         P:    Yeah
         Dr:    Then it didn't
                [[           ]
1→       P:     Hoping it would get better because
                you know I have to work
                     (1.2)
2→       Dr:    ↑ Ka:y I don't know too much about cars,
                tell me (.) how heavy is an intake manifold
```

Following P's "Yeah" response to Dr's initial query, Dr and P simultaneously begin speaking at the next turn-slot: Dr begins to ask a follow-up question precisely when P elaborates by qualifying prior "Yeah" answer—a continuation that repeats Dr's initial query by first correcting and replacing "thinking" with "Hoping...+

---

[4]There are instances, however, where overlap and thus simultaneous speaking is avoided but similar problems remain to be addressed:

Street:2.6:6; (arrows mine)
```
         Dr:   As far as you know no k- kinna twisting of
               your back or anything
                    (0.4)
         P:    No:t that I know of
                    (1.0)
→        Dr:   ↑ Okay
         P:    ↑ No
→        Dr:   pt .hh And since then it's been painful to
               move from side to si:de?
```

As Dr's "↑ Okay" initiates closing down prior, P offers a delayed and more certain answer ("↑ No") that is neither in overlap nor pursuant of fuller turn/continued speaking. Treated as further evidence of an adequate response, Dr moves next to "And-prefaced query" and topic shift.

[explanation regarding work]". Here P's "Yeah" is responsive to Dr's prior query and does, albeit minimally, exhibit attention to the problem of her back "get better." But in (1→) it also apparent that P moves immediately to introduce what appears to be a matter of some importance: one form of reason-giving that could be heard as P's attempt to *solicit* Dr's understanding, perhaps even commiseration, regarding P's predicament. For example, P's "you know" specifically addresses and essentially invites Dr to become a coparticipant, one who at least acknowledges the problems P is facing. (Chapter 10, this volume addresses this issue.)

Notice, however, that following an extended pause Dr (in 2→) neither attempts to recycle and complete prior question withdrawn during overlap, nor address P's elaborated response and reference to "*work.*" Instead, Dr relies on "↑ Ka:y" *not* as an acknowledgment of P's articulated problems, but as a resource for closing down P's introduced topic (i.e., relationships among "back pain" and "work"): in (2→) Dr engages in an activity *other* than treating P's reformulated answer and reason-giving as sufficient, interesting, or otherwise worthy of attention. Rather, and en route to shifting topical focus, Dr's "↑ Ka::y + [question]" essentially disregards and even ignores concerns nominated by P. Through such noticeably absent uptake, and thus by imposing such constraints on the very possibility of P's topic elaboration, Dr sets up and preserves the option of seeking additional information about the apparent cause of the injury (i.e., what P was lifting when the back injury occurred), but now aligned with Dr's concerns and priorities.

And just how this work gets done following "↑ Ka::y" in (2→) should not be overlooked. Here Dr begins by *disclaiming knowledge* about "cars," through which two timely and practical activities are achieved. First, Dr's disclaiming is a particularly innovative (although indirect) method for inviting P to assist Dr and actually collaborate in shifting away from (and thus essentially avoiding) what P had, only moments before, put forth as issues of some importance. Second, Dr's disclaiming is itself a form of reason-giving amounting to a justification for the very actions Dr has initiated. Viewed together, the inviting and reason-giving built into Dr's disclaiming offers a uniquely tailored response to P's own prior reason-giving and solicitation.

For these reasons the delicate character of Dr's disclaiming, initiated via "↑ Ka::y," should not be discounted as merely coincidental. On the contrary, this utterance is precisely and locally occasioned to facilitate a shift *away* from P's concerns and *toward* Dr's priorities. It also sets up Dr's next "tell me (.) how heavy is an intake manifold." No longer an indirect invitation but now an explicit charge prefacing Dr's query, P is now in an obligatory position to be responsive to what Dr has adeptly transformed from P's to Dr's priorities.

Turn-Transitional Environments

Within both Exemplars 12 and 13, brief moments of overlapped and thus simultaneous talk were apparent between physician and patient. Across turn-transitional environments more generally, where bids for floor and speakership are (more or less) competitive and continuous (cf. Beach, 1993a), "Okay" usages may appear free-standing but are typically prefiguring fuller turn and topic shift. In casual and institutional talk alike, "Okays" are routinely placed at or near what might be treated as potential completion points of some prior speaker and thus are potentially transition-ready.

For example, Jensen (1987) suggested that in such turn-transitional environments physicians may routinely propose (via "Okay") that patients' answers are sufficient. One such instance employed by Jensen appears in Exemplar 14. Here S initially overlaps D's question prior to its completion (1→). Next, P continues to speak (2→) even after D's first "ok" (3→), thus beginning to "interjectively delete" (Beach, 1993a) the pre-closing D's "ok" was attempting:

Exemplar 14 (CP-008:#1/#16; Jensen, 1987; arrows mine)
        S= significant other
        D: .hhh ah did yer doctor in [city] do any
               kind of tests of any sort
        P: (hm mm) =
        D: = ekg: or blood tests or anything like that
               [   ]
1→   S: he had planned to th is
            w eek
            [   ]
2→   P: he h ad planned to yo u se e
                            [   ]
3→   D: ok
2→   P: but I didn't go (.) ya know that means I'd had to
            go down (.) earlier than I'd like to n (   )
        D: ya
2→   P: that's where I decided I was goin to get involved
            up the- in this area (you know)
                          [   ]
4→   D: ok
4→   D: what sort of tests did he say he was going to do
            or did he have (any)

More specifically, Jensen (1987, p. 43) suggested that D's two "ok's" (Lines 3→ & 4→) are tokening *acceptance* of P and S's turns, treating them as sufficient answers to questions. This appears to be the case in 3→ (although P's "ok" is still pre-figuring a fuller turn) where both S and P's responses amounted to what D could make out as a "no" answer to prior question (cf. Jones & Beach, Ch. 2, this volume. Yet in (4→) (as with Exemplars 12 & 13) interactional work beyond "acceptance" is involved: D's "ok" sets up the possibility of not having to address matters laid out in P's explanation, essentially shoving off from the background reasoning provided by P. Instead D returns to "tests," incorporating new information by shifting the question from past to present (i.e., "did doctor do → going to do"), at once actively avoiding further elaboration upon topics implied in P's backgrounding while ensuring that "tests" be addressed as efficiently and sufficiently as possible (and again, not coincidentally, on the doctor's own terms).

It is in this way that D's closing "ok" in (4→) is every bit as much a *rejection* of P's potential topic nomination as an *acceptance* of the sufficiency of P's response. This is not to say that clinicians do no rely upon "Okays" for straightforward acceptance of some prior response. But (Exemplar 14 4→) does not appear to be such a case, as little or no acceptance per se is displayed by D.[5]

In terms of whether patients may reject doctors' attempts to close down and shift topics via "Okays"—not unlike P's (2→), in Exemplar 14, described earlier as an "interjective deletion—Jensen (1987) began to address how patients may continue speaking despite what "Okays" might be projecting:

```
Exemplar 15 (CO-014:#19; Jensen, 1987; arrows mine)
        D:      do you walk up the hill daily
                    (     )
        P:      jest about (     ) but I 'n I walk from my house
                (it ah:::) out by {name} park
        D:      m hm =
        P:      = to my office (.) (in my) {name} school every
                day.
                    (     )
1→      D:      OK
                    (     )
        P:      usually both ways (.) (when) in decent weather
2→      D:      OK (     ) tch .h um:: (     ) do you have asthma
```

Put simply, speakers to whom "Okays" are addressed may themselves disattend such pre-closing attempts with continuation, creating points of negotiation over floor and topical boundary issues. Yet it is important to stress that in Exemplar 15, other data provided by Jensen (1987) as evidence of these claims, and further medical diagnostic data available for inspection, patients' continuations are *momentary* problems to be resolved; no cases have been found where patients absolutely refuse to adhere to doctors' attempts to shift topics toward what they prioritize as more important and relevant "official" matters (i.e., when accomplishing such

---

[5]This raises the problematic questions of (a) determining whether "displaying acceptance" and "treating a response as sufficient" are functionally equivalent descriptions, and (b) whether orienting to prior turn as "sufficient" is functionally equivalent to such actions as "closing down, disattending, failing to elaborate upon" and similar ways of accounting for the work of some next speaker's way of managing options available from prior speaker's turn-at-talk. Although an extensive discussion of these issues, and their diverse implications for understanding both casual and institutional interactions would be useful, it rests beyond the focus of this chapter to elaborate on such details.

tasks as "revealing a medical history," "creating a medical record," "retrieving facts for necessary for diagnosis," and so on.) And although Bergmann's (1992) analysis of psychiatric intake interviews has revealed several kinds of "explosive reactions," and at times a lack of cooperation by patients (see also Erickson & Schultz, 1982; Labov & Fanshel, 1977), such has not been found to be the case with the medical interviews examined for this chapter.

By reinspecting Exemplars 14 and 15, several common features become noticeable: (a) P is caught up in producing a fuller description than D may have "preferred"; (b) at transitional/opportunity spaces, D relies on "Okay" in ways treated by P (via continuation) as premature movement to closure; (c) yet in orientation to D's pre-closings, P works to immediately (or in "real time", nearly so) bring unsolicited and elaborated turn to a close. No attempts are made by P to display outright "rejection" of the trajectory initiated by D, if and when "rejection" is taken to be a problem requiring fuller attention and/or continued lack of compliance to topical progression as initiated by D. Rather, P's talk is *designed* to come to a close *as responsive to D's "okay" placement*. And in the very next turn (as in Exemplar 15), P does terminate speaking, giving rise to D's (2→)"OK" repeat + [topic shift via next question concerning "asthma"].

Repeated and recycled "Okay" usages occur routinely across turn-transitional environments, in large part as resources for dealing with ongoing continuations, seemingly until and unless speaking is completed and the way is then made clear for "Okay" producers to initiate next action(s). I have referred to these repeated "Okay" placements as "Okays-in-a-series" (cf. Beach, 1991) that may appear contiguously (typically from two to four in a row; e.g., see Beach, 1993a, and/or as interspersed throughout an extended spate of speaking (the example of two "Okays" in near vicinity in Exemplar 15 being one minor example). In most all cases, these serial "okay" placements are recruited components for attempting to deal with some interactional trouble (e.g., attempting to terminate another's continuation in order to get back on track), and also to terminate what are themselves treated as particularly troubling topics or activities. Across such usages, the rule of thumb appears to be the more "Okay" usages, the greater the trouble requiring resolution ("closure" being only one instance).

This can begin to be seen in a final instance drawn from medical diagnostic interviews, one initially examined by Jensen (1987):

Exemplar 16 (CP-014:#20; arrows mine)
    D: =m hm ( ) have you ever had pneumonia?
            ( )
    P: no
            ( )
    D: tuberculosis skin test do you know?=
    P: =ya ( ) I've had that it (I its all)
            comes back positive

```
           D:     always positive=
           P:     =m hm
    1→     D:     ok
           P:     cause (that way) I guess I been in contact
                  with people that had ( ) active tb
    2→     D:     a ha=
           P:     =or slept next to em in jail
    3→     D:     ok (      ) ha ha    yes::
                     [          ]   [    ]
           P:             (ya know)        but
           P:     it comes up positive every time
    4→     D:     all right ((chuckling)) (  ) .hh um:::
                  (  ) any trouble with your urinary track
```

Here D's initial "ok" (1→) is employed as a third turn receipt to P's confirmation of D's prior question, and as noted previously immediately precedes no-problem topic switches. However, P continues by providing an explanation ("cause ..."; see also Exemplars 12 and 13) which D next receipts ("a ha" in 2→) with a token of special understanding or realization (cf. Beach, 1990a). As P continues speaking, it is worth noting that D's (3→) *escalates* the attempt toward closure in tri-marked fashion (i.e., "ok + laugh token + yes")—one method for integrating alternative resources to increase the likelihood that worked-toward consequences will actually be achieved—in this instance by laughter that betokens appreciation for P's prior and potentially humorous utterance, and a "Yes::" that (as Jensen, 1987, observed and as discussed previously) displays a possible shift-implicative bid for speakership. And finally, as P finally brings his unsolicited contribution to a close D's "all right" (4→) does seem to more forcefully terminate prior extended discussion, albeit not without mitigation and some sensitivity to the gist of P's comments (i.e., by relying on "chuckling" in the midst of closure and transition to "topic shift via next question").

SUMMARY AND IMPLICATIONS

The prior analysis examined diverse and locally occasioned "Okay" usages across selected medical diagnostic interviews. Findings reveal not only the indispensable utility of "Okays" for achieving diverse institutional tasks, but even more centrally how "Okays" are situated within encompassing courses of action involving what are often delicate negotiations between providers and clients. Such negotiations are often reflective of alternative orientations to "official" business at hand, even though occasions as medical interviews are uniquely tailored to (and in search of solutions for) lay persons' problems. Thus, one common set of problems requiring constant resolution involves physicians' attempts to keep the interview "on track" with "official" business at hand—a focus on issues treated by clinicians as important that, apparently, patient-initiated actions such as continuations, indirect answers to questions, and unsolicited comments can essentially "sidetrack" (cf. Beach, 1990a, 1994). Simply put, on such occasions it is not uncommon for clinicians to rely on "Okays" as devices variously designed to constrain clients' talk, and via subsequent queries attempt to bring talk back in line with particular topics and points that, once again, are deemed relevant and worthy of pursuit en route to achieving professional goals and priorities.

Although it was shown how participants may differentially work toward more or less contrasting sets of relevancies and priorities throughout discursive interviews, in the vast majority of cases it is physicians who proactively recruit "Okays." Generally speaking, in the course of guiding and directing topics and activities; seeking clarification and enhanced understandings as apparent prerequisites to topic shift; simultaneously constraining patients' options while preserving physicians' abilities to initiate topic shifts by focusing on specific kinds of next actions and priorities. As interactional resources physicians routinely rely on, "Okays" are especially employed as partial solutions to ongoing problems, particularly those treated as distracting to, or even momentarily in competition with, what "institutional authorities" are working toward in carrying out role-incumbent tasks.

Consequently, even though a physician's "Okay" (as preface to immediate next question and/or as free-standing) may come off as briefly acknowledging receipt of what was taken to be meaningful in P's elaborated utterance, the opportunity to assess just *what* and *how* an utterance (and portions thereof) is deemed relevant, and toward what purposes, is reserved by and for physicians whose "Okay" makes possible the option of following up on, momentarily putting on hold, or even disattending altogether what came prior in favor of moving to some next "official" matter.

Strikingly similar findings are beginning to be generated across a larger corpus of institutional data, including more diverse clinical involvements (including family, behavioral therapy, and pregnancy counseling sessions, as well as 911 phone calls, cf. Beach, 1994; Zimmerman, 1992). Yet in each case "Okays" are adapted to the occasion at hand, replete with situated troubles and solutions reflecting emergent, altogether institutional, contingencies.

The diversity of "Okay" usages across the medical diagnostic interviews examined herein reveals how it is problematic to assume that a given acknowledgment token can be employed to achieve only limited actions. Such diversity was apparent across several discernible (although by no means exhaustive, and at times overlapping) ways. To simplify, these usages are best arrayed on a continuum from achieving work involving no or minor difficulties, on one hand, to increasing troubles requiring remedy on the other. First, physicians may simply treat patients (via "Okay" as third turn receipt) as having been adequately responsive in prior answer to initial question. Second, "Okays" may precede partial repeats and/or direct queries seeking clarification and confirmation of patient's prior answer. In these environments, "Okays" may also display that not only was some or all of patient's prior answer adequately responsive, but that certain unspoken implications are understood and even agreed upon as a prerequisite to topical movement. Third, physicians employ "Okays" as resources for managing turn-transitional environments involving simultaneous speaking and, at times, continuations by patient. In these circumstances, and not uncommonly so, physicians' "Okays" are embedded in the task of not directly addressing patients' elaborated response, essentially disregarding and even ignoring topics raised by patient. Here it is seen that "Okays" make possible physicians' options for following up on a prior answer in a particular (clinically relevant) fashion, putting on hold one portion in favor of another topical issue, and at times altogether disattending what was projected and thus made available by patient in prior turn-at-talk. Of interest in these types of interactional moments are how physicians persevere in retaining the option of assessing the relevancy (and/or lack thereof) of issues raised and concerns held by patients. Moreover, it was shown how physicians may simultaneously display acceptance *and* rejection of various contributions offered by patients, and in so doing preserving and utilizing what is interactionally constructed as an "institutional privilege" to selectively address—even "shove off"—patients' matters while systematically moving toward what are put forth as clinically relevant concerns. And finally, although patients appear to overwhelmingly and immediately align with and adhere to closures and openings initiated by physicians, there are moments where patients continue to speak and elaborate on selected issues. These more persistent continuations gave rise to physicians' "Okays-in-a-series" (and, at times, "Allright"), clearly placed and repeatedly designed to bring such patient-initiated talk to a close.

Taken as a whole, the "Okays" evident within the cross-situational data summarized above provide only partial access to more encompassing, "doubly relevant" activities: preserving and constraining options, closing down and opening up topics, inviting involvements and enforcing focus, soliciting and protecting, accepting and rejecting, checking understandings and making points. These kinds of activities consistently reveal the priorities and concerns of providers and clients, and thus an overwhelmingly important and complex set of clinical problems: how it is possible that "official" clinical priorities get pursued in the face of lay persons' attempts to co-structure interviews. It cannot be overlooked that it is patients who are seeking assistance, just as it is readily apparent that clinicians take on the "authoritative" responsibility for eliciting, regulating, and evaluating information. Understanding just how clinicians interactionally impose their institutional status, invoke certain "privileges" in the course of guiding and directing these activities, and otherwise work toward achieving the business at hand is of practical consequence for practitioners and researchers alike.

Returning to the teaching–learning positions taken by Verby (1991) and addressed at the outset of this chapter, it should now be clear that the kinds of activities within which "Okays" are embedded are considerably more diverse and complicated than clinicians have assumed. Although "Okays" have little if anything to do with "reinforcing some harmful behaviors" throughout interaction, they are implicated in a rather diverse set of interactional moments involving, for example, how or if patients' answers are treated as adequate or sufficient. And although it is certainly the case that "dictionaries" are not analytic replacements for detailed examinations of recordings and transcriptions, it is important to draw attention to the literal "meaning of a word" such as "Okay" versus the "situated and meaningful usage of an utterance" recruited to achieve a host of practical interactional tasks. Similarly, there is some truth to Verby's claim that "an ok response also conditions and prepares patients to wait for the doctor's next question." It is, after all, doctors who are consistently pursuing "official" business by relying on "Okay" as one resource for closing down, and even disattending or ignoring altogether, what patients may be contributing to the diagnostic interview.

Yet treating "Okay" as the "destructive" source of such actions, and assuming that problems arising from such behaviors might be eliminated altogether by exorcising "Okays" from clinicians' lexicon, is not a realistic solution. Rather, the attempted elimination of "Okays" is at best a "quick fix" or "band-aid approach" to more precise understandings of what is at stake given the overall focus, purpose, and procedural manipulation of these clinical activities: matters involving the interactional negotiation of "official" versus "lay" orientations, and their consequences, that requires ongoing and closer inspection.

In this light, it is not surprising that Verby reported the following:

> [by the] third or fourth month of the student-physician's stay, the use of ok has been eliminated by the majority of the students. However, in the last set of videotapings (done at the end of their rural Minnesota experience) a significant retention of the use of ok recurs in the majority of students. However, the intensity and quantity of oks have been significantly reduced. Whether the retention of oks persists or not depends on the student's attitude, behavior, and willingness to change interviewing idiosyncrasies. This change also requires strong support and reinforcement by knowledgeable and emphatic academic and clinical faculty over a long period of time. This would include surveillance into and through residency training.

Here the observation might be made that although "Okays" may be eliminated for a brief period of time, it is natural for them to seep back into clinical practice despite efforts to "change interviewing idiosyncrasies": "Okays" are simply yet deeply implicated in the "asymmetric" and proactive work of structuring interviews in pursuit of clinical agenda and goals, at times in consideration of but, seemingly, just as often at the expense of patients' elaborations, continuations, and related contributions. These and related actions often provide a basis for complaints and actual displays essentially treating doctors as inattentive, impatient, not listening well, and/or failing to appreciate and value the insights and stories offered by patients (cf. Heath, 1986; Jensen, 1987; Mishler, 1984). And notice that such complaints and reactions fall short of attributing malicious intentions to doctors; instead, descriptions of and visible orientations to real time interactional involvements are offered.

Clearly, then, until and unless the focus and priority of "official" clinical business is eliminated altogether, which of course is quite unrealistic given the inevitability and omnipresent features of professional–lay interactions (cf. Drew & Heritage, 1992), the reliance on "Okays" (and other resources) as recruited components for controlling and shaping topical progression will undoubtedly continue. This is so despite recommendations to the contrary by "knowledgeable and emphatic academic and clinical faculty" who, knowingly or not, may be creating additional rather than resolving present troubles: offering prescriptive solutions to recurring interactional difficulties, the real-time specifications of which remain premature and largely underdeveloped.

It is on this basis, however, that clinicians and academicians can mutually benefit from one another's experiences, insights, and findings. Although this chapter began by considering one case study involving "Okays" drawn from the RPAP program at the University of Minnesota Medical School, and through analysis generated alternative and at times competing findings, it is nevertheless laudatory that this program and many others turn directly to videotaping interviews for purposes of better understanding and refining interview techniques. Yet when such difficulties exist with understanding the interactional usages and ramifications of "Okays," which after all reveal only one small, although no less consequential range of phenomena when considering the larger scheme of activities through which talk-in-interaction gets practically accomplished, it takes little imagination to realize the problems inherent in making yet "larger" claims about the organization of casual and institutional conduct (cf. Beach & Lindstrom, 1992; Drew & Heritage, 1992; Schegloff, 1987b;).[6] And especially for clinicians, these troubles hold the potential of becoming exacerbated when attempting to prescribe and thereby alter behaviors that have not been fully and contextually examined "by reference to their placement and participation within sequences of actions . . . to its turn-within-sequence character" (Atkinson & Heritage, 1984, pp. 7, 9).

And it is in this sense that the fact remains, and is clearly evidenced via "Okays" and the activities they are recruited to achieve within medical interviews, that premature movement to prescription is problematic: so doing is tantamount to gener-

---

[6]It is in the concern with "big issues" that Sacks' (1984) basic focus rested with the organization of human interaction, and consequently how such entities as "institutions" exist only through members' concerted activities:

> The search for good problems by reference to known big issues will have large-scale, massive institutions as the apparatus by which order is generated and by a study of which order will be found . . . It is possible that detailed study of small phenomena may give an enormous understanding of the way humans do things and the kinds of objects they use to construct and order their affairs. (pp. 22, 24)

ating a diagnosis prior to understanding the symptomatic nature of an entire range of problems, emerging from and uniquely situated within a fully disclosed medical history.

REFERENCES

Atkinson, J. M., & Heritage, J. (Eds.). (1984). *Structures of social action: Studies in conversation analysis*. London: Cambridge University Press.

Austin, J. L. (1962). *How to do things with words*. Oxford: Oxford University Press.

Beach, W. A. (1990a). Language as and in technology: Facilitating topic organization in a Videotex focus group meeting. In M. J. Medhurst, A. Gonzalez, & T. R. Peterson (Eds.), *Communication and the culture of technology* (pp. 197–220). Pullman: Washington State University Press.

Beach, W. A. (1990b). On (not) observing behavior interactionally. *Western Journal of Speech Communication, 54*, 603–612.

Beach, W. A. (1991). *"Okay" as projection device for fuller turn: Displaying "state of readiness" for movements toward next-positioned matters*. Unpublished manuscript.

Beach, W. A. (1993a). Transitional regularities for "casual" "okay" usages. *Journal of Pragmatics, 19*, 325–352.

Beach, W. A. (1993b). The delicacy of preoccupation. *Text and Performance Quarterly, 13*, 299–312.

Beach, W. A. (1994). *"Okays" and their relevance to "making points" in therapy and counseling sessions*. Unpublished manuscript.

Beach, W. A. (in press). Conversation analysis: "Okay" as a clue for understanding 'consequentiality'. In S. Sigman (Ed.), *The consequentiality of communication*. Hillsdale, NJ: Lawrence Erlbaum Associates.

Beach, W. A., & Lindstrom, A. L. (1992). Conversational universals and comparative theory: Turning to Swedish and American acknowledgment tokens-in-interaction. *Communication Theory, 2*, 24–49.

Bergmann, J. R. (1992). Veiled morality: Notes on discretion in psychiatry. In P. Drew & J. Heritage (Eds.), *Talk at work: Interaction in institutional settings* (pp. 137–162). Cambridge: Cambridge University Press.

Boden, D., & Zimmerman, D. H. (Eds.). (1991). *Talk and social structure*. Cambridge: Polity Press.

Button, G. (1987). Moving out of closings. In G. Button & J. R. E. Lee (Eds.), *Talk and social organization* (pp. 101–151). Clevedon: Multilingual Matters.

Button, G. (1990). On varieties of closings. In G. Psathas (Ed.), *Interaction competence* (pp. 93–148). Lanham, MD: University Press of America.

Byrne, P. S., & Long, B. E. L. (1976). *Doctors talking to patients: A study of the verbal behaviors of doctors in the consultation*. London: HMSO.

Drew, P., & Heritage J. (Eds.). (1992). *Talk at work*. Cambridge: Cambridge University Press.

Drew, P., & Holt, E. (1988). Complainable matters: The use of idiomatic expressions in making complaints. *Social Problems, 35*, 398–417.

Duranti, A., & Goodwin, C. (Eds.). (1992). *Rethinking context: Language as an interactive phenomenon*. Cambridge: Cambridge University Press.

Erickson, F., & Schultz, J. (1982). *The counselor as gatekeeper*. New York: Academic Press.

Frankel, R. (1990). Talking in interviews: A dispreference for patient-initiated questions in physician-patient encounters. In G. Psathas (Ed.), *Interaction competence* (pp. 231–262). Lanham, MD: University Press of America.

Goffman, E. (1981). *Forms of talk*. Philadelphia: University of Pennsylvania Press.

Heath, C. (1984). Talk and recipiency: Sequential organization in speech and body movement. In

J. M. Atkinson & J. Heritage (Eds.), *Structures of social action: Studies in conversation analysis* (pp. 247–265). London: Cambridge University Press.

Heath, C. (1986). *Body movement and speech in medical interaction*. Cambridge: Cambridge University Press.

Heath, C. (1992). The delivery and reception of diagnosis in the general practice consultation. In P. Drew & J. Heritage (Eds.), *Talk at work* (pp. 235–267). Cambridge: Cambridge University Press.

Heritage, J., & Greatbatch, D. (1991). On the institutional character of institutional talk: the case of news interviews. In D. Boden & D. Zimmerman (Eds.), *Talk and social structure* (pp. 93–137). Cambridge: Polity Press.

Heritage, J., & Sorjonen, M. L. (1994). Constituting and maintaining activities across sequences: *And*-prefacing as a feature of question design. *Language in Society, 23*, 1–29.

Jefferson, G. (1980). *End of grant report on conversations in which "troubles" or "anxieties" are expressed* (HR 4805/2). London: Social Science Research Council (mimeo).

Jefferson, G. (1981). *Caveat speaker: A preliminary exploration of shift implicative recipiency in the articulation of topic* (Final Report). The Netherlands: Social Science Research Council (mimeo).

Jefferson, G. (1984a). On stepwise transition from talk about a trouble to inappropriately next-positioned matters. In J. M. Atkinson & J. Heritage (Eds.), *Structures of social action: Studies in conversation analysis* (pp. 191–222). London: Cambridge University Press.

Jefferson, G. (1984b). On the organization of laughter in talk about troubles. In J. M. Atkinson & J. Heritage (Eds.), *Structures of social action: Studies in conversation analysis* (pp. 347–369). London: Cambridge University Press.

Jefferson, G. (1990). List construction as a task and resource. In G. Psathas (Ed.), *Interaction competence* (pp. 63–92). Lanham, MD: University Press of America.

Jefferson, G. (1993). Caveat speaker: Preliminary notes on recipient topic-shift implicature. *Research on Language and Social Interaction, 26*, 1–30.

Jefferson, G., & Lee, J. R. E. (1981). The rejection of advice: Managing the problematic convergence of a "troubles-telling" and a "service encounter". *Journal of Pragmatics, 5*, 399–422. (Reprinted in P. Drew & J. Heritage (Eds.), (1992). *Talk at work* (pp. 521–548). Cambridge: Cambridge University Press.

Jensen, N. M. (1987). *Topic management in doctor–patient conversations: An exploratory analysis of the use of the speech particle "OK"*. Unpublished master's Thesis, University of Wisconsin, Madison.

Jones, C., & Beach, W. A. (1994). Therapists' techniques for responding to unsolicited contributions by family members. In B. Morris & R. Cheneil (Eds.), *Talk of the Clinic* (Ch. 2, this volume). Hillsdale, NJ: Lawrence Erlbaum Associates, Inc.

Labov, W., & Fanshel, D. (1977). *Therapeutic discourse: Psychotherapy as conversation*. New York: Academic Press.

Levinson, S. (1983). *Pragmatics*. Cambridge: Cambridge University Press.

Levinson, S. (1992). Activity types and language. In P. Drew & J. Heritage (Eds.), *Talk at work* (pp. 66–100). Cambridge: Cambridge University Press.

Markova, I., & Foppa, K. (Eds.). (1991). *Asymmetries in dialogue*. Hemel Hempstead: Harvester Wheatsheaf.

Mehan, H. (1979). *Learning lessons: Social organization in the classroom*. Cambridge, MA: Harvard University Press.

Mishler, E. (1984). *The discourse of medicine: dialectics of medical interviews*. Norwood, NJ: Ablex.

Redeker, G. (1990). Ideational and prgramatic markers of dicourse structure. *Journal of Pragmatics, 14*, 367–381.

Sacks, H. (1984). Notes on methodology. In J. H. Atkinson & J. Heritage (Eds.), *Structuring social action:* Studies in conversation analysis (pp. 21–27). London: Cambridge University Press.

Schegloff, E. A. (1984). On some questions and ambiguities in conversation. In J. M. Atkinson & J.

Heritage (Eds.), *Structures of social action: Studies in conversation analysis* (pp. 28–52). London: Cambridge University Press.

Schegloff, E. A. (1987a). Analyzing single episodes of interaction: An exercise in conversation analysis. *Social Psychology Quarterly, 50,* 101–114.

Schegloff, E. A. (1987b). Between micro and macro: Contexts and other connections. In J. Alexander, B. Giesen, R. Munch, & N. J. Smelser (Eds.), *The micro–macro link* (pp. 207–234). Berkeley: University of California Press.

Schegloff, E. A. (1990). On the organization of sequences as a source of "coherence" in talk-in-interaction. In B. Dorval (Ed.), *Conversational organization and its development* (pp. 51–77). Norwood, NJ: Ablex.

Schegloff, E. A. (1991a). Reflections on talk and social structure. In D. Boden & D. H. Zimmerman (Eds.), *Talk and social structure* (pp. 44–70). Cambridge: Polity Press.

Schegloff, E. A. (1991b). To Searle on conversation: A note in return. In J. Searle et. al (Eds.), *(On) Searle on conversation* (pp. 78–91). Philadelphia: John Benjamin.

Schegloff, E. A., & Sacks, H. (1973). Opening up closings. *Semiotica, 7,* 289–327.

Schiffrin, D. (1987). *Discourse markers.* Cambridge: Cambridge University Press.

Sorjonen, M. L., & Heritage, J. (1991). And—prefacing as a feature of question design. In L. Laitinen et al. (Eds.), *Asennonvaihtoja [Changes in footing]: Essays in honor of Auli Hakulinen* (pp. 68–84). Helsinki: Vastapaino.

Searle, J. (1969). *Speech acts.* Cambridge: Cambridge University Press.

Searle, J. (1987). Notes on conversation. In D. G. Ellis & W. A. Donahue (Eds.), *Contemporary issues in language and discourse processes* (pp. 7–19). Hillsdale, NJ: Lawrence Erlbaum Associates.

Silverman, D. (1987). *Communication and medical practice.* London: Sage.

Sinclair, J. McH., & Coulthard, M. (1975). *Towards an analysis of discourse: The English used by teachers and pupils.* Oxford: Oxford University Press.

Streeck, J. (1980). Speech acts in interaction: A critique of Searle. *Discourse Processes, 3,* 133–154.

Verby, J. E. (1991). OK is sometimes not ok. *Learning Resources Journal/University of Minnesota Health Sciences.*

Zimmerman, D. H. (1992). The interactional organization of calls for emergency assistance. In P. Drew & J. Heritage (Eds.), *Talk at work* (pp. 418–469). Cambridge: Cambridge University Press.

13 Implications of Relational Communication for Therapeutic Discourse

Kelly S. McNeilis
Ohio State University

Teresa L. Thompson
University of Dayton

Dan O'Hair
University of Oklahoma

Physicians and patients create a communication context unique to most dyadic encounters. Traditional roles defined by the therapeutic setting are assumed by physicians and patients. Patients seek care and physicians are expected to provide counsel and treatment. Within the context of those roles, physicians and patients are exchanging messages to reveal the nature of the medical condition, negotiate the treatment plan, and establish a relationship that is mutually negotiated. Traditional roles will often give way to negotiated roles that transpire from interaction. How physicians and patients perceive their respective roles and the relationship that ensues can greatly influence various therapeutic outcomes (e.g., satisfaction, compliance, malpractice litigation). Relational definition is an intrinsic component of the medical setting. One of the relational elements that has drawn recent attention involves the process of how physicians and patients attempt to gain control of their relationship. Both physician and patient have reasons for exerting control over the relationship. In this chapter we hope to show that, through relational control analysis, practitioners can understand how their communication of control might influence and have an effect on patients' satisfaction with the physician, subsequent compliance with medical advice, and patients' perceptions of their physician.

Observing how provider and patient use relational control during a medical interview is of particular significance for physicians in light of a trend toward research that takes a microscopic approach to the talk between physician and patient in both the medical and communication fields (see Stiles & Putnam, 1989). These types of analyses can offer practitioners new outlets for becoming more competent communicators during the medical interview. Additionally, this type of research may be used to educate patients. Helping patients understand their responsibility to the relationship, and thus adjusting their communication, should lend assistance to physicians in making the interaction a successful one.

The particular performances addressed in this chapter are those found in the medical interview dealing with the negotiation of the therapeutic plan. There are generally three parts to the medical interview: history taking, medical exam, and negotiation of therapeutic plan (Stiles & Putnam, 1989). Although our concern here is not with the first two parts, physicians should be aware of their control attempts and maneuvers during these episodes. The particular nature of the talk in the third part of the medical interview is of primary interest to communication scholars. During this part of the interaction, patients and physicians will negotiate their roles, plans for treatment, and relational goals. From this perspective, research explores how each interactant seeks control of the interaction—to align the roles as he or she sees fit. Control is managed through their communication, that is to say, seeking to take control, yield control, or remain neutral.

Relational control can be observed most directly through the use of relational coding analysis. This approach assigns numerical codes to each individual utterance of participants as a way of determining control attempts. After developing the background for relational control, a rationale for study is provided, followed by the analysis of actual doctor–patient interactions. The chapter concludes with practical implications for using this technique within the practitioner/physician context.

RELATIONAL CONTROL

The relational perspective is based most directly on the work of Bateson, Bavelas, Jackson, and others who were at least loosely affiliated with the Mental Research Institute in Palo Alto, California. Thus, its applications to therapeutic discourse are extensive.

Background and Description

The relational perspective is based most directly on the work of Bateson, a noted anthropologist. His work was responsible for a shift in the focus of inquiry from the individual to the relationship as the unit of analysis. Such an analytical shift was necessary because, as Bateson and his colleagues reminded us, communication occurs not within an individual, but *between* individuals (Fisher, 1982). Bateson's background as an anthropologist led him to focus on what happens, rather than why things happen.

The perspective from which the relational view is drawn is from a related series of principles, generated by Bateson and others, that has great heuristic appeal, and has provoked much thought and analysis. The perspective is sometimes labeled the *Palo Alto view* because much of the work came out of a group of researchers centered around Bateson's work at the Veterans' Administration Hospital in Menlo Park and Jackson's Mental Research Institute in Palo Alto.

Although the interactional view has caused much interest, it has also been subject to much criticism. There are those who have argued that when we place no limits on a definition of communication, the concept becomes meaningless (Wilder, 1979). They have also complained of the difficulty of operationalizing terms from the relational perspective (Wilder, 1979) and have criticized the conceptual confusion that has occurred as a result of the varying meanings used by those writing within the perspective (see Wilmot, 1980, for an examination of the different meanings attributed to metacommunication; Rogers, 1981, for a discussion of confusion in the concepts of complementarity and symmetry; and Wilder, 1979, for the most thorough summary of this issue). Wilder-Mott (1981) noted Bateson's view of words as dangerous, arguing that labeling something implies an *endstate* (p. 19) that is really inappropriate for this perspective. Indeed, the most popular book on the view, Watzlawick, Beavin, and Jackson's (1967) *Pragmatics of Human Communication* was coldly received by many other members of the team. Nonetheless, the perspective has generated a great deal of interest and some provocative research.

Symmetry and Complementarity

It was during his studies of the Iatmul tribe in New Guinea in the 1930s that Bateson first described the concept of *schismogenesis*. Essentially, it is a process of differentiation in the norms of individual behavior resulting from cumulative interaction between individuals. If the cycle of behaviors focuses on difference, such as assertiveness encouraging submission and vice versa, complementary schismogenesis has occurred. Symmetrical schismogenesis coincides with a focus on similarity, such as when boasting leads to boasting. The concepts of *complementarity* and *symmetry* are applied most properly to the interact which is an act or statement by one person followed by or coupled with an act or statement from a second person. Each act or statement is classified as one-up if it exerts control over the direction of the conversation or the relationship or one-down if it yields control over the direction of the conversation or the relationship. Later researchers (Rogers & Farace, 1975) added the notion of one-across statements, which neither explicitly attempt to gain control, nor explicitly yield control to the other. These concepts are described in more detail when the latest version of the coding scheme typically used to investigate them is discussed. Escalating symmetry (repeated one-up statements) or rigid complementarity (one person repeatedly one-up with the other person repeatedly one-down) are possible pathologies that have been observed.

The perspective termed *relational communication* was derived from the interactional or pragmatic perspective. It focuses, in part, on these notions of complementarity and symmetry, and the newer concept of parallel or transitory interacts, which was required by the addition of one-across acts. Additionally, the relational perspective focuses on how communication creates, defines, and reflects relationships between people. The most notable work on relational communication has been conducted by Rogers and Millar. Their model describes three dimensions to relationships: control, trust, and intimacy. According to Millar and Rogers (1976), the "control dimension is concerned with who has the right to direct, delimit and define the actions of the interpersonal system" (p. 91). Control is the most dynamic and basic of the three dimensions. The control pattern is always defined by both interactants. In addition to coding the interacts, the model looks at the rigidity versus flexibility and stability versus instability of the patterns.

The trust dimension correlates with vulnerability patterns, reward dependability, and confidence patterns. Intimacy is studied by examining the characteristics of transferable versus nontransferable, depending on uniqueness, and degree of attachment, defined as interdependence in terms of mutual self-confirmation. Control, however, has been studied more than trust and intimacy. The control coding scheme focuses on: relational control rather than content; defining message sequences; and mapping transactional patterns over time. Thus, stochastic analysis techniques such as Markov chains are available for complex data sets.

In their research, Rogers and Millar have further distinguished between dominance, asserting one-up relational definitions that are accepted; and domineeringness, asserting one-up relational definitions that are not accepted; (Rogers-Millar & Millar, 1979). They found, for instance, that lower levels of satisfaction and higher levels of role strain are associated with wife domineeringness. However, husband dominance is related to higher levels of satisfaction, lower levels of role strain, and more support.

Coding of relational control has been criticized on several grounds. Folger and Poole (1982) expressed concern over the fact that such coding schemes miss the subjective experience of the interactants by focusing on the interpretation of observers. This argument, however, has been effectively refuted by Rogers and Millar (1982), who relied on some of Folger and Poole's earlier work in formulating their arguments. It is argued that one acceptable approach to research is to ask not what people mean by their behaviors, but what behaviors mean (Fisher, 1982). Other criticisms (nicely summarized by Emmert, 1989, and Trenholm, 1991) focus on validity and reliability concerns. However, "recent research by Poole and Folger (1985) supports the viability of coding schemes that identify the meaning of messages on a general, conventional level. Moreover, the predictive validity of the Rogers and Farace coding scheme is well established" (Fairhurst, Rogers, & Sarr, 1987, p. 402). The coding scheme most commonly used to assess relational control is the latest adaptation of that described by Rogers and Farace (1975), which built upon the earlier work of Sluzki and Beavin (1965) and Mark (1970).

A RATIONALE FOR RELATIONAL CONTROL ANALYSIS IN THERAPEUTIC SETTINGS

In an effort to examine how practitioners and patients define and control their relationships, three recent studies have applied relational coding to the medical/therapeutic context. O'Hair (1989) studied 11 naturally occurring physician–patient interactions and found that, although physicians both attempt and gain control of most interactions, patients also attempt and sometimes succeed at relational control maneuvers. He also found evidence of several transitory dyadic exchanges. O'Hair's research emphasized relational control exchanges and did not focus directly on questions relating to the types of relational control messages exchanged between physician and patient.

Building on O'Hair's research, von Friederichs-Fitzwater, Callahan, Flynn, and Williams (1991) examined transcripts of 30 physician–patient conversations from four contexts. Unlike O'Hair, they found the predominant interact type was neutralized symmetry. They reported a tendency toward domineering behavior on the part of the patient. Like O'Hair, however, they found that physicians tended to control through questioning and topic change.

McNeilis and Thompson (1994) studied dentist–patient interactions utilizing six different dentists. These dyads engaged in more transitory interactions than any other control type. All types of acts (one-up, one-down, or one-across) were more likely to be followed by a one-across statement than by any other type of response. Dentists were no more likely than patients to follow a one-up statement with another one-up.

The studies just reported simply scratched the surface in an area of medical discourse that is seriously underdeveloped. In order to more fully understand how practitioners and patients accomplish relational goals during interaction, relational communication analysis techniques must be maximized beyond previous attempts. There are a number of subtle dimensions operating during physician–patient interactions that can be observed through relational coding schemes. First, patterns of dominance, domineeringness, submissiveness, complementarity, and symmetry can be determined directly from relational exchanges. Dominance may appear as a predominant characteristic of a particular exchange based on a practitioner's tendency to control the relationship, however, the responsibility may lie with an unassertive patient. Haug and Lavin (1979, 1981, 1983) discovered that patients hold critical and challenging attitudes toward physicians, yet rarely communicate their feelings. In the case of a domineering practitioner or patient, repeated, but unsuccessful attempts at relational control may create frustration and result in adverse medical and relational outcomes such as doctor shopping, withdrawal, and noncompliance (Kreps & Query, 1989; Street & Wiemann, 1987).

Relatedly, relational control analysis can help to draw inferences about role expectations and role negotiation between patient and physician. By determining patterns of relational control strategies, researchers can develop suppositions about the success or failure of medical dyads as they negotiate roles. In initial interactions, physician and patient must form role expectations based on contextual predilections and previous experiences (Kreps, 1988). As they come to know one another, role negotiation can be revealed through relational exchanges. Conflict, in the form of competitive symmetry, may reflect a recurring theme in certain medical dyads where physician and patient are vying for control of the relationship (Danziger, 1981). Physicians intent on maintaining power and influence will use one-up strategies defining their expertise, authority, and ability to control information (Beisecker, 1990; Parrott, Burgoon, & Ross, 1992). Patients, viewing their role as an informed decision maker (Ballard-Reisch, 1990), may respond with one-up messages that question, challenge, and impugn physician control efforts. The issue of conflicting role expectations can be especially dramatic when patients anticipate a style of medical delivery based on consumerism, and are faced with practitioners who communicate from a paternalistic perspective (Beisecker & Beisecker, 1993).

Third, specific control maneuvers can be assessed leading to an interpretation of strategy choice for both patients and physicians. Disconfirmation, instructions, questions, assertions, and the like can be coded for frequency and response likelihood among interactants. Once patients and practitioners have come to terms about their relative roles and mutually participate in the decision-making process, relational control analysis can reveal those strategies that are most effective for enhancing medical outcomes. Instructions may be especially useful in verifying treatment regimens among cooperating patients. Questions can serve important functions in clarifying complicated medical treatment. Even disconfirmation, usually thought of as a negative relational strategy, may identify elements of the relationships that need adjusting.

Fourth, relational control analysis could prove useful in identifying global patterns of relational communication. Physicians may begin interactions with a one-down, yielding relational patterns and switch to more controlling maneuvers when perplexed, annoyed, uncertain, or concerned with the patient's condition or their communication behavior. On the other hand, patients may switch from relational control attempts during the diagnostic phase to more yielding patterns of control during the presentation of the treatment regimen. Such "switchpoints" would serve to mark a transition in the relational control exchange, allowing the relational partner to adjust his or her communication behavior, thereby maximizing the relational exchange. Of course, physician or patient may not understand the function of the switchpoint and ignore or deny the maneuver.

In an attempt to demonstrate the applicability of the relational perspective to the therapeutic context, we present exemplars from four medical interviews. We outline three characteristics of relational control in this context and offer some implications based on the perspective.

ANALYSIS

Four interviews were selected from data collected at a family medical center on the campus of a large southwestern university. The three doctors who participated were all residents. The interactions were taperecorded as part of a larger research project not connected with this analysis.

Relational Control Analysis

The instrument used in analyzing the relational dimension of control and patterns in these interactions was relational coding. According to Folger and Poole (1982), the use of this device is helpful in translating utterances by participants into meaningful categories for defining relational control. "It is in the translation from message to control functions that the schemes link interaction to the definition of social relationships" (p. 235). The Rogers and Farace (1975) adapted coding scheme was used for this study. Adaptations to the scheme have been made by Fairhurst (1989). This method allows for the description of control by analyzing the exchange, transactions, or interactions of the speakers and not just single messages in and of themselves. This analysis utilized dominance as a factor of relational control. *Dominance,* which is a component of control, "refers to paired message exchanges" as opposed to *domineering control maneuvers* that "refer to individual message movements" (Courtright, Millar, & Rogers-Millar, 1979, p. 180).

One of the principles of relational communication is that "all of the interaction involves an on-going reciprocal definition of relationships" (Rogers & Farace, 1975, p. 228). This coding scheme relies on the message sequence and not on single utterances. These utterances must be looked at in context. To gain an understanding about what is being said by each interactant, a three-digit code is used first to define the nature of the utterances. The pairing of these three-digit codes provides information more crucial to defining the control dimension examined in this chapter. The three-digit code indicates whether the utterance is controlling (one-up), yielding control (one-down), or neutral (one-across). After each utterance is coded, sequential utterances by each participant are paired to indicate the type of interact produced, whether it be relatively controlling or not.

According to Rogers and Farace (1975), each three-digit code is derived as follows: the first digit represents the speaker, the second refers to the grammatical form of the message, and the third digit reflects the response mode or "metacommunication" of the message in relation to the statement that came before it. Next, to understand the nature of the interaction, "any two-person communication can be represented by a series of sequentially ordered three-digit codes" (Rogers & Farace, 1975, p. 230). So the next step in coding the interaction and also in determining relational control is to "translate" the three-digit codes into control codes. These control codes are derived from a combination of the second two digits, the

	Support	Nonsupport	Extension	Answer	Instruction	Order	Disconfirmation	Topic change	Initiates-terminates	other
	1	2	3	4	5	6	7	8	9	0
Assertion 1	↓	↑	→	↑	↑	↑	↑	↑	↑	→
Question 2	↓	↑	↓	↑	↑	↑	↑	↑	↑	↓
Talk-over 3	↓	↑	↑	↑	↑	↑	↑	↑	↑	↓
Noncomplete 4	↓	↑	→	↑	↑	↑	↑	↑	→	→
Other 5	↓	↑	→	↑	↑	↑	↑	↑	↑	→

FIG. 13.1. Control code schematic from Rogers and Farace (1975). Copyright (1975) by Sage Publications. Reproduced by permission of Sage Publications Inc.

grammatical form of the message and the response mode. The control dimension code is defined in one of three directions: (a) *one-up* is termed as moving in the direction of gaining control of the exchange (e.g., instructions, topic changes, orders, disconfirmations, and answers with substance, etc.); (b) *one-down* is defined as moving in the direction of giving up control, allowing, seeking, or accepting it (e.g., questions that extend and supportive responses, etc.); and (c) *one-across* is defined as moving toward "neutralizing, or control-leveling categories" (e.g., noncomplete phrases and assertions of extension, etc.) (Rogers & Farace, 1975). The result is a scheme (see Fig. 13.1) that represents all possible combinations of the second and third digit variations.

The final step in the relational coding scheme is combining the control code directions of the physician and patient and creating categories of paired utterances or sequences. This step "operationalizes the transactions by the degree of control for each exchange as it 'unfolds'" (Rogers & Farace, 1975, p. 230). Three categories of pairings result. The first one is termed *symmetrical transactions*. This pairing is the result of control directions that are the same. One type of symmetry is called *competitive*, which results from a pair of responses coupled together and both codes are assigned as one-up. Here, speakers are vying for control of the interaction. Another type of symmetry is termed *submissive*. This occurs when both speakers allow control of the exchange and give one-down comments. The final type of symmetry is called *neutralized* and occurs when the speakers neither take control nor give it up and instead give one-across statements. The second type of pairings of control codes is called *complementary transactions*. In this interaction, the speaker attempts control and the other yields or one yields and the other then attempts control of the exchange. The final type of pairing of control codes is called *transitory*. One type of transitory pair occurs when a speaker gives a one-up comment the other returns with a one-across statement or (vice-versa) is called *transi-*

tory dominant. The other type is called *transitory submissive* when one-down statements are paired with one-across. (See Table 13.1 for examples of relational control exchanges.)

For purposes of analysis and due to space limitations, entire interviews were not coded. As mentioned in the introduction, the third part of each interview—negotiation of the therapeutic plan—is the communication of interest. The coding began immediately after the medical examination was concluded and the physician began talking about what he or she thought the patient could do to manage the condition or illness. In all four cases, this section of the interview concluded the interaction.

Of the four cases, three different physicians were recorded. One of the physicians recorded was female. She conducted two of the interviews, whereas two males conducted the others individually. Of the four patient interviews coded, three of the participants were male and the other was female. There were 111 paired

TABLE 13.1
Relational Control Exchanges

Symmetry

Competitive symmetry (one-up; one-up)
    Patient: I want you to renew my prescription.
    Doctor: You need a different type of medication.
Submissive symmetry (one-down; one-down)
    Doctor: Will you let me arrange for a series of therapy sessions?
    Patient: Whatever you think is indicated.
Neutralized symmetry (one-across; one-across)
    Doctor: So, you feel that the treatment hasn't worked?
    Patient: I think, maybe, I am not sure about . . .

Complementarity

One-up; one-across
    Doctor: You will have to remain in the hospital for another week.
    Patient: OK.
One-down; one-up
    Patient: I really appreciate your help in getting my child admitted to ER
    Doctor: In the future, bring her to the East Wing.

Transitory

Transitory dominant (one-up; one-across or one-across; one-up)
    Patient: I don't want to have surgery again.
    Doctor: Well, I think, ugh, . . .
Transitiory submissive (one-down; one across or one-across, one-down)
    Doctor: Are you going to have the lab work done when you leave here?
    Patient: Ugh, I don't know, uhm, . . .

exchanges (interacts) between physician and patient—coded, using an adapted version of the Rogers and Farace relational coding scheme (Fairhurst, 1989).

Although only one coder was used to develop examples for the control exchanges described in this chapter, relational control analysis should employ at least two coders who demonstrated adequate intercoder agreement (see O'Hair, 1989).

The results of the coding are presented in Table 13.2, illustrating the frequency with which each of the possible control types and interacts occurred in these interviews.

Of the 188 utterances coded, physicians contributed 56% of those utterances, whereas patients contributed the other 43%. Of those utterances, the most frequent attempts made by physicians were one-up (37) and one-across (36). Patients chose the one-across move most (37). Both patients and physicians chose the one-down move the least (54). Still, combined control attempts by both patients and physicians demonstrated one-across attempts most often.

Interact Type

The most frequently occurring interacts in these medical interviews were complementary (one-down and a one-up) and transitory (one-across with any other code) interacts. Interestingly, complementary attempts were most frequent when physicians offered a one-down message followed by a patients' one-up message. Both patients and physicians completed equal amounts of transitory-submissive (one-across and one-down) and transitory-neutralized (one-across paired with a one-across) interacts. For example, in the following exchange the doctor has found out some new information near what appeared to be the end of the interview and is

TABLE 13.2
Frequencies of Control and Interact Types

Control and Interact Type	Physicians	Patients
One-up	37	24
One-down	33	21
One-across	36	37
Total	106	82
Competitive symmetry	4	4
One-up Complementarity	6	8
One-down complementarity	12	8
Leveling one-up transition	14	9
One-up leveling transition	5	0
Leveling one-down transition	8	10
One-down leveling transition	4	2
Neutralized symmetry	8	10
Submissive symmetry	4	5
Total	55	56

following up on it. Here, there are two complementary interacts where the doctor offers control and the patient willingly accepts:

Exemplar 1
D: How long has it been since you had an eye exam? (one-down)
P: um, I had one in, like in the beginning of the year. (one-up)
(Silence as doctor examines patients eyes)

Exemplar 2
D: And that's never happened to you before, right? (one-down)
P: No. (one-up) You know that is what was so surprising 'cause it happened and you know I didn't think anything of it. I was there trying to clear my eyes out thinking I just had something in there. (one-across)

This exchange appears to typify a case where the physician allows the patient to maintain some control in the interaction while still being able to direct the flow of discussion by asking questions.

In Exemplar 3, the doctor communicates a one-across and the patient responds with a one-down. This is followed by a neutralized-symmetrical interact (two sequential one-across moves):

Exemplar 3
D: Yeah, (one-down support) when you get a little abscess like that, you really can't . . . (one-across noncomplete extension)
P: Yes, (one-down successful talk-over support) I've had them on my hands where I got stickers and stuff like that and had it drained . . . (one-across noncomplete extension)
D: Yeah, (one-across backchannel) yeah, really can't get well with antibiotics unless you open it up and get that puss out (one-across extension)

Explanations such as these characterize many of the neutralized-symmetry interacts found in these interactions.

Dominance and Domineeringness

It is important to assess how each interactant attempts to control the interaction through his or her communication. Recall that dominance is the ability to control the relationship by sending a one-up message that is accepted with a one-down message. Domineeringness is the attempt at dominance (sending a one-up message) that is either ignored (no response), denied (respondent replies with a reciprocal one-up message resulting in competitive symmetry), or transitionalized through a one-across message. In the data observed here, the one-up moves by physicians were accomplished mostly through the use of instructions and topic changes, for example:

Exemplar 4
D: Okay, I'm going to get you some antibiotics for seven days and hopefully that will help clear up that, ah, bacterial infection in your sinuses. (one-up assertion as instruction)

and,

D: If it gets bad enough you know you might try some Tylenol. If it persists and it worries you that something might be going on wrong, then go ahead and come back. (two one-up assertions as instruction)

On the other hand, the one-up moves by patients tended to be successful talk-overs, nonsupports, and topic changes. Mostly, patients used more one-across moves accomplished primarily by the use of extensions and backchannels. In these cases, patients merely continued the topic of discussion after answering a question brought up by the physician or gave responses such as "uh-huh" or "okay." Examples of this usually occur as patients extend their comments after answering a question. Backchannels occur as indications that one hears the other person or acknowledges one's comment.

Where we think physicians and patients can encounter problems is in the predominance of an interact where the doctor is in the one-up position as a strategy during the entire interview or constantly in a one-down position where the patient does not take control. Over a period of time, this strategy may prove to be an ineffective one, eventually silencing the patient's voice to tell her or his side of the story. If continued, the patient may receive a treatment that is not in synch with his or her lifestyle and eventually may not continue the advice or medications, may use them incorrectly, or may decide not to return to that particular physician again. Take the following example:

Exemplar 5
D: Well, we talked about you quite a bit and I think we're gonna hang on to you. (one-up) I think we might put you in the hospital overnight anyway. (one-up) I think we need to try to find out a little bit better what is going on with you. (one-across)
P: Well what, I don't have time. (one-up disconfirmation)
D: You don't have time, huh? (one-down)
P: No, I got, I got (inaudible) my damn car won't start all week. (one-up) Been worried about that. (one-across)
D: Well, I think you need to get a little bit better before you worry about that other stuff. (one-up nonsupport) We need to make sure there's not anything bad going on in your head. (one-up)

P: (laughs a bit) There's not anything going on that I know of for sure. (one-up) I don't I don't feel too bad, I feel pretty good except when I get up. I just have trouble navigating. (one-across)

D: I need to answer a phone call, (one-up) I'll be right back, but I think we're gonna try and hang on to you. (one-up) Do you have any big objections to that? (one-down)

P: (Pause) No, I guess not. (one-down)

D: Well, hopefully it'll be just a short stay. (one-down)

Here, the patient is told he will be admitted to the hospital immediately without consideration of his current ability to get out of work or any other factors. Perhaps because the patient was elderly—and in that case, an emergency—the physician made no attempt to indicate those concerns to the patient and instead just told him "we're gonna hang on to you." In terms of making an attempt to address relational concerns, it appears this physician treated the patient without regard to his current life situation. Despite this apparent lapse by the physician, here is a case where disconfirmation and nonsupport were used to counter each other's requests. The physician clearly is making an earnest attempt to indicate the severity of the symptoms and the need for immediate attention through the use of controlling moves.

In a similar case dealing with an acute foot problem, the situation also called for immediate care. Here, the doctor gives the patient little opportunity to answer when asked about his ability to stay and get his foot treated immediately. After being told of the treatment needed for his foot, the doctor follows with this:

Exemplar 6

D1: .... and she's (D2) probably gonna need to check it tomorrow or the next day. (one-up) But its gonna have to be opened to get well. (one-up)

P: Okay (one-down)

D2: Okay? (one-down) I'm gonna get a nurse to move you over to another room. (one-up) We'll have to soak your foot and then go ahead with the procedure (one-up), if that's okay with you, alright? (one-down) Do you have any questions? (one-down) Do you understand why I'm doing what we're doing? (one-down)

P: Yeah (one-down)

Despite the frequency of the one-down moves made here by the doctor, the patient, for whatever reason, decides to follow with more one-down moves. It seems apparent that the doctor's approach of firing so many questions at the patient, may have restricted his ability to answer freely.

Role Negotiation

There are also instances in these interviews of how roles are negotiated between the patient and physician via their control moves. Role expectations are rarely discussed in physician–patient relationships, so we looked for exchanges where those expectations were more implied. In the following exemplars, the physicians recognize and use their expertise role to prescribe medication or suggest treatment. Exemplar 7 illustrates how one particular intern communicated her role expectation and implied the role for the patient.

Exemplar 7
P: But you know, the cramping, I've always had that (one-up topic change from a previous comment)
D: Do you take Tylenol for it or anything? (One-down question that extends the topic)
P: No. (One-up answer)
D: If it gets bad enough, you know, you might try some Tylenol. (One-up instruction) If it persists and it worries you that something might be going wrong, then go ahead and come back. (One-up instruction)
P: I'm wondering you know, another thing is that awhile back I was going to come back in here and get myself checked cause I'd noticed that I had trouble (One-up topic change), you know, I thought maybe so on and see one in opthomology, ya know, some doctor with my eyes. (one-across extending the topic)
D: What's wrong with your eyes? (One-down question that extends the topic)

This excerpt shows the physician implicitly communicating her role as the physician by suggesting the proper treatment for the cramping and telling the patient to return in case of further problems. As she does this, the patient refuses to give up by going onto another problem she is experiencing–prompted by something the physician said about coming back. Later on in this interview, the physician tries again, after examining the patient's eyes, to reestablish her expertise role and ability to close the interview.

Exemplar 8
D: Well, certainly I have no objection to your making an appointment over in the opthomology department if you'd like to have your eyes checked. (One-up instruction) But, I WOULD like you to call me immediately if you have any further concerns. (One-up order) In the meantime, I'll talk with the staff to see if we need to put you on an aspirin a day. (One-up instruction)
P: Okay. (one across backchannel)

D: Okay? (one-down question for support)
P: Thank you, Dr. (one-down support)

In another interview, a physician tries fervently to maintain his role as medical expert by correcting the patient several times.

Exemplar 9
D: Uh, there's one that, I think it is called Intep LA and you can buy it over the counter. (One-up answer)
P: Could you write it down for me so I can ... (One-down question of support)
D: Ya (One-down agreement)
P: I'll probably get that and maybe try that and see how it works (One-across extension)
D: You'll take that one or twice a day (One-up instruction)
P: How much, how many milligrams do they come in ... (One-across noncomplete that extends)
D: Ah, I'm not sure (One-up successful talk-over answer) It's ah ... (One-across noncomplete that extends)
P: Twenty four hours a day, that is, one tablet every four hours? (One-down question of assistance)
D: No, one every twelve hours (One-up assertion of nonsupport)
P: Of course (One-down support), like time release tablets. (One-across extension)

This exchange is a constant struggle between the physician and the patient where it appears the patient finally gives in to the physician. The patient uses all one-acrosses and one-downs and relinquishes control to the physician and appears to accept the role negotiation initiated by the physician.

Physicians and patients also make choices about how they will respond to a particular control move or request by the other. The choices and strategies they employ will ultimately impact how they each define their roles. For example, in the Exemplar 10 the patient explicitly relies on the physician for information and the physician returns the request by providing that information and further instruction.

Exemplar 10
P: You know I wonder if that might be aggravating my condition. (One-down question of support)
D: Usually the humidifier is better (One-up instruction) because, uh, it tends to bring the fluids out and you might also be taking more liquid that tends to loosen up the secretions also. (One-across extension)
P: Uhm (One across unsuccessful talkover)

D: Decongestants will help you (One-across extension) basically what you've been doing (One-down support).
P: Well, uh, what do you think about the uh, combination of the prophalgesic that don't make you quite as drowsy. (One-up question topic change) I took some As, huh, Aspe . . . (One-across noncomplete)
D: Aphrin Spray? (One-down question of support)

What is also interesting about this example is that they seem to have negotiated roles very well, as the patient is in a position where he feels comfortable enough to ask questions without being prompted by the physician. There were quite a few of these types of exchanges where the patient asks a number of questions of the physician without prompting. Additionally, these questions occurred in the form of successful talk-overs that were either in support of a previous comment by the physician or were disconfirmations of the physicians' comments.

In terms of other sequences of relational control interacts, when confronted with a one-down message by doctors, patients were more likely to take control with a one-up message. These data seem to indicate that patients felt freer to take control only after the doctor offered or ignored control, not after a one-up attempt by doctor. But they do not use the one-across messages from doctors to take control exclusively since they also respond with equal amounts of one-downs and one-across moves. On the other hand, when negotiating a one-across message from a patient, doctors more often choose one-down or one-across messages.

Switchpoints

Identifying global patterns of relational communication ignores the reality that the physician may begin a segment of the interview with a one-down questioning style and, when met with an unfamiliar or ambiguous situation, may switch his or her style. These and other "switchpoints" occurred relatively frequently in these interviews. The most common instances at which the points occurred were when the physician moved from the history taking segment of the exam and then to the concluding segment of the interaction. The physicians used a comparatively accommodating approach during the history-taking segment while discovering the source of the patient's complaint. Then, during the physical exam, questions became more pointed and there was more control exerted. Finally, the control pattern changed once more during the concluding or treatment/diagnosis component of the medical interview. Although these physician-initiated switches are easily identifiable, others including patient switches are not so evident. Following are a few of the instances where either the physician or the patient used a particular control attempt that caused a major shift or switch in the relational communication pattern. In Exemplar 11, the patient attempts a switch that is successful.

Exemplar 11
D: I'll see you in a year for your pap smear (One-up instruction) . . . Anything I can help you with concerning that well just give a call down here and we'll see if I can help you. (One-across extension)
P: Okay, (One-across backchannel) ah, the pap smear should come out alright, shouldn't it? (One-up question topic change) There shouldn't be any problems (One across noncomplete extension)
D: I don't see any reason why it shouldn't be. (One-down talk-over support)

This switchpoint is key to this exam because, by expressing this concern, this patient was able to bring up quite a few others that eventually led to a heretofore unmentioned eye problem. The interacts up to this point were mostly complementary and after this switch, the interacts turned more neutral and symmetrical whereby the physician asked more questions and the patient made more one-up moves.

In another example noted earlier, the patient had engaged in mostly one-down control moves toward the physician in the earlier segment, but quickly changed his style in the following sequence.

Exemplar 12
D: I think we need to find out a little bit better what is going on with you. (One-across extension)
P: Well, I don't have time. (one-up assertion with disconfirmation)
D: You don't have time? (One-down question with extension)
P: No, I got, I got (inaudible) my damn car won't start all week. (One-up assertion with non support)

In other cases, there appears to be a sequence that is much more likely to allow patients freedom to explain or engage in an open dialogue with the physician where he or she does not assume complete control. In Exemplar 13, a pattern of complementarity emerges where the patient assumes a one-up strategy after the physician offers control. The doctor remains in that mode until she begins to describe some way to deal with the patient's problem of cramping. In this case, they compete for control.

Exemplar 13
D: I don't have good reason for that either, (one-down) but if it doesn't have to do strictly with your menstrual cycle you know if it's in between you menstrual cycle that's, that's. . . . (one-across) You're not having any problems with bowel movements or anything like that? (one-down)
P: No. (one-up) No, as a matter of fact I've taken a laxative a mild one. (one-across) But you know, the cramping, I've always had that. (one-up)

D: Do you take Tylenol for it or anything? (one-down)
P: No. (one-up)
D: If it gets bad enough you know you might try some Tylenol. (one-up) If it persists and it worries you that something might be going on wrong, then go ahead and come back. (one-up)
P: I'm wondering you know, another thing is that awhile back I was going to come back in here and get myself checked cause I'd noticed that I had trouble, ya know, I thought maybe I should go on in ophthalmology, ya know some doctor with my eyes. (one-up)
D: What's wrong with your eyes? (one-down)
P: I started having problems with that and so . . . (one-across)
D: Blurred vision? (one-down)

This example appears to be a failed attempt at a switchpoint. In the end, however, the failure appeared advantageous. Because the doctor let the patient assume some control to interject her thoughts, the doctor found out about an eye problem the patient had been experiencing that eventually led to another appointment with an ophthalmologist. Had the doctor maintained the focus on the line of conversation regarding a lack of reason for the cramping—just to take some Tylenol—the problem with the patient's eye might never have surfaced. This is a good example of how letting the patient control after one-down or one-across attempts can prove advantageous and how failed switchpoints may be necessary.

These and other examples illustrate how the physicians can control the interaction and thus patients' actions through their communication of control by talking more and using more one-up and one-across moves. In spite of these instances, some of the interactions do exhibit good examples of a balanced negotiation of treatment plan between physician and patient. In Exemplar 14, the physician asks the patient if she has made up her mind about getting a tubal ligation and allows her to tell her side of the story before making a decision as to how to proceed regarding the procedure:

Exemplar 14
D: Have you been back up to the ob dept? (one-up) Or what are your plans about the procedure? (one-down)
P: I haven't gone up there yet, (one-up) but I figure I'd go on ahead with it. (one-across) But like I told you, I'm going to have to get like a second opinion because, you know, in order for the insurance to cover they would probably have to go with that. (one-across)
D: Okay. (one-across) Have you talked with anybody up there on the phone or anything? (one-down)
P: No. (one-up)
D: No. (one-across) Okay well, you've just still been kinda mulling it over in your mind. (one-across)

P: Yes, just been thinking about it. (one-across)
D: Thinking about it? (one-down) What does your husband think? (one-down)
P: He thinks I should. (one-up)
D: What are you using for contraception now? (one-up)
P: Condoms. (one-up)
D: That's fine, (one-down) you can use that as long as you want to till you make up your mind (one-up)

It appears that in this instance there was control offered by the physician by giving one-down moves and the patient accepted this by responding with one-up attempts. The natural switchpoint comes after this sequence with a statement that the exam will begin. What is noteworthy about this example is that the physician returns to this relational style after the exam is over when they begin discussing treatment options.

Sequences and switchpoints such as these are found throughout these interactions and point to alternative ways of communicating with patients and for conducting the interview. Implications of using these strategies are discussed next.

PRACTICAL IMPLICATIONS

Although we cannot generalize from these data, the examples illustrated here demonstrate how physicians and patients interact and attempt to control one another through their communication. We found instances where the patient tried to balance the control by making one-up moves after the doctor's one-down moves, as well as cases where the doctor controlled the interaction with more one-up moves overall. Physicians can benefit from understanding how they control patients through their communication. In particular, we think that making adaptations to their current communication style is a way for physicians to make use of this information.

Relational control is an important issue relevant to both participants in the medical interview. First, expectations of both interactants can play a key role in whether or not the interview is successful or satisfactory. Control may interact with expectations in a way that produces a struggle in fulfilling initial expectations, resulting in a "spiraling down" control struggle (Fuller & Quesada, 1973). To counteract this dysfunctional trend, both interactants need to remain aware of one another's expectations and need to maintain some motivation to negotiate how expectations can be mutually achieved.

The following are considered to be various uses served by changes made in physician control style. First, for physician concerns, a change in their communication style may bring about more satisfying interactions with their patients (O'Hair, 1989). By refraining from complete control over the interaction, physicians may find that information offered by patients about lifestyle concerns, and so on, can provide help in putting together the therapeutic regimen the patient will follow. Above all, sharing some control with the patient could mediate the stress some physicians experience during patient interviews.

Patients will benefit from shared relational control by realizing a sense of partnership when dealing with their acute problems. Research suggests that patients sometimes are noncompliant as a way of asserting their power and independence (Beisecker, 1990). This is certainly not a desirable outcome sought by physicians. Balancing and adapting control styles by the patient may also reduce some of the stress they associate with physician communication and assuming a subordinate role so commonly associated with being a "patient." Alternatively, affording patients opportunities for relational control may increase their stress level associated with the medical problem they are experiencing. Physicians need to be aware of each patient's need for control or lack thereof. Adapting to patient styles or needs for control is not a skill developed overnight or solely by reading this chapter. It is, however, a technique developed over time by remaining sensitive to patients' communication needs.

There are several possible advantages that could occur in physician and patient interactions showing more balanced control. Such balanced control would not require total equality, but would involve a much needed exchange of control. These advantages might include the following:

- increased patient satisfaction with the interview,
- greater compliance with treatment regimen,
- reduced stress associated with patient interaction,
- more satisfying relationships with patients, and
- patient levels maintained.

Balanced control might, of course, lead to some short-term disadvantages, such as the following:

- initial added stress at keeping control balanced (physician and patient),
- patient discomfort at being asked to participate fully, and
- struggles over control during the interaction (physician and patient).

Thus, although there are a few disadvantages to assuming this new communication style, they appear to be short lived. Marshall (1993) described an intern's experience with a new interviewing technique to increase patient-centeredness and participation, which is closely associated with balancing control. The intern mentioned that at first he was uncomfortable with the new technique but that with more practice it became part of his repertoire of communication styles and added only a few minutes to each interview.

Although we know that patients desire physicians and other care providers to take some control, the literature almost never reports patient complaints that their doctors take too little control. It is not likely that this is a problem. Patients do complain, however, about physicians who say too little. Physicians can determine if they are controlling too much when the patient is very quiet or exhibits attempts to take a turn such as raised eyebrows, a forward lean, hunched shoulders, a frown, raised finger, open mouth, or utterances that physicians interrupt. Patient cues such as the one listed here are beneficial in managing a productive information exchange (Geist & Hardesty, 1990).

A problem is likely to exist if physicians find themselves spending a lot more time talking than the patient. The potential consequences of excessive control on the part of the provider include (a) inaccurate diagnosis, (b) doctor shopping, and (c) lack of compliance (Beisecker, 1990). Although past research has indicated that this is a likely consequence of too much physician control, such a relationship has not yet been specifically documented. McNeilis and Thompson (1994) attempted to study this relationship, but their subjects evidenced too little variance in compliance rates to provide a meaningful test of the relationship.

If physicians find themselves controlling too much, they need to explicitly relinquish control (e.g., "I'm sure that you have some questions and concerns, too—let me give you some time to ask me about those." "Is there anything else that you would like me to know about, even if it's not directly related to this problem? Anything else that's bothering you?").

The theme of increased awareness and monitoring of potentially controlling behavior is a key concern of physician–patient interaction. This chapter outlined some of the possible effects of control in an attempt to make apparent the need for such awareness and monitoring. Although we are not advocating a relinquishment of control on the part of physicians or other care providers, we are suggesting a recognition of these effects and that care providers may want to seek feedback about their control behaviors and the repercussions of these behaviors. This feedback may be sought: (a) informally, through attendance to nonverbal cues; (b) explicitly, through questions to patients or colleagues; or (c) technologically, through video- or audiotaping of interactions with patients. In any case, it is likely that increased awareness and monitoring of relational control attempts can impact on control struggles between patients and providers and help alleviate the negative effects of these control struggles.

REFERENCES

Ballard-Reisch, D. S. (1990). A model of participative decision making for physician–patient interaction. *Health Communication, 2,* 91–104.

Beisecker, A. E. (1990). Patient power in doctor-patient communication: What do we know? *Health Communication, 2,* 105–122.

Beisecker, A. E., & Beisecker, T. D. (1993). Using metaphors to characterize doctor–patient relationships: Paternalism versus consumerism. *Health Communication, 5,* 41–58.

Courtright, J. A., Millar, F. E., & Rogers-Millar, L. E. (1979). Domineeringness and dominance: Replication and expansion. *Communication Monographs, 46,* 179–192.

Danziger, S. K. (1981). The uses of expertise in doctor-patient encounters during pregnancy. In P. Conrad & R. Kerns (Eds.), *The sociology of health and illness* (pp. 359–376). New York: St. Martin's.

Emmert, V. J. L. (1989). Interactional analysis. In P. Emmert & L. L. Barker (Eds.), *Measurement of communicative behavior* (pp. 218–248). New York: Longman.

Fairhurst, G. (1989). *Supplemental coding rules and modification of the relational control coding scheme.* Unpublished coding manual.

Fairhurst, G. T., Rogers, L. E., & Sarr, R. A. (1987). Manager–subordinate conversation patterns and judgments about the relationship. In M. McLaughlin (Ed.), *Communication yearbook 4* (pp. 395–415). Newbury Park, CA: Sage.

Fisher, B. A. (1982). The pragmatic perspective of human communication: A view from systems theory. In F. E. X. Dance (Ed.), *Human communication theory* (pp. 192–219). New York: Harper & Row.

Folger, J. P., & Poole, M. S. (1982). Relational coding schemes: The question of validity. In M. Burgoon (Ed.), *Communication yearbook 5* (pp. 235–247). New Brunswick, NJ: Transaction Books.

Fuller, D. S., & Quesada, G. M. (1973). Communication in medical therapeutics. *Journal of Communication, 23,* 361–370.

Geist, P., & Hardesty, M. (1990). Reliable, silent, hysterical or assured: Physicians assess patient cues in their medical decision making: *Health Communication, 2,* 69–90.

Haug, M. R., & Lavin, B. (1979). Public challenge of physician authority. *Medical Care, 17,* 844–858.

Haug, M. R., & Lavin, B. (1981). Practitioner or patient—Who's in charge? *Journal of Health and Social Behavior, 22,* 212–229.

Haug, M. R., & Lavin, B. (1983). *Consumerism in medicine: Challenging physician authority.* Beverly Hills, CA: Sage.

Kreps, G. L. (1988). The pervasive role of information in health and health care: Implications for health communication policy. In J. A. Anderson (Ed.), *Communication yearbook 11* (pp. 238–276). Newbury Park, CA: Sage.

Kreps, G. L., & Query, J. L. (1989). Health communication interpersonal competence. In G. M. Phillips & J. T. Wood (Eds.), *SCA 75th anniversary commemorative volume* (pp. 293–323). Carbondale: Southern Illinois Press.

Mark, R. A. (1970). *Parameters of normal family communication in the dyad.* Unpublished doctoral dissertation, Michigan State University, East Lansing.

Marshall, A. A. (1993). Whose agenda is it anyway?: Training medical residents in patient-centered interviewing techniques. In E. B. Ray (Ed.), *Case studies in health communication* (pp. 15–30). Hillsdale, NJ: Lawrence Erlbaum Associates.

McNeilis, K., & Thompson, T. L. (1994). The impact of relational control on patient compliance in dentist-patient interactions. In G. Kreps & D. O'Hair (Eds.), *Communication and health outcomes* (pp. 57–72). Hillsdale, NJ: Lawrence Erlbaum Associates.

Millar, F. E., & Rogers L. E. (1976). *Explorations in interpersonal communication* (pp. 87–103). Beverly Hills, CA: Sage.

O'Hair, D. (1989). Dimensions of relational communication and control during physician–patient interactions. *Health Communication 1,* 97–116.

Parrott, R., Burgoon, M., & Ross, C. (1992). Parents and pediatricians talk: Compliance-gaining strategies; use during well-child exams. *Health Communications, 4,* 57–66.

Poole, M. S., & Folger, J. P. (1985). *How shared are "shared" interpretations?* Unpublished manuscript, University of Minnesota, Minneapolis.

Rogers, L. E. (1981). Symmetry and complementarity: Evolution and evaluation of an idea. In C. Wilder & J. Weakland (Eds.), *Rigor and imagination* (pp. 231–251). New York: Praeger.

Rogers, L. E., & Farace, R. V. (1975). Analysis of relational communication in dyads: New measurement procedures. *Human Communication Research, 1,* 222–239.
Rogers, L. E., & Millar, F. (1982). The question of validity. A pragmatic response. In M. Burgoon (Ed.), *Communication yearbook 5* (pp. 249–257). New Brunswick, NJ: Transaction Books.
Rogers-Millar, L. E., & Millar, F. E. (1979). Domineeringness and dominance: A transactional view. *Human Communication Research, 5,* 238–246.
Sluzki, G. E., & Beavin, J. (1965). Simietriay complemetaridid: Una definicion operacional y una tipologia de parejas. *Acta Psiguiatrica v Psiocologica de America Latina, 11,* 321–330.
Stiles, W. B., & Putnam, S. M. (1989). Analysis of verbal and nonverbal behavior in doctor-patient encounters. In M. Stewart & D. Roter (Eds.), *Communicating with medical patients* (pp. 211–222). Newbury Park, CA: Sage.
Street, R. L., & Wiemann, J. M. (1987). Patient satisfaction with physician's interpersonal involvement, expressiveness, and dominance. In M. L. McLaughlin (Ed.), *Communication yearbook 10* (pp. 591–612). Beverly Hills, CA: Sage.
Trenholm, S. (1991). *Human communication theory* (2nd ed.). Englewood Cliffs, NJ: Prentice-Hall.
von Friederichs-Fitzwater, M. M., Callahan, E. J., Flynn, N., & Williams, J. (1991). Relational control in physician–patient encounters. *Health Communication, 3,* 17–36.
Watzlawick, P., Beavin, J. H., & Jackson, D. D. (1967). *Pragmatics of human communication.* New York: Norton.
Wilder, C. (1979). The Palo Alto group: Difficulties and directions of the interactional view for human communication research. *Human Communication Research, 5,* 171–186.
Wilder-Mott, C. (1981). Rigor and imagination. In C. Wilder & J. Weakland (Eds.), *Rigor and imagination* (pp. 5–42). New York: Praeger.
Wilmot, W. W. (1980). Meta-communication: A re-examination and extension. In D. Nimmo (Ed.), *Communication yearbook 4* (pp. 61–69). New Brunswick, NJ: Transaction Books.

Author Index

A

Abelson, R., 21, 47
Agar, M., 20, 42, 45
Aijmer, K., 174, 183
Alexander, K., 188, 205
Altman, I., 36, 45
Amundson, J., 125, 128
Anderson, H. 72, 87, 109, 124, 128
Arcky, R. A., 6, 12
Atkinson, B. J., 125, 128
Atkinson, J. M., 265, 286, 287
Austin, J. L., 133, 146, 237, 255, 265, 287

B

Baillard-Reisch, D. S., 296, 311
Bandler, R., 5, 12, 13
Barry, M. J., 209, 230
Bateson, G., 4, 12, 76, 77, 85, 87, 126, 128
Baudrillard, J., 72, 87
Baxter, L. A., 36, 45
Beach, W. A., 52, 54, 59, 65, 67, 264, 265, 266, 269, 270, 271, 272, 273, 279, 281, 282, 283, 286, 287, 288
Beavin, J. B., 4, 15
Beavin, J. H., 57, 69, 293, 294, 313
Beck, C., 188, 190, 191, 205
Becker, A. L., 72, 74, 86, 87
Beckman, H. B., 211, 228, 229, 230, 240, 241, 244, 248, 255, 256
Beisecker, A. E., 296, 310, 311, 312
Beisecker, T. D., 296, 312
Bell, R., 175, 183
Ben-Sira, Z., 230
Berg, I. K., 72, 87
Berger, M., 131, 146
Bergmann, J. R., 19, 45, 281, 287
Best, S., 72, 87
Biggs, S. J., 123, 128
Billig, M., 156, 163, 169
Billings, J. A., 6, 12, 187, 189, 205, 233, 256
Bobele, M., 5, 13
Bochner, A. P., 26, 45
Bochner, S., 189, 205, 206
Boden, D., 259, 287
Bolinger, D., 235, 255
Boscolo, J., 123, 128
Boscolo, L., 5, 14, 43, 44, 45, 89, 90, 103
Bosk, C. L., 6, 14, 165, 169, 174, 184
Bradley, P. H., 175, 183
Branch, W. T., 6, 12, 229, 230, 244, 255
Breunlin, D. C., 131, 132, 146, 147
Britt, T., 6, 14
Broadhead, W. E., 209, 231
Brown, B. B., 36, 45

Brown, G., 20, 45
Brown, J. B., 211, 230, 231, 247, 256
Brown, P., 188, 205
Brown, R. H., 43, 45
Browning, L. D., 1, 8, 15
Bruner, E., 126, 128
Bruner, J., 31, 45
Bucher, R., 167, 169
Buller, D. B., 215, 231
Burgoon, M., 296, 312
Burke, K., 76, 87
Buttny, R., 6, 12, 19, 21, 25, 45, 46, 102, 103
Button, G., 65, 67, 269, 287
Byrne, P. S., 260, 287

C

Callahan, E. J., 295, 313
Campbell, J. D., 211, 230
Cantor, N., 23, 45
Carpentier, W., 211, 231
Carter, W. B., 213, 230, 235, 256
Cecchin, G., 5, 12, 14, 43, 44, 45, 89, 90, 103, 123, 128
Chenail, R. J., 3, 5, 12, 14, 77, 87, 123, 128
Churchill, A., 243, 25
Cicourel, A., 237, 255
Cimmarusti, R., 131, 146
Clifford, J., 43, 45
Cohen, J. R., 19, 45
Cohen, L.M., 189, 206
Cole, K., 209, 231
Coleman, L., 42, 45
Condor, S., 156, 163, 169
Conklin, F., 21, 46
Conville, R. L., 19, 36, 37, 45
Coope, J., 189, 205
Corea, G., 187, 189, 202, 205
Corradi Fiumara, G., 74, 87

Coulthard, M., 270, 275, 289
Courtright, J. A., 297, 312
Cox, A., 229, 230
Cradock, R. M., 233, 235, 256
Cronen, V. E., 5, 12, 14, 21, 22, 23, 45, 46
Cutler, J., 81, 87

D

Dammann, C., 131, 146
Danehy, J. J., 4, 14
Danziger, S. K., 296, 312
Davis, D., 5, 12
Davis, F., 189, 205
Davis, K., 53, 67
Davis, S. L. R., 5, 12
de Haes, J. C. J., 209, 231
de Saussure, F., 72, 87
de Shazer, S., 72, 87
Deleuze, G., 72, 87
Derrida, J., 72, 87
Dillon, G. L., 42, 45
Dixon, L., 6, 12
Domar, A., 187, 188, 189, 206
Dotson, D., 126, 128
Douthit, P. E., 5, 12
Dowrick, P. W., 123, 128
Drew, P., 1, 9, 12, 52, 67, 259, 260, 266, 268, 286, 287
Duck, S. W., 36, 45
Duranti, A., 265, 287

E

Edwards, D., 72, 87, 108, 125, 128, 156, 163, 169
Eisenbrg, L., 211, 231
Elbert, S., 53, 67
Elliott, R., 106, 108, 123, 126, 128
Emerson, J., 188, 206
Emmert, V. J. L., 294, 312

Empson, W., 81, 87
Ende, J., 152, 169
Engel, G. L., 6, 12, 255
Erickson, B., 175, 183
Erickson, F., 164, 169, 235, 255, 281, 287
Evans, J. J., 20, 46

F

Fahnestock, J., 42, 45
Fairhurst, G. T., 294, 297, 300, 312
Falzer, P., 125, 128
Fang, W., 188, 206
Fanshel, D., 1, 4, 6, 8, 13, 19, 21, 22, 24, 46, 53, 54, 68, 281, 288
Farace, R. V., 293, 294, 297, 298, 313
Feigl, P., 209, 231
Fennell, D., 131, 146
Fernandez, J. W., 74, 87
Fine, J., 131, 146
Fisch, R., 4, 12, 15, 90, 103
Fisher, B. A., 292, 312
Fisher, S., 6, 12, 186, 187, 203, 206
Flavin, K. S., 209, 231
Flynn, N., 295, 313
Foley, R. P., 152, 169
Folger, J. P., 294, 297, 312
Foppa, K., 65, 68, 260, 288
Foucault, M., 72, 87
Fowler, F. J., 209, 230
Frader, J., 6, 14, 174, 184
Frankel, R. M., 6, 12, 186, 187, 189, 190, 207, 211, 228, 229, 230, 235, 236, 237, 240, 241, 243, 244, 248, 255, 256, 257, 260, 266, 268, 287
Franshel, D., 235, 256

Freeman, S. H., 6, 12, 13
Freidman, H. S., 6, 12
Friedlander, M. L., 54, 67
Friedman, S., 72, 87
Fuller, D. S., 309, 312

G

Gale, J. E., 5, 6, 12, 13, 19, 46, 105, 106, 108, 123, 126, 128, 129
Gall, V., 209, 231
Gane, M., 156, 163, 169
Gardner, R. A., 53, 67, 68
Garfinkel, H., 101, 103, 124, 129
Garvey, C., 237, 256
Geertz, C., 102, 103
Geist, P., 311, 312
Gergen, K. J., 72, 88, 124, 129
Gilgun, J. F., 105, 123, 129
Glaser, B. G., 108, 129
Glenn, L. D., 186, 188, 189, 191, 206
Goffman, E., 23, 46, 125, 129, 164, 169, 188, 206, 240, 256, 270, 287
Gold, W. R., Jr., 214, 231
Good, B., 211, 231
Goodwin, C., 51, 68, 240, 256, 265, 287
Goodwin, M. H., 163, 169
Goody, E., 236, 256
Goolishian, H. A., 72, 87, 109, 124, 128
Greatbatch, D., 260, 288
Greenburg, L., 106, 129
Greene, J., 211, 231
Greenfield, S., 211, 230
Griffin, P., 156, 169
Grinder, J., 5, 12, 13
Guattari, F., 72, 87
Guerney, B., 53, 67

H

Haley, J., 131, 146
Halford, M. M., 6, 14
Hall, J. A., 215, 231
Hall, P. M., 26, 46
Halliday, M. A. K., 24, 46
Handy Bosma, J. E., 172, 184
Hanley, D., 209, 230
Hardesty, M., 311, 312
Harland, R., 72, 87
Harre, R., 24, 46
Harrigan, J. A., 6, 14
Harris, L. M., 36, 46
Hart, G., 131, 147
Hasan, R., 19, 46
Haug, M. R., 295, 312
Hayden, K. A., 209, 231
Hays, R. D., 209, 211, 231
Heath, A. W., 5, 14, 105, 123, 124, 125, 128, 129
Heath, C., 268, 286, 287, 288
Hein, N., 6, 13
Hejl, J., 211, 231
Heller, M., 6, 13
Helman, C. G., 6, 13
Heritage, J. C., 1, 9, 12, 22, 46, 52, 54, 60, 61, 63, 67, 68, 124, 129, 260, 265, 266, 286, 287, 288, 289
Herzog, J., 211, 231
Hewitt, J. P., 26, 46, 173, 174, 175, 184
Highlen, P. S., 54, 67
Hillard, P., 188, 206
Hinds, J., 21, 22, 23, 46
Hobbs, J. R., 20, 42, 45, 46
Hockett, C. F., 4, 14
Hoffman, L., 43, 44, 45, 123, 128
Hoffmann, L., 89, 103
Holt, E., 268, 287
Hoppe, R. B., 210, 231
Hopper, R., 26, 46, 172, 174, 175, 183, 184
Hoshmand, L. T., 3, 13
Hosokawa, M. C., 211, 230
Houtkoop-Steenstra, H., 133, 134, 146
Humphrey, F., 156, 169
Hurst, M., 188, 206
Hyatt, J. D., 211, 230

I

Inui, T. S., 213, 230, 235, 256

J

Jackson, D. D., 4, 15, 57, 69, 293, 313
Jacob, F., 100, 103
Japp, P., 54, 67
Jefferson, G., 12, 14, 20, 46, 52, 61, 68, 160, 161, 162, 169, 243, 256, 268, 269, 270, 288
Jensen, N. M., 264, 266, 270, 273, 279, 280, 281, 282, 286, 288
Johnson, B. C., 175, 183
Johnson, K. L., 21, 22, 23, 45
Johnson, K. M., 5, 12
Johnson, R., 91, 101, 103
Jones, C. M., 52, 53, 54, 55, 68, 279, 288

K

Kagas, D. K., 6, 14
Kagen, N. I., 106, 123, 129
Kaplan, S., 209, 211, 230
Karrer, B. M., 131, 146
Katz, N. R., 215, 231
Keenan, E. O., 22, 46, 237, 256
Keeney, B. P., 5, 13, 125, 129
Kellner, D., 72, 87

Kiebert, G. M., 209, 231
Kirk, J. W., 209, 211, 231
Kleinman, A., 211, 231
Knapp, M., 36, 46
Korsch, B. M., 186, 187, 206
Kreps, G. L., 6, 13, 295, 296, 312
Kriseva, J., 72, 87
Kues, J. R., 6, 14
Kuhn, T., 101, 103

L

Labov, W., 1, 4, 6, 8, 13, 19, 20, 21, 22, 24, 46, 53, 54, 68, 91, 101, 102, 103, 235, 256, 281, 288
Landgraf, J. M., 209, 211, 231
Lannamann, J. W., 5, 12, 13, 19, 21, 22, 23, 25, 25, 45, 46, 102, 103
Larson, R., 189, 206
Lassiter, W. L., 54, 67
Lave, J., 166, 169
Lavin, B., 295, 312
Lee, J. R. E., 268, 288
Leeds-Hurwitz, W., 4, 13
Leonardi, P., 52, 53, 55, 68
Lerner, G. H., 51, 64, 68
Lesserman, L., 186, 187, 188, 206
Levenstein, J. H., 211, 230, 231
Levinson, S. C., 6, 13, 42, 46, 133, 146, 188, 205, 265, 288
Levy, D. B., 6, 12
Levy, D. M., 20, 46
Ley, P., 187, 206
Liang, M. H., 209, 231
Liddle, H. A., 131, 132, 146, 147
Lind, E. A., 175, 183
Lindsay, R., 188, 206
Lindsey, E., 126, 128
Lindstrom, A. L., 286, 287
Lohr, K. N., 209, 231
Long, B. E. L., 260, 287

Longacre, R. E., 23, 46
Ludmerer, K., 151, 169
Luke, S., 186, 187, 188, 206
Lyman, S. M., 27, 47, 174, 184
Lyotard, J-F., 72, 88

M

MacKinnon, R. A., 54, 68
Mahrer, A. R., 106, 129
Malik, T. K., 229, 230, 244, 255
Mamlin, J. J., 211, 231
Manstead, A. S. R., 27, 47
Marcus, G. E., 43, 45
Mark, R. A., 294, 312
Markakis, K., 244, 256
Markova, I., 65, 68, 260, 288
Marshall, A. A., 310, 312
Masheter, C., 36, 46
Mastriano, B. P., 6, 14
Maynard, D. W., 233, 235, 256
Mazza, J., 131, 146
McBride, G. B., 186, 206
McBride, W. L., 186, 206
McBroom, W. H., 189, 206
McCracken, E. C., 211, 230, 231
McCullough, J., 188, 205
McDonald, R., 209, 231
McDowell, A. D., 214, 231
McGill, J. B., 209, 231
McGuire, D. E., 131, 146
McKinley, J., 187, 206
McLaughlin, M. L., 19, 46
McLaughlin, T., 73, 74, 75, 88
McLelland, L., 211, 231
McNamee, S., 5, 13, 72, 88, 105, 123, 129
McNeilis, K., 295, 311, 312
McQuown, N. A., 4, 13, 14
McWhinney, I., 210, 211, 212, 230, 231

Mehan, H., 52, 68, 156, 169, 266, 288
Merrian, S., 234, 256
Metcalf, D., 189, 205
Metch, B., 209, 231
Meyer, B., 20, 46
Michels, R., 54, 68
Middleton, D., 156, 163, 169
Millar, F. E., 294, 297, 312, 313
Miller, J. H., 81, 88
Minuchin, S., 53, 67
Mischel, W., 23, 45
Mishler, E. G., 235, 242, 256, 260, 286, 288
Mitchell, C., 105, 129
Mizrahi, T., 167, 169
Moerman, M., 108, 129
Moinpour, C. M., 209, 231
Montalvo, B., 131, 146
Morris, G. H., 5, 12, 19, 46, 174, 184
Morris, J. P., 5, 13
Mulley, A. G., 209, 230

N

Nadler, W. P., 106, 129
Nagireddy, C., 106, 123, 126, 128, 129
Negrete, V. F., 186, 187, 189, 206
Neikirk, H. J., 211, 230
Nelson, E. C., 209, 211, 231
Newfield, N., 6, 13, 19, 46, 108, 128
Nichols, W. C., 131, 146, 147
Nofsinger, R., 6, 14
Norrick, N. R., 162, 169

O

O'Barr, W. M., 175, 183
O'Hair, D., 295, 300, 309, 312

Odell, M., 106, 123, 129
Olson, B., 188, 206
Osler, W., 151, 169

P

Pagano, M., 191, 206
Park, J. M., 5, 12
Parkerson, G. R., 209, 231
Parrott, R., 296, 312
Patton, M. Q., 123, 129, 234, 256
Pearce, W. B., 5, 14, 21, 46
Pendleton, D. A., 189, 206
Penn, P., 43, 44, 45, 54, 68, 123, 128
Percy, W., 1, 14, 71, 88
Peyrot, M., 19, 46
Pittenger, R. E., 4, 14
Piziak, V. K., 211, 231
Plaja, A. D., 189, 206
Platt, M., 237, 256
Polkinghorne, D. E., 3, 13
Pomerantz, A. M., 6, 14, 154, 169
Poole, M. S., 294, 297, 312
Potter, J., 72, 87, 108, 120, 125, 128, 164, 169
Prata, G., 5, 14, 89, 90, 103
Prince, E. F., 6, 14, 174, 184
Putnam, S. M., 291, 292, 313

Q

Query, J. L., 295, 312
Quesada, G. M., 309, 312

R

Radley, A., 156, 163, 169
Ragan, S. L., 188, 190, 191, 205, 206
Rambo, A. H., 5, 14
Rawlins, W. K., 26, 36, 46

AUTHOR INDEX 321

Ray, W. A., 123, 129
Redeker, G., 270, 288
Rennie, D. L., 107, 125, 129
Rice, L. N., 106, 129
Roberts, J., 131, 147
Rogers, L. E., 293, 294, 297, 298, 312, 313
Rogers-Millar, L. E., 294, 297, 313, 313
Rosman, B., 53, 67
Ross, C., 296, 312
Ross, J. M., 5, 13
Rost, K. M., 209, 231
Roter, D. L., 215, 231
Roth, J. A., 189, 206
Rubin, Z., 105, 129

S

Sacks, H., 12, 14, 20, 46, 52, 68, 161, 169, 236, 237, 242, 256, 269, 272, 286, 288, 289
Samora, J., 189, 206
Sapir, J. D., 76, 88
Sarr, R. A., 294, 312
Sarup, M., 72, 88
Satir, V., 57, 68
Saunders, L., 189, 206
Saxon, W. W., 123, 129
Schaeffer, N. C., 233, 235, 256
Schank, R. C., 21, 47
Scheff, T., 27, 47
Scheflen, A. E., 4, 14, 53, 54, 68
Schegloff, E. A., 4, 12, 14, 20, 46, 52, 65, 68, 161, 169, 236, 256, 265, 266, 269, 272, 275, 286, 288, 289
Schegloff, S., 51, 68
Schieffelin, B. B., 22, 46, 237, 256
Schiffrin, D., 54, 68, 269, 270, 289
Schmer, V., 5, 12

Schön, D. A., 7, 14, 152, 169
Schultz, J., 164, 169, 281, 287
Schwartz, R. C., 131, 132, 146, 147
Schwenk, T. L., 152, 169
Scott, D., 3, 14
Scott, M. B., 19, 47, 174, 184
Searle, J., 236, 237, 256, 265, 289
Segal, L., 4, 12
Selvini-Palazzoli, M., 5, 14, 89, 90, 103
Semin, G. R., 27, 47
Shapiro, D. A., 106, 108, 123, 126, 128
Shapiro, J., 3, 14, 228, 231
Sherbourne, C. D., 209, 210, 215, 225, 231
Shreve, E. G., 6, 14
Shultz, J., 235, 255
Shuy, R., 243, 256
Siegfried, J., 53, 68
Silver, J., 186, 187, 206
Silverman, D., 6, 14, 15, 260, 289
Silverstein, O., 5, 13
Sinclair, J. McH., 270, 275, 289
Skinner, G., 211, 231
Sluzki, G. E., 294, 313
Smilansky, J., 152, 169
Smith, J. M., 186, 187, 206
Smith, R. C., 210, 231
Sommers, P. A., 211, 231
Sorjonen, M. L., 54, 60, 68, 260, 288, 289
Spelman, M., 187, 206
Sridaromont, S., 5, 12
Stamp, G. H., 53, 68
Steele, J. L., 189, 206
Steier, F., 123, 129
Steiner, F., 43, 47
Stelling, R. G., 167, 169
Stewart, K., 125, 128, 211, 230, 231

Stewart, M., 211, 231, 247, 256
Stiles, W. B., 211, 231, 291, 292, 313
Stiven, H., 164, 169
Stoeckle, J. D., 6, 12, 187, 189, 205, 233, 256
Stokes, R., 173, 174, 175, 184
Stormberg, J. L., 5, 12
Strano, J. D., 90, 103
Strauss, A. L., 108, 129
Streek, J., 265, 289
Street, R. L., Jr., 211, 214, 215, 229, 295, 313, 231
Suchman, A. L., 244, 256
Sumney, P., 188, 206

T

Talbot, Y., 3, 14
Tannen, D., 6, 14, 74, 76, 88
Taylor, D. A., 36, 45
Taylor, W. C., 6, 12
ten Have, P., 51, 66, 68
Thomas, F., 145, 147
Thomason, R., 172, 183
Thompson, I. M., 209, 231
Thompson, T. L., 295, 311, 312
Thornton, B. C., 6, 13
Timothy, R. P., 209, 230
Todd, A. D., 6, 12, 14, 199, 200, 202, 207, 210, 212, 231
Todtman, D. A., 90, 103
Tomm, K., 5, 13, 14, 90, 103, 122, 125, 129
Tracy, K., 23, 47
Trenholm, S., 294, 313
Tse, C. J., 209, 231
Tucker, B., 131, 147
Tyler, A. G., 132, 145, 147
Tyler, S. A., 72, 74, 88, 112, 129
Tyler, S. G., 132, 145, 147

U

Underwood, P., 188, 206

V

Valentine, L., 125, 128
van de Velde, C. J. H., 209, 231
Van Dijk, T. A., 20, 22, 23, 47
Verby, J. E., 263, 264, 284, 289
Viaro, M., 52, 53, 55, 68
Vinsel, A., 36, 45
von Foerster, H., 77, 88
von Friederichs-Fitzwater, M. M., 295, 313
Vuchinich, S., 65, 68, 69

W

Waitzkin, H., 6, 14, 210, 212, 230, 231, 233, 235
Waletsky, J., 20, 46
Wallat, C., 6, 14
Ward, J. A., 172, 184
Ware, J. E., Jr., 209, 210, 211, 215, 225, 230, 231
Wasson, J. H., 209, 211, 231
Watson, D. R., 22, 46, 61, 63, 68
Watzlawick, P., 4, 15, 57, 69, 90, 103, 293, 313
Weakland, J. H., 4, 12, 15, 90, 103
Weick, K. E., 1, 8, 15
Weinberger, M., 211, 231
Wenger, E., 166, 169
Wennberg, J. E., 209, 230
West, C., 6, 15, 52, 69, 186, 187, 202, 207, 235, 236, 257
Weston, W. V., 211, 231, 247, 256
Wetherell, M., 108, 129, 164, 169
White, M., 120, 122, 125, 129
Whitman, N., 152, 169
Wiemann, J. M., 291, 292, 313

Wilcox, E. M., 6, 12
Wilcox, J. R., 6, 12
Wilder, C., 293, 313
Wilder-Mott, C., 293, 313
Williams, J., 295, 313
Wilmot, W. W., 36, 47, 57, 69, 293, 313
Wilson, R., 126, 128
Wiseman, H., 106, 129
Wittgenstein, L., 42, 47
Wodak, R., 6, 13, 19, 47
Woo, B., 6, 12
Wright, L., 105, 123, 124, 129, 132, 147

Y

Youssef, V., 6, 15
Yule, G., 20, 45

Z

Zahn, C. J., 162, 169, 175, 183
Zimmerman, D. H., 259, 283, 287, 289

Subject Index

A

Abduction, 76-77, 88-86
Accounting, for behavior, 123, 223
   see also Problematic talk,
   Responsibility
Acknowledgment, 52, 56, 59, 61-62
   weak, 154-155, 161, 195, 269-270, 283
Adjacency pairs, 25
Advice, 183
   see also Suggestions
Aesthetics of Change, 4
Aligning actions, *see* Disclaimers, Problematic talk
Alignment, 188, 198, 268
Alrights, 272-273
Ambiguity, 91, 165
And-prefacing, of queries, 58
Answers, *see* Precepting conversations
Assertions, 95-96, 296
Assessments, 54, 65, 160-161
   erroneous self, 166-167
   negative, 156 (fn 2)
   withholding, 154-156
Attentiveness, 228, 230
Authority, *see* Institutional talk

B

Bad news, revealing, 6, 164
Biopsychosocial approach, *see* Health Care

Blaming, *see* Problematic talk
Burkean criticism, 76

C

Cancer Information Service, 171
Change, Principles of Problem Formation and Problem Resolution, 4
Chain maxim for questions and answers, 242-244
Clarification, seeking, 57-58
Clinical discourse
   analysis of, 1-7, 11, 43, 254
   archives of, 3
   recording and transcription of, 2, 311
Clinical interviews
   affect display in, 244-247
   consequences of, 185-188
   discussing quality of life in, 210-230, 244, 247, 254
   dominance in, 211
   educating patients in, 185-207
   empathic opportunities in, 244-247
   goals in, 186, 190, 192, 247-254, 291
   hierarchical organization of, 248-255
   information-seeking in, 185-187, 190, 196, 223, 226, 228, 238-242, 248
   interact types in, 300-301

legitimizing complaints in, 230, 286
managing, 199-200, 210-211, 216, 217, 223, 268, 271-184, 311
marginalizing patients' concerns in, 220-221, 227-229, 278-280, 302
mitigated correction in, 185, 193
negotiating solutions in, 230
okay usages within, 259-287
patients' discomfort in, 188, 193
patients' participation in, 185, 191, 195-196, 199-200, 203-205, 223, 226, 228-229, 291-292
patients' preferences for, 187, 210-211, 214-215, 217, 225-226, 234, 311
patients' satisfaction with, 186-187, 211, 215, 218, 227-228, 291, 295
patients' understanding in, 186-188, 191, 196, 198, 201, 238-242
phases of, 90, 248-254, 292
practitioners' preferences for, 268, 281
presenting diagnoses in, 252-254
problem assessment in, 248-254
questioning in, 55, 238-255, 260
self-disclosure in, 234-236, 295
suggestions in, 191-194, 221-222, 225
the taken for granted in, 227
teamwork in, 89-90, 97
timing in, 270
topic control in, 260, 269-284
turn-taking in, 55, 235, 277-279
windows of opportunity in, 229, 244

Clinical perspectives, 210, 228, 230, 282
understanding, 86-87, 252-254
Clinical teaching, *see* Medical education
Collaboration, among medical personnel, 166
between clinicians and researchers, 1-3, 11, 43, 86-87
between clients and therapists, 105, 123-124
between clients in therapy sessions, 63-64
between physicians and patients, 187, 189, 204, 226, 230, 277, 281, 309-310
between practitioners of different agencies, 138
Collegiality, 167
Communication, effective, 202
Communication patterns, dysfunctional, 53
Communication research, practitioner use of, 86-87
Communication style, 203, 228, 309-310
Communication theory, 4-5, 20-21
Communicational Structure, 4
Competence, questioning therapists', 92, 94-95
valuing patients', 186, 198
valuing trainees', 137, 153, 160, 162-163
Compliance, 25, 186, 203-205, 211, 291, 311
Comprehensive discourse analysis, 1, 4-6, 53
analyzing interactions in, 101-102
expansions in, 93, 101
methods, 21-22, 101-102
propositions in, 94, 102

SUBJECT INDEX 327

rules in, 98, 101-102
units in, 102
Conceptual therapy, 8
Configuration, 75
  types of, 75-76
  use during therapy, 77
  use during intersession breaks,
Confirmation, 59, 296
Confrontation, 96, *see also* Problematic talk
Consequentiality, 165
Constraint, as a feature of accounts, 26
  clinical time, 205, 230, 247, 310
  conditional relevance of questions as, 236
  on configuration of language in therapy, 74
  on disclaimers in medical encounters, 178 (fn 8)
  on participation in health-care, 185-189
  on speaker order in therapeutic-discourse, 52, 55
  on topics in therapeutic discourse, 52
  on turns in clinical or therapeutic discourse, 52, 268, 283-284
Continuers, 54 (fn 7)
Control, 53, 291
  balanced, 310
  excessive, 311
  monitoring, 311
  relational, 291, 295, 309
  struggling for, 309, 311
Conversation, collaboration in, 73
  colligation in, 160
  suggestions in, 133
  therapy as, 75
  turn taking in, casual, 52
Conversation analysis, 1-2, 6, 168, 254

Conversational technique, expanding, 66
Coordinated management of meaning, the, 4-5
  see also Meaning
Correction, 64 (fn 9), 65, 152-153, 185
  embedded, 161
  mitigated/modulated versus aggravated/explicit, 152, 155, 160-163, 165
  self versus other, 162
  see also Clinical interviews, Precepting conversations
Critical theory, 6, 74
Criticism, receptivity to, 167
Cultural taboos, consequences of, 189-190
Culture, variation in practices across, 66, 72, 163
Cybernetics, 4-5, 123, *see also* Constraint

D

Defense, self, 94, 96
Demographic variation, 189-190
Dependency, 187
Delicacy, 66-67, 97, 134-135, 140-141, 183, 276
Diagnosis, *see* Clinical interviews
Dialogue, 74, 200-201
Directives, 191, 196-200, 204-205
Disagreement, 64 (fn 9), 153, 226-227, 250-251
  prefacing, 94
Discernment, 262-263
Disclaimers, consequences of proforma, 183
  early versus embedded, 171, 176-178, 278

SUBJECT INDEX

medical, 172-173
responses to, 175, 181-182
studying, 171
types of, 173
uses of, 173-175
see also Telephone encounters
Disclosure, self, see Clinical interviews
Disconfirmation, 57 (fn 8)
Discouragement, 52
Discourse analysis, cautions about, 183
generalizing from, 270 (fn 3)
sequential, 108, 237-254
Discourse coherence, 20-24
conditional relevance and, 24
context and, 21, 236-255
global, 20-24, 30, 32, 38, 42, 102, 247-255
local, 20, 27, 125, 183, 265
structures and, 20-23
thermal, 42
Discourse organization, deciding among models of, 42-43
hierarchical, 20-24, 36, 42-43
linear, 20
propositions as units of, 94
rules in, 98, 101-102, 236
sequential, 30, 4
theoretical premises and, 125
units of, 22, 94, 270
Disputables, 98
Dissensus, 91-92
Doctor shopping, 295, 311
Dominance/domineeringness, 294-295, 301-303
Double-bind, the, 3-4

E

Education, patient, 185-205
Egalitarianism, unequal, 164

Empathic opportunities, 244-247
missed, 245
Empowerment, 194-196, 202-204
Encouragement, 52, 55, 164, 223, 228-229
Episodes, 24, 102, see also Discourse organization
Error, physician, 311
therapist, 92
Ethnography of communication, 2, 5, 168, 186
Evaluations, see Assessments
Expertise, see Institutional talk
Explanations, 221, 230, see also Clinical interviews, Suggestions, Therapy sessions

F

Facework, 92-95, 162-164, 186-191, 194-196
Facts, tinkering with, 91-101, see also Midsession breaks
Family discourse, 66
Family Interaction Apperception Techniques, 53
Feedback, 74, 117, 114, 152, 311
Figurative language, combined with the literal, 85
dialectical tensions of in therapy, 73, 75-76
resourceful use of, 74-86
torque and looseness in, 77
types of, 75-76
First Five Minutes, The, 4
Fixing the world with the voice, 1,8
Following up, on prior contributions, 62-63, 266
Formulations, use of "so" to preface, 61-62
Foundations of Family Therapy, 89
Freudian criticism, 74

G-H

Greetings, 238
Health-care, biopsychosocial
  approach to, 230
  communication and, 6, 11
  holistic, 190-191, 193, 201
  hypodermic approach to, 227-228
  models of, 6, 210-211, 226
  patient-centered approach to, 228, 230, 255, 310
Health-care interactions, *see* Clinical interviews
Health communication, the development of, 6
Health status, averting discussion of, 222-223
  dimensions of, 209-210
  measuring, 209, 214
Health perceptions, general, 219
Health outcomes, 188-190, 202-203, 211, 227
Hedges, 174-175, *see also* Disclaimers, Telephone encounters, 153
Hotlines, hazards of, 6
How-are-you's, as initial queries in clinical encounters, 238-242
How-to-say-its, 99, 132, 143-146
  conditions for, 137-146
  negation in, 141
  uses of, 134-135, 144-145

I

Ideological dilemmas, 163-164, *see also* Precepting conversations
Indexicality, 138
Irony, 75-76
Institutional talk, 1

  appropriate roles in, 186-188, 228, 291
  asymmetry in, 260-261, 283, 295
  authority in, 65, 185-188
  contrasts between ordinary conversation and, 52, 176, 178-179, 181-182, 198, 235, 238-239, 242-244, 264, 266, 269-270
  display of experience in, 53
  egalitarianism in, 164
  information-seeking in, 186
  "I" versus "we" in, 177-178, 181-182
  microanalysis of, 286 (fn 6), 291
  n-prefacing in, 54 (fn 7)
  okay usages in, 283
  practitioners' versus analysts' observations of, 259-261
  pro-forma responses in, 171, 177
  rights to formulate in, 61
  role-distancing in, 164
  social construction in, 124
  treatment of expertise in, 53, 164, 186, 195
Instructions, 50, 56, 198, 196
  giving reasons for/warranting, 50, *see also* Suggestions
Interaction, analysis 1, 101-102
  disrupted, 55, 65
  multiple-party, 66
  symmetrical and complementary, 293-294
Interactional view, 292-293
  critiques of, 293
Intersession breaks
  reconfiguration in, 83
  using juxtaposition in, 79-80
  using tropes in, 73-75, 81, 86

330 SUBJECT INDEX

Interviews
 definitions of, 233-235
 framing talk in, 117, 125
 intuition in, 238-242, 244
 origins of, 233
 question-answer sequences in, 242-247
 researching, 233, 235
 roles in, 107, 233-235
 social science versus clinical, 234-235, 247-248
 teaching how to conduct, 126
 see also Clinical interviews, Process recall, Questions
Intimacy, *see* Relationships
Intuition, *see* Interviews
Involvement, 268

J-K

Juxtaposition, of figures, 76-80
Knowing-and-being, 255
Knowledge
 dispensing, 186
 documenting claims to, 264-265, 267-268
 imposing versus eliciting, 163
 practical, 125, 151
 prior, 233
 recipe, 137

L

Lack of communication, 27-28, 40
Language-in-use, 71
 exuberance and deficiency in, 74, 86
 particularities of, 72-73, 86
 sensitivity to, 72-73
 the said and the unsaid in, 72, 74, 84, 86, 93, 109-114
 the taken for granted in, 72

Learning, interactive, 185-186, 201-205
Lessons, discourse of, 156 (fn 1), 163, 185, 190, 198
Listening, 74, 228, 230
Listening-and-talking, basic science of, 1, 71-72
Litigation, malpractice, 211, 291
Logic, 77, 86
 tinkerer's 100
 see also Problematic talk

M

Marriage and family therapy
 accounts in, 6
 goals for sessions of, 19, 53, 66, 77, 99, 116-117
 organization of, 7, 44, 78, 89-90
 problem-talk in, 19-20, 22-43
 studies of therapists' conversation techniques in, 6
 supervision in, 131-132
 systemic, 43, 74, 90
 the intercom in, 90
 the mirror in, 89
 see also Mental Research Institute, Milan Systemic Therapy, Supervision, Therapy sessions
Meaning, 73, 75
 change in, 77-78, 86, 100
 contingent, 237
 rigid, 77
 systems of, 74
 levels of, 22, 27
Medical encounters
 information giving in, 6
 intake process for, 6
 patient education in, 185-205, 291
 see Clinical interviews

Medical education
  assessments of, 166-167
  clinical, 151-152
  dilemmas of, 163-164
  feedback in, 152, 163
  procedures of, 152-153, 259
  use of recordings in, 261-263
  variation in, 165
  see also Clinical interviews,
    Precepting conversations,
    Professional development,
    Supervision
Medical effectiveness, evaluating, 209, 296
Medical interviews, *see* Clinical interviews
Mental Research Institute, 4, 90, 292
Metaphor, 75-76, 142
Metonymy, 75-76
Microanalysis, 2, 4, 66-67, 183, 286 (fn 6)
Midsession breaks
  assertions within, 95
  avoiding confrontation in, 96
  counter-assertions in, 96
  disputables in, 98
  dissensus within, 91-92
  narrative within, 95
  requests in, 92, 97
  tinkering with facts in, 91-101
  use of, 90
Milan Systemic Therapy, 4-5, 43-44, 90, 123
Mind in Therapy, 4
Milestone sayings, 137-138
Miscommunication, 186, 189-190
Misunderstanding, 186-188, 198, 236
Multiple versions, *see* Narrative, Problematic talk
Mutual Storytelling Technique, 53

N

Narrative, 20, 24, 31, 54 (fn 6), 73, 95, 98, 102
  analysis, 81
  collaborative production of, 54
  eliciting in therapeutic discourse, 53-54, 126
  functions of, 31
  logic of, 31
  terminating topics within, 61
Natural History of an Interview, The, 5
Newsmarks, 61
Now-prefacing, 64
N-prefaced queries, 54 (fn 7)
Nursing, 185-207, *see also* Clinical interviews

O

Obstetrics-Gynecology, *see* Clinical interviews
Okays, 54 (fn 7), 59-60, 203, 245, 259-287
  accepting/rejecting by use of, 279-280, 284
  alternatives to, 272-273
  partitioning via use of, 275
  positioning of, 266, 272, 274-276
  proscribing use of, 263-269, 284-289
  recycled, 281-282
  uses of, 260, 283-284
  see also Clinical interviews, institutional talk
Opening up/closing down, 55-65, 260, 269-270
Opportunity spaces, *see* Precepting conversations

P

Paraphrases, *see* Formulations
Pauses, as elicitation cues, 154-155, 158
Perceptions, physicians', 189-190, 210-211
Persuasion, 101
Poetics, 73
Politeness, 50, 164
Power, asymmetrical, 199-201, 210-211, 228
Pragmatics of Human communication, 4, 293
Precepting conversations, 152-168
   ambiguity in, 165
   consequentiality and, 165
   corrections in, 153, 161-167
   giving good hearings in, 158-160
   hinting with questions in, 153
   managing disagreement in, 153
   providing opportunity spaces in, 153-156
   treatment of answers in, 153-154
   treatment of assessments in, 154, 160-161
   outcomes of mitigated correction in, 165-167
   see also Corrections
Prenatal consultations, 185-230, *see also* Clinical interviews
Problematic talk, consequences, 30
   accounts and, 26-27, 31-35, 41
   ambiguity as, 91
   avoiding confrontation in, 96, 117
   blaming and, 27-28, 30, 35, 41, 95, 99
   construction of, 25-36, 66, 92
   dissensus, 36, 39, 91-92, 112-114
   enduring versus momentary problems, 280
   hierarchical structure of, 20, 24, 27, 29, 31-32, 35, 41
   logic of, 22, 27, 29, 38, 40
   multiple versions and, 30, 92
   persistence in, 30, 34
   prefaced queries in, 54 (fn 7)
   solutions in, 29, 40, 101, 136, 144
   see also Marriage and Family Therapy, Relationships
Process analysis
   comprehensive, 106
   reflexive, 105
Process recall, interpersonal, 105
   disagreement in interpersonal, 115
   effectiveness of, 123
   externalizing problems in interpersonal, 120-122, 125
   surfacing clashing expectations in interpersonal, 114-117, 125
Professional development, 131, 138, 145-146, 163-164, 166-167
   leading-edge, 146
Psychotherapy, 89
   process research, 106

Q

Quality of life
   discussing health-related, 209-231
Quantification, 270 (fn 2)
Questions, 55-56, 58-59, 199, 296
   ambiguity in, 238-242
   assessment-prefaced, 54 (fn 7)
   baiting, 92-93

conditional relevance of, 236-237
context of, 236-238
curiosity in, 125
hints in, 153, 156-158
force of, 236-238
interpretations of, 186-187
linguistic analysis of, 235-237, 240, 254
opening windows of opportunity through, 229, 255
teaching, 143
theory of, 235-236
types of, 236
see also Clinical interviews, Interviews

R

Rapport, 185
Reactions, explosive, 281
Reassurance, 201
Recall, stimulated, 106, *see also* Process recall
Receipt, third turn, 266-267, 274
Recommendations, *see* Suggestions
Recursive frame analysis, 5
Reformulations, midcourse, 240
Requests, 50, 92, 97, 134
    preconditioning, 133-134
Reflexive practitioner, the, 7, 11
Reflexivity, 71-72, 86, 105, 108, 122-123, 126, 263
Relational control analysis, 292-311
    procedures of, 297-299
Relationships
    affect display in, 39
    alignment of, 198
    defining, 36, 124, 291, 296

dialectical tensions of, 26, 34, 36, 39, 41
dimensions of, 294
intimacy in, 39
larger system, 138-140
negotiating, 291-292, 296, 304-306
maintenance of, 38
misunderstanding, in, 31
patterns of, 296
problems in close, 19
switchpoints in, 296, 306-309
team member to member, 99, 101
time as a problem in, 26, 40-41
transitions/stages in, 36-38, 43
turning points in, 37-38
validation of, 39-40
working, 66, 89
Repair, *see* Correction
Repetition, as an indicator of salience, 23
    of figures, 81, 85
    as reinforcement, 196
    of questions in precepting conversations, 154, 158-160
    partial, 59-60
Research, as intervention, 105, 117-120, 124
Responsibility, 193, 195, 199-201, 204-205
Retention, 193, 200
Retrospection, 100, 105
    delayed experience via, 111
Roles, negotiation of, *see* Institutional talk, Relationships
Rules, *see* Comprehensive discourse analysis, Discourse organization
Rural Physician Associate Program, 263, 286

S

Salience, means of displaying, 22-23, 27-29, 34, 41
Self-awareness, 203
Sensitivity, 72-73, 230, 252
Sidetracking, 283
Social Constructionism, 72, 124-125
Sociopsychological context of health, communicating about 209, 211-212, 226, 303
Speech acts, critique of theories of, 265
   incompleteness of, 237
   timing of, 237
Speech and Hearing clinics, revealing test results in, 6
Strategy, 296, 302
Structuralism, 72-73
   post-, 72
Structure of Magic, The, 5
Suggestions, 132-146, 164
   detail in, 136
   phrasing recommendations as, 191-194
   sequences of, 133
   warrants for, 134, 194-196, 200
Summaries, *see* Formulations
Supervision
   clinical, 126, 131
   coaching in, 144
   difficulties in, 131-132, 145
   effective, 132
   goals of, 131
   live versus videotape, 131
   phases of, 132-132
   roles in, 131-132
   sharing expertise in, 135
   suggestions in, 132-146
   telling how to say it in, 132, 134-146

Switchpoints, 296, 306-309
Synecdoche, 75-76

T

Tactics of Change, The, 4
Teaching personae, 190, 193, *see also* Clinical interviews
Teamwork, *see* Clinical interviews, Medical education, Therapeutic team
Telephone encounters
   demographic questions in, 172
   disclaimers in, 176-183
   goals of clinical, 172
   phases of, 172
   placement of disclaimers in, 180-181
   practices in, 171
   teaching medical terminology in, 172
Theoretical orientation, variation in practices according to, 66
Therapeutic Discourse, 2, 4, 6, 21, *see also* Clinical discourse, Comprehensive discourse analysis
Therapeutic team, the, 44, 101
Therapeutic techniques, optimizing, 141
Therapy sessions, as multiple-party conversations, 49
   closing down matters for discussion in, 49-50, 55, 57-60
   directing conversation in, 25, 49-67
   disregarding unsolicited comments in, 57-58
   goals of, 19
   handling unsolicited contributions in, 51-67

opening matters for discussion in, 49-50, 59-60, 63
overlapping talk in, 49
redirecting the focus of, 52, 62-63
selecting speakers in, 49-51
speaking for others in, 49-50
the said and the not-yet-said in, 109-114, 125-126
using interpersonal process recall in, 106-127
Time, *see* Clinical interviews, Constraint, Relationships
Topic, *see* Clinical interviews
Transcription, key, 11-12
process, 108
Troubles, normal, 236
Troubles talk, 268-269
"okays" in the marking of, 274-277
variations in, 283
see Problematic talk
Trust, 204-205, 294
Turn-taking, patterns of, 115-116
asynchrony in, 268, 277 (fn 4), 278

U

Unsolicited comments, *see* Therapy sessions

V

Voice of medicine, 252
Voice of the life world, 252

W

Windows of opportunity, *see* Clinical interviews
Withdrawal, 295
Women's health-care, 186-187, 201-202
Words, complex, 81, 85
context of, 75, 265
jargon, 186-187
play with, 75, 83, 86

Y

Yeahs, 269-270